SUPERVISORY
MANAGEMENT
for Healthcare Organizations

FOURTH EDITION

SUPERVISORY MANAGEMENT
for Healthcare Organizations

THEO HAIMANN, PhD

The Mary Louise Murray Professor
of Management Sciences
St. Louis University

THE
CATHOLIC HEALTH ASSOCIATION
OF THE UNITED STATES

ST. LOUIS, MO

To
Ruthe

Contents

Contents

Preface

Healthcare providers are confronted with far-reaching problems about the future of the healthcare system in the United States. They are concerned with a continued stream of revolutionary and sophisticated breakthroughs in medical science and technology, an aging population, and a federal government coping with the need and desire to deliver coverage and fiscal integrity. The possibility exists that the highest quality of care might be replaced with "adequate" quality to meet the strains of a financially driven system. There is great concern that issues are being approached first on the basis of cost and not on need and quality. The challenge to healthcare providers is stronger than ever. Therefore survival has become an issue for many of today's healthcare organizations. Patients, providers, and payors all see the need for a more efficient healthcare system, and it is not surprising that far-reaching changes are taking place. Current market pressures demand new delivery methods, managed care contracting is a burning issue, and the movement to the outpatient side is continuing. Furthermore, medical practice arrangements by physicians and surgeons are changing greatly, the traditional fee-for-service concept is undergoing radical rethinking, and managed fee-for-service is emerging.

One common aspect that is significant for the reader and author of this book is that all these changes are being accomplished in corporate and thus organizational settings. This is true for the users on the one hand, such as patients, health maintenance organizations (HMOs), and preferred provider organizations (PPOs), and healthcare centers, nursing homes, surgical centers, joint ventures, independent practice associations, physicians' offices, home healthcare programs, and so forth on the other hand. At the center of all this activity is the manager, who has to bring and hold together the human resources, physical facilities, professional expertise, skills, technology, information systems, and other support systems. In addition, this all has to be accomplished within the fiscal constraints of a more efficient healthcare system than has prevailed in the past.

Therefore it is necessary that the managers involved in the delivery of healthcare understand the complexities of organizational life, behavior, development, and climate. All managers—from the chief executive officer to the first-line supervisor—must be managers in the most professional sense.

In order to contribute to organizational effectiveness, administrators and managers must understand and know the practice of management. Most executive level positions are filled by individuals who have been exposed to formal health administration education. However, thousands of middle- and lower-level administrative positions, such as department heads and supervisors, are filled by health professionals and others who have not had any formal education or training in administration, management, and supervision per se.

This book is intended for these department heads and supervisors in all types of healthcare facilities, hospitals, surgical centers, HMOs, physician's group practices, extended care facilities, nursing homes, homes for the aged, rehabilitation centers, long term care facilities, or other institutions of this type. They were placed into their supervisory positions primarily because they did an outstanding job in their chosen healthcare professions. Their previous experience and education, however, rarely included the area of supervision. Thus these supervisors who rise from the ranks often find themselves in increasingly demanding positions yet have little or no familiarity with the administrative and managerial aspects of their newly attained rank. Suddenly they are confronted with the need to be an effective manager, to stay on top of a more sophisticated job, to gain new perspectives and insights into human relationships. Their position may have changed from being a good nurse, for example, to becoming a head nurse, supervisor of nursing, or whatever the title may be. The primary function changes from doing things oneself to getting things done through and with employees by motivating them so that they enthusiastically go about achieving departmental goals, institutional objectives, and their personal goals.

This book is written for an introductory course in management to acquaint students with their future roles in an organizational setting. It is intended to be used as a textbook in the education of nurses, medical technologists, dietitians, therapists, medical records administrators, and all other healthcare professionals. It can be used in any of the courses where managerial, supervisory, and leadership concepts are studied.

In addition to this, this text is intended to aid people in the healthcare field who are already faced with such a supervisory task. Its purpose is to demonstrate to the supervisors that proficiency in supervision will better equip them to cope with the ever-increasing demands of getting the job done, will contribute more effectively to the overall goals of the institution, and at the same time will make them more valuable to the facility's chief executive.

This book is introductory in the sense that it assumes no previous knowledge of the concepts of supervision. Although the book does include material of a sophisticated nature, this material is explained in terms that can easily be understood by the inexperienced supervisor. The book will also help newly appointed supervisors become acquainted with the many problems they will confront and offers practical advice for their solution. For experienced supervisors, this book is intended to refresh thinking, to introduce current ideas, and widen horizons by taking a different and challenging look at both their own position and that of their employees.

Even though the text is written for supervisors, not for chief executives and administrators, most of its content would be of great interest to the latter as well. The common denominator of all levels of supervisors is the part they play as managers within the administrative hierarchy of the institution. Without going into the technical details of specific supervisory positions, the book discusses the managerial aspects common to every supervisory job, whether in nursing; the laboratory; radiology; physical, occupational, or respiratory therapy; medical records; medical social work; housekeeping; dietary; pharmacy; security; laundry; maintenance; dispatch; engineering; or any of the other specialties found within the healthcare field.

It is important to realize that the supervisory position in any field is the most critical point in the entire organizational structure. It involves the management of people in the day-to-day running of a department within an organization. In all healthcare activities, the supervisor's position is exceptionally strategic since in most cases the recipient does not elect to receive the services provided, nor does this person understand them. The supervisor must contend with emotional factors involved in the care of the patients and their loved ones under conditions that make effective supervision unusually difficult. In addition to this, the supervisor is often torn between clinical, professional, administrative, legal, moral, and ethical considerations. Above everything else, however, the supervisor's activities must ultimately reflect the welfare of the patient. All these factors make it more imperative for the supervisor to be a capable manager of the department.

Moreover, external factors also affect the supervisor's role. It is an established fact that the healthcare field comprises one of the largest activities in the United States today. Provisions for healthcare services will become more complex because of rapidly expanding areas of concern, growing government interest, an increasing and aging population, advances in medical science and technology, and the challenges of new diseases. In addition, it is essential for all healthcare facilities to keep pace with social and environmental progress. This means an ever-increasing challenge for efficient management capable of coping with more sophisticated problems, whether they are of an economic, professional, scientific, moral, legal, or educational nature.

To create a framework in which management knowledge can be organized in a practical way, the author has chosen to use the *functions* of managers as the primary approach—planning, organizing, staffing, influencing, and controlling. Each function is thoroughly dealt with by breaking it down and explaining its relationship to the knowledge already accumulated. In taking this approach, any new knowledge, whether from behavioral and social sciences, quantitative approaches, or any other field, can easily be incorporated into this open system at any point. All of the managerial functions are closely related; they represent an interlocking, interacting system. In practice such a distinct classification of these managerial functions is not always discernible, but this type of academic separation allows a methodological, clear, and complete analysis of a supervisor's managerial functions. Organizing management around these traditional management functions captures the essence of the manager's job.

The supervisor's job of getting things done with and through people has its foundation in the relationship between the supervisors and the people with whom they work. For this reason the supervisor must have considerable knowledge of the human aspects of supervision, of the behavioral factors that motivate the employees. This book attempts to integrate such behavioral factors into the conceptual framework of managing. Although it is obviously not an all-comprising text on management, the book does try to present a balanced picture. Thus human relations and behavioral aspects are kept in proper perspective in relation to the other aspects of the supervisory job.

In writing this fourth edition, I have retained the basic concepts and the emphasis on the five basic managerial functions. All the chapters of the previous editions have been revised and updated, and some of the subject matter has been rearranged to facilitate the reader's understanding of the concepts and their application. These concepts, however, are expanded and integrated with current practices, new knowledge and research, and recent developments to show the contemporary emphasis of this edition. Completely new materials have been added in many areas to make this book more usable for today's department heads and supervisors. More attention is given to the behavioral sciences, psychology, and sociology as they impact on managing human resources. New material has been added on organizational design, performance appraisal, quality circles, management by objectives, individual and small group behavior, motivation, equal and fair employment practices, employee assistance programs, discipline without punishment, zero base budgeting, and many other aspects of managing.

The chapter focusing on some of the legal aspects of the supervisory job has been revised and updated. Everyone working in the healthcare field is aware of the importance of legal problems and their implications. Therefore, this chapter, written in layman's language, will familiarize supervisors with some of the legal aspects of healthcare activities. It is not intended to advise supervisors what to do or not to do and is certainly not a substitute for consultation with and legal advice by lawyers. Special thanks for writing this chapter go to Carolyn Haimann, JD and general counsel, and Lynn Morgenstern, JD, staff attorney, both of The Jewish Hospital of St. Louis.

Material for this text has come from the writings and research of scholars in the areas of management, behavioral and social sciences, as well as from the practical experience of many supervisors, managers, and administrators in the field. In addition, this text also reflects the author's experiences in teaching management, in consulting, in conducting many supervisory development programs, and in giving lectures to administrators and supervisors at different levels in the managerial hierarchy of hospitals and related healthcare facilities.

In writing the book, I realize that most people working in healthcare facilities are women, and thus I was inclined to refer to supervisors as ''she'' and to use the female gender throughout the book. Since men also are actively engaged in the delivery of healthcare, however, I thought it best to give men and women ''equal time'' by referring to them as supervisors, department heads, or similar terms. This was accomplished by using nouns or plural pronouns or by using the expression ''he or she.'' When it was necessary to refer to an individual, I used the common gender ''he,'' meaning a person of either sex. I hope that those readers who are sensitive to such terminology will forgive me and not interpret this stylist device as prejudicial to the vital managerial role of women in the healthcare field. Another language problem faced in this and previous editions is the use of the term *subordinate;* it is meant to describe a person who is below a supervisor or manager in the organization's hierarchy. The term denotes position only and is not intended disparagingly.

Finally, in writing a book such as this, I am indebted to so many persons that it is impossible to individually give due credit to all who have assisted over the two decades of the book's existence. I also appreciate the searching and stimulating questions that the participants in the development programs brought up. Further, I owe a special obligation to so many members of Barnes Hospital, St. Louis, that it would be impossible to mention all of them by name. This health-care center was a constant source of much information and insight. Among the many who were so helpful, special thanks to Marlene A. Hartmann, Senior Vice President for Patient Care, and Sherlyn Hailstone, Vice President, Nursing Service. I am also indebted to Karen S. Hausfeld, Associate Director of Nursing

Service, St. Mary's Health Center, St. Louis, and to Rose Dunn, Assistant Vice President, Administration, MetLife HealthCare Management Corporation, St. Louis, for many suggestions for this edition. Nancy Angenend Serrot, now a medical student at St. Louis University, was of immeasurable help in verifying quotes and sources of material and in endless hours of proofreading. And special thanks go to my wife Ruthe for her patience and general assistance throughout the years of writing and revising this text. To all these people, I extend my grateful appreciation while bearing full responsibility for any sins of omission or commission.

Theo Haimann

Part One

STEPPING INTO MANAGEMENT

THE SUPERVISOR'S JOB

■ THE HEALTHCARE PERSPECTIVE

The needs and demands for the highest-quality management in all healthcare delivery activities are intensifying to such a degree that survival has become an issue for some of today's healthcare organizations. No let-up is in sight. The current market pressures demand new delivery methods. For example, in the past patients came to the healthcare center; now healthcare facilities are going to the patients with satellite outpatient services, outreach programs, mobile mammography units, health fairs, and so on.

Other changing trends affecting healthcare management include managed care contracting, an increasingly difficult issue for every healthcare institution. The further growth of managed care seems inevitable, and many healthcare centers are lacking the data they need for successful managed care contracting. The format of medical practice arrangements by physicians and surgeons also is changing greatly, and the traditional fee-for-service concept is undergoing radical rethinking. In many instances new joint physician/hospital ventures are being set up. In addition to this, new breakthroughs and technologies are likely to change key services, such as in the fields of cardiology, oncology, orthopedics, neurology, and women's health. Hospitals are creating ''centers of emphasis'' to focus limited resources on the growth and more profitable areas. Another challenge comes from the continuing strong movement to the outpatient side. There also is the danger and growing possibility of a shortage of one of the most needed expertise and assistance in this field, namely, that of nurses.

In addition to these factors, many other changes from all directions are impacting on the delivery of healthcare. All of these forces are likely to continue to impose constraints on healthcare services and set higher expectations. These new developments, trends, and activities have something important in common: new ''corporations'' are created for these new ventures and subsidiaries. This requires extensive and sophisticated long-range planning and good control over internal affairs. In turn, all of this, more than anything else, calls for more and better management. Managers, from chief executive officers down to first line supervisors, are needed to implement these activities and make them function effectively.

As stated, these changes are being achieved in organizational settings. The organization is the most important and critical element providing the means for bringing the resources together. Managing is the process by which healthcare organizations fulfill this responsibility. It is the manager who is responsible for acquiring and combining the resources to accomplish the goals. This applies to all managers, from the chief executive officer down to the first line supervisor. As scientific, economic, competitive, social, and many other pressures change, it is not the nurse or the technologist that the organization depends on to cope with that change; this is the manager's responsibility. Management has emerged as a potent force in our society since the turn of the century and has become essential to the life of all healthcare endeavors.

Today's health services are almost exclusively being delivered in an organizational setting such as a healthcare center, nursing home, clinic, surgical center, health maintenance organization, physicians' offices, home care programs, or any other type of healthcare institution. Only an organizational setting can bring together the physical facilities, professional expertise, skills, information systems, technology, and the myriad of other supports that today's health services delivery requires, whether these services are curative, rehabilitative, or preventive. Therefore, it is absolutely necessary that those involved in the delivery of healthcare services understand the complexities of organizational life, organizational behavior, development, and climate and the importance of expert administration in addition to their own professional areas of expertise.

Traditionally healthcare professionals were primarily concerned with the scientific, technical, and clinical aspects of their work; being a good nurse meant mastering the field of nursing. This was true even of the director of nursing, who was a nurse first and a manager second. Now, because of the increased demands, the health professional must be equally concerned with both aspects of the job, the management and the profession.

Delivery of healthcare is a term that is becoming increasingly common in the daily press, magazine articles, and conversations in the United States. What is generally meant by this term is the problem of providing adequate healthcare services of all types, intended to maintain and improve the health of all people regardless of age, color, locale, or ability to pay. The reason healthcare delivery systems are receiving such attention in the United States is that the cost of healthcare has risen more steeply than any other item in our national economy. Not only have the total expenditures in the field of health services risen by leaps and bounds, but these expenditures have also become an ever-increasing percentage of the overall economy, as expressed in our gross national product. It is understandable that the delivery of healthcare has become a major national issue and that all institutions engaged in this service are receiving continuous and increasing scrutinization.

Moreover, since the delivery of healthcare largely means providing a service, which due to its nature is people intensive, it is understandable that about 60 percent of the total expenditures within the field are for wages and salaries, twice the amount of most industrial enterprises. Therefore, many criticisms have naturally centered around employee productivity to justify such large wage and salary expenditures. What is needed besides many other changes is better and more effective administration of healthcare activities, that is, ultimately better supervision throughout. In the final analysis it is the front-line management—the supervisor of the department regardless of the title and nature of work—who is responsible for the department functioning smoothly and efficiently. It is essential, therefore, that due emphasis be paid to the need for the managerial development of effective supervisors within all phases of the healthcare field.

■ THE DEMANDS OF THE SUPERVISORY POSITION

The supervisory position within the administrative structure of any healthcare activity, such as a medical center, nursing home, free-standing surgicenter, health maintenance organization, urgi-center, intermediate care facility, independent practice organization, or preferred provider organization, has long been acknowledged as a difficult and demanding one. You have probably learned this from your own experience or by observing supervisors in hospitals and related institutions as they go about their daily tasks. The supervisor, whether a head nurse or a chief technologist in the clinical laboratory, can be depicted as "the person in the middle," since he or she serves as the principal link between higher administration and the institution's employees. (See Figure 1-1.)

If we look carefully at the job of almost any supervisor, regardless of who or what he or she supervises, we can see that it involves four major dimensions, four areas of responsibility. First, the supervisor must be a good boss, a good manager,

■ FIGURE 1-1 The administrative pyramid.

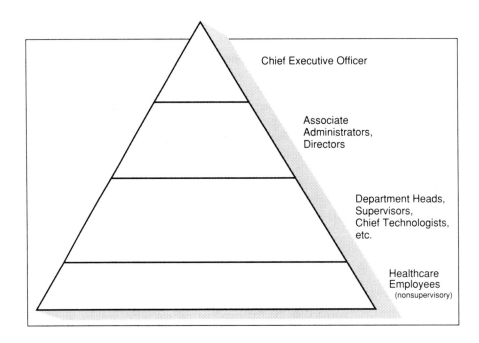

Chief Executive Officer

Associate Administrators, Directors

Department Heads, Supervisors, Chief Technologists, etc.

Healthcare Employees (nonsupervisory)

and a leader of the employees who work in this unit. The supervisor must have the technical, professional, and clinical competence to run the department smoothly and see that the employees carry out their assignments successfully. The first responsibility—not in any order of importance—is toward the employees of the department. Second, the supervisor must also be a competent subordinate to the next higher manager. In most instances this person would be an administrator, associate administrator, or director of a service. The second responsibility is toward administration and the "owners" of the organization.

Between these two dimensions of the supervisor's role is a third area of responsibility in which he or she acts as a connecting link between the employee and the administration. To the employees, such as RNs, LPNs, aides, or unit secretaries, the head nurse can be viewed as being the administration of the healthcare institution, since in this example the head nurse is the primary contact that employees have with the administration. The supervisor is that member of the administration who must make certain that the work gets done.

The fourth and final part of the supervisor's role is to maintain satisfactory working relationships with the heads of all other departments and services. The relationship to these other department heads must be that of a good colleague who is willing and eager to coordinate the department's efforts with those of the other departments to reach the overall objectives and goals of the institution, that is, the best possible service and patient care.

■ FIGURE 1-2 Dimensions of the supervisor's job.

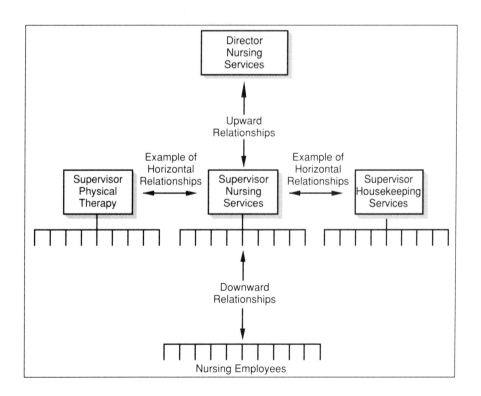

The four dimensions of the supervisor's job are shown more clearly in Figure 1-2. The supervisor must be successful in vertical relationships downward with subordinates and upward with his or her superior. In addition, the supervisor must be skillful in handling horizontal relationships with other supervisors, since this will facilitate getting the job done for the benefit of the client.

Partly because of the complexity of these relationships, it is commonly acknowledged that the role of the first-line supervisor in any industrial or commercial undertaking is a most difficult one. It is even more difficult for supervisors within the healthcare field because their activities directly or indirectly affect people, the quality of patient care, and the smooth overall functioning of the institution. In addition to their many professional obligations, healthcare supervisors must always bear in mind the needs and desires of patients and their relatives who, at the time, are physically and emotionally upset. Thus, the supervisor should be continuously aware of the problems of human relations among medical staff members, the other highly educated professionals and personnel of the institution, and patients. All these considerations make the job of the healthcare supervisor a particularly demanding and challenging one.

For example, let us look at the long list of demands made on a head nurse in charge of a nursing unit. Whether the institution practices team nursing, primary care, or total patient care, the head nurse's duty still is to provide for and supervise the nursing care rendered to the patients in the unit. She does this partly by delegating a certain amount of her authority for the care of patients and the supervision of personnel to an assistant head nurse or team leaders within her area. Still the head nurse must plan, direct, and control all activities within the nursing unit. She must make the rounds of her unit with medical and nursing staff. She also is expected to make rounds for personal observation of the condition and behavior of patients and to assess the need for and quality of continued nursing care. She may even have to assume general nursing functions in the care of those patients who have complex problems.

Furthermore, the head nurse must interpret and apply the policies, procedures, rules, and regulations of the facility in general and of nursing services in particular. She must provide coverage of the unit for 24 hours by scheduling to have the unit properly staffed at all times. She is to communicate and report to her nursing supervisor (assuming that the nursing supervisor is the immediate superior of a number of head nurses) all pertinent information regarding patients in her unit. She must orient new personnel to the unit and acquaint them with the general philosophies of the institution. She is also concerned with continued in-service education in her unit, in other words, with teaching personnel. Likewise, she participates in the evaluation of her subordinates.

In addition, it is part of the head nurse's job to coordinate the activities of her unit with unit managers if they are available. She also must coordinate her patient care with the care and therapeutic procedures of the various departments throughout the institution. Moreover, she is involved in the design and regular reevaluation of the budget. She serves on a number of committees, in addition to attending all head nurses' meetings. She might also be expected to help in the supervision and instruction of student nurses when necessary. Many additional duties are often assigned to a head nurse, depending on what the particular healthcare facility specifies in its description of this very demanding position.

Although it is difficult, if not impossible, to forecast specifically when and how a new scientific or technological event will impact on the supervisory position, every supervisor must continue to be better educated. It is important that supervisors prepare themselves and their employees professionally, scientifically, technologically, and psychologically for changes that will occur inevitably in the delivery of healthcare. In addition to the medical and scientific breakthroughs, the "computer revolution" will continue to affect all supervisors. Adaptations and uses for desktop and personal computers will grow with the development of specialized software so that supervisors will have to be familiar with computer operations as part of their daily routines.

With a growing, complex society and increasing demands for more sophisticated and better healthcare, the job of any supervisor in the field is likely to become even more challenging. This is true whether the title is head nurse, medical record administrator, operating room supervisor, director of maintenance, foreman of the electricians, chief respiratory therapist, laboratory supervisor, chief technologist of radiology, food service supervisor, or supervisor of any one of the many other activities necessary for the smooth functioning of a healthcare center. The one aspect that will help the supervisor cope with all this is the development of his or her knowledge and skill in the managerial part of the job.

This supervisory position is usually the first step in a long career of administrative positions that will make increasing demands for competent management as the individual moves up the administrative ladder. For instance, the staff nurse is made an assistant head nurse. After having served in this capacity for some time, she is promoted to head nurse, then to supervisor of nurses, then possibly to associate director of nursing, and even possibly to director of nursing services. Most of the tens of thousands of managerial positions in healthcare organizations are filled by health professionals who have not had any formal administrative training or study in management or administration per se. It is therefore essential that the supervisor, department head, chief technologist, or whatever the title may be, learn as much as possible about the meaning of being a competent first-line manager because this is his or her first step in the climb up the managerial and administrative ladder.

■ THE MANAGERIAL ASPECTS OF THE SUPERVISORY POSITION

The job of a supervisor can also be viewed in terms of three essential skills. First, the good supervisor must possess *technical skills*. These skills are primarily concerned with things, so that he or she knows the clinical and technical aspects of the work to be done. In addition, two more skills are needed, namely human skills and conceptual skills. *Human skills* are those skills that concern working with people, motivating them, and understanding individual and group feelings. *Conceptual skills* enable the supervisor to visualize something mentally in its entirety, to see the big picture, to understand how all parts of the organization contribute and coordinate their efforts. These human and conceptual skills are essential to the managerial aspects of a supervisor's job.

You may have observed various supervisors on different occasions and noticed that some of them are usually harassed, disorganized, and overly involved in doing the job at hand. They are muddling through and are knee-deep in work. Such supervisors put in long hours and are never afraid of doing anything themselves. They are working exceedingly hard but never seem to have enough time left to actually supervise. On the other hand, you may have observed supervisors who seem to be on top of the job and whose departments function smoothly and orderly. They have found time to sit at their desks at least part of the day and keep their desk work up to date. Why is there such a difference?

Of course, some supervisors are basically more capable than others, just as there are poor and good medical technologists. However, if you compare two chief technologists in two hospitals to discover why one is on top of the job and the other is continuously fixing things herself, you will probably find that one understands her job better than the other. Let us assume that both are equally good professionals, both work in the same subspecialty and have similar equipment, and the conditions under which they perform are similar. Still, the results of one chief technologist are significantly better than those of the other. Why is this? The answer is that the one is simply a better manager. She is able to supervise the functions of her department in a manner that allows her to get the job done through and with the people of her department. The difference between a good supervisor and a poor supervisor, assuming everything else being equal, is the difference in their managerial abilities.

Surprisingly enough, however, the managerial aspect of the supervisor's position has long been neglected. Rather, the emphasis has always been put on the clinical and technical competence for doing a particular job. Consider your own job, for example. It is very likely that you were appointed to this job from the ranks of one of the various professional services or crafts. As a result of your ingenuity, effort, and willingness to work hard, you were promoted to the supervisory level and were expected to assume the responsibilities of managing your unit. Little was done, however, to acquaint you with these responsibilities or to help you cope with the managerial aspects of your new job. More or less overnight you were made a part of administration without having been prepared to be a manager. Ever since, you have done the best you could by imitating and learning from your predecessors, and your department is probably functioning reasonably well. Still, there are likely to be some problems, and these may be lessened by a better understanding of the supervisory aspects of your job, so that you will be the manager running the department instead of the department running you.

It is the aim of this text to show the supervisor how to become a better manager. This does not mean that one can neglect or underestimate the actual work involved in getting the job done. As you know, one of the requirements of a good supervisor is a thorough understanding of the clinical, professional, and technical parts of the operations. Often the supervisor is actually the most skilled individual of the department and can do a more efficient and quicker job. He or she must not be tempted to step in and take over the job, however, except for purposes of instruction or in case of an emergency. Rather, the supervisor's responsibility is to see that the employees can do the job and do it properly. As a manager, the supervisor must plan, guide, and manage. Let us concentrate further on these managerial requirements of the supervisory position.

■ THE MEANING OF MANAGEMENT

First, let us consider what is meant by management. The term *management* has been defined in many ways, generally as a process of coordinating and integrating human, technical, and other resources to accomplish specific results. The following is a more meaningful definition for our purposes: *management is the process of getting things done through and with people, by directing and motivating the efforts of individuals toward common objectives.* You have undoubtedly learned from your own experience that in most endeavors one person can accomplish relatively little alone. For this reason people have found it expedient and even necessary to join with others to attain the goals of an enterprise. In every organized activity it is the manager's function to achieve the goals of the enterprise with the help of subordinates and fellow employees.

Achieving goals through and with people is only one aspect of the manager's job. It is also necessary to create a working atmosphere, a climate, a culture, within which subordinates can find as much satisfaction of their needs as possible. In other words, a supervisor must provide a climate conducive for the employees to fulfill such needs as recognition, achievement, and companionship. If these needs can be met right on the job, employees are more likely to strive willingly and enthusiastically toward the achievement of departmental objectives, as well as the overall objectives of the institution. Thus, we must add to our earlier definition of management by saying that the manager's job is *getting things done through and with people by enabling them to find as much satisfaction of their needs as possible, while at the same time motivating them to achieve both their own objectives and the objectives of the institution.* The better the supervisor performs these duties, the better the departmental results will be.

You may have noticed by this time that we have been using the terms supervisor, manager, and administrator interchangeably. Although the exact meaning of these titles varies with different institutions, the term *administrator,* or *executive, is generally used for top-level management positions, whereas manager* and *supervisor* usually connote positions within the middle or lower levels of the institutional hierarchy. There are some theoretical differences to consider, but for our purposes these terms will be used interchangeably.

Our reason for doing this will become clearer when you understand the somewhat surprising fact that the managerial aspects of all supervisory jobs are the same. This is true regardless of the supervisor's department or section or level within the administrative hierarchy. Thus, the managerial content of a supervisory position is the same whether the position is director of nursing services, head of the housekeeping division, chief engineer in the maintenance department, or chief therapeutic dietician. By the same token, the managerial functions are the same for the supervisor on the firing line (lowest-level or first-line supervisor), middle level of management, or top administrative group. In addition, it does not matter in which type of organization you are working. Managerial functions are the same for an industrial enterprise, commercial enterprise, not-for-profit organization, fraternal organization, government, or hospital or other healthcare facility. Regardless of the activities of the organization, department, or level, the managerial aspects and skills are the same.

■ MANAGERIAL SKILLS AND TECHNICAL SKILLS

These managerial skills must be distinguished from the professional, clinical, and technical skills required of a supervisor. As stated before, all supervisors must also possess special technical skills and professional know-how in their field. Technical skills vary between departments, but any supervisory position requires both professional technical skills and standard managerial skills. Mere technical and professional knowledge would not be sufficient.

It is important to note that as a supervisor advances up the administrative ladder, he or she will rely less on professional and technical skills and more on managerial skills. If you will observe your own institution, you will find that the higher you go within the administrative hierarchy, the more administrative skills are required and the less technical know-how. Therefore, the top-level administrator generally uses far fewer technical skills than those who are employed under him or her. In the rise to the top, however, the administrator has had to acquire all the administrative skills necessary for the management of the entire enterprise.

For example, the chief executive officer of a hospital is concerned primarily with the overall management of hospital activities; his or her functions are almost purely administrative. In this endeavor, the chief executive depends on the technical skills of the various subordinate administrators and managers, including all the first-line supervisors, to get the job done. The chief administrator in turn uses managerial skills in directing the efforts of all these subordinate managers toward the common objectives of the hospital. Therefore, throughout the organization the emphasis, content, and purpose of the managerial skills are the same.

■ MANAGERIAL SKILLS CAN BE LEARNED

At this point you may be wondering how a supervisor acquires these very important managerial skills. First of all, let us emphatically state that the standard managerial skills can be *learned*. They are not something with which you are necessarily born. Although it is often suggested that good managers, like good athletes, are born, not made, this belief is patently false. It cannot be denied that people are born with different physiological and biological potentials and that they are endowed with an unequal amount of intelligence and many other characteristics. It is also true that a person who is not a natural athlete is not likely to run 100 yards in record time. Many individuals who are natural athletes, however, have not come close to that goal either.

A good athlete is made when a person with some natural endowment, by practice, learning, effort, sacrifice, and experience develops this natural endowment into a mature skill. The same holds true for a good manager; by practice, learning, and experience he or she develops this natural endowment of intelligence and leadership into mature management skills. The skills involved in managing are as learnable and trainable as the skills involved in playing tennis. If you currently hold a supervisory position, it is likely that you have the necessary prerequisites of intelligence and leadership and that you are now ready to acquire the skills of a manager. It takes time and effort to develop these skills; they are not acquired overnight. The supervisor has ample opportunity to apply the principles and guidelines discussed in this text to the daily work. By applying the content of this text, the supervisor will certainly prevent many difficulties from occurring, and before too long the supervisor will reap the many benefits from practicing good supervision.

The most valuable resource of any organization is the people who work there, the human resources. It is the first-line supervisor to whom this most important resource is entrusted in the daily working situation. The best utilization of the human assets of the organization depends greatly on the managerial ability and understanding of the supervisor, as manifested by his or her expertise in influencing and directing them. The supervisor's efforts in this respect will lead to the creation of an organizational climate in which the employees will be able to realize the satisfaction of the multitude of their needs. The supervisor's job is to create this climate of motivation, satisfaction, leadership, and continuous further self-development and self-improvement. This is a challenge to every supervisor because it ultimately means the need for his or her own further self-development as a manager.

■ BENEFITS FROM BETTER MANAGEMENT

The benefits that you as a supervisor will derive from learning to be a better manager are obvious. First, you will have many opportunities to apply managerial principles and knowledge to your present job. Good management as a supervisor will make a great deal of difference in the performance of your department. It will function more smoothly, work will get done on time, you will probably find it easier to stay within your budget, and your workers will more willingly and enthusiastically contribute toward the ultimate objectives.

The application of management principles will put you as a supervisor on top of your job, instead of being completely "swallowed up" by it. You will also have more time to be concerned with the overall aspects of your department, and in so doing, you will become more valuable to those to whom you are responsible. For example, you will be more likely to contribute significant suggestions and advice to your superiors, perhaps in areas about which you have never before been consulted but that ultimately affect your department. You will also find it easier to see the complex interrelationships of the various departments throughout the health-care center. This in turn will help you to work in closer harmony with your colleagues who are supervising other departments. Briefly, you will be able to do a more effective supervisory job with much less effort.

In addition to the direct benefits of doing a better supervisory job for the health-care institution, there are other benefits for you personally. As a supervisor applying sound management principles, you will grow in stature. As time goes on you will be capable of handling more important and more complicated assignments. You will be able to fill better and higher-paying jobs. You will move up within the managerial hierarchy and will naturally want to improve your managerial skills as you advance.

As stated earlier, an additional satisfying thought is that the functions of management are equally applicable in any organization and in any managerial or supervisory position. That is, the principles of management required to produce microwave ovens, manage a retail department, supervise office work, or run a repair shop are all the same. Moreover, these principles are applicable not only in the United States, but in other parts of the world as well. Aside from local peculiarities and questions of personality, it would not matter whether you are a supervisor in a textile mill in India, a supervisor in a chemical plant in Italy, a department foreman in a steel mill in Gary, Indiana, or a supervisor of the medical records section in a hospital in St. Louis. By becoming a manager, you will become more mobile in every direction and in every respect.

Therefore, there are great inducements for you to learn the principles of good management. However, you cannot expect to learn them overnight. You can only become a good manager by actually managing, that is, by applying the principles of management to your own work situation. You will undoubtedly make mistakes here and there but will in turn learn from those mistakes. The principles and guidelines of management discussed in this book can be applied to most situations. They will help you avoid errors that often take a long time to correct. Your efforts to become an outstanding manager will pay substantial dividends. As your managerial competence increases, you will be able to prevent many of the difficulties that make a supervisory job a burden instead of a challenging and satisfying task.

■ SUMMARY

The demands on good management in healthcare activities are increasing rapidly, making the role of the supervisor a most challenging one. To the employees in the department, the supervisor represents management. To a superior, he or she is a subordinate. To the supervisors in other departments, he or she must be a good colleague, coordinating efforts with theirs to achieve the institution's objectives. The supervisor must possess technical, human, and conceptual skills. The supervisor must have the clinical and technical competence for the functions to be performed in the department, and at the same time he or she must be the manager of that department.

Management is the function of getting things done through and with people. The way a supervisor handles the managerial aspects of the job will make the difference between running the department and being run by the department. The managerial aspects of any supervisory job are the same, regardless of the particular type of work involved or the position on the administrative ladder. As a supervisor climbs up this ladder, the managerial skills will increase in importance, and the technical and professional skills will gradually become less important. These managerial skills can be learned; a manager is not "born," he or she is made. A supervisor will benefit greatly both professionally and personally if he or she takes the time to study and acquire managerial expertise and excellence.

2

MANAGERIAL FUNCTIONS AND AUTHORITY

The supervisor's managerial role rests on two foundations: managerial functions and managerial authority. In Chapter 1 we discussed the importance of this role, the capability to learn the necessary skills, and the benefits of mastering them. The first benchmark is the managerial functions a supervisor must perform to be considered a true manager. The other major characteristic of the managerial position is the concept of authority inherent to the supervisory position. Authority is discussed briefly later in this chapter and more extensively throughout this book.

■ THE MANAGERIAL FUNCTIONS

Managerial skills are the functions a manager *must* perform to be considered a manager. These skills are the functions necessary to carry out the managerial job. In this text, the five managerial functions are classified in the major categories of *planning, organizing, staffing, influencing,* and *controlling.* The labels used to describe these functions vary somewhat in management literature; some textbooks list one more or one less managerial function. Regardless of the terms or number used, the managerial functions collectively constitute one of the two major characteristics of a manager.

A person who does not perform these functions is not a manager in the true sense of the word, regardless of title. We must discuss more precisely the managerial functions of planning, organizing, staffing, influencing, and controlling. The following explanation is only introductory, general, and brief, since most of the book is devoted to the discussion and ramifications of each of these functions.

Planning

Planning, the first managerial function, determines in advance what should be done in the future. This function consists of determining the goals, objectives, policies, procedures, methods, rules, budgets, and other plans needed to achieve the purpose of the organization. In planning, the manager must think of, contemplate, and select a course of action from a set of available alternatives. Thus, planning is mental work that involves thinking before acting, looking ahead, and preparing for the future. Planning is laying out in advance the goals to be achieved, the road to be followed, and the best means to achieve these objectives.

You may have observed supervisors who are constantly fighting one crisis after another. The probable reason is that they did not plan or look ahead. It is every manager's duty to plan; this function cannot be delegated to someone else. Certain specialists may be called on to assist in laying out various plans, but as the manager of the department, the supervisor must make departmental plans. These plans must coincide with the general overall objectives of the institution as laid down by the chief executive officer (CEO). Within the overall directives and general boundaries, however, the manager has considerable leeway in mapping the departmental course.

Planning must come before any of the other managerial functions. Even after the initial plans are laid out and the manager proceeds with the other managerial functions, the function of planning continues in revising the course of action and choosing different alternatives as the need arises. Therefore, although planning is the first function a manager must tackle, it does not end at the initiation of the other functions. The manager continues to plan while performing the organizing, staffing, influencing, and controlling functions.

Organizing

Once a plan has been developed, the manager's organizing function determines how the work is to be accomplished. The manager must define, group, and assign job duties. More specifically, through organizing the manager determines and enumerates the various activities to be accomplished and combines these activities into distinct groups—departments, divisions, sections, teams, or any other units. Then the manager further divides the group work into individual jobs, assigns these activities, and at the same time provides subordinates with the authority needed to carry out these activities.

In other words, to organize means to design a structural framework that sets up all the positions needed to perform the work of the department and to assign particular duties to these positions. When the manager organizes the structural framework, it is also imperative that the authority relationships between the various subordinates be appropriately aligned. While organizing, the manager necessarily must delegate a certain amount of authority to the subordinate managers, so that they can carry out the duties for which they are responsible. Organizing encompasses the elements of specialization, departmentalization, span of management, authority relationships, responsibility, unity of command, line and staff, and other factors. The result of the organizing function is the creation of an activity-authority network for the department, which is a subsystem within the total healthcare network.

Staffing

Staffing is the manager's responsibility to recruit and select new employees to ensure that there are enough qualified employees to fill the various positions needed and budgeted for in the department. Besides hiring them, staffing also involves training these employees, promoting them, appraising their performance, and giving them opportunities for further development. In addition, staffing includes a wise and appropriate system of compensation. In most healthcare institutions the personnel department helps with and facilitates the technical aspects of staffing. The basic authority and responsibility for staffing, however, remain with the supervisor.

Influencing (or leading, directing or motivating).

The managerial function of influencing means issuing directives and orders to accomplish the job and to help the members of the organization work together. This function is also known as *leading, directing,* or *motivating.* The influencing function of a manager includes directing, guiding, teaching, coaching, and supervising subordinates. It is not sufficient for a manager to plan, organize, and staff. The supervisor must also stimulate action by giving directives and orders to the subordinates, then supervising and guiding them as they work. Moreover, it is the manager's job to develop the abilities of the subordinates by leading, teaching, and coaching them effectively. Influencing is concerned with motivating people at work to achieve their maximum potential, satisfy their needs, and stimulate them to act in ways they may not on their own.

Thus, influencing is the process around which all performance revolves; it is the essence of all operations. This process has many dimensions, such as employee needs, morale, job satisfaction, productivity, leadership, and communication. Through the influencing function the supervisor seeks to create a climate conducive to employee satisfaction while achieving the objectives of the institution. As you know from personal experience, much and perhaps most of your time is spent in influencing subordinates.

Controlling

Controlling is the function that ensures that plans are followed and objectives achieved. In other words, to control means to determine whether the plans are being carried out, if progress is being made toward objectives, and whether other actions must be taken to correct deviations and shortcomings. Again, this relates to the importance of planning as the primary function of the manager. A supervisor could not check on whether work was proceeding properly if there were no plans to check against. Controlling also includes taking corrective action if objectives are not being met and revising the plans and objectives if circumstances require it.

■ THE INTERRELATIONSHIPS OF MANAGERIAL FUNCTIONS

It is helpful to think of the five managerial functions as a continuous circular movement, a management cycle. A cycle is a system of interdependent processes and activities. Each activity blends into another and each affects the performance of the others. In daily supervisory activities you may have often thought that your job is a vicious cycle, without a beginning or an end. If you think of the managerial process as a cycle consisting of the five different functions, however, this idea will greatly simplify your job of supervising. As shown in Figure 2-1, the five functions flow into each other, and at times there is no clear line indicating where one function ends and the other begins. Because of this interrelationship, no manager can set aside a specific amount of time each day for one or another function. The effort spent on each function will vary as conditions and circumstances change. The planning function, however, undoubtedly must come first. Without plans the manager cannot organize, staff, influence, or control. Throughout this text, therefore, we shall follow this sequence of planning first, then organizing, staffing, influencing, and controlling.

■ **FIGURE 2-1 Cycle of supervisory functions.**

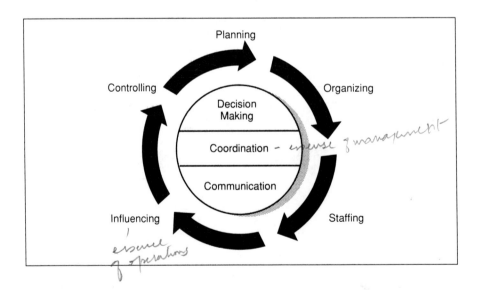

It should be emphasized that although the five managerial functions can be separated theoretically, in the daily job of the manager these activities are inseparable. Again, each function blends into the other, and each affects the performance of the others. The output of one provides the input for another, which is why these functions can be viewed as elements of a system. (See Figure 2-2.)

■ FIGURE 2-2 Elements of the supervisory system.

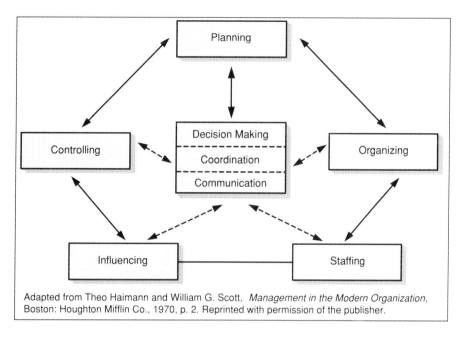

Adapted from Theo Haimann and William G. Scott, *Management in the Modern Organization,* Boston: Houghton Mifflin Co., 1970, p. 2. Reprinted with permission of the publisher.

■ UNIVERSALITY OF THE MANAGERIAL FUNCTIONS AND THEIR RELATION TO POSITION AND TIME

As stated earlier, the managerial functions are universal. These functions are the responsibility of all managers, regardless of whether they are the chairman of the board, the president of the healthcare center, the vice-president for patient care, or the supervisor on the firing line. All of these managers perform all five functions. This idea is known as the principle of *universality of managerial functions.*

The time and effort that each manager devotes to a particular function will vary, however, depending on the individual's level within the administrative hierarchy. For example, a CEO will usually spend more time in planning, organizing, and controlling and less time in staffing and influencing. On the other hand, a supervisor of a department will probably spend less time in planning and organizing and more time in staffing and especially influencing and controlling. The CEO is likely to plan, for example, 1 year, 5 years, or even 10 or 20 years ahead. A supervisor will make plans of much shorter duration. At times a supervisor will have to make plans for 6 or 12 months but more frequently will just make plans for the next month, week, or even for the next day or shift. In other words, the span and magnitude of plans will be smaller.

The same is true of the influencing function. The CEO will normally assign tasks to subordinate managers, delegate authority, depend on their accomplishing the task, and spend a minimum of time in direct supervision. As a supervisor, however, you are concerned with getting the job done each day and throughout the day, and you will have to spend much time in this influencing or directing function. And similar observations can be made for organizing, staffing, and controlling. Therefore, we can conclude that all managers perform the same managerial functions, regardless of their level in the hierarchy, but the time and effort involved in each function will depend on their position on the administrative ladder. (See Figure 2-3.)

■ **FIGURE 2-3 Amount of time spent on each function.**

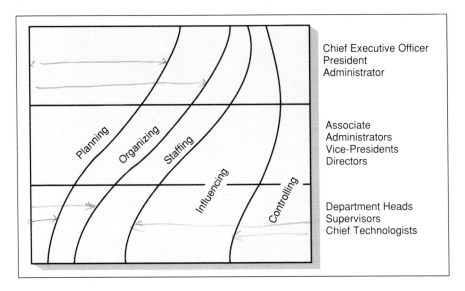

■ MANAGERIAL AUTHORITY

The second factor that characterizes a manager is authority. Without authority a person in an organizational setting cannot be a manager. What is this authority that makes a supervisor a manager? Why is authority a characteristic that makes the managerial position? Briefly, authority can be defined as legal or rightful power, the right to act and to direct others. It is the power by which a manager can ask subordinates to do or not do a certain task that the manager deems appropriate and necessary to realize the objectives of the department.

One must realize that this managerial authority is not actually delegated to people but to positions within the organization. The authority belongs to the formal position a manager holds and not to the manager as an individual. Therefore, one usually speaks of the manager's authority, rather than the authority of the managerial position. This form of managerial authority ceases when the manager resigns from the job or is discharged. The manager's successor will then have this authority.

This formal, organizational authority gives the supervisor the power and right to give directives to the members of the department to achieve the objectives and tasks assigned to it. Our concept of authority must also include the possession of power to impose sanctions when necessary. Without such power to enforce an order, the enterprise could become disorganized, and chaos could result. If a subordinate refuses to carry out the manager's directive, this authority must include the right to take disciplinary action and possibly to discharge the employee.

This aspect of authority obviously has many restrictions. These may be in the form of legal restrictions, union contracts, or consideration of morals, ethics, and human behavior. For example, legal restrictions may make it necessary to take and fulfill many steps before an employee can be dismissed. Also, every successful manager knows that to influence and motivate subordinates to perform required duties, it is best not to depend on this formal managerial authority but to use other ways and means to accomplish the job. In other words, it is far better not to depend on the negative aspects of dominance and authority. In practice most managers do not speak of authority at all. They prefer to speak of the "responsibility," "tasks," or "duties" they have. Such managers correctly consider it better human relations to say that they have the responsibility for certain activities instead of saying that they possess the authority within that area. Using the words responsibility, tasks, and duties in a loose sense allows the manager to avoid the "big stick."

As a supervisor, however, you should not be misled by the loose use of these terms. Having authority means having the power and right to issue directives. You should know that tasks and duties have been assigned to you and that you have accepted the responsibility for getting them done. This responsibility has been exacted from you by your superior. It is important to understand that the concept of responsibility is always connected with authority. These concepts go hand in hand; one cannot exist without the other. Regardless of how the supervisor applies authority, we emphasize again that the supervisory position must have this authority. Otherwise, chaos would follow.

Our discussion in Chapter 9 referring to the meaning and various bases of authority will shed additional light on this concept of authority. In Chapter 11 the concepts of authority and responsibility will be discussed. At that time, how subordinates and workers react to authority and how authority is delegated will be examined. Delegation of authority means the process by which a supervisor receives authority from the superior manager, as well as the process by which some of the authority assigned to this position is delegated to subordinates. Just as authority is the lifeblood of any managerial position, delegating authority to the lower ranks within the managerial hierarchy makes it possible to build an organizational structure with effective managers on every level. This point will be discussed more fully throughout this text because it plays such an important role in supervisory management. This concept of formal positional authority will merge into an entire spectrum of influence, power, and authority.

At this point, however, you need only to remember that authority is one of the basic characteristics of the managerial job. Without authority, managerial functions and the supervisor-subordinate relationship would be weakened and become meaningless.

■ SUMMARY

The five managerial functions of planning, organizing, staffing, influencing, and controlling are one of the two benchmarks of the manager's job. Each blends into another, and each affects the performance of the others. The output of one provides the input for another. These five functions are universal for all managers, regardless of position in the managerial hierarchy. The time and effort involved in each function will vary depending on the position on the administrative ladder the manager occupies.

The second benchmark of the managerial job is authority; it makes the managerial position real. This organizational authority is delegated to positions within the organization. Since these positions are staffed by people, one usually speaks of the manager's authority rather than the authority of a managerial position.

· *Part Two* ·

CONNECTIVE
PROCESSES

■ CONNECTIVE PROCESSES

The benchmarks of the managerial job are authority and the performance of the five managerial functions. These five functions are interrelated and interconnected. Binding the five managerial functions together are three connective processes: decision making, coordination, and communication. These connective processes are not functions in and of themselves; rather, they link the five functions together into a continuous management system. These processes allow the manager to run the department as a smoothly working unit that is a subsystem within the larger system of the healthcare organization.

Decision making, coordination, and communication are essential to the performance of each of the managerial functions. For example, when the manager plans, decisions certainly must be made. These decisions must also be coordinated to not contradict one another or result in duplication of effort. Finally, these decisions must be communicated to those who are to carry them out. Similarly, when the manager performs the organizing function, decisions as to the type of organizational structure to be set up are needed. This structure must be coordinated with that of the rest of the institution. Communications and explanations to the subordinates are essential so that they will understand their place and their duties in relation to each other and to the whole institution. The same pattern of deciding, coordinating, and communicating holds true for the other functions of staffing, influencing, and controlling.

Thus, the three connective processes are a vital force for all the managerial functions and must be developed to hold the managerial system together. Since they overlay the functions, these three processes will be discussed in separate chapters before analyzing each of the managerial functions.

3

DECISION MAKING

Decision making can be defined as the process of selecting one alternative from among a number of other alternatives. Decisions are an integral part of all five managerial functions, but they are most closely associated with the planning function. Although the manager acts within an organizational environment, managerial decision making is considered in this text as an individual process. At the heart of this process is the individual manager, whose decisions will be influenced by many other persons, various departments, the total organization, and environmental factors such as the economy, technology, governmental requirements, and politics.

If practicing managers were asked to define in one or two words the essence of their jobs, they probably would reply "making decisions." This process of decision making is the core of all managerial activities. Making decisions is a substantial part of everybody's daily activities. All of us have to solve problems in many areas of endeavor. Therefore, decision making should not be foreign to us. Decision making is a basic human activity that begins in early childhood and continues throughout a person's life.

■ PROGRAMMED AND NONPROGRAMMED DECISIONS

For many of the decision-making situations that confront us in our daily lives, we have a standard solution. Solving these problems does not usually cause us much difficulty because we are quite familiar with them. These decisions are called *programmed decisions* because they refer to repetitive routine problems that have fixed answers, methods, rules, and standardized operating procedures.

For instance, a staff nurse finds that a patient has an elevation of temperature. To verify the finding, the nurse measures it again with a different thermometer and finds out whether the patient just had a cup of hot coffee or a cigarette. The elevation registers the same degree. Reinforced with these facts, the nurse has a solution for the problem, namely, to check again after a period of time. Again the results are the same. The next decision is to see whether the attending physician left orders to cover this problem; if not, the nurse automatically decides to consult the physician for further action. The staff nurse had to make several decisions up to this point. All of them were programmed; a standard procedure had anticipated these kinds of problems.

For other decision-making situations the application of computers and operations research are a great aid in developing programmed decisions, such as with the reorder point and the quantity to be ordered by the purchasing agent. A program has been designed for this particular problem, and the computer is called on to come up with the answer.

However, frequently supervisors are confronted with new or unusual problems—decision-making situations for which no standard solutions exist and no program has been designed. These situations call for the making of *nonprogrammed decisions*. In these instances the manager should use a logical, rational decision-making process. The following discussions are directed to these managerial, nonprogrammed decision-making situations.

■ THE IMPORTANCE OF DECISION-MAKING SKILLS

As a supervisor you are constantly called on to find practical solutions to problems that are caused by changing situations or unusual circumstances. Normally you are able to arrive at a satisfactory decision. One reason why you are in a supervisory position is that you have made many more correct decisions than wrong decisions as problems presented themselves.

All managers, at all levels of the organization in all functions, make decisions. Decisions are not made in a vacuum, since each has some effect on the entire system. All managers go through, or should go through, the same process of decision making that you go through as a supervisor. The only difference is that the decisions made at the top of the administrative hierarchy are usually more far reaching and affect more people and areas than those decisions made by a supervisor. Thus, decision making, as with the five managerial functions, is an essential process that permeates the entire administrative hierarchy.

Once a decision has been made, effective action is necessary. Every decision made should be put into practice and carried out. A good decision is useless if nobody does anything about it. Obtaining effective action, however, is not our concern in this chapter. Other chapters will deal mainly with ways the manager can achieve effective action. This discussion will explain the process that should come before the action, the process that you as a manager should go through to decide what action to take.

Let us be more specific about the timing of this decision-making process. When viewing a person as a decision maker, a picture often comes to mind of an executive with horn-rimmed glasses bent over some papers, pen in hand, ready to sign on the dotted line. Or we may see a person in a board of directors meeting, raising an arm to vote a certain way. Such images have one point in common: they portray the decision makers at the very moment of choice, ready to select one alternative that leads from the crossroads down a particular path of action. This moment of decision making should not be emphasized here, since it does not describe the long, difficult process that must come before the final moment of selecting one alternative over the others.

Although long and difficult, the decision-making process is worthwhile learning and knowing. As with the managerial skills, the skills involved in decision making can be learned, and once learned they provide great benefits for the manager. These benefits will accrue to the manager, no matter what position he or she holds, because the decision-making process is used on all levels of the administrative hierarchy.

Moreover, it is important to note that your managerial job involves not only making decisions yourself, but also seeing that those who work under you make decisions effectively. Obviously a supervisor cannot make all the decisions necessary for running the department. Many of the daily decision-making activities you are responsible for as a supervisor will be delegated to your subordinates. It is therefore necessary that you also teach and train your subordinates in this process of making decisions.

■ STEPS IN DECISION MAKING

The decision-making process involves several steps, and the decision maker must follow these steps in the sequence in which they are arranged:

1. Define the problem.
2. Analyze the problem.
3. Develop alternatives.
4. Evaluate the alternatives and select the best.
5. Take action and follow-up.

Define the Problem

Supervisors have often been heard to say, "I wish I had the answer," "I wish I had the solution to this," or "I wish I knew what to do about this." All these "wishes" indicate that the supervisor is overly concerned with having an answer. Instead of seeking an *answer*, however, the supervisor should be looking for the real problem. The first task is always to find out what the problem is in the particular decision situation; only then can one work toward the solution, the answer. As someone has put it, "There really is nothing as useless as having the right answer to the wrong question."

In most cases defining the problem is not an easy task. What often appears to be the problem might be merely a symptom of it that shows up on the surface. It is necessary to dig deeper to locate the real problem and define it. For example, a supervisor might seem to be confronted with a problem of conflicting personalities within the department. Two employees are continually quarreling and cannot get along together. On checking into this situation, however, the supervisor may find that the problem is not one of personalities, but that the functions and duties of each employee have never really been delineated.

Thus, what appeared on the surface to be a problem of personal conflict was actually a problem of organization and structure. Only after the true nature of the problem has been realized can the supervisor do something about it. In this case the chances are good that once the activities and duties of the two employees are delineated, the friction will stop. Defining a problem such as this may be a time-consuming chore, but it is time well spent. The process of decision making cannot proceed further until the problem is clearly defined.

Analyze the Problem

After the problem, not just the symptoms, has been defined, the manager can set out to analyze it. The first thing in this analysis is to assemble the facts, to gather all pertinent information. Only after a clear definition of the problem is found can the supervisor decide how important certain data are and what additional information may be needed. In certain situations some of this is done simultaneously while defining the problem. The supervisor will then gather as many facts as possible.

Many supervisors complain, however, that they never have enough facts. Although it is normal for a supervisor to think that he or she does not have all the facts, this complaint is often just an excuse to delay a decision. A manager will never have *all* the facts available. Therefore, it is necessary to make decisions on those facts that are available and also on those additional facts that can be gathered without undue delays or costs.

At the same time it is wise to consider the behavioral impact on problem definition and to remember that what is believed to be a fact is somewhat colored by subjectivity. One cannot be completely freed of the subjective elements involved. As much as we may want to exclude prejudice and bias, we are only human, and subjectivity will creep in somehow. Of course, we should make an effort to be as objective and impersonal as possible. This process of analysis, however, requires the supervisor to think not only of objective considerations, but also of intangible factors that may be involved. These factors are difficult to assess and analyze, but they do play a significant role, especially in healthcare institutions. Such intangibles may be factors of reputation, quality of patient care, morale, discipline, perception, etc. It is hard to be specific about such factors, but they should nevertheless be considered in analyzing the problem.

Develop Alternatives

After having defined and analyzed the decision situation, the manager's next step is to search for and develop various alternative courses of action. An absolute rule is that all possible alternatives will be taken into consideration. Always bear in mind that the final decision can only be as good as the best of the alternatives considered. The decision can never be better than the best alternative.

It is almost unthinkable that a situation should not offer at least several alternatives. These choices, however, might not always be obvious, yet it is the duty of the decision maker to search for them. Also, some of the alternatives may not be desirable, but the manager should not decide this until all of them have been carefully considered. If this is not done, one is likely to fall into the "either-or" kind of thinking. You have often heard it said after one minute's deliberation: "There is only one of two things that we can do, either...or..." The type of manager who says this is too easily inclined to see only one of these two alternatives as the right one to follow.

Consider the following situation. Hospital regulations state that patients leaving their rooms after 10 AM will be charged a late-stay charge. This time limit is necessary to have the room vacated and cleaned in time for the new admission influx at 1 to 2 PM. The patient was admitted on July 1 at 2 PM to the room and left at 11 AM on July 2. The bill arrived with an additional day's charge as the late-stay charge, but the patient stayed less than 24 hours and refuses to pay for 48 hours. Even in this unpleasant dilemma, several alternatives exist, although none of them is completely desirable. The hospital could insist on having the patient pay the bill, although this would cause ill will. Second, one could ask the attending physician to justify why the patient could not be discharged earlier if the reason is medically related. This may be sufficient to have insurance coverage pay the charge if an insurer is involved. Third, the hospital could write off the charge.

Also, it is not enough for you as a supervisor to decide between the various alternatives that have been presented by subordinates. The routine alternatives normally suggested by them may not include all the possible choices. It is your job as a manager to conceive of more, and possibly better, alternatives. Even in the most discouraging situations there are several choices, and although none of them may be desirable, the manager still has a choice to make.

Brainstorming is a tool often used to increase creativity in problem solving.[1] If the decision situation is particularly vexing and if time permits, a brainstorming session with other supervisors or employees is a good tool to come up with as many alternatives as possible. This is likely to result in novel, unusual, unorthodox alternative solutions. Although a thorough discussion of brainstorming is beyond the scope of this text, the manager should know some of the main ideas. The participants must feel free to contribute as many alternatives as possible, no matter how extreme and wild these may be. The participants can build on ideas presented by others. Criticisms, ridicule, and evaluations must be withheld in order to hear all ideas. This creative problem-solving process is likely to increase the number of alternatives.

Evaluate the Alternatives and Select the Best   *Make a decision*

The purpose of decision making is to select or choose from among the various alternatives the course of action that will provide the greatest number of wanted consequences and the smallest number of unwanted consequences. After developing the alternatives, the manager should test each of them by imagining that each has already been put into effect. Each alternative must be examined as to how feasible and satisfactory it is and what the consequences will be if it is chosen. Once the alternatives have been thought through and appraised along these lines, the decision maker will be in a position to select one.

In this process the supervisor should bear in mind the degree of *risk* involved in each course of action. One must remain aware that no decision is without risk; one alternative will simply have more or less risk than another. It is also possible that the question of *time* will make one alternative preferable to another. There is usually a difference in the amount of time required to carry out each alternative, and this should be considered by the supervisor. Moreover, in this process of evaluating the different alternatives, the supervisor should also bear in mind the *resources, facilities, know-how, equipment,* and *records* that are available. Finally, the manager should not forget to judge the different alternatives along the lines of *economy of effort,* in other words, which action will give the greatest result for the least amount of effort and expenditure.

It is important that the decision be of high quality, but it must also be *acceptable* to the group affected by it. If the highest-quality decision is not acceptable to the group, its effectiveness probably is diminished, since it will be carried out at best grudgingly, or it might even be quietly sabotaged. In such a situation it might be advisable for the supervisor to choose a more acceptable decision that is not of the highest quality. Acceptability is one more consideration in this process of choice.

Using these criteria of feasibility, satisfactoriness, risk, timing, acceptability, resources, and economy, the manager often can see that one alternative clearly provides a greater number of desirable consequences and fewer unwanted consequences than any other alternative. In such cases the decision is a relatively easy one. The best alternative, however, is not always so obvious. It is conceivable that at certain times two or more alternatives may seem equally desirable. Then the choice is simply a matter of the manager's personal preference. On the other hand, the manager also may believe that no single alternative far outweighs any of the others or is sufficiently stronger. In this case it might be advisable to combine two of the better alternatives and come up with a compromise solution.

But what about a situation where the manager finds that none of the alternatives is satisfactory and that all of them have too many undesirable effects? As a supervisor, you might have been in a situation where the undesirable consequences of all the alternatives were so overwhelmingly bad that they paralyzed any action. You might have thought that there was only one available solution to the problem, namely, to take no action at all. Such a solution, however, is deceptive. A supervisor is wrong to believe that taking no action will get him or her "off the hook." In practice, taking no action is as much a decision as deciding to take a specific action, although few people are aware of this. Most people think that taking no action relieves them of making an unpleasant decision. The only way for the manager to avoid this pitfall is to try to visualize the consequences of inaction. The manager needs only to think through what would happen if no action were taken and will probably see that, in so doing, an undesirable alternative is chosen.

Having ruled out inaction in most cases, you may still be in a position where all alternatives seem undesirable. In such a case you should search for new and different alternatives. Be a bit creative and try to develop at least a couple of new solutions. Also check to see that all the steps of the decision-making process have been followed. Has the problem been clearly defined? Have all the pertinent facts been gathered and analyzed? Have all possible alternatives been considered? Has the brainstorming technique been used? Chances are that some new alternatives will come up, and a good decision can then be made. In making this decision, however, you might have to employ some additional factors, such as experience, intuition, and actual testing, or you may have to resort to scientific decision making.

Experience

The manager's final selection from among the various alternatives is frequently influenced and guided by past experience. History often repeats itself, and the old saying that "experience is the best teacher" still holds true. Managers undoubtedly can often decide wisely on the basis of their own experience or that of other managers. Knowledge gained by past experience can frequently be applied to new situations, and no manager should ever underestimate the importance of such knowledge. On the other hand, it is dangerous to follow past experience blindly.

Therefore, whenever the manager calls on experience as a basis for choice among alternatives, the supervisor should examine the situation and conditions that prevailed at the time of the past decision. Current conditions may still be very much the same, and thus the present decision should be the same as the one made on that previous occasion. More often than not, however, conditions have changed considerably, and the underlying circumstances and assumptions are no longer valid. In these cases, of course, the decision should not be the same.

Previous experience can also be helpful if the manager is called on to substantiate the reasons for making a particular decision. Experience is a good defense tactic, and many superiors use it as valid evidence. There is still no excuse, however, for following experience blindly. Past experience must always be viewed with the future in mind. The underlying circumstances of the past, present, and future must be considered. Only within this framework is experience a helpful approach to the selection from alternatives.

Hunch and Intuition

Managers will at times admit that they have based their decisions on hunch and intuition. At first glance, certain managers may seem to have an unusual ability for solving problems satisfactorily by intuitive means. A deeper search, however, will disclose that the "intuition" on which the manager thought a decision was based was actually past experience or knowledge. In reality, the manager is recalling similar situations from the past that are now stored in the memory; this type of recall is labeled "having a hunch." No superior would look favorably on a subordinate who continually justifies decisions on the basis of intuition or hunch alone. These factors might come into play occasionally, but they must always be supplemented by more concrete considerations.

Experimentation

The avenue of experimentation, or testing, is a valid approach to decision making in the scientific world; conclusions reached through laboratory tests and experimentation are essential. In management, however, to experiment and see what happens is inappropriate and often too costly and time consuming. Moreover, it is difficult to maintain controlled conditions and test various alternatives fairly in a normal work environment. There may be certain instances, however, when a limited amount of testing and experimenting is admissible, as long as the consequences are not too disruptive. For example, a supervisor might decide to test out different work schedules or different assignments of duties. In this small restricted sense, experimentation may at times be valid. In a supervisory situation, however, experimentation usually is at best a most expensive way of reaching a decision.

■ QUANTITATIVE DECISION MAKING

During the last four decades or so a new group of highly sophisticated tools has become available to aid the manager in decision making. These tools are quantitative, involving linear programming, operations research, probability, and simulation. They are sophisticated mathematical techniques applied by mathematicians, statisticians, programmers, systems analysts, or other scientists working with computers. A discussion of this tool is beyond the scope of this text. A short description could not do justice to this important and well-documented field of scientific decision making. The overall process is known as scientific decision making, or operations research.

Only certain types of management problems lend themselves to this type of quantitative analysis and solution. In a healthcare situation, for example, it could be applicable to problems involving scheduling, inventory, arranging for the best possible use of facilities and employees during various shifts, planning for the most effective utilization of existing resources, and so on. Such scientific problem solving is a complicated and costly way of reaching decisions, however, and it should be used only with the permission and knowledge of top administration when the magnitude of a problem warrants considerable effort and expenditure. The problems confronting a single supervisor usually are not of this magnitude. If a major problem is affecting the entire organization, however, or if similar problems are found in several departments, it may be advisable for top management to employ the quantitative approach. Since many healthcare centers today have easy access to a computer, it should not be difficult to contact someone within this center to see if they could lend some assistance in solving the problem. The programmers and systems analysts may produce not only an optimum solution, but their research may also lead to other findings that are welcome by-products. Management, however, should not forget that it could be a long and tedious, as well as an expensive, process. If the problem is of sufficient magnitude, such effort and expense are certainly worthwhile.

Take Action and Follow-Up

No matter what method has been used to arrive at the solution, effective action is necessary once the decision has been made. Going through the lengthy and tedious decision-making process is pointless unless the manager goes all the way and sees the decision carried out effectively. As stated before, nothing is so useless as a good decision that is not carried out. In other words, decision making is only one aspect of the manager's job; achieving effective execution of the decision is at least as important. Even after action has been taken, decision making is not complete without follow-up to evaluate the effectiveness of the decision. If all is well and the results are as expected and satisfactory, we can stop here. If the results are not as expected or if unanticipated consequences arose, however, or if something did not work out as decided, then the supervisor should look at the situation as a new problem and go through all the steps of the decision-making process again from a new point of view.

Action and follow-up are impossible without two other essential processes, communication and coordination. Unless a decision is clearly communicated to the people who must carry it out and unless it is coordinated with other decisions and other departments, it will be meaningless. Thus, the two additional connective processes that are vital to management's overall task of "getting things done through and with people" must be examined.

■ SUMMARY

Selecting the best alternative by facts, study, and analysis of various proposals is still the most generally approved avenue of making a managerial decision. If an objective, rational, systematic method is used in the selection, the manager is likely to make better decisions. The first step in such a method is to define the problem. After a problem is defined, you must analyze it. Then you must develop all the alternatives you possibly can, think them through as if you had already put them into action, and consider the consequences of each of them. Each alternative must be evaluated on the basis of past experience. By following this method, you will most likely be able to select the best alternative, the one with the greatest number of wanted and the least number of unwanted consequences.

Not only can you learn this sound method of decision making, but as a supervisor you can teach the same systematic step approach to your subordinates. In so doing, you have the assurance that whenever subordinates are confronted with a situation where they have to make a decision, they also will decide in a systematic and rational manner. Although this is not always a guarantee for arriving at the best decisions, it is likely to produce more good decisions than would otherwise be the case.

Scientific decision making, or operations research, is an approach to problem solving that involves quantitative analysis, models, and computers. If the problem is of sufficient magnitude to warrant such an effort, sophisticated scientific decision-making techniques involving mathematicians, statisticians, systems analysts, and other specialists should be used.

NOTES

1. See Alex F. Osborn, *Applied Imagination,* 3d ed., New York: Charles Scribner's Sons, 1963.

4

COORDINATING ORGANIZATIONAL ACTIVITIES

A major problem facing every organization is the coordination of organizational activities. Division of work and specialization, as discussed in Chapter 10, involves separating employees into departments, divisions, units, sections, etc., based on shared expertise. This is particularly true of healthcare activities, where continuous advances in medical and related sciences and technology bring about increasingly greater specialization and fragmentation. This leads to large and complex organizational structures in terms of differentiation of activities and specialization. This proliferation of specialties has clear advantages for patients and clients in terms of scientific care. However, it creates additional problems for the management of healthcare institutions, namely, the need for coordination—the process of linking the activities of all these units in the organization.

The reason for coordination is that all these areas are interdependent; they depend on each other for information, activities, resources, and communications. The interdependence is particularly great in a hospital because it is reciprocal, meaning that activities flow both ways between units, e.g., from ward to surgery, from surgery to intensive care, and from intensive care to radiology. Clearly the need for coordination is great in such a complex situation. The greater the degree of interdependence, the more attention must be devoted to coordination.

■ THE MEANING OF COORDINATION

Supervisory management was defined as the process of getting things done through and with people by directing their efforts toward common objectives. This means that management involves the coordination of the efforts of all members of an organization. Some writers have even defined management as the task of achieving coordination, or more specifically, of achieving the orderly synchronization of employees' efforts to provide the proper amount, timing, and quality of execution so that their unified efforts lead to the stated objectives. Other writers have preferred to look at coordination as a separate managerial function.

32

We prefer to view coordination, however, not as a separate function of the manager and not as *the* defining characteristic of management, but as a *process* by which the manager achieves orderly group effort and unity of action in pursuit of the common purpose. The manager engages in this process *while* performing the five basic managerial functions of planning, organizing, staffing, influencing, and controlling. The resulting coordination, the resulting synchronization of efforts, should be one of the goals that the manager keeps in mind when performing each of the five managerial functions. Coordination, therefore, is a *by-product* the manager brings about while performing the five managerial functions appropriately. Coordination is a part of everything the manager does.

It is evident that the task of achieving coordination is much more difficult on the top administrative level than on your supervisory level. The chief executive officer (CEO) has to achieve the synchronization of efforts throughout the entire organization. As a supervisor of only one department, you have to be concerned with coordination primarily within your own department and its relations to the other divisions. The achievement of coordination is necessary, regardless of the scope of your division. We have suggested that you view coordination as a natural outgrowth of performing your five managerial functions appropriately. Coordination should result as a by-product and should not be looked on as a separate managerial function. As a supervisor, you should bear coordination in mind in everything you do. Thus, synchronizing the efforts of subordinates should be a prominent consideration whenever you plan, organize, staff, influence, and control.

Coordination and Cooperation

The term *coordination,* however, must not be confused with *cooperation,* since there is a considerable difference between them. Cooperation merely indicates the willingness of individuals to help each other; it is the result of a voluntary attitude of a group of people. Coordination is much more inclusive, requiring more than the mere desire and willingness of the participants.

For example, consider a group of people attempting to move a heavy object. They are sufficient in number, willing and eager to cooperate with each other, and trying to do their best to move the object. They are also fully aware of their common purpose. In all likelihood, however, their efforts will be of little avail until one of them, the manager, gives the proper orders to apply the right amount of force at the right place and time. Only then will their efforts be sufficiently coordinated to actually move the object.

It is possible that by coincidence mere cooperation could bring about the desired result, but no manager can afford to rely on such coincidental occurrence. Although cooperation is always helpful and its absence could prevent all possibility of coordination, its presence alone will not necessarily ensure that process. Coordination is therefore superior to cooperation in order of importance. Coordination is a conscious effort to tie the activities together.

■ DIFFICULTIES IN ATTAINING COORDINATION

Coordination is not easily attained, and the task of coordination is becoming increasingly difficult as the various duties become more complex. With the growth of an organization, the task of synchronizing the daily activities becomes more and more complicated. As the number of positions in your department increases, the need for coordination and synchronization to secure the unified result increases. As stated before, specialization is another source that may cause problems of coordination. Also, human nature presents additional problems of coordination. Your employees are preoccupied with their own work because their evaluation is based on how they perform their jobs. Thus, they have a narrow perspective and hesitate to become involved in other areas.

■ COORDINATION AND THE MANAGERIAL FUNCTIONS

Coordination cuts across each of the managerial functions. We have already stated that as a manager performs the managerial functions, coordination is one of the desired by-products. Let us look more carefully at how this important by-product is related to each of the five functions, as well as to the other connective processes.

When the manager *plans,* efforts for coordination must be made immediately. The planning stage is the ideal time to plan for coordination. As a supervisor, you must see that the various plans within your department are properly interrelated. You should discuss these plans and alternatives with the employees who are to carry them out so that they have an opportunity to express any doubts or objections. The earlier you include employees of the department in the process, while plans are still flexible, the better the chances for coordination.

The same concern for coordination should exist when the manager *organizes.* Indeed, the whole purpose of organizing is to ensure coordination. Thus, whenever a manager groups activities and assigns them to various subordinates, coordination should be in his or her mind. By placing related activities that need to be closely synchronized within the same administrative area, coordination will be facilitated.

Moreover, in the process of organizing, management defines authority relationships in such a way that coordination will result. Often poor coordination is caused by a lack of understanding of who is to perform what or by the failure of a manager to delegate authority and exact responsibility clearly. Such fuzziness can easily lead to duplication of efforts instead of synchronization.

Coordination should also be an aspect of the *staffing* function. It is important that the right number of employees are in the various positions to ensure the proper performance of their functions. The manager should see that they have the proper qualifications and training.

When a manager *directs* and *influences,* he or she is also concerned with coordination. The essence of giving instructions, coaching, teaching, and supervising subordinates is to coordinate their activities so that the overall objectives of the institution will be reached in the most efficient way. As some writers have stated, coordination is that phase of supervision devoted to obtaining the harmonious and reciprocal performance of responsibilities of two or more subordinates.

Finally, coordination is directly connected with the *controlling* function. By checking whether or not the activities of the department are proceeding as planned and directed, any discrepancy will be discovered and immediately corrected to ensure coordination after that point. Frequent evaluation and correction of departmental operations help to synchronize not only the efforts of employees, but also the activities of the entire organization. Thus, by its nature, controlling is the last process to bring about the overall coordination.

■ COORDINATION AND DECISION MAKING

Since the process of decision making is at the heart of all managerial functions, achieving coordination must be an overriding thought in every manager's mind whenever decisions are made. When choosing from the various alternatives, the manager must never forget the importance of achieving synchronization of all efforts. Thus, that alternative most likely to bring about the best coordination will be selected. At times a certain alternative *taken by itself* may seem to constitute the best choice. A second choice, however, might result in better coordination. This is why the previous chapter stresses the importance of the solution's acceptability as one of the supervisor's considerations in choosing from alternatives. The supervisor would be better advised to follow the second solution, since achieving coordination is an important, if not overriding, objective.

■ COORDINATION AND COMMUNICATION

In all coordination efforts good communication will be of immeasurable help. It is not enough for a manager to make decisions that are likely to bring about coordination; having decisions carried out effectively is at least as important. To achieve successful execution, the supervisor must first communicate the decisions to the subordinates so that they understand them correctly. Therefore, good communication is essential for achieving coordination. The importance of effective communication for achieving coordination will become even more obvious as we discuss this in Chapter 5.

Personal, oral, face-to-face contact is probably the most effective means of communicating to obtain coordination. Other means, however, such as written communications, reports, procedures, rules, bulletins, as well as numerous modern mechanical devices, also ensure the speedy dissemination of information to employees. Recent developments in electronic data processing and the use of computer systems can also be helpful in communicating and coordinating.

■ INTERNAL COORDINATION IN HEALTHCARE CENTERS

Because of the proliferation and specialization of medical sciences and technologies, healthcare centers have become large and complex organizational structures. More and more positions have had to be created, and this increasing specialization and division of work has generated a need for more and better coordination. As a result of such specialization, however, the synchronization of daily activities has become extremely complicated, and coordination has become increasingly difficult to attain. This is especially true in the healthcare field. You know that as the number of positions in your department and in the hospital increases and as more specialized and sophisticated tasks are performed, the greater is your need and effort for coordination and synchronization to secure the unified result, namely, the best possible patient care.

Of course, the process of bringing about total coordination of *all* divisions and levels within a healthcare facility is ultimately the concern of the chief administrator. The CEO must deal with the fact that each special departmental interest in the healthcare center is likely to stress its own opinion of how the best possible patient care should be accomplished. Each department is likely to favor one route or another, depending on its particular functions and experience. This problem of different viewpoints also holds true among the numerous levels of the administrative hierarchy. Considerable thoughtfulness and understanding is required of all managerial and supervisory personnel to coordinate the working relationships of the groups above, below, and alongside each department. Even with cooperative attitudes, self-coordination, and self-adjustment by most members of the healthcare center, duplication of actions and conflicts of efforts may still result unless good administration carefully synchronizes all activities. Only through such coordination can management bring about a total accomplishment that exceeds the sum of the individual parts. Although each part is significant, the result can be of greater significance if management achieves coordination.

■ TECHNIQUES AND METHODS OF COORDINATION

The techniques and methods to be used in an organizational setting will vary with the dynamics of the environment and the degree of specialization. Lawrence and Lorsch conducted some of the best recent studies on coordination and integration. They examined various managerial coordinating efforts in different industrial environments, i.e., in highly dynamic settings, in relatively dynamic settings, and in a predictable and stable environment. Their findings could be taken into consideration in certain healthcare settings.[1]

When managerial hierarchy is used to achieve coordination, all the subjects under discussion in Chapters 9 through 12, such as authority, span of management, delegation, and line and staff relationships, are the techniques employed to achieve coordination. Policies, standard procedures, methods, rules, and performance standards are additional techniques to integrate activities. Good communications act as necessary lubricants in all these processes. If the manager cannot achieve coordination because of the dynamic nature of the environment, an individual in a liaison role might be called on to coordinate two or more independent units. That person, although without any formal authority, nevertheless is familiar with problems of both units and would facilitate coordinating needs. Some organizations engaged in high-performance and dynamic industries even have had to introduce an entire coordinating department into the organizational structure.

■ DIMENSIONS OF COORDINATION

Working in any organization, one can see the need for coordination in three directions: vertical, horizontal, and diagonal coordination.

Vertical Coordination

Coordination between the different levels of an organization can be considered as vertical coordination, such as between the CEO and the director of nursing and between the director of nursing and a supervisor of nursing. Vertical coordination is achieved by delegating authority, assigning duties, and supervising and controlling. Although authority carries great power, effective vertical coordination is better achieved by performing the managerial functions wisely instead of relying on the weight of formal authority. (See Figure 4-1.)

■ **FIGURE 4-1 Vertical coordination.**

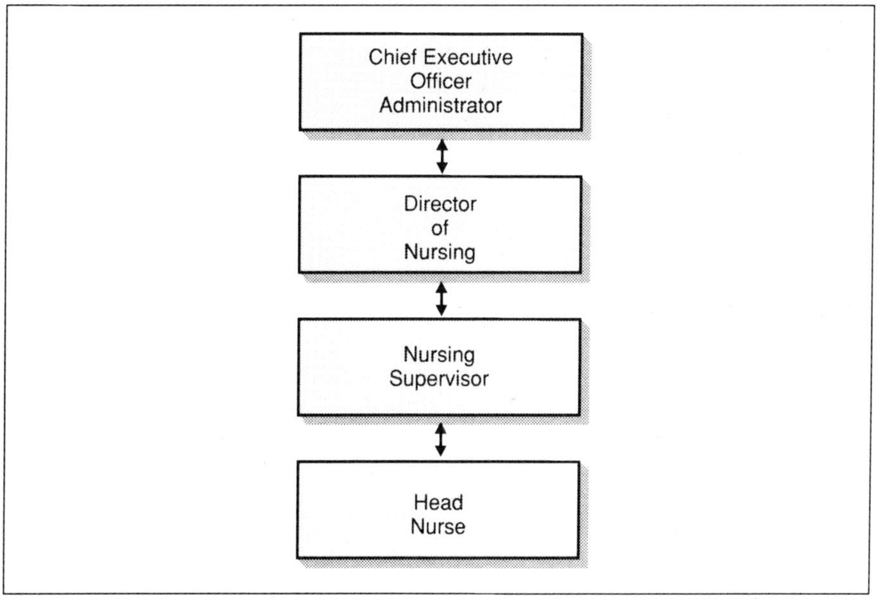

Horizontal Coordination

Horizontal coordination exists between persons and departments on the same organizational levels. For example, to achieve better hospital room utilization, the need for an earlier checkout hour has been targeted as the solution. To work out this problem, new arrangements have to be made between the various managers of the activities affected. Therefore, the director of admissions, together with the director of nursing, chief of the pharmacy, head of patient accounts, executive housekeeper, and director of ancillary escort services, who are all involved in the discharge process, will try to coordinate their activities to achieve this goal. (See Figure 4-2.)

Each of the executives involved manages his or her own department and has no authority over the other executives. Horizontal coordination obviously cannot be ordered by any one of them. It is achieved by a policy and procedure stating that when necessary, the departments must interact, cooperate, and adjust their activities to achieve coordination. If horizontal coordination cannot be achieved, such a problem must be referred to a higher level in the managerial hierarchy with authority over all these departments. In all likelihood this is the CEO, who will simply issue the necessary directives to achieve the earlier checkout hour.

■ **FIGURE 4-2 Horizontal coordination.**

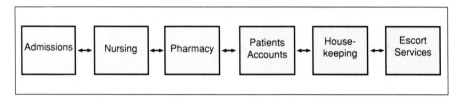

Diagonal Coordination

Diagonal coordination cuts across the organizational arrangements, ignoring positions and levels. In a small day-surgery center, for example, close working relationships and short lines of communication make diagonal coordination easier than in a large organization. Even in this case, however, this process must be operative. For instance, in a hospital all departments need access to the engineering and maintenance department, a centralized service. This access has to be coordinated by negotiations between the users and the provider, who are responsible for working this out. (See Figure 4-3.) Coordination cannot be accomplished simply by referring the problem up the line in the chain of command.

■ **FIGURE 4-3 Diagonal coordination.**

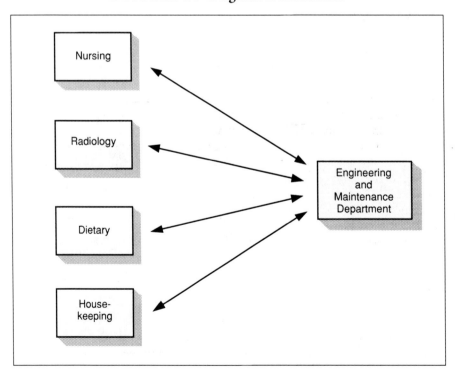

■ THE COORDINATOR

Some hospitals do have positions labeled coordinator; these are often regular managerial and supervisory jobs and should be named as such. In these cases the title "coordinator" is a misnomer. For instance, instead of having a group of nurses known as nursing supervisors, they might be called "nursing coordinators." Their positions, as defined in their job descriptions, are likely to be managerial, regardless of the title. Some healthcare centers simply prefer the word coordinator to that of supervisor.

As stated before, however, the task of securing harmonious action and internal coordination within a healthcare center belongs primarily to those in managerial positions. This task should not be assigned to a specialist, often called a "coordinator." The managers are in a far better position than any special coordinator to view the various functions and determine how they should be coordinated to bring about the desired objective and get the job done. The important point is that all managers must coordinate as they perform their five managerial functions. Therefore, it is questionable whether the task of securing internal coordination within the healthcare center can be shifted or assigned to a special department or a number of individuals.[2]

On the other hand, several positions in many healthcare centers are properly known and labeled coordinator, such as in-service coordinator or education and training coordinator. These are usually staff positions providing service and assistance to whomever would need and benefit from their area of expertise.

■ EXTERNAL COORDINATION

In addition to this need for internal coordination, however, a need exists for coordination with factors *external* to the institution, such as changes in the general economy; governmental activities; medical, scientific, and technological advances; other providers; new user groups; joint ventures; and the social interests of the general public in healthcare. External coordination must exist among each hospital, other healthcare institutions, and the many new aspects of the total healthcare system. In those situations where a hospital is trying to coordinate some activities with other healthcare institutions or with any other external factor (long-term healthcare facility, surgicenter, joint venture, social work agency, visiting nurses agency, etc.), a special coordinator or liaison person may be used. Such persons should be thoroughly familiar with the conditions and thinking of their institution, be able to explain these to the others, and communicate the findings and intentions back to their institution. Normally, however, an external coordinator does not have any authority to commit the institution to action. In most instances it is necessary to check back with the administrator or executive director as to how far the institution will go to support whatever action has been chosen. In this situation, therefore, we are not dealing with a manager in the sense of the term used in this text.

Nevertheless, the importance of such external coordination should not be underestimated. The more external coordination among healthcare centers and related institutions, the better will be our overall healthcare system. Thus, much is being said today about interface relationships, i.e., analyzing behavior among healthcare providers and users at the point where they are tangent to one another.

In the final analysis management's ever-increasing problems of coordination, both internal and external, can only be offset by ever-increasing knowledge of how to perform the managerial job. Fortunately this knowledge is becoming broader because of the emergence of new tools and devices and a more thorough understanding of the overall dependence and relationships among healthcare systems within the community, state, and country.

■ SUMMARY

Coordination is a part of everything the manager does. Coordination is the orderly synchronization of all efforts of the members of the organization to achieve the stated objectives. It is not a separate managerial function but a by-product that results when the manager performs the five managerial functions. Coordination cuts across each of the managerial functions. A significant difference exists, however, between cooperation and coordination. Cooperation is always helpful in achieving coordination, but coordination is more important.

As a supervisor plans, organizes, staffs, influences, and controls, it must be remembered that the ultimate goal is to achieve coordination or the synchronization of all efforts. The same overriding thought permeates the manager's mind whenever decisions are made and communicated to the employees. Achieving coordination is a valid consideration for all managers, regardless of their positions, level within the administrative hierarchy, or the type of enterprise in which they work. Because of the proliferation and specialization of medical sciences and technologies, the task of obtaining coordination in a healthcare center has become increasingly difficult.

In addition to the need for internal coordination, a need exists for coordination with factors external to the institution, such as government activities, local health councils, users, and other provider groups. To achieve this external coordination, a liaison person or special coordinator can be used to provide the necessary contacts between the institution and outside factors.

NOTES
1. Paul R. Lawrence and Jay W. Lorsch, *Organization and Environment, Managing Differentiation and Integration,* Homewood, IL: Richard D. Irwin, Inc., 1969; first published in 1967 by Division of Research, Graduate School of Business Administration, Harvard University, Cambridge, MA, "New Management Job: The Integrator," *Harvard Business Review* 45, November-December 1967, pp. 142-151; and "Differentiation and Integration in Complex Organizations," *Administrative Science Quarterly,* March 1967, pp. 1-47.
2. Lawrence and Lorsch.

5

COMMUNICATING

Communicating is the process of transmitting information and understanding from one person to another. Almost all daily managerial activities involve communication; most of the manager's time is taken up by some sort of communication, giving and receiving information. Communicating involves two or more persons. Therefore, behavioral processes such as motivation, attitudes, perception, leadership, experience, and feelings play an important role.

As with all organizations, a healthcare center needs valid information as one of its important resources. Communication provides the key for this. A hospital devotes much activity to gathering and processing information from the moment the client enters the facility until discharge. Serious consequences can arise when communications are minimal, become misunderstood, break down, or do not exist. The following incident is a spectacular example of the impact of no communication.

A few years ago a patient was "lost" for 25 hours in a Chicago area hospital. The patient, whose condition left him unable to speak or otherwise communicate and who needed support to sit up in a wheelchair, was secured to a wheelchair with a restraint belt, pillow, and lapboard. He had been in the occupational therapy department in the lower level of the hospital and was wheeled by a volunteer escort, supposedly back to his ward. The escort wheeled him, along with another patient, to the passenger elevator(s). The volunteer escort was to complete the assignment. About 45 minutes later, a nurse, assuming the patient was back in his ward, could not locate him there. Intensive investigation began immediately, searching the hospital and adjoining buildings with the assistance of the hospital police unit, ward staff, physicians, nurses, etc. The patient could not be located.

The search continued for 25 hours, when a hospital employee stepped onto an elevator in the basement to find the patient secured in a wheelchair and bent over. This person was unaware that the patient had been missing and leaned over to speak to him, offering assistance. The employee quickly observed that the patient was unable to respond, and after reading forms attached to the chair, returned the patient to his floor, where he was recognized by a medical student and returned to his proper ward. During the "lost patient's" absence, several hospital employees who would have recognized the patient told investigators they rode the elevator on which he was later found and did not see him. An elevator repairman also said he and an inspector took the elevator out of service for some time during the patient's absence and that no one was on the elevator. Despite a thorough month-long investigation, the hospital was unable to account for the patient's whereabouts during the 25-hour period.

Unfortunately the patient died from cerebral hemorrhage after undergoing brain surgery several weeks later. The hospital stated that his death was in no way connected with any ill effects caused by this incident.

Communication is the third process that serves to link the managerial functions in an organization. Employees look for and expect communication, since it is a means of motivating and influencing people. Communication is vital to them not only for purposes of social satisfaction, but also to carry out their jobs effectively. Thus, the communication process fulfills both human needs and institutional needs.

You already know that as a supervisor your job is to plan, organize, staff, influence, and control the work of the employees and to coordinate their efforts for the purpose of achieving departmental objectives. To accomplish these goals, however, you must explain and discuss the arrangement of the work. You must give directives. You must describe to each subordinate what is expected of her or him. You probably will need to speak to your employees regarding their performance. All this is communication.

As you continue supervising employees, you probably will come to realize that your skill in communication determines your success. Communication is the most effective tool for building and keeping a well-functioning team. Just consider your own job and you will quickly see why communication is essential to successful supervision. Communication is the only means a supervisor has to take charge of and train a group of employees, direct them, motivate them, and coordinate their activities. This ability to communicate is essential to leadership. Is there any area of responsibility within your job as a supervisor that you could fulfill without communicating? Without effective communication, the organizational structure cannot survive.

■ THE NATURE OF COMMUNICATION

Communicating is the process of transmitting information and understanding from one person to another. Communication, fundamental and vital to all managerial functions, is a means of imparting ideas and making oneself understood by others. The exchange is successful only when mutual understanding results, i.e., when the meaning the sender wishes to convey has been transmitted. Agreement is not necessary, as long as the sender and receiver have successfully exchanged ideas and understand each other and the message received is close in meaning to the message intended.

As a supervisor, you spend most of your time in either sending or receiving information. One cannot assume, however, that real communication is occurring in all these exchanges. Also, being constantly engaged in sending and receiving messages does not ensure that a supervisor is an expert in communicating.

Communication was defined as the process of passing information and understanding from one person to another. The significant point here is that communication always involves two persons: a sender and a receiver. Communication is not merely a matter of sending. There must be a receiver. One person alone cannot communicate; communication is not a one-way street. For example, a person stranded on a deserted island who shouts for help does not communicate because there is no receiver. This example may not be so obvious to managers who send out a large number of memoranda. Once a memorandum has been sent, many are inclined to believe that communication has occurred. However, communication does not occur until information and understanding have passed *between the senders and the intended receivers.*

This understanding aspect of communication is another important part of our definition. A receiver may hear a sender but still not understand what the sender means. Understanding is a personal matter between people. If the message received is close in meaning to the one intended, then communication has taken place. However, people may interpret messages differently. If the idea received is not the one intended, then communication has not taken place; the sender has merely spoken or written. "Simply telling" somebody something is not enough to guarantee successful communication. As long as there is no reception or imperfect reception of the idea intended, we cannot speak of having communicated.

As stated before, communication does not require the receiver to agree with the statement of the sender. Communication occurs whenever the receiver at least understands what the sender means to convey. Two persons can fully understand each other and still not agree. Thus, your subordinates do not have to agree with everything you as a supervisor communicate to them, but they must understand it. No subordinate can be expected to comply with a directive unless he or she understands it. Similarly, supervisors must know how to receive knowledge and understanding in the messages sent to them by their subordinates, fellow supervisors, and superiors.

Only through effective communication can policies, procedures, and rules be formulated and carried out. Only with such communication can misunderstandings be ironed out, long-term and short-term plans achieved, and activities within a department coordinated and controlled. The success of all managerial functions depends on effective communication.

■ COMMUNICATION NETWORK

In every organization the communication network has two distinct but equally important channels: the formal channels of communication and the informal channel, usually called the "grapevine." Each channel carries messages from one person or group to another in downward, upward, horizontal, and diagonal directions. (See Figure 5-1.)

Formal Channels

The formal channels are established mainly by the organizational hierarchy. These channels follow the lines of authority from the chief administrator all the way down to employees. You are probably familiar with the expression that messages and information "must go through channels." This refers to the formal flow of communication through the organizational hierarchy.

Downward Communication

When it moves in a downward direction, this formal flow of communication flows from superiors to subordinates. The flow begins with someone at the top issuing

■ **FIGURE 5-1** The directions of information along formal communications channels.

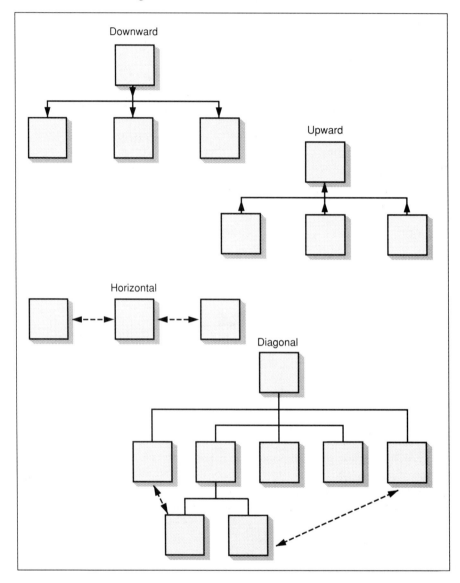

a message, the next person in the hierarchy passing it along to those who report to him or her, and so on down the line. The downward direction is the one management relies on the most for its communication. Generally, downward communication starts action by subordinates; its content is mostly of a directive nature. This communication is used to convey not only directives, but also information, objectives, policies, procedures, etc. The manager should transmit the right amount of information, neither too little nor too much. Downward communication helps to tie the levels of the organizational structure together and to coordinate activities.

Upward Communication

Upward communication is a second but equally important direction in which messages flow through the official network, but from subordinates to superiors. Any person charged with supervisory authority accepts an obligation to keep the superior informed. Moreover, the subordinates must feel free to convey their opinions and attitudes to their superior and to report on activities and actions regarding their work. Management should encourage a free flow of upward communication, since this is the only means by which supervisors can determine whether their messages have been transmitted and received properly and whether appropriate action is taking place.

As a supervisor, you should encourage and maintain upward communication channels and pay proper attention to the information transmitted through them. You must show that you want the facts and want them promptly. Unfortunately the reaction of many managers to upward communication is still similar to that of ancient tyrants who executed the "bearer of bad news." In your supervisory capacity you must make a deliberate effort to encourage upward communication (1) by showing a genuine desire to obtain and use the ideas and reports of your subordinates, (2) by being approachable, and (3) by recognizing the importance of upward communication. Lack of an effective upward flow will throttle the natural desire of your employees to communicate, lead to frustration, and ultimately cause your employees to seek different outlets, such as the grapevine.

In addition to encouraging your employees to communicate upward to you, you must likewise communicate upward to your own superior. Persons who have been put into a supervisory position accept the obligation to keep their superiors informed. As stated at the outset, supervisors are the people in the middle. They are not only responsible for providing good communication downward *to* their employees. They are also responsible for stimulating good communication upward *from* their workers and then passing this and other information to the next higher level in the administrative hierarchy. However, most supervisors will agree with the statement that it is much easier for them to "talk down" to their subordinates than to "speak up" to their superior. This is especially true if supervisors have ever had to tell their boss that they did not meet a certain schedule because of bad planning or that they forgot to carry out an order.

Nevertheless, it is the supervisor's job to keep his or her superior advised of up-to-date facts concerning the department. The supervisor should inform the superior of any significant developments as soon as possible after they occur, even if the information reveals errors. If the boss were to learn such news elsewhere, this would indicate that proper upward communication was not allowed or that the supervisor was not providing it. Superiors have a right to complete information, since they are still responsible if anything goes wrong.

Your superiors may have to act on what you report. Therefore, they must receive the information in time and in a form that will enable them to take the necessary action. As a supervisor, you must assemble all facts that are needed and check them carefully before passing them on to your boss. Bear in mind that upward messages are more subject to distortion than downward communication. Try to be as objective as possible. This may be difficult at times, since all subordinates want to appear favorably in the eyes of their boss. Thus, you may want to soften the information so that facts will not look as bad as they are. However, sooner or later the full extent of the malfunctioning probably will be discovered. When difficulties arise, it is best to tell your superior the complete score, even if this means admitting mistakes. Always keep in mind that your boss depends on the supervisors for upward communication, just as you depend on your employees to pass along their information to you.

Horizontal Communication

In addition to downward and upward communication, a third direction of communication is essential for the efficient functioning of an enterprise. This horizontal, sideward, or lateral communication is concerned mainly with communication across departments or among people on the same level in the hierarchy but in charge of different functions. Horizontal communication occurs more among managers than nonmanagerial personnel. For example, lateral communication will often occur between the operating room supervisor and the head nurse on the surgical floor. This channel facilitates coordination. Horizontal communication also plays an important role in matrix and project organizations, as discussed in Chapter 10.

Diagonal Communication

Diagonal communication, on the other hand, is the flow of messages between positions that are on different lateral planes of the organizational structure. Communication between line groups, such as nursing personnel, and between staff groups, such as the laundry department, are examples of diagonal communication, as are messages between the floor nurse and radiology, therapy, dietary, or laboratory departments. (See Chapter 12.) To achieve coordination among the various functions in any organization, especially in a healthcare organization, a free flow of both horizontal and diagonal communication is essential. Without it, good patient care would be difficult to achieve.

■ THE COMMUNICATION MEDIA

The media mostly used for communication are verbal communication (oral and written words), visual media, and nonverbal communication. Although spoken and written words are the most widely used media, one cannot ignore or underestimate the power of visuals and nonverbal communication.

Verbal Communication

Words are the most effective and most widely used forms of communication. This communication can be a real challenge to the supervisor, since words can be tricky and messages that mean something to one employee can have a completely different meaning to another. Therefore, supervisors must make an effort to improve their skills in speaking, writing, listening, and reading. You may have heard the story about the maintenance foreman who asked the new worker to paint the canopy in the front of the hospital green. When the foreman checked on the job an hour later, he found that the waste container had been painted bright green. The new employee did not know what a canopy was. Perhaps he should have known, but no one had ever told him.

Oral Communication

The most prevalent communication in any organization is oral. Oral communication is superior to the written medium, since it normally saves time and achieves better understanding. This is true of both face-to-face and telephone communication. In daily performance face-to-face discussions between the supervisor and subordinate are the principal means of two-way communication. Such daily contacts are at the heart of an effective communication system. Face-to-face discussions provide the most frequently used channels for the exchange of information, points of view, instructions, and motivation. No other form of communication can equal oral communication, especially the face-to-face type.

Oral communication is simple and can be done with little preparation and without pencil, paper, typewriter, etc. Therefore, effective supervisors will use this medium more than any other. They know that subordinates like to see and hear their boss in person. Also, oral contact is usually well received because most people can express themselves more easily and more completely by voice than by writing.

Aside from these features, the greatest single advantage of oral communication is that it provides immediate *feedback,* even if the feedback is only an expression on the listener's face. By merely looking at the receiver, the sender can judge the reaction to what is being said. Oral communication thus enables the sender to find out immediately what the receiver is hearing or not hearing. Oral communication also enables the receiver to ask questions immediately if the meaning is not clear. Then the sender can explain the message more thoroughly and clarify unexpected problems. Moreover, the manner and tone of the human voice can endow the message with meaning and shading that even long pages of written words simply could not convey. The manner and tone create the atmosphere of communication, and the response is influenced accordingly.

There are some minor drawbacks to oral communications. No permanent record of what has been said exists. The sender may forget part of the message, or some noise or random disturbance may interfere. The many benefits, however, far outweigh these shortcomings.

Written Communication

Regardless of the speed and effectiveness of oral communications, a well-balanced communication system will include both the written and the oral media. Although oral communication is used more frequently, written messages are indispensable and are especially important in healthcare activities. Often, detailed and specific instructions may be so lengthy and cumbersome that they must be put into writing so that they can be studied for a longer period. It is advisable to use the written medium for widespread dissemination of information that may concern a number of people. Furthermore, a degree of formality is connected with "putting it in writing," which orally delivered messages usually do not carry.

Written messages provide a permanent record that can be referred to as often as necessary. The spoken word, in contrast, generally exists only for an instant. Another advantage of written communications is that they are typically more accurate. The sender can take the necessary time and choose precise terminology when the information is being written down; it can be reread and redrafted before it is finalized. Written communication is preferable when important details are involved and a permanent record is necessary as "evidence." Many situations arise in the healthcare field where the written form is absolutely necessary.

Visual Media

Sometimes managers will also make use of visual aids as a way to communicate. Pictures are particularly effective in connection with well-chosen words to complete a message. Even without any words, however, visual media are a useful tool to convey a message. Many enterprises make extensive use of the pictorial language in the form of blueprints, charts, drafts, models, posters, color coding, cartoons, slides, etc. Motion pictures and comic strips offer clear proof of the power of the pictorial language to communicate and bring about understanding.

Nonverbal Communication

Although nonverbal communication does not use words, it can carry the same and even more meaning than words themselves. *Actions* and *behavior* are the other media playing a part in nonverbal communication. In their role of managers, supervisors must not forget that what they *do* is interpreted as a symbol by their subordinates and that often actions *do* speak louder than words. Because of their managerial status, all observable acts communicate something to employees, whether supervisors intended them to or not.

The setting for the communication also can play a role as a nonverbal medium, expressing symbols of familiarity, power, etc. For example, consider the manager sitting in a manager's chair behind the desk and the receiver in the visitor's chair or standing up; this setting connotes power and control.

Purposeful silence, gestures, a handshake, a shrug of the shoulder, body movements, eye contact, a smile, and a frown all have meaning. For instance, a frown on the supervisor's face at times may mean more than 10 minutes of oral discussion. These are examples of nonverbal communication, sometimes also referred to as *body language*. Studies have shown that a large percentage of the meaning of a message is transmitted by these media.

By the same token, a manager's *inaction* is also a way of communication. An unexplained action can often communicate a meaning that was not intended. Suppose, for example, that a piece of equipment has been removed from the laboratory for overhaul without telling the employees why. To the technologists apprehensive of a reduction or change in procedures, such unexplained action could convey a message that the supervisor probably had no intention of sending.

■ THE MANAGER'S ROLE IN COMMUNICATION

Since organizational effectiveness largely depends on the successful functioning of its communication network, every manager must become familiar with what can be done to minimize the problems in the communication process and ensure its success. Most organizational structures today are intricate and create many layers of supervision and long lines of communication. Breakdowns and distortions of communication can occur at any level of supervision.

All of you are familiar with the confusions, frictions, and inconveniences that arise when communications break down. These breakdowns are not only costly in terms of money, but they also create misunderstandings that may hurt your teamwork, morale, and even patient care. Indeed, many of a supervisor's problems are caused by faulty communication. That is, the way you as a supervisor communicate with your subordinates is the essence of your relationship, and most problems of human relations grow out of poor or nonexistent communication. Always remember that no communication occurs until and unless the meaning received by the listener is the same as the meaning the sender intended to convey. The effective communicator must realize that the speaker and the listener are two individuals with separate backgrounds, experiences, values, attitudes, and perceptions. Both live in different worlds, and many factors can interfere and play havoc with the messages that pass between them.

■ BARRIERS TO COMMUNICATION

The supervisor must realize that there are many barriers to effective communication. First we will discuss those factors that may create roadblocks to the intended meaning of a communication, then examine the means of successfully overcoming these barriers. Although many communication barriers exist, the more important ones can be grouped into three general categories: language barriers, status and position barriers, and general resistance to change.

Language

Normally, words serve us well and we generally understand each other. Sometimes, however, the same words suggest different meanings to different persons. The words themselves create a barrier to communication. It is often said that people on different levels "speak a different language." Many instances occur when a frustrating conversation ends with the admission that "we are just not speaking the same language," yet both participants have been conversing in English. To avoid such a breakdown in communication, the communicator should use the language of the receiver and not his or her own style of language. The sender should speak a language that the receiver is accustomed to and understands. It is not a question of whether the receiver *should* understand it; the question is simply, does he or she understand the language? The supervisor must therefore use plain, simple words and direct, uncomplicated language.

This is difficult at times because the English language assigns several meanings to one word. This problem is often referred to as one of *semantics*. For example, the word "round" has many meanings. We speak of round as a ball, he walks round and round, a round dozen of eggs, a round trip, a round of beef, a round of boxing, round as a cylinder, etc. When administration speaks of "increased productivity," these words may have positive meaning to the manager and probably less positive connotations for the employees. When using words that have such different meanings, the communicator must clarify the exact meaning intended. The sender should not just assume that the receiver will interpret the word in the same way he or she does.

Many words in our language have reasonably similar meanings, but they convey different messages, as evidenced in the following two lists:[1]

List A	List B
Firm	Unyielding
Aggressive	Ruthless
Compassionate	Weak
Concerned with detail	Nit-picking
Certain	Cocky
Easygoing	Unconcerned
Selective	Arbitrary
Respects line of authority	Bureaucratic
An independent thinker	A nonconformist
Blunt and direct	Tactless

For most people, the words in list B convey a less favorable message than those in list A. When describing someone you care for, you are likely to use the words in list A. However, the listener tends to listen and interpret the language based on his or her own experience and frame of reference, not yours.

Status and Position

An organizational structure and the resulting administrative hierarchy create a number of different status levels among the members of the organization. Status refers to the regard and attitude displayed and held toward a particular position and its occupant by the members of the organization. A difference in status certainly exists between the level of the president and that of the supervisors and between the level of the supervisors and that of their employees. This difference in status and position creates barriers that distort the sending and receiving of messages.

For example, when employees listen to a message from the supervisor, several factors become operative. First, the employees evaluate what they hear in relation to their own position, background, experience, and perception; they also take the sender into account. It is difficult for a receiver to separate what he or she hears from the feelings he or she has about the person who sends the message. Therefore, the receiver often adds nonexistent motives to the sender. Union members are frequently inclined to interpret a statement coming from administration in a negative manner because they are often convinced that management is trying to weaken and undermine the union. Often a hospital's newspaper is considered a propaganda organ and mouthpiece of administration, and its contents are viewed with suspicion. Such mental blocks and attitudes obviously do not make for good communication or understanding.

The supervisor who is trying to be an effective communicator must realize that these status and position differences influence feelings and prejudices of the employees and thus create barriers to communication. Moreover, not only might the employee evaluate the boss' words differently, but they might also place undue importance on a superior's gesture, silence, smile, or other nonverbal expressions. Simply speaking, the boss' words are not just words; they are words that come from a boss. This is how barriers caused by status work in the *downward* flow of communication.

Similar obstacles resulting from status and position also arise in the *upward* flow of communication, since all subordinates are eager to appear favorably in their boss' eyes. Therefore, employees may conveniently and protectively screen the information that is passed up the line. A subordinate, for example, is likely to tell the superior what the latter likes to hear and will omit or soften what is unpleasant. By the same token, supervisors are anxious to cover up their own weaknesses when talking to a person in a higher position. Thus, supervisors often fail to pass on important information because they believe that such information would reflect unfavorably on their own supervisory abilities. After two or three selective filterings of this sort by different echelons of the administrative hierarchy, you can imagine that the message is likely to be considerably distorted.

Resistance to Change

Resistance to change can constitute a serious barrier to communication because often a message is meant to convey a new idea to the employees, something that will change either their work assignment, position, daily routine, working environment, or social networks. Most people prefer things as they are and do not welcome changes in their working situation. Without going into the various reasons for this resistance to change at this point, many employees resist such a change, feeling that it is safer to leave the existing environment in its present state. (See Chapter 19 for a discussion of the reasons for resistance to and facilitation of change.)

Ultimately each of us lives in our own world. Although it may not be a perfect world, we sooner or later learn to make peace with it and live within it more or less happily. Consequently a message that will change this world is greeted with suspicion, and the listeners' receiving apparatus works as a filter, rejecting new ideas if these conflict with what listeners already believe. They are likely to receive only the portion that confirms their present beliefs and ignore anything that conflicts. Sometimes these filters work so efficiently that in reality the receivers do not hear at all. Even if they hear, they will either reject that part of the message as false, or they will find some convenient way of twisting its meaning to fit their preconceived ideas. In the end, the receivers hear only what they wish to hear. If they are insecure, worried, or fearful in their position, this barrier to receiving communication becomes even more powerful.

As a supervisor, you may have been confronted with situations in which it appeared that your subordinates only half listened to what you had to say. Your employees were so busy and preoccupied with their own thoughts that they paid attention exclusively to the ideas they had hoped to hear. They simply selected those parts of the total communication that they could readily use. The information your employees did not care for or considered irreconcilable was conveniently brushed aside, not heard at all, or easily explained away. The selective perception of information constitutes a serious barrier to a supervisor's communications, particularly when the message was intended to convey a change, a new directive, or anything that could conceivably interfere with the employees' routine or working environment.

Additional Barriers

In addition to the barriers already mentioned, many other roadblocks to communication arise in specific situations. For example, obstacles are caused by emotional reactions, such as deep-rooted feelings and prejudice. Other obstacles result from physical conditions, such as inadequate telephone lines, overload of messages, lack of a private place to talk, heat, or noise. Indifference, the "don't care" attitude, also may prevent communication. In such a case the message may get through, but it is acted on only halfheartedly or not at all. The subordinate's complacency may prevent the message from getting across as well.

All these and many other barriers form serious roadblocks to good communication. Unless managers are familiar with such barriers, they are in no position to overcome them. Supervisors should not just assume that the messages they send will be received as intended; it may be more realistic, although discouraging, to assume the opposite. Since the effectiveness of the supervisory job depends largely on the accurate transmission of messages and orders, managers must do everything possible to overcome these barriers and improve their chances for enhancing their communication effectiveness.

■ OVERCOMING BARRIERS TO IMPROVE COMMUNICATION EFFECTIVENESS

Major communication barriers can be prevented and overcome in numerous ways: with adequate preparation, credibility, feedback, direct language, effective listening, sensitivity, appropriate actions, and some repetition. Familiarity and utilization of these techniques will increase the likelihood for successful communication.

Adequate Preparation and Credibility

Do not initiate communication before you know what you are going to say and what you intend to achieve. You must think the idea through until it becomes solid in your mind; do not just proceed with imprecise thoughts and desires that you have not bothered to put into final form. Only if you understand your ideas can you be sure that another person will understand your instructions. Therefore, know what you want to communicate and plan the sequence of steps necessary to attain it.

For example, if you want to make a job assignment, be sure that you have analyzed the job thoroughly so that you can explain it properly. If you are searching for facts, decide in advance what information you will need so that you can ask intelligent, pertinent, and precise questions. If your discussion will entail disciplinary action, be certain that you have sufficiently investigated the case and have enough information before you reprimand or even penalize.

If supervisors are not a reliable source of information, problems of credibility may arise; the supervisor may not be trusted. If communication senders are well prepared and honest, however, credibility will not be a problem. Supervisors must overcome the barriers caused by their managerial position and by the employees' likely perception and interpretation of the message's meaning. Some reactions should be anticipated, and the message should include clarifications of some questions it may cause.

Feedback

Probably the most effective tool for improving communication is feedback. Managers must always be on the alert for some signal or clue indicating that they are being understood. Merely asking the receiver and getting a simple "yes" is not usually enough. Usually more feedback is required to make sure that the message is received as intended and that understanding is actually taking place. The medium used in the communication affects the type of feedback.

The simplest way to obtain such reassurance is to observe the receiver and judge the responses by nonverbal clues, such as a facial expression of understanding or bewilderment, the raising of an eyebrow, or a frown. This form of feedback is only possible in face-to-face communication, of course, which is one of the outstanding advantages of using such communication.

Another way of obtaining feedback in any oral communication is for the senders to ask the receivers to repeat in their own words the information that has just been transmitted. This is much more satisfactory than merely asking the receivers whether or not they understand or if the instruction is clear, both of which require only a yes answer.

If the receiver can restate the content of the message, then the sender will know what the receiver has heard and understood. At the same time the receiver may ask additional questions that the sender can answer immediately. This direct feedback is probably the most useful way to make certain that a message has gotten across. Additional feedback can be obtained by observing whether or not the receivers behave in accordance with the communication. If direct observation is not possible, such as occurs with a written message, the senders must watch for responses, for reports, and as a last resort, for results. If these are as expected, the sender can assume that the message was received correctly.

Direct, Simple, and Adult Language

Another helpful way to overcome blocks in communication is for the manager to use words that are as understandable and simple as possible. The communication should be on an adult basis, and the supervisor should not "speak down" to the employees. Long, technical, complicated words and jargon should be avoided, unless both the sender and the receiver are comfortable with them. The sender should also be aware of the possible different meanings that words can have for different receivers, as discussed earlier. Again, the single, most important question is not whether the receiver should have understood it, but, did he or she understand it?

Effective Listening and Sensitivity

An additional means for overcoming barriers to communication is to spend more time listening to the receiver effectively. Because of different backgrounds, the world of the subordinate is often significantly different from that of the superior. Some common ground still is necessary for understanding. Therefore, you must give the other party a chance to tell what is on his or her mind. The only way you can convince the other party of your interest in and respect for his or her opinions is to listen carefully and completely; this means putting the other party at ease and not interrupting. Good listening means more than a mere expression of attention. It means putting aside biases, listening without a fault-finding or correcting attitude, and paying attention to the meaning of the idea rather than to only the words. (See Figure 5-2.)

   The supervisor who pays attention and listens to what the subordinate is saying learns more about the employee's values and relationships to the working environment. Understanding, not agreement, is essential. It may even be advisable for the supervisor to state occasionally what has been expressed by asking the common question, "Is this what you mean?" The listener must patiently listen to what the other person has to say, even though it may seem unimportant. Such listening will greatly improve communication, since it will reduce misunderstandings. Being sensitive to the receiver is necessary in order to communicate effectively. This means sensitivity to the receiver's perspective and position and possibly even empathy. Careful listening and sensitivity allow a speaker to adjust the message to fit the responses and world of the receiver. This adjustment opportunity is another advantage of oral communication over written messages.

Actions Speak Louder Than Words

Supervisors communicate by actions as much as by words. In fact, actions usually communicate more than words. Therefore, one of the best ways to give meaning to a message is to behave accordingly. Managers who fail to bolster their talk with action fail in their job as a communicator, no matter how capable they are with words. Whether supervisors like it or not, their superior position makes them the center of attention for the employees. The boss communicates through all observ-

■ FIGURE 5-2 Effective listening guides.

1 Stop talking!
You cannot listen if you are talking.
Polonius *(Hamlet):* "Give every man thine ear, but few thy voice."

2 Put the talker at ease.
Help a person feel free to talk.
This is often called a permissive environment.

3 Show a talker that you want to listen.
Look and act interested. Do not read your mail while someone talks.
Listen to understand, rather than to oppose.

4 Remove distractions.
Don't doodle, tap, or shuffle papers.
Will it be quieter if you shut the door?

5 Empathize with talkers.
Try to help yourself see the other person's point of view.

6 Be patient.
Allow plenty of time. Do not interrupt a talker.
Don't start for the door or walk away.

7 Hold your temper.
An angry person takes the wrong meaning from words.

8 Go easy on argument and criticism.
These put people on the defensive, and they may "clam up" or become angry.
Do not argue; even if you win, you lose.

9 Ask questions.
This encourages a talker and shows that you are listening.
It helps to develop points further.

10 Stop talking!
This is first and last, because all other guides depend on it.
You cannot do an effective listening job while you are talking.

• Nature gave people two ears but only one tongue,
which is a gentle hint that they should listen more than they talk.

• Listening requires two ears,
one for meaning and one for feeling.

• Decision makers who do not listen
have less information for making decisions.

From Keith Davis and John W. Newstrom, *Human Behavior at Work: Organizational Behavior,* 7th ed., New York: McGraw-Hill Book Company, 1985, p. 413. Reprinted with permission of the publisher.

able actions, regardless of whether or not it was intended. Verbal announcements backed up by appropriate action will help the supervisor overcome barriers to communication. If the supervisor says one thing but does another, however, sooner or later the employees will "listen" primarily to what the boss "does." For example, the director of nursing services who says she is always available to see a subordinate will undermine the verbal message if the door to the office is kept closed or if she becomes irritated whenever someone comes in.

Repetition

At times it is advisable for a supervisor to repeat the message several times, preferably using different words and means of explanation. A certain amount of redundancy is especially advisable when the message is important or when the directives are complicated. The degree of redundancy will depend both on the content of the message and on the experience and background of the employee. The sender must be cautioned, however, not to be so repetitious that the message may be ignored because it sounds overly familiar. If in doubt, a degree of repetition is safer than none.

■ THE GRAPEVINE: THE INFORMAL COMMUNICATIONS NETWORK

Although it is essential to develop sound formal channels, the dynamics of organizational life tend to create additional channels of communication. An informal communication network among people in the organization commonly referred to as the grapevine then emerges. Every organization has its grapevine, a network of spontaneous channels.

Informal communication is a logical and normal outgrowth of the informal groupings of people, their social interaction, and their natural desire to communicate with each other. The grapevine must be looked on as a perfectly natural activity. It fulfills the subordinate's desire to be "in the know" and to be kept posted on the latest information. The grapevine also gives the members of the organization an outlet for their imagination and an opportunity to relieve their apprehensions in the form of rumors.

Attempts to eliminate the grapevine are in vain. An efficient manager will acknowledge the grapevine's presence and possibly put it to good use. For example, by learning who the key members are, the manager can sound out employee reactions to contemplated changes before making a decision. An informal communication network also enables the manager to surreptitiously feed some information into this channel and obtain some valuable information from it. The grapevine offers the supervisor excellent insight into what the subordinates think and feel.

Operation of the Grapevine

Sometimes the grapevine carries factual information and news, but most often it carries inaccurate information, half-truths, rumors, private interpretations, wishful thinking, suspicions, and other various bits of distorted information. The grapevine is active 24 hours a day and spreads information with amazing speed, often faster than most official channels could. The grapevine has no definite pattern or stable membership. It carries information in all directions, up, down, horizontally, and diagonally. The news is carried in a flexible, meandering pattern, ignoring organization charts. Its path and behavior cannot be predicted, and the path followed yesterday is not necessarily the same as today or tomorrow.

Most of the time only a small number of employees will be active participants in the grapevine. Most employees hear information through the grapevine but do not pass it along. Any person within an organization is likely to become active in the grapevine on one occasion or another. However, some individuals tend to be active more regularly than others. They believe that their prestige is enhanced by providing the latest news, and thus they do not hesitate to spread the news or even change it, so as to augment its "completeness" and "accuracy." These active participants in the grapevine know that they cannot be held accountable, so it is understandable that they exercise a considerable degree of imagination whenever they pass information along. The resulting "rumors" give them, as well as other members of the organization, an outlet for getting rid of their apprehensions. During periods of insecurity, upheaval, and great anxiety the grapevine works overtime. In general the grapevine serves as a safety valve for the emotions of all subordinates, providing them with the means to say freely what they please without the danger of being held accountable. Since everyone knows that tracing the origins of a rumor is nearly impossible, employees can feel quite safe in their anonymity as they participate in the grapevine.

Uses of the Grapevine

Because the grapevine often carries a considerable amount of useful information, in addition to distortions, rumors, and half-truths, it can help to clarify and disseminate formal communication. Informal communication often spreads information that could not be disseminated through the official channels of communication. For instance, the nursing director "resigns" suddenly. Although top administration does not want to say publicly what happened, it does not want to leave the impression that she was treated unfairly or discriminated against. In such a situation someone in administration may tell someone in the hospital, who "promises" not to spread it further, what really happened.

Managers should accept that they can no more eliminate the grapevine than they can abolish the informal organization that develops among employees. It is unrealistic to expect that rumors can be stamped out; the grapevine is bound to flourish in every organization. To deal with it, the supervisors must tune in on the grapevine and learn what it is saying. They must look for the meaning of the grapevine's communication, not merely for its words. They must learn who the key members are and who is likely to spread the information. They must also learn that by feeding the grapevine facts, they can counter rumors and half-truths. This is one way to use the grapevine's energy in the interest of management.

Rumors can be caused by several different factors, such as wishful thinking and anticipation, uncertainty and fear, or even malice and dislike. For example, it is common for employees who want something badly enough to start suddenly passing the word. If they want a raise, they may start a rumor that management will give everybody an across-the-board pay increase. No one knows for certain where or how it started, but this story spreads like wildfire. Everyone wants to believe it. Of course, it is bad for the morale of a group to build up their hopes in anticipation of something that will not happen. If a story is spread that the supervisor realizes will lead to disappointment, the manager should move vigorously to debunk it by presenting the facts. A straight answer is almost always the best answer.

The same prescription applies to rumors caused by fear or uncertainty. If, for example, the activities of the institution decline, and management is forced to lay off some employees, stories and rumors will quickly multiply. In such periods of insecurity and anxiety the grapevine will become more active than at other times. Usually the rumors are far worse than what actually happens. Here again, it is better to give the facts than to conceal them. If the supervisor does not disclose the facts, the employees will make up their own "facts," which are usually a distortion of reality. In many instances much of the fear and anxiety can be eliminated by maintaining open communication channels. Continuing rumors and uncertainty are likely to be more demoralizing than even the most unpleasant facts. Thus, it is usually best to explain immediately why employees are being laid off. When emergencies occur, when new procedures are introduced, when policies are changed, explain why. Otherwise your subordinates will make up their own explanations, and often they will be incorrect.

Other situations may arise, however, where you as a supervisor do not have the correct facts either. In such instances let your superior know what is bothering your employees. Ask your superior for specific instructions as to what information you may give, how much you may tell, and when. Next, meet with your chief assistants and lead employees. Give them the story and guide their thinking. Then they can spread the facts before anyone else can spread the rumors.

Although this procedure may work with rumors caused by fear or uncertainty, it might not be appropriate for rumors that arise out of dislike, anger, or malice. Once again, the best prescription is to try to be objective and impersonal and to come out with the facts, if this is possible. Sometimes, however, a supervisor will find that the only way to stop a malicious rumor peddler is to expose him or her personally and then reveal the untruthfulness of the statement.

A superior should always bear in mind that the receptiveness of any group to rumors is directly related to the strength of the supervisor's leadership and the respect the subordinates have for the manager. If employees believe in your fairness and good supervision, they will quickly debunk any malicious rumor once you have exposed the person who started it or given your answer to it. Thus, although there is no way to eliminate the grapevine, even its most threatening rumors can be counteracted to management's advantage. Every supervisor, therefore, will do well to listen to the informal channels of communication and develop the skill in dealing with them.

■ SUMMARY

Communication is the process of transmitting information and understanding from one person to another. As long as two persons understand each other, they have communicated, although they may not agree. Agreement is not necessary for communication to be successful. To perform the managerial functions, a supervisor must realize the crucial importance of good communication.

Throughout every organization there are formal and informal channels of communication. These channels carry messages downward, upward, horizontally, and diagonally. The formal channels are established mainly by the organizational structure and authority relationships. The position of the supervisor plays a strategic role in the communication process in all these directions.

Although words are the most significant media of communication, one must not overlook the importance of nonverbal language as another meaningful medium. In addition, action is a communication medium that often speaks louder than words. In the healthcare field the written word is also a major medium of communication. Of all media, however, oral face-to-face communication between supervisors and employees is still the most widely used and the most effective, since it provides immediate feedback.

There are many reasons why messages frequently become distorted or do not come across. The manager must be aware of the major barriers to effective communication; some can be attributed to the sender, the receiver, their interaction, or the environment. Efforts must be made to be aware of these obstacles and how to overcome them.

In addition to the formal channels, an informal network exists, usually referred to as the grapevine. This is the communication network among the people in the organization; it is a natural outgrowth of the informal organization and the social interactions of people. The grapevine serves a useful purpose in every organization. Instead of trying to eliminate it, the supervisor should accept the grapevine as a natural outlet and safety valve of the employees. The supervisor should tune in on it and at times even feed, cultivate, and put it to good use.

NOTES

1. From Steve Altman, Enzo Valenzi, and Richard M. Hodgetts, *Organizational Behavior: Theory and Practice,* Orlando, FL: Harcourt Brace Jovanovich, Inc., 1985, p. 534. Reprinted with permission.

6

LEGAL ASPECTS OF THE HEALTHCARE SETTING

Carolyn A. Haimann, JD, and Lynn Morgenstern, JD

Current conflicting pressures on the healthcare industry have created a legal environment of change and uncertainty. In recent years courts have increasingly demonstrated a willingness to accept new theories of liability for healthcare institutions as providers of medical services and as employers. Government agencies continue to issue regulations that constrain hospital activities in an attempt to meet two distinct and possibly conflicting goals: holding down healthcare costs and improving the quality of care.

As medical technology has advanced rapidly, medical ethicists, the public, and the courts are facing legal concerns about such subjects as termination of artificial life support, nutrition and hydration, embryo freezing and transfer, and predetermination of genetic diseases and disorders. Complex issues of confidentiality and selective treatment as well as patient and employee safety surround the AIDS epidemic. Advertising and marketing projects developed to address the present competitive climate in the industry require reflection on their legal implications. There is no question that in order to function effectively in this atmosphere, today's healthcare managers must be aware of the legal considerations that may arise from their activities and decisions.

All persons involved with the operation of a healthcare institution are cognizant of the importance and effect of law in healthcare delivery. All apply laws and legal principles at times in their daily routines, and legal aspects have become of major importance. This is true with the problems faced not only by the members of the board, administrators, physicians, and surgeons but also by all supervisors, department heads, and possibly everyone involved in healthcare delivery in a private healthcare setting.[1]

The contents of this chapter are intended to provide very general and basic information in lay language and should not be used in place of the advice or consultation with legal counsel. The purpose is to give department heads and supervisors an overall general perspective of some of the legal aspects of their positions. The reader should be aware that problems of hospital liability evolve from court decisions based on principles of common law and vary from jurisdiction to jurisdiction. As with all aspects of law, hospital law and court decisions applying these principles evolve and change on a continuous basis.

For example, for a long time the courts protected hospitals and other charitable institutions from lawsuits that might infringe on the assets of a charitable institution. This was generally known as the doctrine of charitable immunity. As discussed later in this chapter, nearly every state has now established the doctrine that charitable organizations have the obligation for compensation for injuries caused by them.

■ LIABILITY

Liability is a word and a problem that has become increasingly familiar to healthcare administrators, supervisors, and employees in recent years. Managers and employees at all levels are constantly being reminded of the potential for liability and its resulting costs to the institution permeating their everyday activities and decisions. In-house legal counsel, risk managers, consent forms, incident reports, and numerous requirements for documentation are constant reminders of the litigious environment within which the healthcare team works. Liability is on everyone's mind, and the burgeoning number of multimillion dollar judgments against institutions and their staffs has become an albatross around the necks of management and physicians. This chapter will discuss some of the various aspects of liability for the healthcare institution, the supervisor, and the employee.

The Institution's Direct Responsibility

Although liability is frequently imposed on institutions for negligence resulting in injuries to visitors and employees, most lawsuits filed against healthcare facilities involve patient injuries and allegations of negligent care. Therefore, this discussion focuses on the institution's liability for injuries to its patients and its responsibility for the medical care rendered by its physicians.

The law requires that any organization, such as a hospital, because of its actions allowing the public to rely on it for its safety, has a duty to exercise ordinary care to prevent injury. The duty owed by the hospital to its patients varies to some degree from jurisdiction to jurisdiction and also varies depending on the particular circumstances involved. Generally speaking, however, in most jurisdictions a hospital owes a duty of due care to its patients to provide that degree of skill and care and diligence that would be provided by a similar hospital under the same or similar circumstances. More specifically, a hospital has a legal duty to provide its patients with, among other things, premises kept in a reasonably safe condition, appropriately trained and skilled staff, reasonably adequate equipment, and proper medications. Whether the hospital has breached any of its duties to the patient in a particular situation usually will be decided by a jury. If a jury finds that a hospital has failed to meet the various standards of care owed to its patients thereby breaching its duty, then the hospital will be found negligent.

Respondeat Superior

As discussed, the institution is directly responsible for its actions in relation to the patient. In addition to this, however, the institution is indirectly liable for patient injuries in that it is legally responsible for the actions of those persons, employees and staff, over whom it exercises control and supervision. This vicarious liability arises from the doctrine of respondeat superior. Under this doctrine, the institution-employer is legally responsible for the negligent or wrongful acts of the employee even though the facility itself committed no wrong; the negligence of the employee is imputed to the employer. If an employee commits a negligent act that is the direct cause of injury to a patient, then the employer may be liable for the damages awarded to the injured party. The doctrine of respondeat superior applies only to civil actions, and an employer is not responsible for the criminal actions of its employees.

In order for the institution to be liable under respondeat superior, it is necessary that the employer have the right to control the actions of employees in the performance of their duties. If the jury determines that the employer has the right to control the actions of its employee (i.e., the method, time, and manner of work performance) and that the employee (or agent) was acting within the scope and course of employment, then the institution will be liable. An act will generally be considered within the scope of employment when the employee is acting on behalf of or perceives himself or herself to be acting for the benefit of the institution.

The theory of respondeat superior, however, does not absolve the employee of liability for his or her wrongful act. The employee, as well as the employer, may be found liable in damages to an injured third party. Under the law the employer may pursue indemnification from the employee for damages paid on his or her behalf under respondeat superior. In other words, the institution can seek recovery for the financial loss from the employee when his or her actions caused the facility to be responsible for the loss.

A hypothetical example will illustrate the application of liability under respondeat superior. Let us assume Joe Smith has been employed by hospital X for the past five years as a full-time, registered nurse on its medical floor. He has a good job record with no incidents of poor performance or poor exercise of nursing judgment. While Joe Smith is on duty during his assigned shift on his assigned floor, he is responsible for passing evening medications to the patients. Joe fails to check carefully the order for patients, Mrs. Jones and Mrs. Brown, and administers the medication ordered for Mrs. Jones to Mrs. Brown instead. As a direct result of the wrong medication being administered to her, Mrs. Brown suffers a severe and sudden drop in blood pressure resulting in shock. Mrs. Brown recovers, but not until after an extended hospital stay in the intensive care unit.

Mrs. Brown sued the nurse and the hospital for negligence. The jury found the nurse liable for negligence and found the hospital vicariously liable because it was the employer. The jury awarded a single sum of money, $50,000, against both the hospital and the nurse jointly, even though the nurse was negligent and the hospital's responsibility was based solely on the theory of respondeat superior. The hospital paid the $50,000 to Mrs. Brown and, in accordance with its policy, did not exercise its right of indemnification and did not ask Joe Smith to pay the hospital $50,000.

In this example the employer-employee relationships existed; Joe Smith was a salaried employee, and his hours of work, type of duties, and procedures for carrying out those duties were all controlled by his employer, the hospital. Further, the wrongful act, giving the wrong medication to the wrong patient, occurred while Joe was on his assigned shift performing his assigned duties, and thus the act was "within the scope and course of his employment."

Just as the hospital in this example was responsible for the acts of its nurses, it is also responsible for the acts of all other employees, professional and non-professional, over whom it exercises the requisite degree of control. Thus, an institution will be liable for the negligent acts of technicians, orderlies, transporters, housekeepers, dietary personnel, etc.

The "borrowed servant" theory and the related "captain of the ship" doctrine are often mentioned in connection with the principle of respondeat superior. The "borrowed servant" doctrine applies in certain situations when a private physician clearly has the right to control and direct a facility's employee in the performance of a duty or task. Thus, the physician and not the facility-employer will be liable for that employee's negligent acts.

The "captain of the ship" doctrine, a narrower concept than the "borrowed servant" theory, applies in the operating room setting. Under this doctrine the surgeon is considered the "captain of the ship"; that is, he or she has complete and total control and supervision over the personnel assisting him or her. Thus, the surgeon is responsible for the employee's negligent acts that occur during the procedure. The "captain of the ship" doctrine does not apply outside the operating room setting. It is important to note that the "captain of the ship" doctrine has been increasingly rejected by the courts in various jurisdictions. The current trend is to hold the institution, rather than the surgeon, responsible under respondeat superior for the actions of its operating room personnel.

In both the "borrowed servant" and "captain of the ship" situation, the key element is the extent and right of control the physician has over the employee whose acts caused the alleged injury. Courts carefully examine and juries decide whether or not an employee truly has become the "borrowed servant" of the physician before vicarious liability can be imposed on the physician for the employee's negligent acts. Generally speaking, in non-operating room settings, a physician will not be held liable for negligence of an institution-employed nurse in carrying out the physician's order in the regular course of the nurse's duties. If a physician issues a medically inappropriate order, a court may apportion a measure of the liability to the nurse, and therefore to the institution, if a nurse possessing the same skill and training would have questioned the order rather than carry it out.

The concept of respondeat superior also plays an important role in the question of the institution's responsibility for actions of certain members of its medical staff. The facility is liable under respondeat superior for the actions of those physicians who are employed by the facility or are under its direct control and supervision. Interns and residents in a training program, for example, are considered hospital employees. They are salaried by the hospital to render care to its patients, they do not have private patients, and they are under the control and supervision of the hospital usually through a chief physician who is a hospital employee. Because interns and residents fall within the "employee category," because they do not contract privately for services with their patients, and because the hospital has a right of control over them, hospitals are almost always held vicariously liable for their actions.

Usually, however, hospitals (and other healthcare institutions) are not held liable for the actions of their private physicians practicing in the hospital or other physicians who act as "independent contractors" and over whom the hospital has no direct control. The private physician is considered an independent contractor because he or she has an independent relationship with the patient apart from the hospital. They make independent judgments regarding care of the patient. The private physician is merely making use of the institution's facilities and support staff for the benefit of the patient, and the facility has no right of control over the physicians' actions regarding their patients.

There is, however, an exception to this. A recent trend has emerged in which the hospital has been held vicariously liable for the actions of an independent-contractor physician when no employer-employee relationship exists. In these situations the courts have held that if it appeared to the patient that the physician rendering care to him or her was a hospital employee, and if the patient did not choose the physician himself or herself, then the hospital will be held responsible for the physician's acts under the theory of "ostensible agency."

This principle is most often applied in circumstances where a group of private physicians has contracted with the hospital to render special services, such as anesthetic, radiologic, or emergency room coverage. These physicians are considered independent contractors, not hospital employees. Some courts have held, however, that patients who come for treatment to the emergency room of a hospital that uses these contracted services do not know that the physicians are not hospital employees and do not choose which physician they want to attend them. In fact, the courts hold, it appears to the patient that the physician is the hospital's employee. The same applies when a hospitalized patient is taken for tests to the radiology department staffed by private physicians who have contracted with the hospital to provide services. In most cases the patient does not select an individual radiologist to conduct the test; the patient accepts treatment from the radiologist assigned. Although a private physician and an independent contractor, this radiologist appears to the patient to be a hospital employee and provided to him or her by the hospital to render care.

As hospitals increasingly contract with outside entities to provide services formerly rendered entirely by hospital departments, the risk of this type of exposure increases. A carefully drawn contract can afford a modicum of protection for the institution, although a contract's provisions cannot constitute an absolute bar to a court finding the institution liable for the acts of an independent contractor.

Institutional Responsibility for Medical Care and Treatment Rendered to Patients

Traditionally, healthcare institutions, most often hospitals in this context, were not considered legally responsible for the negligent actions of those private physicians, chosen by the patients themselves, who used the hospital facilities. The hospital was considered to be merely the provider of the physical premises where the physician carried out his or her work. The hospital did not "practice medicine," only the physician did. The hospital's legal responsibility for the quality of care rendered by private physicians in its facility, however, has expanded greatly in recent years.

This new legal responsibility partly is the result of emerging case law beginning in 1965 with the Illinois Supreme Court case of *Darling v. Charleston Community Memorial Hospital*, 33 Ill.2d 326, 211 N.E.2d 253, 14 A.L.R.3rd 860 (1965), cert. denied, 383 U.S. 946 (1966). In this case the plaintiff, Darling, sustained a fracture in his leg during a football game and was taken to Charleston Community Hospital for treatment. There the leg was casted, but severe complications arose, resulting in the eventual necessity for amputation of the plaintiff's leg. Plaintiff brought suit against the physician and the hospital. The Illinois Supreme Court held the hospital liable for the patient's injuries and held that the hospital owed a direct duty of care to the patient. This is a landmark decision because it imposed on the hospital the duty to monitor the quality of patient care.

The *Darling* case has been cited, followed, and expanded on by courts in various other states. The implications of the *Darling* decision for hospitals has been widely debated. The general trend since the *Darling* decision, however, has been toward holding the institution directly responsible for the medical care rendered to its patients. The court in the *Darling* case said:

> The conception that the hospital does not undertake to treat the patient, does not undertake to act through its doctors and nurses, but undertakes instead simply to procure them to act upon their own responsibility, no longer reflects the fact. Present-day hospitals, as their manner of operation plainly demonstrates, do far more than furnish facilities for treatment. They regularly employ on a salary basis a large staff of physicians, nurses, and interns, as well as administrative and manual workers, and they charge patients for medical care and treatment, collecting for such services, if necessary, by legal action. Certainly, the person who avails himself of "hospital facilities" expects that the hospital will attempt to cure him, not that its nurses or other employees [sic] will act on their own responsibility.

Clearly at this point, although the hospital is not legally responsible for the negligent acts of its private physicians acting as independent contractors, a hospital must monitor the quality of patient care and the care given by its private physicians. A hospital usually will be held directly liable under the theory of corporate negligence for failing to select its medical staff carefully, periodically review the activities of its physicians, and take necessary action against those physicians when the hospital has knowledge or reason to know that they are not performing according to set standards or are incompetent or endangering patient welfare.

In fact, recent federal and state legislation impose peer review responsibilities on hospitals that include reporting disciplinary actions and lawsuits against physicians on the hospital's staff to government agencies. Some states have extended the reporting requirements to include nurses.

A new area of liability exposure has resulted from changes in reimbursement for hospital services. Under Medicare's diagnosis-related groups (DRGs), the hospital is paid a set amount for a patient based on that patient's diagnosis. If the patient requires more care and a longer stay than that covered by the specified DRG amount, the hospital loses money on that patient. A similar situation arises where third-party payors practice utilization review. Typically a medical insurance company will designate a specified number of days for hospitalization of a plan enrollee. If complications develop, and the patient requires a longer stay, the physician must seek third-party payor approval for the additional time. If that request is denied, the hospital will not be paid for the extended stay. These developments have given rise to the perception, whether or not it is true in practice, that patients are being discharged "sicker and quicker." Suits for injuries caused by premature discharge are just beginning to reach the courts. These actions may not only be brought against hospitals, but against physicians and third-party payors as well.

The current healthcare reimbursement and regulatory setting, the growth of the use of computers, and the increased demand for data mean that more outsiders have access to hospital information. As it becomes increasingly difficult for hospitals to maintain the confidentiality of patient records, patients are becoming more concerned with release of what they consider to be personal information. Hospitals must consider all these factors in developing procedures to provide the maximum protection of patient information. It is a supervisor's responsibility to make employees aware of these procedures and to monitor compliance.

■ NEGLIGENCE AND MALPRACTICE

"Malpractice" is a term often used synonymously with "negligence" in reference to the actions or wrongful acts of physicians, nurses, and other medical professionals. In fact, these terms are not identical but are similar. *Negligence* is defined in *Black's Law Dictionary* as:

> The omission to do something which a reasonable man, guided by those ordinary considerations which ordinarily regulate human affairs, would do, or the doing of something which a reasonable and prudent man would not do.[2]

Malpractice is the term for negligence of professional persons. *Malpractice* is defined in *Black's Law Dictionary* as:

> Professional misconduct or unreasonable lack of skill. This term is usually applied to such conduct by doctors, lawyers, and accountants. Failure of one rendering professional services to exercise that degree of skill and learning commonly applied under all the circumstances in the community by the average prudent reputable member of the profession with the result of injury, loss, or damage to the recipient of those services or to those entitled to rely upon

them. It is any professional misconduct, unreasonable lack of skill or fidelity in professional or fiduciary duties, evil practice, or illegal or immoral conduct.[3]

Any individual may be negligent, such as when one drives carelessly and strikes another vehicle or when a homeowner fails to rope off a hole in his front walk that is not easily visible. Only a professional person such as a physician, however, can commit malpractice.

To determine what does or does not constitute negligence, the law has developed a measuring scale called the "standard of care." Generally speaking, this standard of care is determined by what a reasonably prudent person would do under similar circumstances. This "reasonably prudent person" is, more specifically, a hypothetical person with average skills, training, and judgment. This is the yardstick for measuring what others should do in similar circumstances. The person's performance that is being accused of being negligent is then measured against what the reasonably prudent person would have done in similar circumstances. If someone's performance fails to meet the standard, then there is negligence. Also, if it was foreseeable that failure to meet that standard would cause injury and if the negligence was the direct and proximate cause of injury, then liability will be imposed.

Elements of duty of due care, breach of duty, foreseeability, causation, and damages apply in any situation where a medical professional's acts are challenged as wrongful or negligent by a plaintiff. The standards of care that medical professionals must meet are higher than those imposed on laypersons. An example of how these elements of negligence apply in the hospital setting in reference to a professional person will be helpful.

Let us assume Jane Doe is a registered nurse in a jurisdiction that permits recovery against nurses for malpractice. Ms. Doe is assigned to give medicine to Mr. James, a patient under her care. She misreads the order, which is for 40 mg of gentamicin, an antibiotic, and instead gives him 400 mg of gentamicin. This drug is extremely potent, and Ms. Doe knows that an excessive dose can cause renal problems. Mr. James suffers renal shutdown and has to be hospitalized for several more weeks. Applying the elements as previously outlined, Nurse Doe has a duty to the patient to possess that degree of skill and learning ordinarily possessed by nurses. She also has the duty to meet the standard of care for nurses in this same situation, that is, to act as a reasonably prudent nurse would have acted. In this case, specifically, this means meeting that requisite standard of care, she should have given the ordered medication to the right patient, in the ordered dose, at the ordered time, and by the ordered mode of administration. This is what a reasonably prudent nurse would have done in this same situation. Ms. Doe deviated from the standard of care (breaching her duty) by failing to give the correct dosage and was thus negligent. If her negligence was the proximate cause of harm to the patient, then she will be liable for damages. The burden is on the plaintiff to prove the standard and deviation from that standard. The jury must decide whether the negligent act was in fact the proximate cause of the injury.

It is important to recognize, however, that not all bad results or unexpected outcomes are the result of negligence or mean liability for the person committing the act. Let us assume Jane Doe gave the correct dosage of medication to the patient. Let us assume further that Mr. James had never taken the medication before and on inquiry had said he had no known allergies to any drugs. Five minutes after he received the medication, he suffered a severe, unanticipated allergic reaction resulting in a cardiac arrest. In this case, although the medication caused injury to Mr. James, Ms. Doe will not be liable. She met her duty of care. She gave the correct dose to the right patient, at the right time, in the correct manner of administration. She had no reason to know that Mr. James would have an allergic reaction. She did not breach her duty; she was not negligent. Without committing negligence, she cannot be found liable.

It is also important to know that one may be negligent but not held liable if the negligent act does not result in harm to the other party. If Jane Doe gave the wrong dose of medication to Mr. James but he suffered no ill effects, she is still negligent. Because her negligent act caused no harm, however, she probably will not be held liable for damages.

We have taken a brief look at some of the various types of liability for the healthcare institution, corporate negligence, and respondeat superior. General reference has also been made to the employee's own liability for his or her acts. Let us now turn our attention to the liability of the supervisor.

■ SUPERVISOR'S LIABILITY

The healthcare professional, as we have seen, can be held personally liable for his or her actions. Many members of this group are supervisors by title and supervise others as a regular part of their job duties. What about that aspect of their job? Can the supervisor be held personally liable for his or her negligent actions as *a supervisor* as well?

The supervisor is not liable for the acts of those supervised on the basis of respondeat superior because the supervisor is not the employer of those he or she supervises. The institution is the employer, and the supervisor has only administrative responsibility for those he or she directs. A supervisor is also not liable just because someone under his or her supervision acts negligently and causes injury to a third party.

A supervisor's performance, however, will be measured against the standard of care for a reasonably prudent person in the same or similar supervisory position. If a supervisor fails to meet the standard, he or she might be held liable as a supervisor for the harm caused. If a supervisor permits or directs someone to perform a duty that the supervisor knows or reasonably should know the person is not trained to perform, then the supervisor may be held liable for negligent supervision if that person causes harm.

Let us assume Betty Green is a head nurse in hospital X. The hospital has a provision stating that no nurse employed less than three months shall be allowed to do endotracheal suctioning with no assistance unless the head nurse is familiar with and has reviewed and approved the new employee's performance of that task. Ms. Burnside, a new employee, has been working under Ms. Green's supervision for one month. Ms. Green has observed Ms. Burnside help another nurse to suction a patient; the head nurse concluded that Ms. Burnside does not perform the task adequately and needs some additional in-service training. Mr. Kane, a patient, has an order to be suctioned, if needed, and Ms. Green tells Ms.

Burnside to suction Mr. Kane. Ms. Burnside does so, but incorrectly, causing injury to the patient's tracheal wall. Ms. Green will probably be held liable for negligent supervision. She had reason to know that Ms. Burnside by herself could not yet adequately and skillfully perform suctioning on a patient.

Liability for the nursing supervisors frequently arises as a result of the actions of nursing students under their direct control and supervision. Supervisors need to exercise particular care in not permitting nursing students and others in training to perform tasks and duties for which they are not yet trained or do not have adequate skill, information, or experience.

Remember the example given earlier where Joe Smith gave the medication intended for Mrs. Jones to Mrs. Brown? In this case Joe had worked on his floor for five years with a good record and no incidents of poor performance or faulty nursing judgment. His head nurse, as supervisor, would not be liable for Joe's negligent act. Since the head nurse is not Joe's employer, she is not liable under respondeat superior. Also, she is not liable as a supervisor because she had no reason to think Joe was not able to perform properly the task of passing out medications. If, on the other hand, Joe had made 10 similar mistakes in the past several months and the supervisor was aware of this and took no action to counsel or make sure Joe was performing properly, then the supervisor might be held liable for negligent supervision.

■ ADDITIONAL POTENTIAL CAUSES FOR LIABILITY

Many other areas of healthcare activities have potential for liability of the institution, its supervisors, and its employees. These include obtaining informed consent from patients; following proper admission and discharge procedures to avoid charges of false imprisonment, negligent failure to render treatment, or abandonment of care; and ensuring a safe work environment for employees. Institutions and personnel must also deal with controversial issues fraught with philosophical, moral, legal, and ethical complexities, such as abortion, sterilization, and the right to die with dignity. A discussion of these and other issues, however, is beyond the scope of this chapter.

■ EMPLOYEE LITIGATION

Employees are becoming increasingly aware of their legal rights, resulting in an explosion in the number of legal actions brought by employees against their current or former employers. Most typically these claims involve a former employee alleging unlawful discharge by the employer. This is a recent phenomenon, since historically the law viewed the employment relationship as one "at will." That is, if there was no contract for a specific term, an employer could terminate an employee at any time, for any reason. An employee, for his or her part, was free to leave at any time.

The first exceptions to this legal principle originated with statutory and constitutional prohibitions against discrimination based on race. More recently sex, national origin, age, handicap, and pregnancy discrimination have been prohibited by statute and regulation. Following on the heels of these legislated exceptions, the courts in many states have begun to acknowledge other situations where an employer cannot rely on the "employment at will" doctrine. Courts have recognized claims where an employee was discharged for refusing to perform an illegal act, for "whistle-blowing" against the employer, or for breaching what the employee alleged to be an express or implied contract. Employees have successfully claimed that employee handbooks contain the terms of express written contracts or that statements made during job interviews constitute implied contracts.

The surge in employee litigation places additional burdens on supervisors, since it is their responsibility to treat an employee fairly, to follow institutional policy regarding discipline, and to monitor and document the employee's performance accurately. If a supervisor fails to follow proper procedures and to document incidents and the manner in which employees discharge their duties, the institution is left open to claims that an employee was disciplined for discriminatory or wrongful reasons and not for poor performance.

■ SUMMARY

The healthcare institution's legal responsibility for what occurs on its premises is increasing rapidly and is cause for concern by administrators, supervisors, and employees alike. The professional members of the healthcare team also are being held to stricter and higher standards of care and are being held liable for their negligent acts. Those practicing in the healthcare field are well advised to familiarize themselves with the various aspects of their job that could result in liability to themselves or their institution. They must exercise caution and care in the performance of their duties.

NOTES
1. Our discussion does not cover situations in facilities operated by the Veterans Administration, Army, Navy, Air Force, and Public Health Service.
2. *Black's Law Dictionary*, 5th ed., St. Paul; MN: West Publishing, 1979, p. 930.
3. *Black's Law Dictionary*, p. 864.

Part Three

PLANNING

7

MANAGERIAL PLANNING

Planning is deciding in advance what is to be done in the future. Planning is the primary managerial function and the primary task of every manager. Logically planning must come before any of the other functions because it determines the framework in which the other functions—organizing, staffing, influencing, and controlling—are carried out. Planning begins with decision making, the process of selecting from alternatives. Modern healthcare activities operate in an environment that is always changing in ways institutions can neither control nor predict precisely. This increases the need for planning. The only way institutions can survive is to plan rationally and prepare for change.

Every organization must plan ahead because it dare not face the future unprepared. In planning management is concerned with formulating strategy, establishing the objectives to be achieved, and determining how to achieve them. Planning information is assembled, the external and internal environments are studied, planning premises are set out, and decisions are made to reach organizational goals. These decisions made in planning provide the other functions with their objectives and standards against which performance is measured.

Thus, when the manager plans a course of action for the future, an attempt is made to achieve a consistent and coordinated structure of operations aimed at the desired results. Plans alone do not bring about these results; to achieve them, the operation of the healthcare center is necessary. Without plans, however, random activities would prevail, producing confusion and possibly even chaos.

■ THE NATURE OF PLANNING

Planning as a Continuous Mental Process and Primary Function

Planning is mental work and therefore may be difficult to perform. No substitute exists, however, for the hard thinking that planning demands. It is necessary to think before acting and base action on facts rather than guesses. For this reason, planning is the primary function that must come before the manager can intelligently perform any of the other managerial functions. Only after having made the plans can the supervisor organize, staff, influence, and control. How could a supervisor properly and effectively organize the workings of the department without having a plan in mind? How could the department head effectively staff and supervise the employees without knowing which avenues, policies, procedures, and methods to follow and without knowing what the objectives are? And how could the activities of the employees possibly be controlled? None of these functions could be performed without having planned first.

However, planning does not end abruptly when the supervisor begins to perform the other functions. It should not be a process used only at occasional intervals or when the manager is not too engrossed in the daily chores. Rather, planning is a continuous process that must be used consistently every day. With day-to-day planning the supervisor realistically anticipates future problems, analyzes them, determines their probable effect on the activities, and decides on the plan of action that will lead to the desired results.

Planning as a Task of Every Manager

The question often has been raised, who does the planning? The managers do the planning, and it is the job of every manager, whether chairman of the board, chief administrator of a hospital, or supervisor of a small department. By definition, all of them are managers and therefore all of them must do the planning. As noted in Chapter 2, however, the importance and magnitude of plans will depend on the level on which plans are determined. Planning on the top level of administration is more fundamental and more far-reaching. In the supervisory levels of management the scope and extent of planning become narrower and more detailed. Thus, the chief administrator is concerned with the overall aspects of planning for the entire healthcare center, such as constructing new facilities, adding new specialties, and enlarging outpatient services. Planning for new buildings encompassed most of the long-range planning during the 1960s. Today's long-range planning must make certain that the healthcare center's services are appropriate, timely, and competitive; it probably will also include plans for shared services and linkages with other healthcare providers and user groups. In descending the managerial hierarchy, an example of long-range planning for the nursing director includes setting objectives for patient care, defining priorities, writing new procedures, and determining activities to fulfill these objectives. A supervisor is concerned with plans for getting the job in the department done promptly and effectively each day.

Although planning is the manager's function, this does not mean that others should not be called on to give advice. Some healthcare institutions have full-time employees known as "planners," usually in a staff position. They are normally employed to help the chief executive officer (CEO) in his or her long-term strategy and planning decisions. It is unlikely that supervisors would need such planners' help. However, at times a supervisor may think that certain areas of planning require special knowledge, such as with human resources, nursing shortages, computer and accounting procedures, or professional and technical aspects. In such instances the supervisor must feel free to call on specialists within the organization to help with the planning. In other words, a manager should avail himself or herself of all possible help to plan effectively. In the final analysis, however, it is still the manager's and no one else's personal responsibility to plan.

Planning as a Cost Saver

Planning is efficient; it makes for purposeful organization and activities, which in turn minimize costs and reduce waste. Deciding in advance what is to be done, how, by whom, where, and when promotes efficient and orderly operations. All efforts are directed toward a desired result; haphazard approaches are minimized, activities are coordinated, and duplications are avoided. Minimum time is needed for the completion of each planned activity because only the necessary amount of work is done. Facilities are used to their best advantage, and guesswork is eliminated. Thus, by its very nature planning has many benefits that no manager can afford to neglect.

Effective management demands optimum use of the organization's resources. As a supervisor, you are entrusted with the management of both employees and physical resources of the department. You have to work with people and such factors as space, equipment, tools, and materials. How all these resources are used is your primary responsibility and the basis on which your managerial performance is judged.

Only by planning will you be able to make the best possible use of these resources. Only by planning will you as a supervisor be able to bring out the best in your employees, the most valuable resource you have. Plans for the proper use of physical resources are also essential because of the capital investment that the healthcare center has made in them. Even in the smallest department, the total investment in working space, equipment, tools, materials, and supplies is substantial. Only by planning can all of these resources be used most effectively.

■ THE MAJOR PLANNING CONSIDERATIONS

The Planning Period

A major question is, for how long a period should the manager plan? Usually a distinction is made between long-range, intermediate, and short-range planning. The exact definitions of long-range and short-range planning depend on the manager's level in the hierarchy, the type of institution, and the kind of activity in which it is engaged. For all practical purposes, however, *short-term* planning can be defined as planning that covers a period up to 1 year. *Long-term* planning usually involves a considerably longer interval. In recent years an increasing trend has been to plan 5, 10, or even 20 years ahead. The board and CEO must plan along these lines, in addition to making short-term plans. Planning for 1 to 5 years is often called *intermediate* planning.

The supervisor's planning period probably will be short range, that is, planning for 1 year at the most or perhaps for 6 months, 1 month, 1 week, or even 1 day. There are activities in certain departments for which a supervisor can definitely plan 3, 6, 9, or 12 months in advance, such as the planning of preventive maintenance. With certain activities in a health facility, on the other hand, supervisory planning will be for a shorter time—a week, a day, or only a shift. Such short-range planning is frequently needed in nursing services. It is more desirable if the supervisor is able to make longer-range plans, but for practical purposes, proper attention must be given to seeing that the work of each day is accomplished. Such short-range planning for the day is always necessary. This planning requires the supervisor to take the time to think through the nature and amount of work that is to be done each day by the department, who is to do it, and when. Furthermore, this daily planning must be done ahead of time; many supervisors prefer to do it at the end of the day or shift, when they can size up what has been accomplished to formulate plans for the following day or shift.

Occasionally a supervisor will also be involved in long-term plans. For example, the boss may want to discuss planning for new and additional activities for the institution. A supervisor may be informed of a contemplated expansion or the addition of new facilities and will be asked to estimate what the department can contribute or what will be needed. If a hospital plans for an enlarged outpatient surgical center, the director of nursing, as well as the operating room supervisor, will be deeply involved in such a plan.

From time to time the administrator might request the supervisor to look into the future and project the long-term trend of a particular activity, especially if it is apparent that such activity will be affected by major breakthroughs in medical science and technology. It is important for the supervisor to participate in such long-range planning because the plans may require some employees to be reassigned or others to acquire additional skills. The long-range plans also may indicate that subordinates with completely new skills and education are needed and that a search for them must start now. Learning new procedures and techniques might be necessary as a result of new equipment that will be introduced. In these situations the supervisors must participate in long-range planning. Usually, however, their primary planning period will be shorter.

The Integration and Communication of Plans

The supervisors' short-range plans must be integrated and coordinated with the institution's long-range plans. Long-range planning should not be viewed as an activity separate from or contrary to short-range planning. Therefore, it is essential for top-level administration to keep all managers well informed of the new and existing long-range plans of the institution and to make certain that the short-range plans of lower-level management are in accordance with them. The better informed the supervisors or lower-level managers are, the better they will be able to integrate their short-range plans into the overall plans.

All too often, however, there is a gap between the knowledge of top management and lower-level management concerning planning. This gap is often justified by the claim that many of the plans are confidential and cannot be divulged for security reasons. Most employees know that very little can be kept secret in any organization; therefore, internal security cannot always be used as an excuse. On the other hand, supervisors should realize that some limitations exist and that top-level administration does not have to disclose all their plans as long as lower-level managers are informed of those plans that will directly affect their particular activities.

To this extent, therefore, plans should be communicated and fully explained to subordinate managers so that they are in a better position to formulate derivative plans for their departments. By the same token, supervisors should always bear in mind that their own employees will be affected by the plans that they make. Since employees are needed to execute whatever has been planned, the supervisor is well advised to take them into his or her confidence and explain in advance what is being planned for the department. The manager may even want to consult the employees and ask for suggestions, since some may be in a position to make helpful contributions. The supervisor should also remember that well-informed employees always are better employees who appreciate that they have not been kept "in the dark."

■ TYPES OF PLANS

Organizational Goals and Objectives

The first step in planning is to develop a statement of the goals and objectives for the institution that becomes the target toward which all activities are directed. These goals and objectives must be expressed clearly and communicated fully so that all managers have a common understanding around which to coordinate their activities. The objectives will largely determine how the managers go about their organizing, staffing, and influencing functions. Also, controlling would be meaningless without objectives as guidelines. Effective management is always management by objectives. This holds true for the CEO of a hospital, for the supervisor on the "firing line," and for all managers on the levels between the CEO and supervisor. Formulating objectives should therefore be foremost in every manager's mind. Once the goals have been established, additional plans, such as policies, standard procedures, methods, rules, programs, projects, and budgets, are then designed to achieve the objectives.

Primary Objectives

As noted earlier, the first step in planning is a statement of the overall, or primary, objectives to be achieved by the enterprise. Every member of the organization should be familiar with this statement of objectives, since it outlines the multiple goals and end results toward which all plans and activities are directed. These objectives constitute the purpose of the healthcare center, and without them no intelligent planning can take place. Setting these overall objectives is a function of top-level administration—the board and the CEO.

In general, many healthcare centers have such primary objectives as providing primary, secondary, or even tertiary care to the sick and injured; doing research; working toward advancement of medical knowledge; helping in the maintenance of health and in the prevention of sickness; providing education; and training employees in all the professional and nonprofessional activities customarily associated with a healthcare institution.

effective & efficient services

In addition to these goals, a healthcare facility can have many other objectives: maintaining a fine reputation among hospitals, practicing the best possible medicine, establishing a good image in the community, discharging numerous social and charitable responsibilities, achieving cost effectiveness and cost containment, etc. Moreover, another essential objective of even not-for-profit healthcare facilities is to ensure fiscal integrity, operate within available financial resources, and balance a preset budget. For those healthcare activities organized as a for-profit undertaking, profit certainly is also one of the major objectives.

A healthcare institution also will strive toward many other less tangible objectives. In relation to its employees, for instance, the goal is being a good and fair employer. The objective in this case is to establish the reputation in the healthcare field of being a good place for people to work.

Any organization has many objectives, and the real difficulty lies in ranking and balancing them. This is especially true for healthcare facilities. Although it would be beyond the scope of this book to discuss all the objectives of the different types of healthcare facilities, the previous examples show sufficiently well the multiplicity and complexity of objectives and why top-level administration has a continuous challenge in balancing and achieving them. If the CEO would choose a single objective to the exclusion of all others, the effectiveness of the institution's overall performance could be jeopardized. All this is becoming increasingly difficult because healthcare activities must function in a continuously changing environment, making it necessary to reevaluate past objectives and add new ones.

Secondary or Departmental Objectives

Although the goals established for an institution as a whole are called the primary objectives, those set up for each of the institution's various departments can be called secondary, supportive, or derivative objectives. Since each department or division has a specific task to perform, each must have its own clearly defined goals associated with the functions as a guide. These secondary goals and objectives of the departments must stay within the overall framework set by the primary objectives and must contribute to the achievement of the overall institutional objectives.

Because they are concerned with only one department, however, the secondary objectives are necessarily narrower in scope. Whereas the overall objectives *(primary)* are broad and general, the objectives of a department have to be much more specific and detailed to serve as specific guides for subordinate units. They enable departmental managers to operate at their own discretion, although always within the limits of the overall institutional goals. For instance, the objective that "the welfare of the patients is the foremost concern in our institution" will permeate all secondary goals.

This may become clearer if we use as an example the stated objectives of the facility's medical records department, also known as medical information services. The objective is to collect systematically and maintain all patient demographic and medical data and facilitate analysis of the data such that the resulting information benefits the user. The medical record is compiled during the treatment of each patient and preserves all information about a person's illness or injury as noted by, and in the treatment rendered by, the medical team. It is used as a permanent record of conditions treated and may serve as an aid in treating future illnesses. Further, the patient's record is the primary data source for (1) clinical and statistical research, (2) administrative planning and program evaluation, and (3) litigation for the patient, institution, and physician. Additional objectives of the medical information services department are (1) to collect, analyze, and publish various hospital and diagnostic statistics and (2) to review concurrently and retrospectively the quality of care and utilization of services.

In another example, the nursing department's objectives may state that its mission is to provide superior patient care within selected specialties in which it has demonstrated ability. This might include primary care, secondary care, and possibly tertiary care.[1] The objectives may state further that this care is to be provided in the context of a medical education program and possibly in an academic medical center setting. Figure 7.1 gives an example of the objectives and philosophy of the nursing service in a large teaching hospital.

Obviously these departmental objectives are specific, but their fulfillment contributes significantly to the achievement of overall institutional goals. In fact, the primary objectives could not be achieved if these and all other departmental objectives were not fulfilled.

Integration Between Objectives

It is essential for all supervisors and their employees to understand clearly not only the objectives of their own department but also those of the entire institution. The two sets of objectives must be carefully defined and stated so that they can be integrated, coordinated, and explained on the departmental level. The supervisor must bear in mind that the successful completion of a task depends on the full understanding of its purpose by those who have to carry it out. It is therefore good management to make certain that all employees at all levels are thoroughly informed and indoctrinated about the objectives to be achieved.

Review of Objectives

Since all healthcare activities operate in an increasingly ever-changing environment, contingencies will arise that might necessitate a change in the thrust of the enterprise. This will create the need for a change in the objectives. Objectives must be flexible and able to adapt to changes in the internal and external environments. Therefore, reviewing the objectives from time to time is a managerial duty on all levels.

■ MANAGEMENT BY OBJECTIVES

To achieve specific results from setting these departmental objectives, more and more organizations are using a process called *management by objectives (MBO)*. The term and concepts were first introduced by Peter Drucker in the early 1950s and have become very popular since then.[2] Managers in healthcare organizations

■ **FIGURE 7-1** Barnes Hospital nursing service philosophy.

Page 1 of 1

Document Number _____
NSAB Approved _____
Implemented _____
Supersedes _____
Next Review _____

Policy Statement

Nursing is the individualized process of assisting patients and families as they progress through changing levels of health, and helping them gain either an improved level of independence or a peaceful death.

We are committed to the provision of patient-centered nursing care based upon an established model of standards of nursing practice. The standards of care provide a framework in which individual professional nurses utilize the nursing process. This process includes assessment of patients' healthcare problems, identifying nursing diagnosis, planning for and implementing goal-directed nursing therapies and critically evaluating the outcomes of that care on a continual basis. Effective discharge planning, beginning at the time of patient's admission, is integral to assuring a patient's smooth transition from hospital to the community.

We support the dignity of the individual and believe that patients have the right to respectful care. We believe that nurses are patients' advocates and must make ethical nursing decisions while delivering care. Nurses play a central role in the communication of various aspects of patient care as well as coordination of that care through collaboration with members of the healthcare team. We believe that patients and/or their significant others should participate in the development, delivery, and evaluation of their care.

We are committed to health teaching to promote an optimal level of functioning for patients and families. We believe that professional growth of nurses is related to the development of competency in nursing practice and the acceptance of accountability for one's own actions and judgments. We provide experiential and educational opportunities which support professional growth and recognize that nursing research activities are necessary to improve and develop nursing practice.

In response to expressed health needs of the community, we accept the responsibility to share relevant knowledge and information. We recognize the community has the right to expect that care be provided in a manner which demonstrates concern for cost effectiveness.

Reprinted with special permission of Barnes Hospital, St. Louis. For illustrative purposes only.

---

should be familiar with the MBO concept, since its use in their activity is increasing.

MBO is an integrative management concept, containing elements of the planning function, together with participative management, motivation, and controlling. MBO demonstrates the interrelationships of the managerial functions and the systems approach to management. Therefore, MBO will also be discussed in other appropriate sections of this text. At this time, however, we are primarily concerned with the meaning of MBO in connection with setting and achieving departmental objectives.

MBO is concerned with goal setting for individual managers. In this process a manager at any level and that individual's immediate subordinate jointly develop goals in accordance with the organizational goals. Once institutional goals are clarified, the manager and the subordinate together should develop and agree on the subordinate's goals to be achieved during a stated period. To be operational, these performance objectives set must be *specific, measurable (quantifiable), challenging,* but realistically *attainable* by the subordinate within the *time frame* established. This means that each objective must provide a plan showing the work to be done, the time frame, and the individual who will accomplish it. There must be quantitative indicators to measure the work achieved. To be realistic, it should be possible to carry out the activity within the time frame set, a period long enough to get the objective done, but short enough to provide timely feedback and still permit intervention if necessary. It is understood that the degree to which these goals are achieved will be a major factor in evaluating the subordinate's performance.

The important point is that these goals are jointly established and agreed on ahead of time. At the end of the period, both supervisor and employee participate in the review of the subordinate's performance to see how results for the period compare with the objectives he or she set out to accomplish. If the goals were achieved, new goals will be set for the next period. If a discrepancy exists, efforts are made to find steps to overcome these problems, and the manager and subordinate agree on new goals for the next period. MBO clearly is a powerful tool in achieving involvement and commitment of subordinates.

■ ADDITIONAL TYPES OF PLANS

Once the objectives have been determined, managers must design numerous plans necessary to achieve fulfillment of the goals. Several different types of plans are devised to implement objectives: policies, procedures, methods, rules, programs, projects, and budgets. All these plans must be designed to reinforce one another; that is, they must be integrated and coordinated. Since every manager will probably have to devise or at least use each type of plan at some time, he or she should be familiar with the meaning of all of them. The major plans are formulated by the CEO, but all department supervisors will have to formulate their own departmental plans accordingly. The purpose of all these plans is to ensure that the thinking and actions taken on different levels and in different departments of the institution are consistent with and contribute to the overall objectives.

The different type of plans just referred to can be divided into two major groups: repeat-use plans and single-use plans. Objectives, policies, procedures, methods, and rules are commonly known as repeat-use, or standing, plans because they are followed each time a given situation is encountered. In other words, they are used again and again. Repeat-use plans are applicable whenever a situation presents itself that is similar to the one for which the standing plan was originally devised.

The opposite of repeat-use plans are single-use, or single-purpose, plans. These plans are no longer needed once their objective is accomplished. Once the goal is reached, the plan is used up. Within this single-use plan category are programs, projects, and budgets.

■ REPEAT-USE OR STANDING PLANS

Policies

Policies are probably the most frequently used and mentioned plans among the various plans a manager must depend on and devise. *Policies are broad guides to thinking.* They are general statements that channel the thinking of all personnel charged with decision making. Although they are broad, policies do have definite limitations. Policies reflect constraints, and as long as a supervisor stays within these limitations, he or she will make an appropriate decision, one that conforms to the policy. Thus, policies serve to keep decision makers on the right track, and in this way they facilitate the job of both managers and subordinates. Policies ensure uniformity of decision making throughout the organization. They help to coordinate activities and, as the organization grows larger and more complex, the need for policies increases.

Policies as an Aid in Delegation

Policies cover the various areas of the organization's activities: some relate to the managerial functions (e.g., a promotion-from-within policy); others relate to operational functions (e.g., patient care policies, public relations, marketing). By issuing all these policies, top-level administration sanctions in advance the decisions made by subordinate managers, as long as they stay within the broad policy guidelines. After having set policies, a higher-level manager should feel reasonably confident that whatever decisions the subordinate managers make will fall within the limits of the policies. In fact, the subordinates will probably come up with decisions comparable to those the manager would have made. Thus, policies make it easier for the higher-level manager to delegate authority to the subordinates.

Policies are a great help to the subordinate managers as well. Policies provide specific guidelines for subordinates' thinking that facilitate decision making and at the same time ensure uniformity of decisions throughout the enterprise. Therefore, the clearer and more comprehensive the policy guides are, the easier and more effective it will be for the higher-level managers to delegate authority and for the subordinate managers to exercise authority.

The Origin of Policies

Policies do not come about by chance; they are determined by management, particularly by the higher administrative levels. Formulating policies is one of the most important functions of top-level management. These managers are in the best position to establish the various types of policies that will facilitate achievement of the enterprise's objectives. Once the corporate policies have been set by the top-level administrator, they in turn will become the guides for various policies covering divisions and departments, such as patient care policies. Such divisional and departmental policies are *originated* by the various managers lower in the managerial hierarchy. This type of policy formulation, originated by the top administrative level and pursued by the lower managerial levels, is the most important source of policies.

Occasionally, however, a supervisor may have a problem situation not covered by existing policy. In such a dilemma the supervisor has only one choice: go to the boss and simply ask whether or not any of the existing policies are applicable. If none applies, then the supervisor should appeal to the boss to issue a policy to cover such situations.

For instance, suppose that one of your employees asks for a leave of absence. To make the appropriate decision, you would prefer to be guided by policy so that your decision would be in accord with all other decisions regarding leaves of absence. You may find, however, that the administrator never issued any policies on granting or denying a leave of absence. Instead of making an ad hoc decision (for this case only), you ask your boss to issue a policy, a broad guide for thinking to be applied whenever leaves of absence are requested. You probably will not have to make such a request very often because a good administrator usually foresees most of the areas in which policies are needed. On occasion, however, you may have to appeal to your own boss, stimulating the formulation of what is known as *appealed policy.*

In addition to originated and appealed policies, some policies are *imposed* on an organization by external factors, such as the government, accrediting agencies, trade unions, and trade associations. The word "imposed" indicates compliance with a force that cannot be avoided. For instance, to be accredited, hospitals and other healthcare facilities must comply with certain regulations issued by the accrediting agency. These regulations must be translated into institutional policy, and all employees must abide by them.

The Joint Commission on Accreditation of Healthcare Organizations now requires hospitals to have formal policies specifying, for example, when physicians and nurses may refrain from trying to resuscitate patients who are terminally ill. Although most hospitals had such a policy prior to this request, many had not announced one or had avoided a policy on this issue. Another example of an *externally imposed* policy is being an equal opportunity employer. Unless the healthcare center practiced such a policy before federal and state fair employment legislation was promulgated, such a policy statement today can be regarded as one that was externally imposed on the hospital.

Clarity of Policies

Because policies are such a vital guide for thinking and thus for decision making, it is essential that they be stated simply and clearly. Policies must be communicated so that those in the organization who are to apply them will fully understand their meaning. This is no easy task. It is difficult to find words that will be understood by all people in the same way, since different meanings can be attached to the same word. Although there is no guarantee that even the written word will be properly understood, it still seems more desirable to put all policies in writing. This at least will avoid the added ambiguity of spoken words.

In addition to better comprehension, other benefits are derived from written policies:

1. The process of writing policies requires the top-level administrator to think them out clearly and consistently.
2. Written policies are easily accessible; the subordinate managers can read them as often as they wish.
3. The wording of a written policy cannot be changed by word of mouth because the written policy can always be consulted.
4. Written policies are especially helpful for new managers who need immediate help in solving a problem.

Although these advantages are significant, one disadvantage is connected with written policies. Once policies are written down, management may become reluctant to change them. Thus, some enterprises prefer to have their policies communicated by word of mouth because they believe that this is more flexible, allowing the verbal policies to be adjusted to different circumstances with greater ease than written policies. The exact meaning of a verbal policy might become scrambled, however, making it difficult to apply the policy properly. For this reason, written policy statements are generally considered far more desirable and necessary.

The Flexibility of Policies

Defining a policy as a broad guide to thinking requires a certain amount of flexibility. Although policies must be consistent to coordinate the activities of each day successfully, they must also be flexible. Some policies even have flexibility explicitly stated by such words as "whenever possible," "whenever feasible," or "under usual circumstances." For instance, one of the most widely practiced policies today is: "Our enterprise believes and practices promotion from within whenever possible." If these clauses are built in, then the manner in which the supervisor applies the policy will determine its degree of flexibility. The supervisor must intelligently adapt the policy to the existing set of circumstances. Such flexibility, however, must not lead to inconsistency; policies must be administered by supervisors in a consistent manner.

The Supervisor and Policies

Although supervisors seldom have to issue policies, they must continuously use them. Supervisors primarily apply existing policies in making their daily decisions. It is also the supervisors' job to interpret and explain the meaning of policies to the employees of their departments. Therefore, it is essential that supervisors clearly understand the policies and that they learn how to apply them appropriately.

A manager who heads a major department, such as the director of nursing services, which normally comprises half of the institution's employees and has many subdivisions within it, may find it necessary to issue and write policies for the department. In fact, the Joint Commission on Accreditation of Healthcare Organizations will examine these "nursing policies." All of them must reinforce and be in accordance with the overall policies of the entire healthcare center.

Among these policies will probably be a nursing policy stating that the welfare of the patient is the foremost concern of the nursing service and that it takes precedence over all other considerations. In all likelihood the institution's overall policy of fairness and nondiscrimination will also show up in a nursing policy. The policy may state that patients shall be accorded impartial access to treatments or accommodations—to the extent that these are available and medically indicated—regardless of race, color, creed, or national origin. The policy also may state that the patient's right to privacy shall be respected, consistent with medical needs, etc.

The director of nursing services certainly will see that a policy exists for cardiopulmonary resuscitation, also referred to as "code," "no code," or "DNR" (do not resuscitate). This policy in some healthcare centers will simply state that cardiopulmonary resuscitative measures must be initiated on all patients experiencing cardiac arrest unless a "no code order" has been written by the attending physician. In some hospitals the policy will be broader by reaffirming the traditional role of the physician. With appropriate regard for the wishes of the patient and concerned family, the physician may determine that heroic resuscitative measures, contrary to the principles of human dignity and humane medical care, should not be carried out. (See Fig. 7-2.)

Periodic Review of Policies

Policies must be changed when the organization or environment changes, regardless of how well thought out the policies were when originated. Because of changing contingencies, the thrust of the enterprise may be altered, and this will create the need for a change in policies. It is therefore necessary to review and appraise policies periodically to see whether new ones should be issued or existing ones changed, modified, or completely abandoned. Such an investigation may uncover situations that are complete contradictions to current written policies, or it may uncover policies that have become so outdated that no one follows them. In such cases top-level administration must either rewrite or abandon the questionable policies, since an institution certainly cannot afford to let its various subordinate managers decide whether policies are still current or whether they should be observed any longer. Thus, it is essential for policies to be periodically reviewed by top-level management and kept up-to-date.

Procedures

Another type of standing plans are procedures; they are repeat-use plans for achieving the institution's objectives. Procedures are derived from policies, but they are much more specific than policies. *Procedures are guides to action,* not guides to thinking. Procedures show the sequence of definite acts. They outline a chronological order for the acts that are to be performed. (See Figure 7-2.) Procedures specify a route that will take subordinates within the guideposts of the policies and lead them to the final objectives. In brief, procedures prescribe a path toward the objectives; they describe in detail how a recurring activity is to be performed.

■ **FIGURE 7-2** Barnes Hospital nursing service cardiopulmonary resuscitation (CPR).

Document Number _____
NSAB Approved _____
Implemented _____
Supersedes _____
Next Review _____

I. Policy
  A. Cardiopulmonary resuscitation will be initiated on all patients unless there is an order written not to resuscitate.
  B. Guidelines for "Do Not Resuscitate" orders are as follows:
    1. *On covered services:* The intern or resident may write "Do Not Resuscitate" orders following discussion with the attending physician. The house officer must indicate in the medical record that the attending physician has been contacted and that the plan of care has been discussed with the patient and/or family.
    2. *On uncovered services:* The attending physician may give a telephone "Do Not Resuscitate" order only to another member of the Medical Staff on the hospital premises. He/she will record it in the orders. This order must be signed by the attending physician within 24 hours and a note placed in the medical record indicating that the plan of care has been discussed with the patient and/or family.
  C. Any CPR trained employee may initiate CPR.
  D. Annual re-certification in Cardiopulmonary Resuscitation (CPR) is required of all RNs. EXCEPTION: Those RNs who attend a CPR class and are evaluated by a CPR instructor to be physically unable to perform mannikin skills. The extent of the physical limitation will be indicated by the instructor and forwarded to the respective nurse manager.

II. General Information
  A. Principles to be followed for restriction, limitation, or cessation of therapy:
    1. The patient's own desires, if willing or able to express them, or as understood by concerned, responsible family members, take precedence.
    2. The attending physician bears the ultimate responsibility for the management of the patient.
  B. Recommended procedures for restriction, limitation, or cessation of therapy:
    1. In order to clarify as precisely as possible for the professional staff the intent and scope of the planned therapy, the Medical Advisory Committee recommends that the medical record indicate as precisely as possible what measures are to be excluded, e.g.:
Cardiopulmonary resuscitation (Standard "CPR")
Endotracheal intubation
Mechanical ventilation
Administration of blood products
Infusion of vasoactive drugs for the purpose of maintaining arterial pressure
Antibiotics
Parenteral nutrition
Dialysis
Invasive hemodynamic monitoring
Withdrawal of blood for body fluids for laboratory analysis
Return admission to the ICU
Other (Specify)

Reprinted with special permission from Barnes Hospital, St. Louis. This procedure is for illustrative purposes only and should not be considered the recommended procedure.

■ **FIGURE 7-2 Barnes Hospital nursing service cardiopulmonary resuscitation (CPR). (cont.)**

2. Recognizing that the care of critically ill patients, including those who are severely impaired and terminally ill, is a group effort and that the ethical, emotional, and legal implications and responsibilities for all of the group are legitimate issues, a review of the therapeutic plan in such situations can be properly initiated either by the attending physician, by the intensive care unit director, or via the head nurse, by other attendants.

   After thorough review and discussion, which should include discussion between the attending physician and the patient, if possible, and with the immediate family and, if uncertainty exists after obtaining additional appropriate consultation when indicated, the planned restrictions, limitations, or cessations of therapeutic measures should be outlined in the hospital record and the necessary orders written by the attending physician.

3. Because unanticipated improvement in the clinical course occasionally occurs, it is essential that ongoing re-assessment by the involved professional attendants be carried out. Such significant improvements in the clinical course, together with the subsequent necessary appropriate alterations in therapy, should also be documented on the hospital record.

III. Procedure
  A. Purpose: To re-establish and maintain circulation and ventilation in the event of a cardiac or respiratory arrest.
  B. Precaution:
    1. The jaw thrust maneuver should be used in the presence of neck of possible C-spine injury. Do not hyperextend neck.
    2. Any patient with oral Herpes Simplex or on blood and body fluid precautions should be resuscitated with a "Pocket Mask" to avoid mouth-to-mouth contact.
  C. General Information:
    1. Barnes Hospital standards for basic life support (CPR) are those established by the American Heart Association and set forth in *JAMA* (June 6, 1986: Volume 255, Number 21, pages 2909-2931).
    2. Basic life support measures (CPR) can and should be initiated immediately without additional equipment.
    3. Sustained resuscitative efforts in the hospital setting require the equipment carried on the Emergency Cart.
  D. Method: Mouth-to-Mouth or Mouth-to-Stoma resuscitation.
    1. Determine that the patient has arrested. Signs of arrest include:
      a. Unresponsiveness
      b. Apnea
      c. Absence of a carotid pulse
      d. Cyanosis
    2. Call out for help. DO NOT LEAVE THE PATIENT.
    3. Begin resuscitative measures:
      a. Place patient in supine position on a hard surface.
      b. Establish an open airway. Clear the airway, tilt head, lift chin, and observe for spontaneous resumption of respirations.
      c. If no spontaneous respirations, ventilate two times using mouth-to-mouth or mouth-to-stoma, as appropriate. DO NOT WAIT FOR AN AMBU BAG.
      d. Check for carotid pulse.
      e. If pulse is absent, begin one-rescuer CPR (15 compressions to 2 breaths). If pulse is present, observe for respiratory activity and continue to support as necessary.

■ FIGURE 7-2 Barnes hospital nursing service cardiopulmonary resuscitation (CPR). (cont).

4. On arrival, the assisting staff member(s) will:
   a. Summon the arrest team:
      (1) Call 22700 and state, "Code 7" and the location.
      (2) Outside of PCAs, call the Emergency Department (Ext. 22604) who will also respond.
   b. Bring emergency equipment to the arrest.
   c. Insert an oral airway and begin two-person CPR (5 compressions to 1 breath).
      NOTE: Because of the difficulty in maintaining a seal with the mask, it may not be possible to use an ambu bag with two-person CPR. Use of mouth-to-mouth or mouth-to-mask techniques may be required until a third person is available.
5. On arrival, the arrest team will implement further measures:
   a. The patient's managing resident will assume charge of the medical aspects of the resuscitation. In his/her absence the medical resident on the arrest team will assume control.
   b. The charge nurse will assume charge of the nonmedical aspects. In a nonpatient area, this responsibility passes to the Clinical Director of Nursing and/or Nursing Supervisor:
      (1) Assignment of staff.
      (2) Removal of excess furniture and equipment and nonessential personnel from the area.
      (3) Disposition of any roommates, visitors, and other nonstaff people.
      (4) Determination that all members of the arrest team (medical resident, surgical resident, anesthetist, respiratory therapist, EKG technician, dispatch) have arrived. (Central Paging, Ext. 21242, will call the PCA to check if all the arrest team has arrived. If not, Central Page will reach those who have not arrived.)
      (5) Initiation of call to house staff, if not present, and the attending physician of any private patient.
      (6) Assurance of physician's notification of family, if not present.
   c. Other nursing responsibilities:
      (1) Set-up of IV fluids.
      (2) Preparation and administration of IV medications.
      (3) Maintenance of the cardiac arrest worksheet.
      (4) Disposition of specimen.
      (5) Supportive care for family members present.
E. Method: Artificial Airway Resuscitation
   1. Same as III. D. Method, 1. and 2.
   2. Begin resuscitative measures:
      a. Place patient in supine position on hard surface.
      b. If metal or uncuffed trach tube is in place, remove and replace with cuffed trach. Portex trach tubes are available on Emergency Carts.
      c. Inflate cuff.
      d. If no spontaneous respirations, ventilate two times using mouth-to-trach.
      e. Check for carotid pulse.
      f. If pulse is absent, begin one-rescuer CPR (15 compressions to 2 breaths). If pulse is present, observe for respiratory activity and continue to support as necessary.
   3. On arrival, the assisting staff member(s) will:
      a. Summon the arrest team.

■ FIGURE 7-2 Barnes Hospital nursing service cardiopulmonary resuscitation (CPR). (cont.)

---

       (1) Call Ext. 22700 and state, "Code 7" and the location.
       (2) Outside of PCAs, call the Emergency Department (Ext. 22604) who will also respond.
     b. Bring emergency equipment to the arrest.
   4. Same as III. D. Method, 5. a., b., c.

IV. Charting
  A. The nursing note should contain the fact of the arrest, initiation of CPR, and a reference to the cardiac arrest worksheet. A second note should contain the outcome and/or disposition of the patient.
  B. The cardiopulmonary resuscitation worksheet should be used to record patient condition, therapeutic interventions and their outcomes. The "Response to Treatment" section is to be used to note vital signs and other information not recorded elsewhere and to expand upon data charted in other areas. It is to be signed by both the physician and the nurse in charge.

Reference:
  A. Medical Staff Bylaws Rules and Regulations, Rule Number 29, approved by Medical Advisory Committee September 17, 1982, amended November, 1986.
  B. *JAMA*, June 6, 1986: Volume 255, Number 21, pages 2909-2931.

For example, let us recall the policy that stated "Our institution promotes from within whenever possible." The purpose and objectives of this policy are clear. The procedure designs the steps to be taken in a chronological sequence to fulfill the meaning of the policy. These steps might be stated as follows:

1. Every opening in the institution must be posted on the employees' bulletin board in the employees' cafeteria for two weeks.
2. The potential candidates should be able to obtain a job description from the manager in whose department the job is open.
3. Potential candidates must inform their present boss before arranging for an interview.
4. An interview between the applicant and the head of the department where the opening is will be arranged with the assistance of the personnel department.

There are literally hundreds—if not thousands—of procedures in a healthcare center. Just think of the amount in nursing services alone: the procedures for administering medications, intravenous medications, radiologic techniques, examination of critically ill patients, epidermal injections, discharge of patients, etc. Consider, for instance, the need for cardiopulmonary resuscitation in connection with the nursing policy that resuscitative measures must be initiated on all patients who have experienced cardiac arrest unless a "no code order" has been written by the attending physician. As previously stated, such a procedure is shown in the boxed material.

Although supervisors will not have much opportunity to issue policies, there will be many occasions for them to devise and issue procedures. Since supervisors are the managers of the department, they are the ones to determine how the work is to be done. If supervisors were fortunate enough to have only highly skilled employees under their direction, they could largely depend on these subordinates to select an efficient procedure. This is very unlikely, however, and most employees look to their supervisors for instructions on how to proceed. Effective work procedures designed by the supervisors for the institution will result in definite advantages.

One of these advantages is that the process of preparing a procedure necessitates analysis and study of the work to be done. Moreover, once a procedure has been established, it ensures consistency and uniformity of action. Procedures give a predictable outcome. In addition to these benefits, procedures provide the supervisor with a standard for appraising the work of the employees. Since a procedure specifies the sequence of actions, it also decreases the need for further decision making. This makes the supervisor's job, as well as that of the employees, easier. The supervisor is also more likely to assign work fairly and to distribute it evenly among the employees.

A good supervisor will spend considerable time and effort in devising efficient procedures for the department. From time to time, of course, it will be necessary for the supervisor to review and revise departmental procedures, since some are likely to become outdated, just as policies do. Because of the advances in medical science, new activities frequently are introduced into the department; then the supervisor's first duty is to write appropriate procedures for them.

Methods

A method is also a standing plan for action, but it is even more detailed than a procedure. Whereas a procedure shows a series of steps to be taken, a method is concerned only with a single operation, with one particular step. The method tells exactly how this particular step is to be performed. (See Figure 7-3.)

For instance, one of the nursing procedures specifies step by step how controlled substances are to be accounted for at the beginning of each shift by a nurse going on duty and a nurse going off duty. For each step in this procedure there exists a method. For example, one method tells exactly what is to be done in case of unavoidable waste or accidental destruction of a controlled substance; this must be recorded on the narcotics form by the nurse involved, and another professional nurse must witness the form. The remnants, if possible, are to be returned to the pharmacy.

For most work done by the employees of a department there exists a "best method," a best way for doing the job. Again, if the supervisor had only highly skilled subordinates, they would probably know the best method without having to be told. In most cases, however, it is still necessary for the supervisor to specify for the employees exactly what is considered the best method in their healthcare center. Indeed, a large amount of the supervisor's time is spent in devising

■ **FIGURE 7-3 The relationship of policies, procedures, and methods.**

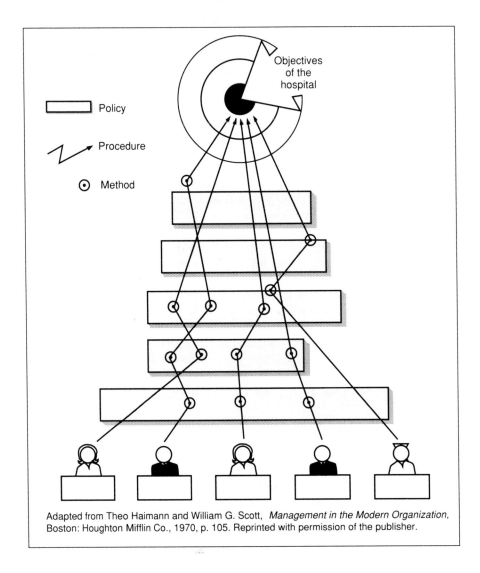

Adapted from Theo Haimann and William G. Scott, *Management in the Modern Organization,* Boston: Houghton Mifflin Co., 1970, p. 105. Reprinted with permission of the publisher.

methods. Once a method has been devised, it carries with it all the advantages of a procedure already cited: uniformity of action, predictability of outcome, standard for appraisal, etc. In determining the best method, a supervisor may occasionally need to enlist the help of another professional, such as a physician, surgeon, pathologist, biochemist, methods engineer, or a specialist in motion and time study, if such a person is available in the organization. Most often, however, the supervisor's own experience is probably broad enough to allow him or her to design the "best" work methods.

Standard Procedures and Practices

In some healthcare activities there will be less need for the supervisor to be overly concerned with devising procedures and methods because the employees will already have been thoroughly trained in standard practices and procedures. For example, nurses, therapists, technologists, technicians, and medical specialists receive many years of schooling and training, during which great emphasis is placed on the proper procedures and methods for performing certain tasks. In managing a department in which such highly skilled employees are at work, the supervisor's job is simplified. One of the main concerns is to ensure that good, generally approved procedures and methods are performed in a professionally accepted way.

However, even then, most healthcare centers "do things differently from everyone else." Even after many years of good schooling and experience in other healthcare settings, new employees have to become familiar with the procedures, methods, and idiosyncrasies of the new facility. The same holds true for recent baccalaureate graduates of nursing programs. Regardless of how much experience a nurse had in another hospital, and regardless of how much a nurse has been taught in school, each healthcare center has its own way of "doing things": documentation and charting, collecting specimens, administering medication, handling emergency measures, etc. Therefore, new employees probably will go through an indoctrination program of many weeks to familiarize them with the procedures and methods of the institution. This is often done by placing them under a preceptor on the nursing unit to which they are assigned.

Rules

A rule is different from a policy, procedure, or method, although it is also a standing plan that has been devised to attain the enterprise's objectives. A rule is not similar to a policy because it does not provide a guide to thinking; it does not leave any discretion to the party involved. A rule is related to a procedure, however, insofar as it is a guide to action and states what must or must not be done. But a rule is not the same as a procedure because it does not specify a time sequence for the particular action. Rules pertain whenever and wherever they are in effect. "No smoking," for instance, is a rule that was made by management, probably just one of a long list of safety rules. This rule is a guide to action, or more precisely a guide to inaction. No order of steps is involved, however; it is simply "no smoking" wherever and whenever it is in effect.

Rules develop from policy; they are not part of it. For example, the institution's safety policy is to make the facility a safe place for the patients, employees, and visitors. Safety considerations play an important role in all procedures and methods, and the "no smoking" rule is just an outgrowth of the original safety policy. The same applies to the rule issued by the supervisor of the clinical laboratories that all employees are to wear gloves at all times when they are in contact with any potentially infectious specimen.

It is the supervisor's duty to apply and enforce the rules and regulations of the healthcare center uniformly, whether they are defined by higher management or set by the supervisor. There will be many occasions when supervisors have to set their own departmental rules. For example, the dress code may state that employees must come to work "appropriately attired" for their job. This broad, general rule gives the director of nursing services the right and obligation to devise a more detailed dress code for the nursing personnel. The operating room supervisor in turn would decide on a special dress code for those working in the surgical areas. Since supervisors have the obligation to see that rules are observed, they should be involved in the design of these rules. Again, these rules are developed from overall hospital policies and must reinforce and support them and not contradict them.

■ SINGLE-USE PLANS

In the preceding sections we have discussed various repeat-use plans, such as objectives, policies, procedures, methods, and rules, which are followed each time a given situation is encountered. The opposite of repeat-use plans are single-use plans, plans that are no longer needed once their objective is accomplished or the time is over. Once the goal is reached, the plan is used up. Single-use plans include programs, projects, and budgets.

Programs and Projects

A *program* is a single-use plan for a large, complex set of activities to reach a specific major undertaking within the organization's overall objectives. The program may have its own policies, procedures, and budgets and may extend over several years. For instance, building a new extended care facility within a healthcare system is a major one-time undertaking. Such a program necessarily involves many derivative plans, each of which can be considered a project. Such plans would include selecting the architects and contractors, securing the financing for the new construction, arranging publicity for the local community, providing information for the local medical society, and recruiting the needed personnel.

A *project* therefore is similar to a program but is smaller in scope. It is an undertaking that can be planned and executed as a distinct entity within the overall program; all projects must be coordinated and synchronized so that the major program will become reality. Programs and projects are single-use plans; once they are achieved, they are filed away. Occasionally someone may look at them again but probably only for historical reasons. Once accomplished, these single-use plans have served their purpose and are finished. Planning such a program is usually top-level administration's concern, whereas supervisors and department heads will primarily be involved only in one of its many projects, such as recruiting the nursing personnel.

Budgets

Budgets are usually thought of only in connection with the controlling function, but this is too narrow a view. Budgets are also plans, plans that express the anticipated results in numerical terms. Such terms may be dollars and cents; nursing hours, hours per patient day, or kilowatt hours; tests to be run; materials; or any other unit used to perform work or measure specific results. Since most values are ultimately convertible to monetary terms, however, and since the overall budgets for the entire institution are expressed in the one common denominator, money, all budgets are eventually translated and expressed in monetary terms. Although budgets are an important tool for controlling, preparing and making a budget certainly are part of the planning function. As we know, planning is the duty of every manager. Using the budget and living with it is part of the manager's controlling function, which will be discussed in Chapter 26.

Since a budget is a plan expressed in numerical units, it has the distinct advantage that the goal is stated in exact and specific terms instead of in generalities. The figures put into a budget represent actual plans that will be seen as goals and standards to be achieved. These plans are not mere projections or general forecasts; they will be considered as a basis for daily operations, cost effectiveness, and the bottom line.

A healthcare center designs a number of budgets, such as income or revenue budgets, capital expenditure budgets, and expense budgets. Of all these, the *expense budget* is the supervisor's major concern because it defines the limits of the various departmental expenditures for a stated period, usually one year. All the following comments refer to budgets of this type because the departmental expenses for salaries and wages, materials, supplies, utilities, equipment rentals, travel, etc., are a challenge and of great concern to the department head.

Because budgets are so important for the daily operations of every department, supervisors who have to use them must participate in their preparation. It is only natural that people resent arbitrary orders, and this applies to budgets. Thus, it is necessary that all budget objectives and allowances be determined with the full input of those who are responsible for executing them. All supervisors should actively participate in the budget-making process for their units, and this should not be mere pseudoparticipation. They should participate in what is commonly known as grass roots budgeting. The subordinate managers also should be allowed to submit their own budgets. (This becomes even more involved with zero base budgeting practices, as discussed in Chapter 26.)

Each supervisor will have to substantiate the budget proposals in a discussion with the boss and possibly with top-level administration, where the budgets are finalized. This is what is meant by active participation in budget making, and this ensures the effectiveness of the process. Such participation, however, should not be construed to mean that the suggestion of the supervisor will always or completely prevail. The supervisor's budget should not be accepted if the higher-level manager believes it is based on plans that are inadequate, overstated, or incorrect. Differences between budget estimates should be carefully discussed by the supervisor and higher-level manager, but the final decision rests with higher management. Nevertheless, if a budget is arrived at with the participation of the supervisors, then the likelihood that they will live up to the budget is better than if it had been handed down to the supervisors by their boss.

In conclusion, it is important to remember that the budget is a single-use plan. It will serve only for the period for which it is drawn up. When the period is over, the budget is no longer valid. A new budget will have to be drawn up, and a new planning period will be established. In traditional budgeting, last year's budget serves as a guideline for next year's budget, unless the healthcare center practices zero base budgeting. Zero base budgeting (see Chapter 26) is a fairly new concept. Instead of accepting current expenditures as a base for the new budget, zero base budgeting requires that all expenditures—new and existing—must be justified, reassessed, and approved from the very beginning.

■ SUMMARY

Planning is the managerial function that determines in advance what is to be done in the future. It is the function of every manager, from the top-level administrator to the supervisor of each department. Planning is important because it ensures the best utilization of resources and economy of performance. The planning period on the supervisory level is usually much shorter than the period on the top administrator's level. Nevertheless, the short-range plans of the supervisor must coincide with the long-range plans of the enterprise.

Setting objectives is the first step in planning. Although the overall objectives are determined by the top-level administration, many secondary objectives must be clarified by the supervisor and must be in accordance with the primary objectives of the overall undertaking. To reach all the objectives, different types of plans must be devised. The broad range of plans can be grouped into repeat-use and single-use plans.

Policies, the major type of repeat-use plans, are guides to thinking; most originate with the chief administrator. In most cases the supervisor's concern with policies primarily is interpreting them, applying them, and staying within them whenever decisions are made for the department. Although supervisors do not usually originate policies, they will often be called on to design procedures, methods, and rules, which are other repeat-use plans. These plans are guides for action, not guides for thinking. Supervisors also will participate in the establishment of budgets, which are single-use plans expressed in numerical terms. Occasionally supervisors are involved with programs and projects, two more examples of single-use plans.

NOTES
1. Primary care means ambulatory, emergency, and initial physician contact; secondary care refers to high-morbidity, low-mortality, inpatient care provided by specialists; and tertiary care means high-mortality, low-morbidity, and highly sophisticated and specialized inpatient care. For a more detailed definition, see Taber's *Cyclopedic Medical Dictionary*, 15th ed., Philadelphia: F.A. Davis Co., 1985, pp. 1379, 1538, and 1709.
2. Peter F. Drucker, *The Practice of Management*, New York: Harper & Row, Inc., 1954; John W. Humble, *Management by Objectives in Action*, New York: McGraw-Hill Book Co., 1970; George S. Odiorne, *Management by Objectives*, New York: Pitman Publishing Corp., 1965; George S. Odiorne, *MBO II: A System of Managerial Leadership for the 80s*, Belmont, CA: Fearon Pitman Publishers, Inc., 1979.

8

SUPERVISORY PLANNING

The managers' skills in foreseeing and preparing for the future will significantly determine the survival and growing success of the healthcare institution. Planning, as we have said, is deciding in advance what is to be done in the future. Although the future is fraught with uncertainties, managers must make certain assumptions about it in order to plan. These assumptions are based on forecasts of what the future will hold. Since the appraisal of future prospects is inherent in all planning, the success of an enterprise greatly depends on the skill of management first in forecasting and then in preparing for the future conditions.

■ FORECASTS AS THE BASIS OF PLANNING

Administrative Forecasts

To plan intelligently, all managers must make some assumptions about the future. The chief executive officer (CEO), however, must forecast the future in a much more far-reaching manner and scope than a supervisor. Since both are managers, however, both must make forecasts. Such forecasts are possible in widely diverse areas. Management typically confines its forecasting effort to factors that experience suggests are important to its own planning. Thus, the chief administrator within the healthcare field would select and use primarily those forecasts that have a direct material bearing on the healthcare field in the broadest sense.

In the endeavor to predict the outlook of things to come, some of the factors the administrator will be concerned with are the general economic, political, and social climates in which the healthcare institution must operate during the next few years. These include forecasts of government policies, legislation and regulation, government spending, and how these might ultimately affect the activities of healthcare providers. The administrator will try to predict the general trends for the delivery of healthcare as it affects the various providers, the more enlightened and aggressive users, cost effectiveness, and so forth. There will be forecasts of monetary policy, the overall economic activities within the United States, inflationary trends, etc.

Top-level management will be vitally interested in forecasts of changes in our population. In the year 2000, for example, the U.S. population is expected to reach 268 million people, about 305 million in 2030, and approximately 311 million people in the year 2080.[1] Projections showing this increase from 232 million in 1982 are based on middle-series assumptions for future fertility, mortality, and net immigration levels. (See Figure 8-1.) We will see the impact of these factors on every organized activity because population trends are critical planning premises that affect long-range strategies of most organizations, especially those in the healthcare field. The breakdown of population figures by age and sex will be even more meaningful, depending on whether administrators are planning for a general short-term hospital, long-term healthcare facility, nursing home, etc.

All these environmental, economic, and political conditions will affect the future operations of a healthcare facility. Since the administrator's job is to take the broad and long-term outlook, forecasts in these far-reaching fields are necessary.[2] Although not directly concerned with making such overall assumptions, all middle- and lower-level managers will ultimately be affected by them.

Supervisory Forecasts

Scientific and Technological Developments

When supervisors make departmental forecasts, their assumptions about the future will cover a much narrower field than will those of administrators. A supervisor should forecast only those factors that may have some bearing on the future of his or her department. For example, supervisors should determine whether there is a growing trend for more sophistication or simplification of the function they oversee or whether this function seems to be of increasing or decreasing significance. It is important to keep abreast of developments in science, technology, and automation. For example, much of the operating room nurses' time formerly was spent in preparing instruments and supplies for sterilization. With the advent of prepackaged, sterilized supplies, all this time is now used in different endeavors.

Based on what has happened in the past, the supervisor should venture some assumption as to what the future will hold. In making such an assumption, one can look to the sources of supplies and equipment used for assistance. Much can also be learned by attending lectures, national meetings, and exhibitions and by reading journals. Advances in medical sciences and technology are progressing so rapidly that in several years the department's functions may be significantly different from what they had been or are today. Consider, for instance, the impact of further mechanization and automation in laboratories, where current automated analyzers are likely to be obsolete in three to five years. Such projections of the future are essential for supervisors in the clinical laboratories for their planning: Will more, less, or about the same number of employees be needed with the same or different education or additional training? Should the equipment be bought or leased? The supervisor must consider these and similar questions.

■ **FIGURE 8-1** Estimates and projections
of total population: 1950 to 2080.

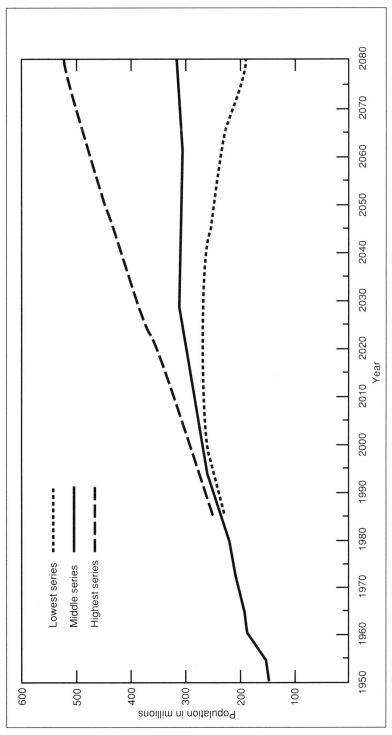

From U.S. Department of Commerce, Bureau of the Census, "Population Estimates and Projections," *Current Population Reports*,
Series P-25, No. 952, July 1984.

Employees and Skills

Supervisors will also have to make forecasts in relation to the types of employees who will be working in the department in the future. Most healthcare activities probably will create a need for employees who have been educated and trained in new and advanced scientific fields capable of coping with the new state of the arts. These employees may possess knowledge and skills unknown and unneeded at present. For example, conceivably in the not too distant future, more knowledge in chemistry, physics, genetics, electronics, mechanical engineering, use of computers, etc., could be helpful to nursing personnel.

The forecast may include the need for employees who are better educated, more skilled, and whose increasing demands the department must be ready to meet. This refers both to monetary demands and to demands that the position offer enough of a continuous challenge. For example, supervisors may find that the current pattern of hours, wages, and fringe benefits will not be satisfactory in the future, and they would be well advised to plan accordingly at an early time. Similarly, supervisors should be aware of the noneconomic demands that young people coming out of school—whether a university, junior college, vocational training program, or high school—expect to fulfill on their jobs. Meeting both types of demands, material and psychological, will be particularly important if supervisors have to look for people who possess skills that up to now have never been required in the department or perhaps anywhere in the institution.

A supervisor may also discover a trend toward upgrading or changing of certain duties. For instance, the supervisor of the operating rooms might foresee an increasing number of operating room technicians. Plans must be made for the impact that this will have on the position of graduate operating room nurses. The director of nursing services might have to view the future in terms of more nurse specialists, more certifications, and more physicians' assistants. If a shortage of nurses in a few years is in the forecast, plans should be made now on how to cope with such an event.

■ BENEFITS OF FORECASTING

One should always remember that at the base of all forecasts lie certain assumptions, approximations, opinions, and judgments. Forecasting is an art, not a science. As yet no infallible way of predicting the future exists; however, forecasting accuracy increases with experience. As time goes on, making assumptions about the future should become a normal activity for all managers, from the administrator down to the supervisor. Managers should exchange ideas, help each other, and supply information whenever available. They most likely will act as a check on each other, and their final analysis of what the future holds will probably be quite reliable.

Even if some of the events that have been anticipated do not materialize or do not occur exactly as forecast, it is better to have foreseen them than to be suddenly confronted with them. Having foreseen these events, supervisors have readied their minds and state of affairs to be able to incorporate changes whenever they are needed. Although this task may sound formidable for supervisors, their job is to be alert to all possible changes and trends. This is the only way supervisors can prevent their own and their employees' obsolescence. In this way supervisors will not have to recall with hindsight the time when certain trends were already visible on the horizon, wishing they had taken them seriously at that time.

■ TACTICAL CONSIDERATIONS IN PLANNING

Supervisors must realize that they do not plan in a vacuum. While planning, they must keep in mind the impact of these plans on others. Success or failure of planning will depend largely on the reaction of those involved in the plans, whether employees, supervisors of other departments, the boss, top-level administration, the medical staff, or many others. Several tactical or political strategies are at the supervisor's disposal to help minimize negative reactions and facilitate the success of the plans. One or a combination of these political, tactical considerations may be used, depending on the situation at hand.

Since timing is a critical and essential factor in all planning, the manager may choose the strategy that tells him or her to *strike while the iron is hot*. This strategy obviously advocates prompt action when the situation and time for action are propitious. On the other hand, the supervisor may want to invoke the old saying that *time is a great healer*. This is not an endorsement of procrastination, but it is often advisable to move slowly and create an opportunity for cooling off because many factors take care of themselves after a short while. This is also known as the *wait and see* strategy.

When significant changes are involved in planning, the supervisor may use the strategy known as *concentrated mass offensive*. This strategy advocates quick radical action all at once to have immediate results. On the other hand, the supervisor may prefer to just *get a foot in the door*. This tactic implies that it may be better to propose merely a portion of the plan in the beginning, especially if the program is of such magnitude that its total acceptance would be doubtful.

Sometimes one supervisor's plan may involve changes that could come about more easily if supervisors of other departments would join in the action. It may therefore be advisable to seek allies to promote the change, that is, to adopt the strategy that states there is *strength in unity*. For example, if a supervisor plans to try to increase the salaries of the employees, it may be expedient to try to get the other supervisors to join the effort in presenting a general request for higher remuneration to the management. This may involve another strategy that is well known in politics: *You scratch my back and I'll scratch yours*. This tactic of reciprocity is practiced not only in political circles and in the activity of purchasing agents, but also among colleagues who wish to present joint action on a particular issue.

The choice and application of these political tactics will depend on the people involved, magnitude and urgency of the objective, timing, means available, and various other factors. Many other political strategies can frequently be helpful in initiating and carrying out plans. Mentioning these tactical considerations, however, should not be construed to mean that they are always recommended. Properly applied, however, they can minimize difficulties and increase the effectiveness of the supervisor's planning.

■ PLANNING THE UTILIZATION OF RESOURCES

Every supervisor is entrusted with a large number of valuable resources to accomplish the job. The supervisor has a duty to plan specifically how to use the resources available so that the work of the unit can be carried out most efficiently and cost effectiveness can be achieved. This means that detailed plans must be made for the proper utilization of the equipment, instruments, space, materials and supplies, and the supervisor's and employees' time.

Utilization of Equipment, Analyzers, and Instruments

The supervisor must plan the proper utilization of the equipment, analyzers, and instruments provided for the department. The equipment represents a substantial investment that the institution has made. Therefore, plans for its efficient use must be made to ensure the proper utilization and return on the investment. In many departments much of this will depend on the activities of the medical personnel. However, it is the supervisor's job to see that employees respect the equipment and instruments and treat them carefully.

Furthermore, the supervisor must ensure that the equipment of the unit is properly maintained. Equipment that is poorly maintained and does not function properly, such as the side rails on the patient's bed, could possibly lead to an incident resulting in a patient's lawsuit for damages. The head nurse or team leader, on learning of such a malfunction, should immediately determine whether the employee is operating the equipment properly and if a maintenance problem exists. The proper steps to remedy the malfunction should be taken at once. Supervisors should work closely with the maintenance department and plan for periodic maintenance checkups.

It is the supervisor's job to ascertain if the equipment serves its purpose and if better facilities are available for doing the work. This does not mean that a supervisor must always have the very latest model available; on the other hand, plans should be made to replace inefficient equipment. The medical specialists working in this area should be actively involved in this as well.

Once supervisors decide to replace old or introduce new equipment, they must plan such replacements very carefully, frequently with the help of the medical staff. They must read professional journals and literature circulated by hospitals and related associations, listen to sales presentations of equipment and instruments, and keep themselves abreast of current developments within their fields. Only with this type of background can the supervisor submit intelligent plans and alternatives for the replacement of equipment to the immediate superior or the administrator. The recommended changes should be well substantiated and supported. The proposal should include projections of better patient care, utilization, cost effectiveness, etc., including considerations of leasing versus buying.

The final decision, however, remains with higher management. Even if the request is turned down, the supervisor has demonstrated that he or she is on top of the job, planning for the future. Eventually the plans for replacing equipment probably will be accepted, and the administrator will realize that the supervisor planned for the department's equipment with foresight.

Work Methods and Procedures

In discussing the planning process, we pointed out that the supervisor is deeply involved in designing, developing, and writing procedures and methods. The supervisor should continually review and, if necessary, revise procedures and make plans concerning improved work methods and processes in the department. The difficulty is that many supervisors work under considerable pressure and find little time for this type of planning. Moreover, the supervisor is often so close to the jobs performed in the department that he or she believes the prevailing work methods are satisfactory and not much can be done about them.

Nevertheless, to maintain high efficiency and the best possible patient care, the supervisor occasionally must study the operations performed so that improvements can be planned. If the department begins doing something that has not been done before, then the supervisor has to write a complete set of new procedures and methods for this new activity. For example, if lithotripsy is to be performed in the hospital, the manager of that unit has to develop new procedures for this recent medical advancement. This will be done with the help, information, and support from medical specialists, technologists, and possibly the maker of the equipment.

The supervisor should try to look at all of the department's operations from the point of view of a stranger coming into the department for the first time. In other words, he or she should look at the current operations with a detached point of view, observing all methods and processes objectively. The supervisor should ask: Is each operation really necessary? What is the reason for it? Could the procedure be combined with another operation? Are the various steps necessary? Are they performed in the best possible sequence? Are there any avoidable delays?

In this effort to devise more efficient work methods, the supervisor may be able to enlist the help of a staff specialist, such as a nurse clinician, systems analyst, or methods engineer. The supervisor should also seek ideas from employees who are doing the job, since they often can make valuable suggestions for improved methods and procedures.

Safety

Healthcare centers have traditionally been very much aware of the need for safety of the patients, employees, and visitors; after all, many accident victims end up in hospitals. This makes every employee in a healthcare center doubly aware of the importance of safety. Also, a safe environment for patients, employees, and visitors of a healthcare center is an ever-present consideration in the training and education of most healthcare professionals.

Although almost all healthcare facilities have a safety committee, or even a safety department, this alone cannot fulfill the institution's obligation to create and maintain a safe environment for clients, visitors, and employees. As part of their responsibilities, managers and supervisors must keep a diligent watch on their areas and attempt to eliminate safety hazards. The recent flood of liability suits against hospitals has put additional emphasis on the need for safety.

A hospital patient is entitled to expect the hospital to keep its premises reasonably safe. Furthermore, since hospitals are used by people who are disabled or infirm, "reasonable care" requires a somewhat higher standard than for other public places or for persons who are healthy. The same care must be taken regarding equipment, instruments, and appliances so that they are adequate for use in the diagnosis or treatment of patients. If defective equipment causes injury to a patient, the hospital may be liable. Cases against hospitals have involved defective beds, broken thermometers, inoperative patient call systems, improperly calibrated x-ray equipment, etc.

Another impetus for safety came with the Occupational Safety and Health Act (OSHA) of 1970, which places greater responsibility on employers to provide employees with a safe and healthy work environment. Since OSHA covers far-reaching areas with many ramifications, implications, and changes of interpretations, the supervisor cannot possibly be familiar with all of it or its most important aspects. Therefore, supervisors should be in close touch with that person in the healthcare center who is the expert, such as the safety director or someone in that office. In any event, OSHA has added to the supervisor's responsibility for planning and maintaining a healthier and safer work environment.

Although many healthcare centers have a safety director, safety committee, or committee for claim prevention and loss control, the true responsibility for safety lies with every manager, from the CEO down to the supervisors. The supervisors, being the persons on the spot, must stress safety more than anyone else and plan for it. The supervisors must be alert to unsafe practices, correct them, and in general enforce safety procedures. Safety must be an integral part in everything and uppermost in supervisors' and the employees' thoughts. Safety must be a continuous consideration in all supervisory planning. It must be integrated in all policies, procedures, methods, practices, directives, etc., so that accidents and incidents do not occur or at least are significantly reduced.

If the healthcare center employs a safety director, this person can be helpful to the supervisor in planning for safety. Ultimately, however, it is the supervisor's job to make certain the employees think and practice safety in everything they do. In the final analysis, people cause far more accidents than faulty equipment.

Use of Space

Supervisors must also plan for the best utilization of space. First, they should determine whether or not the space assigned to the department is being used effectively. Some industrial engineering help, if available, may be requested to make this determination. If such help is not available, the supervisor should make a layout chart, showing the square feet the department has to work with, the location of equipment and supplies, and the work paths of the employees as they carry out their tasks. Such a chart can then be studied to determine whether the allocated space has been laid out appropriately or whether areas need to be rearranged so that the department's work can be done more efficiently.

For example, the chief technologist of the clinical laboratories can show that the annual workload has been increasing by approximately 10 percent annually, which would result in doubling the workload in approximately 9 years. He or she would also point out that 40,000 to 75,000 tests equate to so many square feet and that the laboratories now occupy the same space they had for many years. The chief technologist should also draw up a typical laboratory plan for a same-size hospital, showing a layout for separate work units for all technical sections—hematology, urinalysis, biochemistry, histology, serology, bacteriology, immunology, blood bank, support areas, etc. At the same time the supervisor may also want to point out that laboratory facilities should preferably be on the first floor near the emergency room and admissions and easily accessible to surgery, rather than on the present upper-floor location.

This type of layout planning would show the need for additional space and/or a different location. If such a request is placed before the administrator, based on thorough planning of the space currently allotted, then the likelihood that it will be granted is greater. In this case the chief technologist must realize, however, that he or she has to compete with many other managers who probably also request more space and another location. Even if the request is denied, these plans will not have been drawn up in vain. They most likely will alert the supervisor to some of the conditions under which the employees are working, and perhaps that information can be used to plan more efficient work methods according to the existing conditions.

Use of Materials and Supplies

The supervisor must plan for the appropriate use, security, and conservation of the materials and supplies entrusted and charged to the department. These would include such supplies as gloves, masks, cotton balls, tongue blades, alcohol wipes, syringes, needles, medicine cups, and paper goods at a nursing station. In most departments the quantity of materials and supplies used is substantial. Even if each single item represents only a small value, the aggregate of these items adds up to sizable amounts in the budget of a healthcare facility. Proper planning will ensure that materials and supplies are used as conservatively as possible, without compromising sterility, asepsis, and sanitary requirements. Supervisors must teach their employees proper use of supplies because many workers are careless and do not realize the amount of money involved. Another problem is the loss and theft of materials, often done by the employees themselves. Supervisors must take adequate precautions to minimize this source of loss. Although proper planning for the utilization of materials and supplies will help significantly in performance, it will not prevent all waste.

Management of Time

Supervisors also must plan the use of time. The old saying "time is money" applies to both the supervisor's and the employees' time. Thus, managers must not only plan their employees' time, but they must also consider at least as carefully the management of their own time.

The Employees' Time

When planning for the effective use of the subordinates' time, much will depend on the supervisors' basic managerial strategy and their assumptions about human nature. According to Douglas McGregor, a well-known author and professor of management, most managers base their thinking on one of two sets of assumptions about human nature, which he calls Theory X and Theory Y.[3] The Theory X manager believes that the average employee dislikes work, will avoid work, and tries to get by with as little as possible. The employee has little ambition and has to be forced and closely controlled in each and every job.

The Theory Y manager operates with a drastically different set of assumptions regarding human nature. He or she believes that most employees consider work natural and that most are eager to do the right thing, will seek responsibility under the proper conditions, will exercise self-control, and do not need to be continually urged. Theory Y further states that external controls and threats are not a good means for producing results. Rather, since work is as natural to people as play or rest, it will not be avoided.

Although there may be some situations in which a manager has no choice but to follow Theory X, practice and belief in Theory Y is preferred. Much more will be said about McGregor's theories in Chapters 19 and 21, but it is appropriate to bring them up now because they are important when planning for the effective utilization of employees' time.

For example, if a supervisor is a Theory Y manager, he or she will expect employees to do the right thing and to turn in a fair day's work. Since one cannot expect employees to work indefinitely at top speed, however, the plans for their time will be based on a fair output instead of a maximum output. Allowances will be made for fatigue, personal needs, unavoidable delays, and a certain amount of unproductive time during the workday.

In planning employees' time, as in other aspects of planning, the supervisor may be able to get assistance from a specialist employed by the healthcare provider, preferably a motion and time specialist. However, most supervisors usually can figure out themselves what can be expected of their employees. Managers are capable of planning reasonable performance requirements that their employees accept as fair. Such requirements are based on average conditions and not on emergencies. These reasonable estimates of employees' time are necessary because the supervisor must depend on the completion of certain tasks at certain times. The supervisors themselves may have been given deadlines, and to meet them, they must have a reasonable estimate or idea of how fast the job can be done.

In some situations the subordinate's time is paced and set by someone other than the supervisor because of the nature of the activity performed. For instance, the time an operating room nurse or technician spends on a case is determined by the type of surgery and the speed and skill of the surgeon. In the clinical laboratories the time required is set by the speed of the automated equipment. Furthermore, unexpected complications may add to the time normally necessary to complete the job. In these cases average time estimates can still be made, but the time allotted must allow for the various contingencies that can arise.

In addition to planning for the normal employee time, it may be necessary to plan for overtime. Overtime should be considered only as an emergency matter. If the supervisor finds that overtime or working a double shift is regularly required, then plans need changing by altering work methods, obtaining better or more equipment, or hiring more part-time and full-time employees. The supervisor must also plan for employee absences. One cannot plan for those instances in which employees are absent without notice, but one can plan for holidays, vacations, leaves of absence, layoffs for overhaul, etc. Plans for these absences should be worked out in advance so that the functioning of the department will suffer as little as possible.

Flexible Work Schedules

Work schedules for many employees in different organizations have become more flexible. The leading thought is that employees should have some autonomy to adjust their work schedule to fit their life styles and to choose the hours they would prefer to work. The plans are designed to give employees greater opportunities to enjoy their life *off,* as opposed to *on,* the job. "Flex time" enables employees to choose a schedule that fits into their off-the-job activities. It enables working parents or others with responsibilities at home the opportunity to combine work with family life. The concept of flex time has been successfully introduced into various private and public organized activities and in healthcare centers. Flexible work schedules probably will become even more popular in the future, especially for professional and clerical work.

It is well known that some healthcare professionals, especially nurses, have left their field of expertise because they were dissatisfied with several factors, among which grueling hours and schedules loomed large.[4] Many nurses cannot or do not want to work the traditional 5-day, 40-hour week of rotating shifts, 7 to 3, 3 to 11, and 11 to 7. Therefore, it was necessary to do away with the traditional pattern of nursing staff scheduling. To alleviate these dissatisfactions, flexible work hours have been introduced. Varied plans are available, including 4-40, which means 4 days at 10 hours; 7 days on and 7 days off, using the 10-hour workday; 24-hour weekend shifts; two 16-hour shifts on a weekend; or the 3-day weekend plan.[5] In this situation the introduction of flexible work schedules certainly has been a good idea and probably will be expanded.

Flexible working schedules undoubtedly create some additional scheduling and planning problems for supervisors. Furthermore, such schedules cause problems for proper supervision of the employees during different shift arrangements and in supervisors' coordination of activities with other departments. There also is the real concern that schedules with long hours can potentially cause fatigue and an increase in errors. These and others are additional challenges for supervisors. However, as long as flexible working schedules produce good results (e.g., easier staff recruitment, better staff retention, higher morale, fewer absences, less tardiness, less dissatisfaction, better patient care), supervisors will make every effort to overcome these problems by better supervision.

The Supervisor's Time

Time is life. It is irreversible and irreplaceable. To waste your time is to waste your life, but to master your time is to master your life and make the most of it.[6]

Time is one of the most valuable resources that cannot be renewed or stored. The supply of time is flexible; if supervisors want more time, they have to "make" it themselves. The supervisor's own time is one of the resources for which he or she is responsible. Every supervisor has probably experienced days that were so full of pressures and demands that he or she began to feel as though all the matters that needed attention could never be resolved. The days and weeks were just too short. The only way to keep such days at a minimum is for the supervisor to plan the time for the most effective use.

Unfortunately the supervisor's problems come up on a continual basis but without any order of importance or priority. Thus, the first thing the supervisor must do is to triage, sort, and grade them, that is, decide between those matters that he or she must attend to personally and those that can be assigned to someone else. The supervisor cannot delegate some matters, but most can be assigned to one of the employees. Every time the supervisor dispenses with one of the duties by assigning it to an employee, time is gained for more important matters. This is worthwhile even if some valuable time must be spent training one of the employees in a particular task. In case of doubt, therefore, the supervisor should be inclined to delegate. Then the available time must be planned so that it is divided among those matters to which the supervisor alone can attend. These matters again have to be classified according to their urgency.

Unless supervisors distinguish between those matters that *must* be done and those that *ought* to be done, they are inclined to pay equal attention to all matters before them. Then the more important items may not receive the attention they truly deserve. By distinguishing, supervisors will be giving priority to those matters that need immediate attention. A supervisor should therefore plan the time so that the most important things to attend to will appear at the top of the schedule. The supervisor must make certain, however, that some free time is left in the time schedule because not every contingency can be anticipated. There will be some emergencies that a supervisor must deal with when they arise. The flexibility will make it possible to take care of these situations without significantly disrupting the other activities planned on the time schedule.

Many techniques have been devised to help supervisors control their time schedules. One of the simplest methods is to use a desk calendar to schedule those items that need attention, such as appointments, meetings, reports, discussions, etc. The supervisor should schedule these events far in advance; then they will automatically come up for attention when they are due.

Another effective way of planning each week's work in advance, as well as knowing what is being accomplished as the week progresses, is to keep a planning sheet. Such a planning sheet is prepared at the end of one week for the week to follow. It shows the days of the week divided into morning and afternoon columns and a list of all items to be accomplished. Then a time for accomplishment is assigned to each task by placing it in the morning or the afternoon blocks of the assigned day. Since most people cannot get much work done in fits and starts, substantial blocks of time should be set aside. As a task is accomplished, its box is circled. Those tasks that have been delayed during the day must be rescheduled for another time by placing them in an appropriate block on a subsequent day. Those tasks that are planned but have not been accomplished during the week (they are still uncircled) must be rescheduled for the following week.

Such a record will show how much of the original plan has been carried out at the end of the week and will provide a good answer to the question of where the supervisor's time went. Based on this record, the supervisor will then be able to plan the next week and so on. Regardless of whether this particular system or another is used, the supervisor must schedule the time periods each week and have some method of reporting the tasks that are planned and those that have been accomplished. (See Figure 8-2.)

■ **FIGURE 8-2 Sample planning sheet.**

MONDAY 10/23	TUESDAY 10/24	WEDNESDAY 10/25	THURSDAY 10/26	FRIDAY 10/27
AM	AM *work on job descriptions*	AM *see Personnel Director about Helen. Talk to maintenance about new elec. outlets.*	AM *Arrange dates for evaluation interviews.*	AM *Work on dress code revisions.*
PM *check of leave of absence policy.*	PM	PM *Read minutes, last meeting of infection com.*	PM *Start work on new budget.*	PM *Attend Management Seminar.*

Time-Use Chart

Among the many tools for using time effectively, a supervisor should consider the type of work his or her time is spent on at present. A time-use chart will help. The supervisor should create some broad classifications for daily activities, such as routine duties, regular supervisory duties, special duties, emergencies, and innovative thinking. After each day the supervisor should write down how much time was spent in these categories; having done this for several weeks, he or she will learn much about where the time went.

The supervisor may find that 20 percent of the time was spent on *routine work,* which could and should be assigned to some of the subordinates. A large percentage of time was devoted to *regular supervisory duties,* such as checking performance, giving directives and instructions, evaluating and counseling employees, promoting and maintaining discipline. These are supervisory duties that the manager alone should do, and no time can probably be gained from this area. Then the supervisor will find out how much time was spent in *special duties:* serving on committees, attending professional meetings, planning next year's budget, changing the dress code, reviewing procedures, etc. Again, all this time is probably spent wisely. A certain amount of time also will be spent on *emergencies,* a subject that is unpredictable and will demand some of the supervisor's attention. In addition, some time should be open for *creative and innovative thinking,* which is essential for the climate of the department and the progress of the institution. Although the boss evaluates the supervisor on how well the department's job gets done, somehow the supervisor is also appraised about his or her innovative changes, suggestions, and constructive new ideas.

Such a time-use chart will illustrate where the time went and in which areas a supervisor can ''make'' some more time. Unless the supervisor has a clear picture of this, routine tasks probably will creep in and reduce the time available for the truly supervisory duties.

Another interesting approach to managing time is suggested by Oncken and Wass.[7] They examine three different kinds of management time:
1. *Boss-imposed time*—to accomplish those activities that the boss requires and the manager cannot disregard.
2. *System-imposed time*—to give support to peers and to cooperate and coordinate activities.
3. *Self-imposed time*—to accomplish the items the manager originates and agrees to do himself or herself.
The managers cannot do much about the boss and system-imposed times. The self-imposed time, however, becomes the major area of the manager's concern. Within this area, some of the manager's time is taken up by the subordinates; this can be called *subordinate-imposed* time, and the remaining time is called *discretionary time.* To increase discretionary time, the manager must reduce the subordinate-imposed time.

Most of this discussion was concerned with achieving the best utilization of the manager's time. Although these groupings by Oncken and Wass offer a different approach to the problem, they attempt to bring about the same results: to increase the manager's discretionary time for managerial tasks and innovative thinking.

Utilization of Work Force

The employees in a department are the most valuable resource. Therefore, planning for their full utilization must be uppermost in every manager's mind. Although a supervisor must plan for the use of equipment, tools, and space, improved work methods and processes, conservation of materials and supplies, and proper use of time, the most important planning of all is that connected with utilization of the work force.

This, of course, does not mean planning to squeeze an excessive amount of work out of each employee. Rather, utilization means giving employees as much satisfaction as possible in their jobs. To plan for the best utilization of the work force also entails developing methods for recruiting good employees, searching for all available sources of employees, and working for their retention. Furthermore, proper utilization means to search continually for the best ways to group employees' activities and includes the problems and plans of training, supervising, and motivating employees. Finally, effective use of workers means the continual appraisal of their performance, appropriate promotions, adequate plans for compensation and rewards, and at the same time fair disciplinary measures.

All these considerations play an important role when the supervisor plans for the best utilization of the department's employees. Only through such human resource planning can a situation be created in which workers willingly contribute their utmost to achieve both personal satisfaction on the job and attainment of the department's objectives. The supervisor may feel confident that the efforts made in this regard will be rewarded amply by the employees. Planning for the best utilization of employees is at the heart of expert supervision. It is discussed here only briefly, but this entire book is concerned with bringing about the best possible utilization of employees.

■ SUMMARY

All planning must be done with forecasts of the future in mind. Since the future is uncertain, one must make various assumptions as to what it holds. Overall forecasts or assumptions are made by the top-level administrator, and the supervisor narrows these down to forecasts for the departmental activity. Based on such forecasts, the supervisor will then make plans for the department.

Plans must be made for the full utilization of all the resources at the supervisor's disposal. More specifically, he or she must plan for proper use of equipment and instruments and work methods and processes. There must be plans to utilize effectively the space available and the materials and supplies under supervision. The efficient use of time also must be planned. Even more important, the supervisor must plan for the best overall utilization of the employees in the unit. This means, among other things, seeing that employees are able to find satisfaction in their work.

Throughout all planning, the supervisor should be concerned with the effects of these plans on other members of the organization. At times the manager may need to resort to various tactical considerations that will be helpful in getting the department's plans accepted and effectively performed.

NOTES

1. U.S. Department of Commerce, Bureau of the Census, "Population Estimates and Projections," *Current Population Reports,* Series P-25, No. 952, July 1984.
2. Top level administrators do not, of course, have to actually perform the research and statistical analysis for all forecasts. They frequently use already published statistics and economic forecasts made available by government publications and experts in various fields.
3. Douglas McGregor, *The Human Side of Enterprise,* 25th Anniversary Printing, New York: McGraw-Hill Book Co., 1985, Chapters 3 and 4.
4. The same considerations are applicable to other healthcare employees.
5. The M.D. Anderson Hospital and Tumor Institute in Houston gives nurse applicants about 30 different work schedules from which to choose. See *Time,* Aug. 24, 1981, p. 37.
6. Alan Lakein, *How To Get Control of Your Time and Your Life,* New York: Peter H. Wyden, Inc., 1973, p. 1. See also R. Alec MacKenzie, *The Time Trap,* New York: McGraw-Hill Book Co., 1972; George R. Carnahan, Brian G. Gnauk, David B. Hoffman, and Bruce C. Sherony, *To Improve Management Effectiveness,* Cincinnati: South-Western Publishing Co., 1987; and Walter Kiechel, III, "Beat the Clock," *Fortune,* June 15, 1984, pp. 147-148.
7. William Oncken, Jr., and Donald L. Wass, "Management Time: Who's Got the Monkey?" *Harvard Business Review,* Vol. 52, No. 6, 1974, pp. 75-80.

Part Four

ORGANIZING

9

FUNDAMENTAL CONCEPTS OF ORGANIZING

Authority and Span of Management

Organizing is closely related to planning. Planning defines the goals and objectives of the institution, the expectations. Organizing defines and arranges the activities needed to accomplish these objectives and establishes the relationships among various functions. These activities and functions form subsystems that are synchronized and coordinated into a larger system, called the *formal organization*. Organizing means setting up this formal structure of activities and authority relationships.

How this structure looks and how it works depends on the organization's objectives and size, state of the arts and science, technology, and many other factors. The managerial function of organizing is an impersonal function, which means that the organization is designed with the activities in mind and not around individual personalities to perform them. Of course, the organization must be a structure that can be inhabited by people, the most valuable asset of any organization. It must be a structure in which people can function and thrive. The human element obviously is important, and we will put all these considerations to work in the staffing and influencing functions. When the manager designs the structure, however, this is done without thinking of specific persons. Organizing means setting up a formal structure of activities and authority relationships based on major principles.

Formal organizational theory rests on several major principles or premises:

1. *Authority* is the lifeblood of the managerial position, and the *delegation of authority* makes the organization come alive.

2. The *span of management* sets outside limits on the number of subordinates a manager can effectively supervise.
3. The *division of work* is essential for efficiency.
4. The *formal structure* is the main network for organizing and managing the various activities of the enterprise.
5. *Unity of command* must prevail.
6. *Coordination* is a primary responsibility of management and is fulfilled by performing the managerial functions properly.

These major principles of organization are a primary concern of the chief executive officer (CEO). He or she must translate them into a formal organizational structure so that the institution operates smoothly and accomplishes its objectives.

Since the application of these formal organizational principles involves all levels of management, it is also necessary for you as a supervisor to understand them and know how they are used. This knowledge will help in organizing your own department and in coordinating its activities with those of the rest of the institution. As a supervisor, you will certainly be asked to carry out and may even be asked to help make decisions involving reorganization, departmentalization or the division of work, the span of supervision, the delegation of authority, etc. As you move up the managerial hierarchy, you will probably be called on to participate in more and more such organizational decisions. Thus, although the CEO initially applies the formal principles to establish the organization's overall structure and activities, the department heads, supervisors, and other middle- and lower-level managers must make these principles and the resulting structure work. This is why it is essential for us to discuss the organizing process on an overall, or institutional, basis before we can discuss it on the departmental, or supervisory, level.

The many contingencies facing management are a continuous challenge, and the dynamic nature of organizing enables the manager to bring about change and to absorb and accommodate change as the need arises. This will enable the enterprise to pursue and achieve its objectives continuously. Although organizing is a dynamic process, it rests on two fundamental concepts, *authority* and *span of management*.

This chapter will examine these two fundamental concepts. Authority, the right to direct others and to act and give orders, is one of the bases through which the manager gets the job done. The span of management deals with another dimension, the scope of supervision.

■ AUTHORITY

A brief reference to the importance of authority to the managerial position was made in Chapter 2. Our discussion of authority at that point merely stated that authority is the lifeblood of the supervisory position and one of the characteristics of a manager. Also the process of delegation of authority breathes life into an organization; without it, an organization cannot and does not exist. Therefore, we must examine and understand first the concept of authority.

The Meaning of Authority

Authority is a difficult concept; it has many interpretations and meanings, including the one we have used before: an attribute of the managerial position, the key to the managerial job. In this sense authority refers to the formal or official power of a manager to obtain the compliance of the subordinate with directives, communications, policies, and objectives. Such authority is associated with the manager's function in the organization; it is vested in organizational roles or positions. As long as an individual holds the position, he or she has the privilege of exercising the authority that is inherent in it. Since positions are meaningless unless they are occupied by someone, we generally speak of the authority of the manager, the authority that is delegated to the manager, and so forth. Although it would be more precise to speak of the authority of the managerial *position* itself or the authority delegated to that position rather than to the person who occupies it, the difference is generally regarded as semantic. As long as we understand that authority in this sense resides in the position, we may speak rather loosely of the authority of the manager, supervisor, etc.

Source and Nature of Authority

As stated, authority is a difficult concept with many interpretations and meanings. The definition of authority as "legitimate power" to give orders was first clearly expressed by Max Weber.[1] The subordinates' compliance rests on the belief that it is legitimate for managers to give orders and illegitimate for subordinates not to obey them. Other writers, such as Fayol, have expressed similar views. This kind of authority is vested in organizational roles and positions, not in the individuals who occupy these positions. As long as an individual holds the position, he or she has the privilege of exercising the authority that is inherent in it. Once a manager leaves an organizational position, he or she loses the authority inherent in it, and the authority will go to the successor.

While examining the foundation for this organizational authority, Weber identified three bases of authority: *tradition, rules and regulations,* and *charisma.* Traditional authority "rests on the belief in the sacredness of the social order."[2] For instance, in a patriarchal society the father receives legitimacy through custom. Rules and regulations form a second base. Subordinates will comply with orders because, in a bureaucratic organization, superior-subordinate authority relationships are defined by rules and regulations. In charismatic authority the compelling personal characteristics and charisma of the leader make the subordinates and followers carry out the orders. The concept of leadership will be discussed in Chapter 21.

In addition to these explanations of the meaning and sources of authority, other views have been developed and expressed. In reference to the *source of authority, there are two contradictory views: the formal authority theory and the acceptance theory.* In *formal authority theory,* authority originates at the top of the organizational hierarchy and is delegated downward *from superiors to subordinates.* In *acceptance theory,* authority originates at the bottom of the organizational pyramid and is conferred upward from subordinates to superiors. Let us look at each of these theories more carefully to gain further insight into the difficult authority concept.

Formal Authority Theory

The formal authority theory is the top-down theory. It traces the flow of authority downward from top-level management to subordinate managers. You can trace your authority directly from your boss, who has delegated it to you. He or she in turn receives authority, for example, from an associate administrator, who receives authority from the chief administrator, who traces authority directly back to the board of directors, who receive their authority from the owners or the stockholders. In private corporations, therefore, one may say that the actual source of authority lies in the stockholders, who are, loosely speaking, the owners of the corporation. These owners delegate their power to administer the affairs of the corporation to those whom they have put into managerial positions. From the top administrator that power flows down through the channel of command until it reaches the supervisor.

Limitations of Authority

There are limitations to the authority that a manager has by virtue of his or her position in an organization. These limitations can be either explicit or implicit. Moreover, some of them stem from internal sources and others from external sources. *External limitations* on authority include such factors as our codes, folkways, and life-style, along with the many political, legal, ethical, moral, social, and economic considerations that make up our society. For example, laws referring to collective bargaining and resulting contractual obligations, fair employment practices, etc., are specific examples of external limitations on authority.

Internal limitations on authority would be set mainly by the organization's articles of incorporation and bylaws. In addition to these overall internal restrictions, each manager is subject to the specific limitations spelled out by the administrator when duties are assigned and authority delegated. Generally there are more internal limitations on the scope of authority the further down one goes in the managerial hierarchy. In other words, the lower the rung on the administrative ladder, the narrower is the area in which authority can be exercised. This is known as the *tapering concept of authority,* as shown in Figure 9-1.

All these limitations are explicit, fairly obvious restrictions on authority. In addition to these, a number of more implicit limitations, such as biological restraints, exist simply because human beings do not have the capacity to do certain things. No subordinate should be expected to do the impossible. Thus, physical and psychological restrictions on authority must be recognized and accepted. In today's society such considerations significantly limit the scope of authority of every manager.

Thus far, our discussion has centered on the formal way of looking at the origin of authority as a power that results from our recognition of private property. According to this theory, then, the ultimate source of all managerial authority in America would be the constitutional guarantee of the institution of private

■ FIGURE 9-1 The tapering concept of authority.

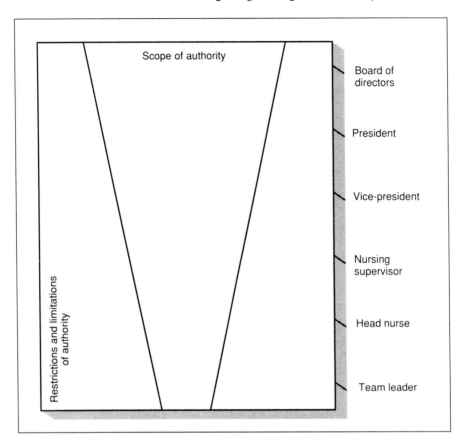

property. Since the Constitution was created by the people and is subject to amendment and modification by the will of the people, it follows that society is the source from which authority flows.[3]

This theory is an agreement with Weber's definition of formal authority, since management's right to give orders is legitimate and the employees are obliged to carry out these orders because they are legitimate. There could be a problem, however, when such an order seems unethical to the employee or outside the limits of the job. This raises the question of whether the subordinate has some say in this matter.

Acceptance Theory of Authority

The acceptance theory of authority addresses the role of subordinates and managerial authority. It is a bottom-up approach in which employees give managers their authority. A large group of writers who do not agree with the formal theory maintain that management has no meaningful authority unless and until subordinates confer it. These writers claim that formal organizational authority is effective only to the extent that subordinates accept it. They state that unless your subordinates accept your authority, you, as a manager, actually do not possess that authority. In reality, subordinates often do not have a choice between accepting or not accepting authority. The only choice they have is to leave the job. Nevertheless, this is a worrisome thought, indicating that there is considerable merit in looking at authority as something that must be accepted by your employees.

Advocates of the acceptance theory state that in most cases a manager does not have a real problem; an employee, on accepting a job, knows that the boss of the department has the authority to give orders, take disciplinary action, and do whatever else goes with the managerial position. Whenever an employee decides to work for a healthcare institution, he or she agrees, within the limits of the job, to accept orders given by the organization. The decision whether an order has authority, however, lies with the person to whom it is addressed and does not reside in "persons of authority" or those who issue these orders.[4]

Formal Authority Theory versus Acceptance Authority Theory

To repeat, the origin of authority can be considered from two viewpoints. The formal way views authority as something that originates with private property, formally handed down from the owners at the top to the lowest line supervisor. In contrast, the acceptance idea views authority as something that is conferred on the supervisor by the subordinates' acceptance of this authority. It is not the author's intention to go further into this academic argument here. This difference of opinions is discussed because it significantly influences the practice of supervision, that is, the manner and the attitudes with which supervision is approached.

This will become more obvious when we realize that adherence to the acceptance theory does not necessarily rule out the downward delegation of authority from upper to lower levels of management. The acceptance theory can be thought of as merely adding another dimension to the formal concept of organizational authority. That is, in addition to having formal authority delegated from above, managers must also have such authority accepted from below. All managers must be aware that they possess formal authority, and, if need be, they can resort to it as a final recourse. Today no one wants to rely exclusively on the weight of this formal authority to motivate workers to perform their jobs. At times, however, every manager will have to make full use of this authority and power; it is hoped that these occasions will be the exceptions and not the rule. Even when the manager must invoke this authority, the manner in which it is done will make a difference in whether it is resented or accepted without resentment. If such actions are accepted graciously most of the time, the manager will know that the subordinates have chosen to recognize and respect the authority that superiors have formally delegated to him or her.

Types of Authority

In the past it might have been sufficient for a manager to rely on authority based on the legitimacy of the social institution—the concept of property rights—to get the job done. This approach alone, however, is no longer appropriate for a manager in any organized activity, especially in a healthcare institution. Therefore, it is necessary to examine the various types of organizational authority: positional, functional, and personal.

Positional authority is based on organizational position and, as stated, rests on the legitimacy of the manager's position as the agent of a socially valid organization. This authority is vested in the position and in the organization and is impersonal. Positional authority exists in all types of organizations: healthcare, educational, business, military, religious, fraternal, etc. We may not prefer a particular individual, but we recognize and accept the legitimacy of that person's position and authority.

Functional authority is based on expertise and knowledge. We accept expert advice and recognize that this person is an "authority" in a particular specialty. Functional authority exists in all branches of learning and crafts and comes from specialization. Healthcare institutions are a prime example of the role and importance of functional authority. The "specialist's" statements and directives are accepted because he or she is the "authority in this field" and carries the weight and power of functional authority. Whereas positional authority is impersonal, functional authority in this sense is highly personal. It adheres to the individual whose knowledge and expertise make him or her the "authority." Whereas positional authority can and must be delegated, functional authority cannot be delegated; it remains with the individual wherever he or she may be and work. Although it is highly personalized, functional authority has some aspects of positional authority because some organizations, especially healthcare centers, demand that certain positions can only be filled by individuals with special skill and expertise. A hospital abounds in examples and applications of functional authority, probably more than any other organized activity. Functional authority rests on acceptance, but it stems from an individual's knowledge and not from society.

Personal authority is based on an individual's characteristics, magnetism, and charisma. Subordinates and followers accept personal authority because their needs are consistent with the leader's goals. Personal authority motivates the subordinates to work willingly and enthusiastically toward the achievement of the objectives. This concept of personal authority can be equated with leadership, which will be discussed in Chapter 21.

Integrated Approach to Authority

To be an effective manager in a healthcare institution, it is not enough to depend on the weight of positional authority based on legitimacy, although occasionally this may be the last resort. It is much more desirable if the manager relies on a combination of all three types—positional, functional, and personal—to manage effectively. This is even more important in the healthcare field because of the occupational and professional character of the people involved; new fields of scientific advances and new technologies make greater expertise a necessity, leading to more and more functional authority. For instance, the chief medical technologist should not rely on only positional authority as the "chief" of the department; he or she should also use personal expertise in this field and leadership ability and charisma. Reliance on all three types of authority will create a highly desirable and motivating organizational climate.

■ THE SPAN OF MANAGEMENT (contor)

The optimum span of management, also known as *span of authority, span of supervision,* or *span of control,* has been a challenge to managers and leaders since biblical times. This concept deals with the scope of supervision, the number of people any one person can supervise effectively. Because this number is limited, organizations must create departments in different areas of activities and place someone in charge of each.

The establishment of departments in an organization is not an end in itself. It is not desirable per se because departments are expensive; they must be headed by various supervisors and staffed by additional employees, all of which runs into large sums of money. Furthermore, departments are not intrinsically desirable because the more there are, the more difficulties will be encountered in communication and coordination. As discussed earlier, departments do make the division of work possible. Equally important, they allow an organization to incorporate what is commonly known as the *principle of the span of management,* or the span of supervision. This principle states that *there is an upper limit to the number of subordinates a manager can effectively supervise.* This is a very crucial factor in structuring organizations.

The Relationships of Span to Levels

Almost every manager knows that a limit exists to the number of employees he or she can effectively supervise. The problem is caused by the many superior-subordinate interactions that are possible: (1) *direct relationships* between the superior and the immediate subordinates, (2) *direct group interactions* between the superior and different groupings of the subordinates, and (3) *cross-relationships* among the subordinates themselves. The number of superior-subordinate interactions that can be handled is limited. Since no one can manage an infinite number of subordinates, the administrator must create departments, or distinct areas of activities over which a manager is placed in charge. The administrator delegates authority to this manager. The manager in turn will redelegate authority to some subordinates, who in turn will supervise only a limited number of employees. In this manner, not only are departments and subdepartments created, but also the *span of supervision,* or the number of employees under each manager, is established. The number of managerial *levels* in the organization is determined as well.

To examine this relationship between the span of supervision and the levels of an organization, imagine a hypothetical organization in which 81 subordinates report to one chief executive, thus representing one organizational level. Then let us assume that 81 subordinates are too many and that only three should report to the top administrator. Under each of these three associate administrators there would now be 27 employees. By creating associate administrators, however, we have established two levels of organization and have a total of four executives. Now, assuming that 27 subordinates are still too many, and that this number is reduced to nine, the organization will require a third managerial level, increasing the total number of managers to 13. Each of the four executives on the upper two levels will have three subordinates, and each of the nine supervisors on the lowest level will have nine subordinates. The span of supervision has thus been reduced drastically from the original 81 to a maximum of nine.

■ **FIGURE 9-2 Relationship between the span of supervision and the levels of an organization.**

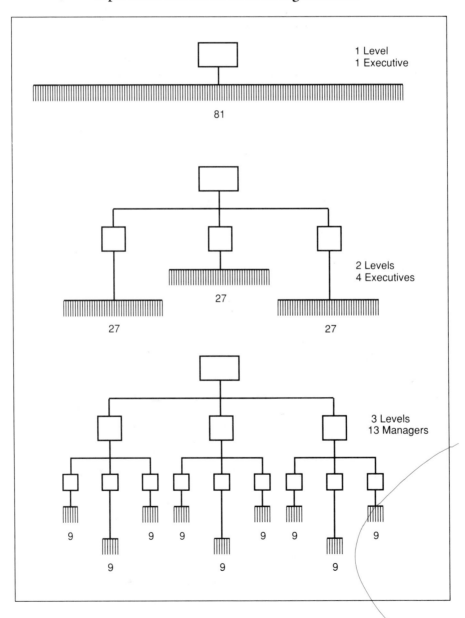

This obviously extreme example is illustrated in Figure 9-2, which shows very clearly what occurs when one begins to narrow the span of supervision. The narrower the span becomes, the more levels of management have to be introduced into the organizational setup. As with departments, this is not desirable per se because it is expensive. Every manager costs money, not only in salaries, but also in supporting salaries. Many levels complicate communication, since the dangers of distortion, omission, and misinterpretation are increased. Finally, levels create problems with morale because the addition of levels increases the distance between employees and upper administration. Therefore, a constant conflict exists between the width of the span and the number of levels: the narrower the span, the more managerial levels. The problem is whether to have a broader span of supervision or more levels, or vice versa. This problem is one that all managers face throughout their entire career.

Moreover, the problem of span versus levels is as old as the human race; an example is cited in the Old Testament. We have still not found a clear solution to the problem. One simply cannot state a definite figure as to how many subordinates a manager can have. One can only say that there is an upper limit to this figure.

Although we do not know exactly what the upper limit should be, it is interesting that in many enterprises the top-level administrator has only from five to eight subordinate managers reporting directly to him or her. Descending down the managerial hierarchy, we find that the span of supervision generally increases. It is not unusual to have anywhere from 15 to 20 people reporting to the supervisor. On closer inspection, we find that the number of subordinates who can be effectively supervised by one manager actually depends on numerous different contingency factors. These factors determine not only the actual number of relationships, but also their frequency and intensity. Therefore, before deciding the proper span of supervision in a particular organization, it is necessary to examine the more important contingencies that influence the magnitude of the span.

Factors Determining the Span of Supervision

One of the factors that influences the magnitude of the span is the competence of supervisors—their quality of management, experience, and know-how. Some supervisors are capable of handling more subordinates than others. Some are better acquainted with good management practices; others have had more experience and are simply better all-around managers. A person who is a "good manager" probably can supervise more employees. Limitations still exist, however, on the human capacity and the amount of time available during the working day.

What the manager does with this time is of utmost importance in determining the span. For example, a supervisor needs more time to make an individual decision for every problem that arises than to make initial policy decisions that anticipate problems that might arise later. Clear and complete policy statements reduce the volume of, or at least simplify, the personal decision making required of a manager and thus can increase the span of supervision. The same applies to other managerial processes that determine in advance definitions of responsibility and authority, performance standards, programs, procedures, and methods. Pre-determinations such as these reduce the number of decisions the manager has to make and likewise increase the potential span of management.

Another factor that will determine how broad a span a manager can handle is the *competence and makeup of the subordinates*. The greater the capacities and self-direction of the employees, the broader the manager's span can be. The training possessed by the subordinates is also important. The better their training, the less they will need their supervisor, thus freeing the manager to increase the span.

Another contingency on the manager's span is the amount and availability of *help from staff specialists* within the organization. If a hospital has a range of experts who provide various kinds of advice and service, then the manager's span can be wider.

The number of subordinates who can be supervised will also depend on the *nature and importance of the activities* performed by them. If these activities are complicated, are highly important, carry critical consequences, or frequently are changing, the span of supervision must necessarily be small. The simpler, uncomplicated, or more uniform the work, the greater can be the number of persons supervised by one supervisor.

Closely related factors that have a bearing on the span of supervision are the *dynamics and complexity of a particular activity*. Some aspects of a hospital routine are most certainly dynamic, whereas others are more stable. In those departments engaged in dynamic, critical, and unpredictable activities, the span will have to be very narrow. In those departments concerned with more or less stable activities, such as food production in the dietary department, the span of supervision can be broader.

Another factor that will determine the span of supervision is the degree to which *objective standards* are or can be applied. If enough objective standards are available for subordinates to gauge their own progress, they will not need to report to and contact their boss constantly. Objective standards will result in less frequent relationships, freeing the manager for a broader span.

Although we have now discussed most of the major factors that influence the span of supervision, we still cannot state a definite number of subordinates that a supervisor can effectively manage in each case. The optimum span will always depend on the particular circumstances, operative contingency factors, and the relative weight of each factor. The solution to this important question is a tradeoff, a balance between levels and span.

■ SUMMARY

Authority and the span of management are two basic concepts that permeate the organizing function.

Authority is the right to give orders and directives and to expect that they are carried out. Much has been said and written about the source of authority. The formal top-down opinion views authority as coming from our Constitution, social institutions, owners, stockholders, board of directors, higher management, and so on down the line to the supervisor. The opposite view, the acceptance theory, views authority as coming from the bottom up. Managers have no authority unless and until the subordinates accept their authority, and they will normally accept only those directives they perceive to be legitimate. Several bases of authority exist: traditional, rules, and charisma. These bases lead to three major types of organizational authority. Positional authority is based on the position in the organization; functional authority is based on knowledge and expertise; and personal, or charismatic, authority is synonymous with leadership.

A second basic concept in the organizing process is to determine the span of supervision at each level and the number of managerial levels. The span of supervision states that there is an upper limit to the number of employees a manager can effectively manage. The actual width of this span is determined by such factors as the capability of the supervisor, previous training and experience of the subordinates, nature and dynamics of the work to be performed, and availability of special staff support. No definite figure can be quoted as the ideal number of subordinates to be supervised by one manager. The manager knows, however, that when the span of supervision is decreased, meaning that the number of employees to be supervised is reduced, an additional supervisor has to be introduced for the excess employees. In other words, the smaller the span of supervision, the more levels of supervisory personnel are needed. This will shape the organization into either a tall, narrow pyramid or, in the case of a broad span of supervision, a shallow, wide pyramid.

NOTES

1. Max Weber, *The Theory of Social and Economic Organizations,* ed. Talcott Parsons, trans. A.M. Henderson and Talcott Parsons, New York: Oxford University Press, 1974, pp. 324-363.
2. Max Weber, "The Three Types of Legitimate Rule," trans. Hans Gerth, *Berkeley Journal of Sociology,* Vo. 4, 1985, pp. 3-10.
3. Elmore Peterson, E. Grosvenor Plowman, and Joseph M. Trickett, *Business Organization and Management,* 5th ed., Homewood, IL: Richard D. Irwin, Inc., 1962, p. 83.)
4. Chester I. Barnard, *The Functions of the Executive,* Cambridge, MA: Harvard University Press, 1956, p. 163.

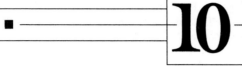

10

DIVISION OF WORK *(Decentralized)* AND DEPARTMENTALIZATION

Formal organization theory, as stated earlier, rests on several major principles or premises. Two of them are division of work and departmentalization. *Division of work,* or *work specialization,* means the degree to which the task of the organization is broken down into component parts. This is essential for efficiency, for the over-all performance of healthcare activities, and for the achievement of objectives. *Departmentalization* is the process of grouping the many activities into distinct units according to logical arrangements. Departmentalization is the building block for the formal structure, the main network for managing the various activities of the enterprise. In this chapter we will discuss the division of work and the design of the formal structure.

These two major premises of organization are a primary concern of the chief executive officer (CEO). He or she is the one who must translate them into a formal organizational structure for the institution. Since the application of these formal organizational principles involves all levels of management, it is also neces-sary for you as a supervisor to understand them and to know how they are used. This knowledge will help in organizing your own department and in coordina-ting its activities with those of the rest of the institution. In your supervisory capacity, you will certainly be asked to carry out, and maybe even help make, decisions involving departmentalization and division of work. As you move up in the managerial hierarchy, you will probably be called on to participate in many more such organizational decisions.

■ DIVISION OF WORK: WORK SPECIALIZATION

The practice of division of work is as old as the human race. From the earliest times we have examples of the practice of specialization in military and civilian activities. In the eighteenth century specialization was tied into efficiency, and since then division of work and specialization have prevailed with increasing momentum. The division of work, as stated, simply means to break down a total

124

job into smaller, more specialized tasks. Human beings have been dividing work in this manner for thousands of years because a group of people, each performing a small specialized part of the overall job, could accomplish more than the same-size group in which each individual was trying to do the whole job alone. In other words, the division of work results in greater efficiency and higher production.

This is particularly true in healthcare institutions. Continuous advances in medical sciences and technology resulted in greater specialization of professionals, facilities, and equipment and increased fragmentation of the delivery of care. Because of the proliferation and specialization of medical sciences and technologies, healthcare centers have become very large and complex organizational structures in terms of differentiation of activities and specialization. Institutions use the talents of a tremendous array of people who have developed particular specializations.

This proliferation of specialties has clear advantages for patients in terms of scientific care. However, it creates additional problems for the administration of healthcare institutions, namely, the need for new and varied organizational structures to coordinate the specialties to achieve objectives. Since the purpose of the organization is to get the job done, specialization and division of work play an important role in designing the type of organizational structure of task and authority relationships conducive for achieving desired results.

■ DEPARTMENTALIZATION

Because the division of work into such specialized tasks produces a much more efficient operation, almost every organization must departmentalize. As stated, departmentalization is the process of grouping various activities into natural units according to logical arrangements. A department is such a unit; it is a distinct area of activities over which a manager or supervisor has been given authority and has accepted responsibility. The terminology may vary and a department may be called a division, service, section, unit, office, or similar term, but it still represents a closely related set of activities.

For all practical purposes the major departments in an organization are established by the CEO. The top-level administrator is the one who groups the various activities and assigns them to be a distinct department. Some departments established this way will be small and will require no further subdivision. In a healthcare institution, however, many departments will be sufficiently large that their managers will have to further subdivide, that is, set up subdepartments or smaller units within the overall department. For this reason, every manager must become acquainted with the various alternatives available for grouping activities. The process of departmentalization can be done on the basis of (1) functions, (2) process and equipment, (3) territory (location), (4) customer (patient), (5) time, or (6) product. We will now explore each of the six alternatives more fully.

Functions

The most widely accepted practice of departmentalizing is to group activities

■ **FIGURE 10-1 Barnes Hospital organization chart.**

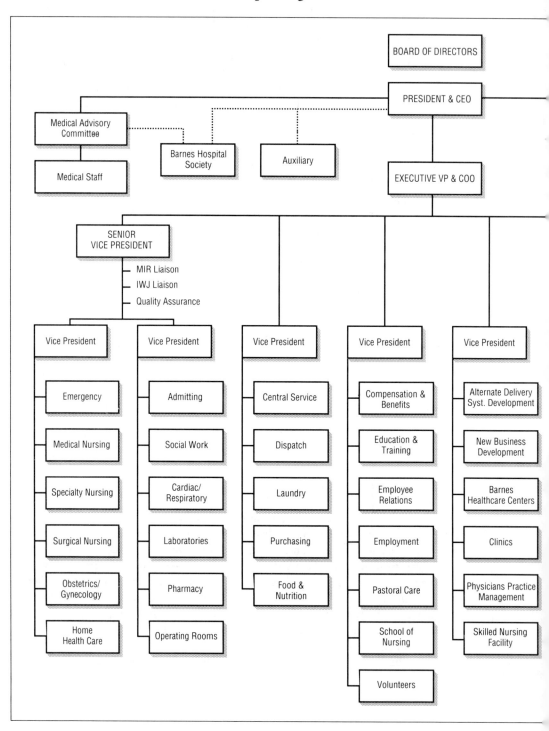

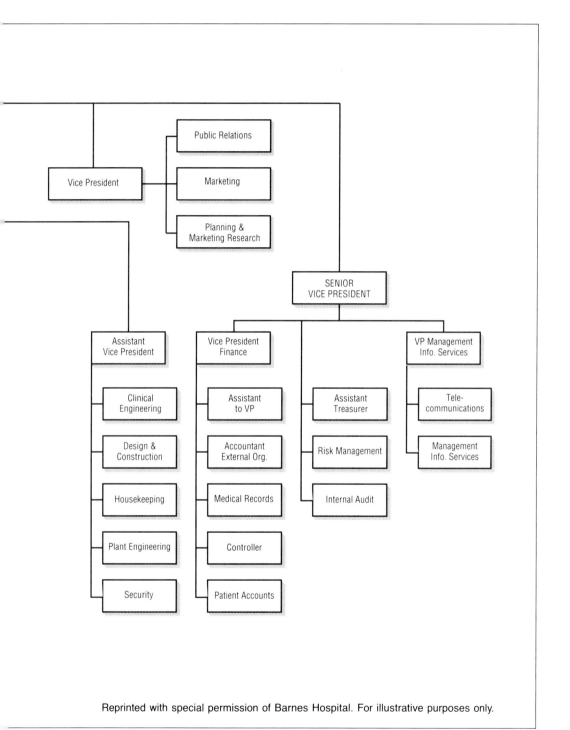

Reprinted with special permission of Barnes Hospital. For illustrative purposes only.

■ **FIGURE 10-2 St. Mary's Health Center organization chart.**

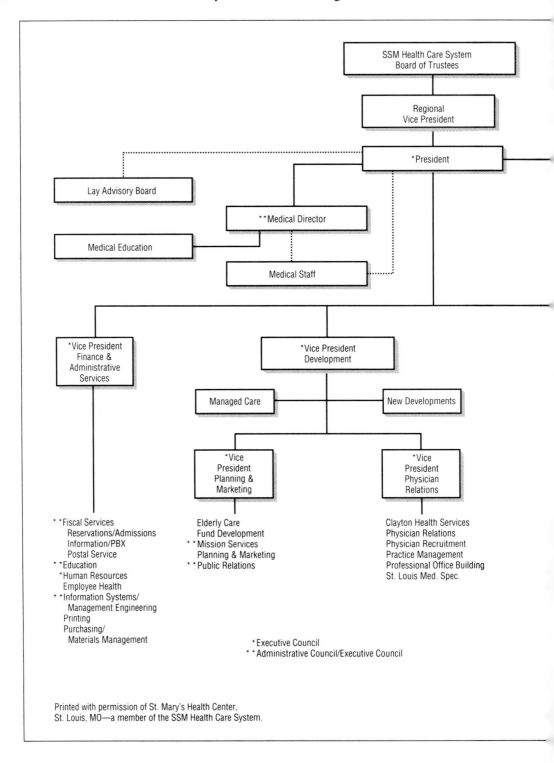

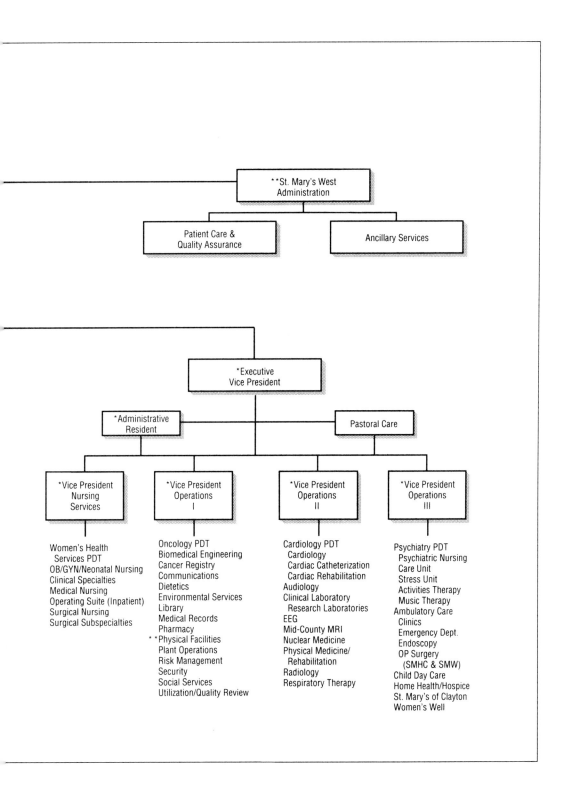

according to functions,[1] or according to the jobs to be done. This is the guiding thought in the establishment of departments in most organized activities and in hospitals and related medical facilities. All activities that are alike or similar and involve a particular function are placed together into one department under a single chain of command. For instance, a director of nursing services would be put in charge of all nursing activities throughout the center, and a director of dietary services is put in charge of all food- and nutrition-related activities. (See Figures 10-1 and 10-2.)

As the institution grows and undertakes additional work, these new duties are added to the already existing departments. For instance, when a hospital adds an outpatient surgical center, performing surgery with reasonably low risk on patients who do not stay overnight, this new activity would logically be assigned to the operating rooms department and its supervisor. Such increased activities, however, might necessitate the addition of more employees and levels of supervision within the functional departments, a topic that was discussed in Chapter 9.

To departmentalize by function is a natural, logical way of arranging the various activities in any enterprise and certainly in hospitals. This kind of departmentalization takes advantage of specialization by combining the functions that belong together and that are performed by experts in that functional field with the same type of education, background, equipment, and facilities. Each supervisor is concerned with only one type of work and concentrates all of his or her energy on it. Functional departmentalization also facilitates coordination, since one manager is in charge of one type of activity. Coordination is easier to achieve in this way than it would be in an organization where the same function is performed in several different divisions. Another advantage of functional departmentalization is that it makes the outstanding abilities of one or a few individuals available to the enterprise as a whole. Because functional departmentalization is a simple and logical method, it is the most widely used way of setting up departments.

Process and Equipment

Activities can also be grouped around the equipment, process, and technology involved. This way of departmentalizing is often found in hospitals because they usually operate certain types of equipment and handle certain processes that require special training and expertise. Everything involving the use of the particular equipment and technology would be referred to its special department. It is important to note that this type of organizational structure is similar to functional departmentalization, the major difference being the emphasis on person-machine relationships. For instance, in an x-ray department, specific equipment is used but also only certain functions are performed. Therefore, departmentalization by function and by equipment become closely allied.

Territory (Location)

An alternative way to departmentalize is according to location. Again, this type of departmentalization is more important in industrial enterprises, but applications of it are made within healthcare institutions. For example, a hospital may be confronted with a setup in which several physically dispersed units exist, such as St. Mary's East and St. Mary's West. If the same functions are performed in different locations and different buildings, then geographic departmentalization may be feasible and necessary. The same considerations are applicable even if all activities are performed in one building, but on different floors and wings, such as a medical-surgical nursing unit, third floor, west wing, and another on the fourth floor, south. One of the advantages of territorial departmentalization is placing decision making close to where the work is done. This departmentalization has the disadvantage of possible duplications of efforts; on the other hand, it provides opportunities for the development of more managerial talent.

Customer (Patient)

At times management may find it advisable to group activities based on customer (patient) considerations. This is commonly known as customer departmentalization, which means that the organization responds to consumers' needs and characteristics. Two examples of nonindustrial organizations that have departmentalized along customer lines are a university and hospital. In the university night programs and day programs comply with the requests and special needs of the "customers," namely, part-time and full-time students. In the hospital certain services and activities are grouped for outpatients and inpatients, such as outpatient surgery. In so doing, the healthcare center delivers its services to more people, especially in such supporting services as the laboratory, x-ray, or physical therapy departments. Work on an outpatient basis is on the rise and is a significant factor in a hospital's revenue picture. This is "customer" departmentalization, which emphasizes the characteristics and needs of the patient.

Time

Some organizations find it helpful and necessary to group activities according to the period during which they are performed. An enterprise such as a hospital or public utility, which of necessity is engaged in a continuous process and operates around the clock, must departmentalize activities on the basis of time, at least to a certain extent. In other words, the institution must set up different time shifts, usually day, afternoon, and night. Activities typically are grouped first on some other basis, such as by function, and then these activities are organized into shifts. The activities to be performed on the other shifts are largely the same as those performed during the regular day shift. Thus, such groupings often create serious organizational questions of how self-contained each shift should be and what relationships should exist between the regular day shift supervisors and the off-shift supervisors.

Product

Industry frequently uses the concept of product departmentalization; however, this does not seem to be applicable in healthcare institutions. To departmentalize on a product basis in industry means to establish each product or groups of closely related products as a product line, which is a relatively independent unit within the overall framework of the enterprise. In product departmentalization the emphasis is shifted from the function to the output, or product. For example, a hospital supply company may have a separate department for furniture, another for surgical supplies, and a third for uniforms.

Product departmentalization in a healthcare facility would involve dividing it into departments based on the "product" turned out, for example, maternity, surgery, intensive care, and psychiatry. Each such department would have its own supervisor of nursing, its own dietary supervisor, its own maintenance staff, etc., and each such "product" department would have its own boss, the director of surgery, the director of intensive care, the director of maternity, etc. These directors would be in charge of all functions within their product departments, including nursing activities, therapy, food services, laundry, and maintenance.

As you can see, such product departmentalization would result in duplication of effort. Instead of a single director of nursing, there would be as many as there are departments. Moreover, coordination among all nursing services would be difficult, since each supervisor reports to a different boss. The same difficulties would be found in every department. Thus, product departmentalization, as practiced in industry, does not seem to be applicable in a healthcare institution.[2]

Mixed Departmentalization (Composite Structure)

Departmentalization is not an end in itself. In grouping activities, management should not attempt to merely draw a pretty picture. Its prime concern should be to set up departments that will facilitate the realization of the institution's objectives and the coordination of its functions. There are advantages and disadvantages to each method of departmentalization. Choosing is a question of balance and deciding which works most effectively. In so doing, management will probably have to use multiple bases of departmentalization and end up with a hybrid structure—mixed departmentalization; for example, a nursing supervisor (functional) on the surgical unit (subfunction), west wing, third floor (location), of the night shift (time). In practice, almost all hospitals have this composite type of departmental structure, invoking function, location, time, and many other considerations. Any mixture is acceptable, as long as it works and is consistent with the overall objectives of the institution.

Organizational Design

So far our discussion of organizational structure has centered around what is often called *traditional structure*. There are many reasons to discuss and understand this approach first and foremost. Traditional structure is the most often used structure in all types of organized activities in the real world. It is the most studied and researched form of organization and has a long history of successful performance. Traditional structure is a contemporary design; it is not "old fashioned," and is not inflexible or rigid. This structure functions successfully under most prevailing conditions and is capable of producing and accommodating change and adapting to contingencies as they arise.

Of course, even the best-designed organization cannot be left without change forever. Changes in the state of the arts, the environment, human and social processes, organizational size, the work force, economic trends, regulatory activities, and so forth have to be accommodated. The institution must design a structure that works best under these contingencies. The organization is an open system: every change in one part of it affects the activity in another part. The organizational concepts discussed thus far are applicable even under those new contingencies.

An example of this flexibility is the recent matrix design of organization, basically a combination of functional and product departmentalization.

Matrix Organization (Matrix Design)

One of the newer organizational structures building on traditional concepts is the matrix organization. Matrix organization, also known as *project* or *grid organization*, does not do away with the traditional organization; it simply builds on it and, under certain contingencies, improves on it. It is superimposed on functional organization, creating a matrix that provides horizontal dimensions to the traditional vertical orientation of the functional organization.

During recent years high-technology industries found a need to create project organizations to focus resources and special talents for a given time on a specific project. Management and the customer became increasingly interested in the end result. The essence of matrix management is a compromise between functional and product departmentalization in the same organizational structure. Figure 10-3 shows possible matrix arrangements in a healthcare institution in which the functional managers are in charge of their professional function, with an overlay of project managers who are responsible for the end product—a specific project. The concept of matrix organization gives an enterprise the potential of conducting several projects simultaneously. For example, the president of the hospital sees the need for three projects to be phased into the institution within the next two years, such as a unit-dose pharmaceutical system, a hospital-wide information system, and preparation for the hospital's accreditation. These three projects could be assigned to three different project managers, and matrix organizations could be established for obtaining these objectives.

By establishing a project organization, better coordination can be achieved than would be possible in a traditional organizational structure. As the project proceeds, it is assigned to a project manager from the beginning to its completion, and people from the functional areas needed for this project are assigned either on a full- or part-time basis to this project. The matrix is an overlay on conventional structure; it draws on traditional structure for the various skills required for this project. The project manager sees the project through from the

■ FIGURE 10-3 Matrix organization.

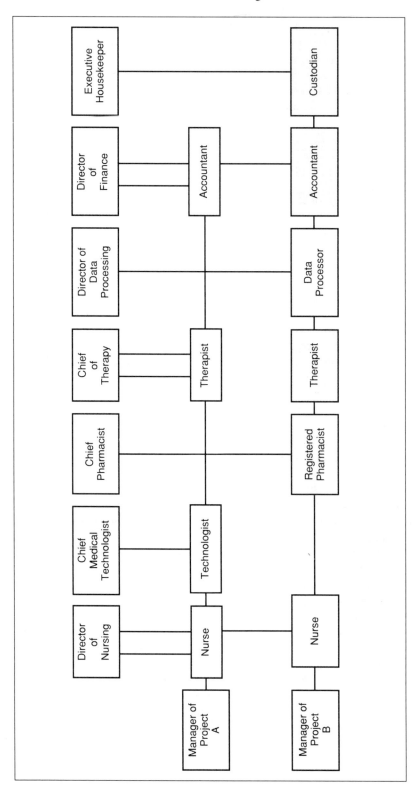

beginning to the end. When the project is finished, the specialized personnel needed return to their functional departments or are reassigned to a new project; the same occurs with the project manager.

There are many advantages to matrix organization:

1. Offers an effective way to phase new projects in and out of operation
2. Improves coordination and establishes lateral relationships
3. Offers greater flexibility to innovative ideas
4. Creates teams quickly to cope with a sudden change or need
5. Dissolves teams without too much repercussion on the overall structure
6. Exposes members of a project to interaction with experts from other areas, thus offering an opportunity for personal development
7. Affords top-level management an additional way to delegate and decentralize

Matrix design also creates a number of problems. Most result from the ambiguity of the role in which the members of the team find themselves while the project lasts. The professional, when assigned to a project, often is faced with duality of command because directives will come from the project manager, whereas conflicting ideas may flow from the functional superior. For instance, the project manager may ask the professional member of the team to perform a task in a way that does not conform to the functional manager's guidelines. While assigned to the project, the professional also may feel isolated from the mainstream of his or her expertise. Further sources of frustration are that the assignment is only temporary, and evaluations and possible promotions are usually still vested in the functional department head and not in the project manager. Dual command probably causes the most difficulties; employees on the project may not be certain to whom they are supposed to report. This is even more confusing when one person is assigned part-time to two or more projects.

Most of these problems are caused by poor project preparation and a lack of concise and clear statements of authority relationships; they can be avoided by the CEO at the start of the project. It is important to clarify the authority and responsibility of the functional managers, for example, those of the chief medical technologist in Figure 10-3 and those of the manager of project A. The project manager should have full authority and responsibility over the integrity of the design and over the budget; he or she must act as decision maker and coordinator for the duration of the project. There must be clear statements about the project manager's frequency of reporting and the scope of the project. The project manager must decide on schedules and work out priorities with the functional managers. The functional managers should be responsible for the integrity of the service or products their departments supply to the project. Statements concerning these decisions and responsibilities are necessary for the guidance of the project manager and the guidance of the functional managers whose departments are involved in the project.

Despite the best preparations and clarifications, misunderstandings may still arise. For example, the priorities between the project managers of two projects who are both vying for a functional manager's services may become an issue. Provisions to resolve such a dilemma should probably be made by referring such a dispute to higher management for a decision. Thorough preparation and clarifying authority and responsibility when the project is established will minimize most of these problems. Some borderline cases involving problems of dual command may come up, however, especially in questions of accuracy and integrity of the project. Remember that all organizational structures can create some problems occasionally. Matrix organization provides an institution with a contemporary proven method of implementing a complex new task of relatively short duration.

Figure 10-4 is an example of a matrix organization where the project involves the computerization of the laboratories. This is a one-time undertaking, a project that is to be completed within a certain time. To phase this project into the organization and have it completed within the allocated period, the administrator decides that a matrix, or project, organization would be the best vehicle to get the job done. After appointing the project manager, several functional specialists needed to accomplish this task are assigned to it. A project manager is put in charge of this project with a clear objective as to what should be accomplished and when it should be finished.[3] To implement this laboratory computerization project, it is necessary to have input and coordination from the laboratories, data processing, pathology department, accounting, and administration. These specialized employees work under the supervision and guidance of the project manager; therefore, several employees from the functional areas involved are assigned to the project on either a full- or a part-time basis. The administrator is able to draft these specialists for the duration of the project; he or she clearly states that the project manager is in charge and is their line superior on this project. The project manager sees the project through from the beginning to the end. On completion, the specialized personnel return to their functional departments, as does the project manager, or some may go on to another project where their special skills are needed.

■ SUMMARY

Management's overall organizing function is to design a formal structural framework that will enable the institution to achieve its objectives. The CEO establishes this framework initially, using the basic principles of formal organizational theory as guidelines. The CEO begins with the principle that specialization, the division of work, is necessary for efficiency. This means grouping the various activities into distinct departments or divisions and assigning specific duties to each.

The administrator can approach this departmentalizing task in several ways. The most widely used concept of departmentalization is grouping activities according to functions, that is, placing all those who perform the same functions into the same department. Besides departmentalization by functions, it is possible to departmentalize by process and equipment, geographical (territorial) lines, customers (patients), time (shift), or product. A composite structure made up of several of these alternatives is most often used.

These guides lead to the design of an organizational structure that sometimes is referred to as "traditional." This traditional structure is as contemporary as the manager wants it to be. Besides having a long history of successful performance, this conventional form of organizational structure can accommodate contingencies and changes as they occur.

■ **FIGURE 10-4** Project organization.

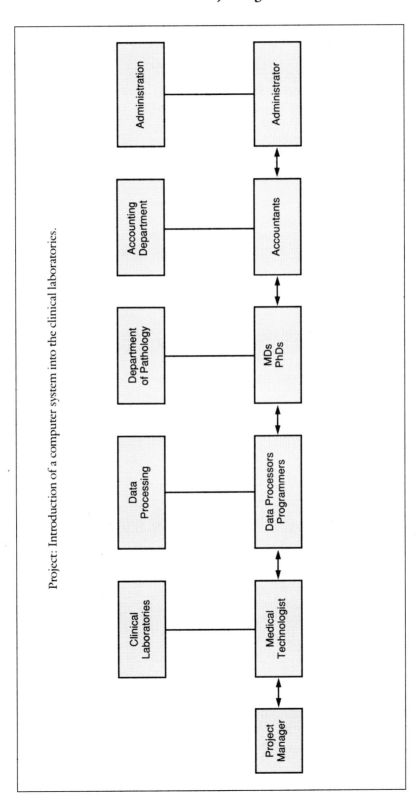

Project: Introduction of a computer system into the clinical laboratories.

One of the newer developments in organizational design is the matrix organization. This stresses horizontal relationships and combines functional and product departmentalization. Matrix design is employed for achieving a special project with a definite result by superimposing a matrix over the traditional organizational structure. At the project's inception, the CEO must clearly state the authority relationships among the project manager in charge, the functional personnel assigned to the project for the duration, and their functional department heads. This is necessary to avoid and minimize possible problems of dual command, dual allegiance, and other conflicts.

NOTES

1. The term function in this context is used to connote organizational activities such as nursing, pharmacy, and laboratories rather than the basic managerial functions of planning, organizing, etc.
2. However, the advent of the diagnosis-related group (DRG) regulations could possibly be considered an approach along the concept of product departmentalization. The DRG concept is a capitative payment for inpatient services rendered to federally insured and some other third-party-payor patients. Discussing DRGs in this or any other context would clearly be beyond the confines of this text.
3. In this discussion we are merely referring to the organizational structural arrangements. The project manager may use a PERT network for the timing of activities and events.

DELEGATION OF ORGANIZATIONAL AUTHORITY

Departmentalization based on division of labor and the concept of span of management is the first task in building the organization. The second step in creating an organization is delegation of authority. As stated before, authority is the lifeblood of the managerial position; without authority the manager's job is meaningless. The process of delegation of authority breathes life into the organizational structure. The same process of delegation that brings authority to the manager is used to delegate it farther down the line of command. As one divides managerial responsibilities, one creates additional levels in the chain of command. The degree to which authority is delegated throughout the institution will indicate the extent of decentralization. Some institutions are at one end of the centralization-decentralization continuum, whereas others will lean to the other end.

■ THE MEANING OF DELEGATION

Just as authority is the key to the managerial position, delegation of authority is the key to the creation of an organization. Although the formal structure of an organization may have been meticulously designed by the chief administrator and carefully explained in manuals and charts, the organization still will not have life until and unless authority is delegated throughout its entire structure. Delegation of authority makes the organization operative. Through this process of delegation, *the subordinate manager receives authority from the superior.* In other words, if authority were not delegated, there would be no subordinate managers and thus no one to occupy the various levels, departments, and positions that make up the organizational structure. Only by delegating authority to subordinate managers is the organization actually created. Only with such delegation can the administration vest a subordinate with a portion of its own authority, thereby setting in motion the entire managerial process and organizational life.

Delegation of authority, however, does not mean that the boss surrenders all of his or her authority. The delegating manager always retains the overall authority to perform his or her functions. If necessary, all or part of the authority granted to a subordinate manager can be revoked and reallocated. A good comparison can be made between delegating authority and imparting knowledge in school. A teacher in school shares knowledge with the students, who then possess this knowledge, but the teacher still retains the knowledge as well.

The Scalar Chain

The line of vertical authority relationships from superior to subordinate is the *scalar chain,* or the *chain of command.* Through the process of delegation, as we have said, formal authority is distributed throughout the organization. It flows downward from the source of all authority at the top, through the various levels of management, to the supervisor, and from there possibly to lower line supervisors. The broad authority necessary to run a private healthcare center is usually delegated by the board of directors or trustees to the president (also known as the administrator or chief executive officer [CEO]), who in turn must delegate authority to subordinate managers (vice presidents, etc.), who delegate farther down the line, and so forth.

This line of direct authority relationships throughout the organization is commonly known as the scalar chain. It is a clear line from the ultimate source of authority to the lowest managerial ranks. This chain of command must be clearly understood by every subordinate. The scalar chain must be closely adhered to, or the risk exists of undermining authority. By the time this "flow of authority" reaches the supervisory level, it probably has narrowed down to a discreet "trickle" of delegation rather than a continuous stream. Nevertheless, it can be traced directly upward to the ultimate source. Scalar relationships are based on positional authority, as discussed in Chapter 9. They are also based on another important managerial principle—unity of command.

Unity of Command

As stated, delegation of authority flows from a single superior to a single subordinate. Each subordinate reports and is accountable to only one superior, namely, that person from whom he or she receives authority. This is known as *unity of command,* the important organizational principle briefly referred to in Chapter 9. A superior manager can have a number of subordinates reporting to him or her, but for each of these subordinates, the one-to-one relationships (unity of command) still prevail.

The scalar chain provides the major route along which the process of delegation moves. Unity of command is a critical organizational concept; it enables the administration to coordinate activities, pinpoint responsibility and accountability, and define and clarify superior-subordinate relationships. Whenever this principle of unity of command is violated or compromised, management must anticipate complications.

■ THE PROCESS OF DELEGATION

Every manager must be thoroughly familiar with the process of delegation, which is the lifeblood of an organization. It consists of three components, all of which must be present. These three components are inseparably related, so that a change in one of them will require an adjustment of the other two. The three essential parts of the delegating process are:

1. The assignment of duties by a manager to the immediate subordinates
2. The granting of permission (authority) to the subordinates to make decisions and commitments, use resources, and take all the actions necessary to perform their assigned duties
3. The creation of an obligation (responsibility) on the part of each subordinate to the delegating superior to perform the assigned duties satisfactorily

Unless all three of these component steps are taken, the success of the delegating process cannot be ensured. This is true no matter which level of management is doing the delegating. It is important to realize that all managers, from the chief administrator down to the line supervisors, must do their part in delegating authority throughout the entire organization. The chief administrator does the initial delegation when he or she groups activities, sets up line and staff departments, and assigns them their duties. Then the managers of each department or division must subdivide and reassign these duties within their own section and at the same time delegate the appropriate amount of authority and exact responsibility to carry them out. Whether it is the chief administrator who delegates authority to the associate administrators and directors or the line supervisor who delegates authority to the nonmanagerial subordinates, the steps in the process of delegation are the same. In the following discussion of these essential steps, we will approach the delegation process mainly on the departmental level rather than on the administrative level, since this book is primarily written for departmental supervisors.

Assigning Duties

In the assignment of duties the supervisor determines how the work in the department is to be divided among the subordinates and the supervisor. All the tasks that must be accomplished in the department will be considered; the supervisor decides which of them can be assigned to a subordinate and which he or she must do. First, many duties are routine, and the manager should assign these to the regular subordinates. Second, other functions can be assigned only to those subordinates who are particularly qualified for them. Third, there are some functions that a supervisor cannot delegate but must do himself or herself.

In all likelihood, however, many duties could be delegated to the two subordinate groups. In such cases much will depend on the manager's general attitude and the availability of subordinates, but some logical guidelines can aid the manager when assigning duties. It is better that the assignments be justified and explained on the basis of such logical guidelines, rather than on personal likes and dislikes or hunch and intuition. This is important because the supervisor will be subject to pressures from different directions when assigning duties. Some subordinates will want to acquire more activities, whereas others will believe that they should not be burdened with certain duties. Thus, despite the guidelines, it will often be difficult for the supervisor to decide where best to place a given activity.

One way of doing this is to assign the activity to those employees who will make the most use of it most of the time. One also may be inclined to assign an activity to employees who are already particularly skilled or primarily interested in it. If they have special interests, these employees probably will carry out the activity best.

By considering such factors, the supervisor should be able to assign work so that everybody gets a fair share and can do his or her part satisfactorily. To achieve this, the supervisor must clearly understand the nature and the content of the work to be accomplished. Furthermore, one must be thoroughly acquainted with the capabilities of the employees. All this is not as simple as it might appear at first. The supervisor is often inclined to assign heavier tasks to those employees who are more capable because it is the easiest way out. In the long run, however, it would be far more advantageous to train and bring up the less capable employees so that they also can perform the more difficult jobs. If too much reliance is placed on one or a few persons, the department will be in a bad situation if they are absent or leave the scene. Thus, it is always a good idea to have a sufficient number of available employees who have been trained in the department's most difficult tasks. Also, the supervisor's problems of assigning various duties will become simpler by building up the strength and experience of all the employees.

The manner and extent to which the supervisor assigns duties to the employees will significantly affect the degree to which they respect and accept the supervisor's authority. Much of the manager's success will depend on the skill in making assignments. This function will be discussed further throughout the text. It must be emphasized again that the first step in the process of delegating authority is to assign certain tasks or duties to each subordinate; each must have a job to perform to warrant a delegation of authority.

Granting Authority

The second essential part in the process of delegation is granting authority— granting permission to make decisions and commitments, use resources, and take all those actions necessary to get the job done. As pointed out earlier, duties are assigned and authority is delegated to *positions* within the institution rather than to people. Since these positions are staffed by people, however, one typically refers to the delegation of authority to subordinates instead of to subordinate positions.

To be more specific, granting authority means that a supervisor confers on the subordinates the right and power to act and make decisions within a predetermined and limited area. The manager always must determine in advance the scope of authority that is to be delegated. The range of delegated authority is usually specific when a task is routine and more general when the task is less formalized.

How much authority can be delegated will depend on the amount of authority that the delegating manager possesses and on the type of job to be done. Generally, enough authority must be granted to the subordinate to perform what is expected adequately and successfully. There is no need for the degree of authority to be greater than necessary, but it must be sufficient to get the job done. If employees are expected to fulfill the tasks assigned to them and make reasonable decisions for themselves within this area, they must have enough authority to perform.

The degree of authority delegated is intrinsically related not only to the duties assigned but also to the results expected. Whenever management delegates authority, it is necessary to inform the subordinate of the expected results, for example, how fast the employee is expected to accomplish the job or how "perfect" the work is expected to be. For this purpose, standards of performance are established to provide a basis for judging work done and to facilitate management's control. These standards will be discussed more fully in the section on control in Chapter 25.

At this point, it is sufficient to say that you as a supervisor must be specific in telling each employee just what authority he or she has and what results are expected while exercising that authority. If this is not stated clearly, the subordinate will have to guess how far the authority extends, probably by trial and error and experimentation. As a supervisor, you may have experienced this when your own boss was not explicit as to how much authority you really had. To avoid this happening to your subordinates, it is necessary that the scope of authority and results expected be clearly defined and explained. As time goes on, less explanation will be necessary. Remember, however, that if you change an employee's job assignment, at the same time you must check to see that the degree of authority you have given is still appropriate. Perhaps it is more than needed; then you may have to revoke some of the delegated authority. Whenever conditions and circumstances of the job change, additional clarification of the scope of authority also becomes necessary.

Limitations to Authority

As discussed in Chapter 9, a manager's authority has limitations because of his or her position in an organization. These limitations can be either explicit or implicit; some stem from internal sources and others from external sources. Generally, more internal limitations on the scope of authority are present the farther down one goes in the managerial hierarchy. In other words, the lower the rung on the administrative ladder, the narrower is the area in which authority can be delegated and exercised. This is known as the tapering concept of authority, as referred to in Figure 9-1.

The Exception Principle

Although the scope of authority clearly delineates the area of decision making, the supervisor may be confronted by a problem beyond and outside of that area. Then the *exception principle* becomes active; these problem situations are exceptions and must be referred to the delegating manager higher up for decision making. The latter must make certain that this is truly an exception, since a danger exists that some subordinate managers may refer too many decisions upward when their own authority would be sufficient. In those situations the superior should refrain from deciding and refer the problem back to the subordinate manager. If it is truly an exception, however, beyond the scope of the subordinate's authority, the superior manager must decide.

Only One Boss

In granting authority, the principle of unity of command must be followed. Employees must be reassured that all orders and all positional authority can come only from the immediate supervisor, the only boss they have. It is very important that this principle be constantly stressed, since situations do occur in which two superiors issue directives and delegate authority to one subordinate. Since Biblical times it has been pointed out that it is difficult, if not impossible, to serve two masters. This sort of dual command is bound to lead to unsatisfactory performance by the employee, and it definitely results in confusion about lines of formal authority. The subordinate does not know which of the two "bosses" has the authority that will contribute most to his or her success and progress within the organization. Eventually such a situation will result in conflicts and organizational difficulties.

Revoking Delegated Authority

As stated before, delegating authority does not mean that management has divested itself of its authority. The delegating manager still retains authority and the right to revoke whatever part of the authority that was delegated to a subordinate. Occasionally, as activities change, there is a definite need to take a fresh look at the organization and to realign authority relationships. Managers frequently speak of reorganizing, realigning, reshuffling, and so forth; what is meant by this is the revoking of authority and reassignment of it elsewhere. Naturally such realignments of authority should not take place too often, since frequent changes create uncertainty, which affects morale. However, periodic reviews of authority delegations are not merely advisable, they are necessary in any organization. This applies to top-level administration as well as to the lowest-level manager.

Creating Responsibility

The third major aspect of the delegation of authority is creating an obligation on the part of the subordinate toward the boss to perform the assigned duties satisfactorily. The acceptance of this obligation creates responsibility. Without responsibility, the process of delegation would not be complete.

The terms *responsibility* and *authority* are closely related. Both terms are often misused and misunderstood. Although one frequently hears such expressions as "keeping subordinates responsible," "delegating responsibility," etc., these phrases do not describe the actual situation because they imply that responsibility is handed down from above, whereas it really is accepted from below.

Responsibility is the *obligation of a subordinate* to perform the duty as required by the superior. By accepting a job, by accepting the obligation to perform the assigned tasks, an employee implies acceptance of responsibility. This responsibility cannot be arbitrarily imposed on a person; rather, it results from a mutual agreement in which the employee agrees to accomplish the duties in return for rewards. Thus, although the authority to perform duties flows from management to subordinate, the responsibility to accomplish these duties clearly flows in the opposite direction, from the subordinate to management.

It is essential to bear in mind, however, that responsibility, unlike authority, cannot be delegated. Responsibility cannot be shifted. Your subordinate accepts responsibility, but you still have it. The supervisor can assign a task and delegate to a subordinate the authority to perform a specific job. However, the supervisor does not delegate responsibility in the sense that once the duties are assigned, the supervisor is relieved of the responsibility for these tasks. A manager can delegate authority to a subordinate, but not responsibility.

The healthcare administrator must delegate a great deal of authority to the associate administrators in order for them to oversee the performance of various tasks and services. These associate administrators, in turn and of necessity, have to delegate a large portion of their authority to the managers below them, but none of them delegates any responsibility. Each still accepts all the responsibility for the tasks originally assigned.

Similarly, when you as a supervisor are called on by your boss to explain the performance within your department, you cannot plead as a defense that you have "delegated the responsibility" for such activity to some employee. You may have delegated the authority, but you have remained responsible and must answer to your boss. It is essential that every supervisor clearly understand this vital difference between authority and responsibility. You must understand that when managers delegate the authority to do a specific job, they reduce the number of duties that they have to perform. They also conditionally divest themselves of a certain amount of authority, which can be taken back at any time if conditions are not fulfilled. In this process, however, managers do not reduce the overall amount of responsibility originally accepted. Although subordinates also accept a certain amount of responsibility for duties assigned them, this does not in any way diminish the manager's responsibility. It does add another layer or level to the overall responsibility, thereby creating *overlapping obligations*. Such overlapping obligations provide double or triple insurance that a job gets done correctly and responsibly.

Thus, although responsibility is something you accept, you cannot rid yourself of it. This thought may cause you anxiety and worry. After all, delegations and redelegations are necessary to get the job done. Although as a supervisor you will try to follow the best managerial practices, you cannot be certain that each of your subordinates will use his or her best judgment all the time. Therefore, allowances must be made for mistakes. In evaluating your performance as a supervisor, some attention will be paid to how much you must depend on your subordinates to get the work of your department accomplished. Although the responsibility has remained with you, your boss will understand that you cannot do everything yourself. In appraising your skill as a manager, your boss will consider how much care you have shown in the following areas: selecting your employees, training them, supervising them continuously, and checking their activities. All these matters will be taken into consideration in evaluating your ability in the event that something goes wrong in your department.

Equality of the Three Essential Parts

Always bear in mind that these three components must blend together to make delegation of authority a success; duties, authority, and responsibility must be commensurate. There must be enough authority (but not more than necessary) granted to your subordinates to do the job, and the responsibility you expect them to accept cannot be greater than the area of authority you have delineated. Subordinates cannot be expected to accept responsibility for activities if they have not been handed any authority. In other words, do not try to "keep your subordinates responsible" for something that you have not actually delegated to them.

Inconsistencies between delegated authority, responsibility, and assigned tasks will generally result in difficult and undesirable outcomes. You may have worked in organizations where some of the managers had much authority delegated to them but had no particular jobs to perform. This created misuses of authority and conflicts. You also may have been in positions where responsibility was exacted from you when you did not have the authority to fulfill an obligation. When responsibility exceeds authority, it is nearly impossible to do the job. This, too, is a most embarrassing and frustrating situation. Therefore, you must make certain that the three essential elements for successful delegation are of equal magnitude and that whenever one is changed, the other two are changed simultaneously.

Some rare occasions occur when responsibility and authority are not equal. For example, in emergencies managers are often inclined and even forced to exceed their authority. One hopes this will be the exception and not the normal state of affairs.

■ DECENTRALIZATION: THE DEGREE OF DELEGATION OF AUTHORITY

As discussed earlier, delegation of authority is the key to the creation of an organization. If no authority has been delegated, one can hardly say an organization exists. Thus, from an organizational point of view, the problem is not whether to delegate or not delegate authority, but rather *how much* authority will be delegated to middle- and lower-level managers. The question involves the *degree* of authority to be delegated. Centralization and decentralization represent opposite ends of this delegation continuum.

This question about the degree of delegation is extremely important because it will determine the answer to another highly significant organizational question: To what extent is the organization decentralized? How much of what authority should be given to whom and for what purpose? Variations in the extent of decentralization are innumerable, ranging from a highly centralized structure, in which the concept of an organization barely exists, to a completely decentralized organization, in which authority has been delegated to the lowest possible levels of management. In the first instance the chief executive is in close touch with all operations, makes almost all decisions, and gives almost all instructions. Hardly any authority has been delegated and, strictly speaking, it cannot be said that an organization has been created. Many small enterprises regularly operate along these lines. Often such one-man shows will collapse if their chief executive becomes incapacitated, dies, or for some other reason leaves the enterprise.

A much less extreme situation is found in organizations where authority has been delegated to a limited degree. In such organizations the major policies and programs are decided by the top-level manager of the enterprise, and the task of applying these policies and programs to daily operations and daily planning is delegated down to the first level of supervision. Few or no other levels exist between the top-level manager and the supervisors. This type of arrangement is often found in medium-sized enterprises. It is obviously advantageous because it limits the number of managers that the general manager must hire, thus keeping expenses down. Furthermore, the unusual knowledge and good judgment the general manager possesses can be applied directly. A considerable number of enterprises in the United States have this type of organization with a limited degree of delegation of authority.

At the other end of the centralization-decentralization continuum, we find those organizations in which authority has been delegated as far down the chain of command as possible. To find out if an organization is this decentralized, one must determine the type of authority that has been delegated, how far down in the organization it has been delegated, and how consistent the delegations are. In other words, one must ask how significant a decision can be made by a manager and how far down this occurs within the managerial hierarchy. The more important the decisions made farther down in the hierarchy, the more decentralization is prevalent. The number of such decisions and the functions affected by them also serve as indicators of decentralization. Also, the less checking that is done with upper-level management, the greater the degree of decentralization.

The answers to all these questions will indicate whether or not you are dealing with an organization that has delegated authority to the greatest extent possible. Most healthcare institutions probably find broad delegation of authority and decentralization advisable and necessary because of the nature of the activities involved and the background and expectations of the personnel. Today's better educated and more sophisticated healthcare work force wants and expects more authority and responsibility to use individual judgment.

It should also be pointed out that timing plays a role in solving the degree of delegation problem. Although centralization of authority or limited decentralization may be the most logical organizational forms to use in the early stages of an enterprise, later stages will usually require the CEO to face the problem of delegating more authority and decentralizing the organization to a greater extent. Such decentralization of authority becomes necessary when centralized management finds itself so burdened with decision making that the top executives do not have enough time to perform their planning function adequately or maintain a long-range point of view. This type of situation usually occurs when an organization expands. It should indicate to top-level management that the time has arrived to delegate authority to lower echelons. In other words, there should be a gradual development toward decentralization of authority commensurate with the growth of the enterprise.

Advantages and Disadvantages of Delegation

There are numerous advantages to delegating and decentralizing authority; these advantages become even more important as the enterprise grows in size. By delegating authority, the senior manager is relieved of much time-consuming detail work. Subordinates can make decisions without waiting for approval. This increases flexibility and permits more prompt action. In addition, such delegation of decision-making authority may actually produce better decisions, since the manager on the job usually knows more pertinent factors than the manager higher up, and speedy decisions are often essential. Delegation to the lower levels also increases morale and interest and enthusiasm for the work. It also provides a good training ground. All these advantages serve to make the organization more democratic and more responsive to the needs and ideas of its employees, which ultimately will result in delivery of better patient care.

Some disadvantages to considerable delegation also may exist. For example, the supervisor of a department may believe that he or she no longer needs the help of upper-level managers and can develop his or her own supporting services. This could easily lead to duplication of effort and suboptimization. Another disadvantage could be a possible loss of control, although the delegating manager can take steps to see that this does not happen. In most situations, however, the advantages of broad delegation far outweigh the disadvantages.

As stated before, the environment and contingencies of healthcare institutions are such that to deliver the best possible patient care, authority must be delegated broadly. It is a question of balance, of finding the degree of decentralization that works. No two healthcare centers are alike. Each has its own tradition, history, problems, challenges, work force, and environment to integrate into an organizational structure that works. This is an ongoing process. One must monitor and adjust the degrees of delegation and decentralization continuously as the environment and the institution change.

■ SUMMARY

In earlier chapters we defined authority as the power that makes the managerial job a reality. Authority is the lifeblood of the managerial position, and the process of delegation of authority breathes life into the organizational structure. Good managers must know how to use formal authority and how to delegate it to their subordinates. Through the process of delegation of authority, management actually creates the organization. This process of delegation is made up of three essential parts: assigning a job or duty, granting authority, and creating responsibility. All three are inseparably related, and a change in one will necessitate a change in the other two.

This process of delegation is the only way to create an organization. Thus, the question is not whether top-level management will delegate authority, but rather how much or how little authority it will delegate. A centralization-decentralization continuum exists in all organizations. If authority is delegated freely all the way down to the lowest levels of supervision, then the organization is highly decentralized. If most authority is hoarded at the top, the organization is highly centralized. Although centralization might be appropriate when an enterprise is just getting started, far greater advantages in many areas arise from decentralization, or broad delegation of authority.

LINE AND STAFF AUTHORITY RELATIONSHIPS

First in this part of the book, we organized horizontally, meaning we divided the work to be done into departments. Then we divided the managerial work to be done vertically by delegating authority. Now, as another consequence of specialization, there is the need to add staff to the organization. We are creating lateral and diagonal relationships by adding line and staff relationships.

In healthcare facilities one usually speaks of the nursing staff, medical staff, dietary staff, administrative staff, etc. In this context the word "staff" applies to a group of people who are engaged primarily in one activity to the exclusion of others. That is, staff is used to define all those people who perform somewhat the same job, such as nurses, physicians, and dietitians. In the general field of management and administration, however, the meaning of the term *staff* is very different. "Staff" is spoken of in connection with "line," and both these terms refer to authority relationships, which will be discussed in this chapter. In the following discussion, any reference to "staff" will mean *line/staff,* not the meaning that most people working in healthcare centers usually associate with staff.

Since no one, not even the chief executive officer (CEO), could possibly have all the knowledge, expertise, skills, and information necessary to manage a modern organization, staff becomes an essential and critical part of the institution. Staff plays an increasingly important part in the successful decision making in today's organizations. This is even more evident in the delivery of healthcare. Line managers retain the administrative and authoritative parts of the activities, whereas staff supplies the scientific, technological, technical, and informational aspects. Without these aspects, the institution could not function properly.

■ ORIGIN OF STAFF

The concept of staff is not new; there have been applications of it since the days of ancient Athens and Rome, in the College of Cardinals, and in the military throughout history. Even today we can see examples of the need for and use of staff in the highest office of the country, the Presidency. Today staff plays a major and critical role in all organized activities.

As organizations grow in size and complexity, the duties of the managers increase and they try to do more and more. Then managers add subordinate managers by creating more departments and delegating authority. Sooner or later, however, their span of management is so large that no more can be added because the managers cannot pay proper attention to them. At this point they add personal staff, which means one or more assistants to do the work that cannot be delegated. Again, sooner or later the assistant's knowledge is too general and not sufficiently qualified. Furthermore, other members of the organization also need the help of experts in many difficult areas, such as, fair employment practices and law. This is where organizational staffs are added to advise and support any member of the institution who needs their help. Today staff activities are increasing, as is the number of people working in them.

■ LINE AND STAFF ORGANIZATION

Much has been written and said about the concepts of line and staff, and probably no other area in the field of management has evoked as much discussion as these concepts. Many of the difficulties and frictions encountered in the daily life of an organization probably result from line and staff problems. Misconceptions and lack of understanding as to what line and staff really are can cause bitter feelings and conflicts of personalities, disunity, duplication of effort, waste, and lost motion.

As a supervisor of a department, you should know whether you are attached to your organization in a line capacity or a staff capacity. You might be able to find this out by reading the job description, and, if that does not clarify it, by asking your superior manager. Line and staff are not characteristics of certain functions; rather, they are characteristics of authority relationships. Therefore, the ultimate way to determine whether a department is related to the organizational structure as line or staff is to examine the intentions of the CEO. The CEO confers line authority on certain departments and places others into the organizational structure as staff. Staff is not inferior to line authority, or vice versa; they are just of a completely different nature. As we discuss these differences, keep in mind that the objectives of the staff elements are ultimately the same as those of the line organization, namely, achievement of the institution's overall goals—delivery of the best possible patient care.

Line Organization

The simplest of all organizational structures is the line organization. The line organization depicts the primary chain of command and is inseparable from the concept of authority. Thus, when we refer to line authority, we mean a superior and a subordinate with a direct line of command running between them. In every organization this straight direct line of superior-subordinate relationships runs from the top of the organization down to the lowest level of supervision. Figure 12-1 depicts an example of one direct line of authority running from the board of directors to the president of the institution, the director of nursing services, a nursing supervisor, a head nurse, a team leader, and finally to the other nursing employees.

■ **FIGURE 12-1 A direct line of authority.**

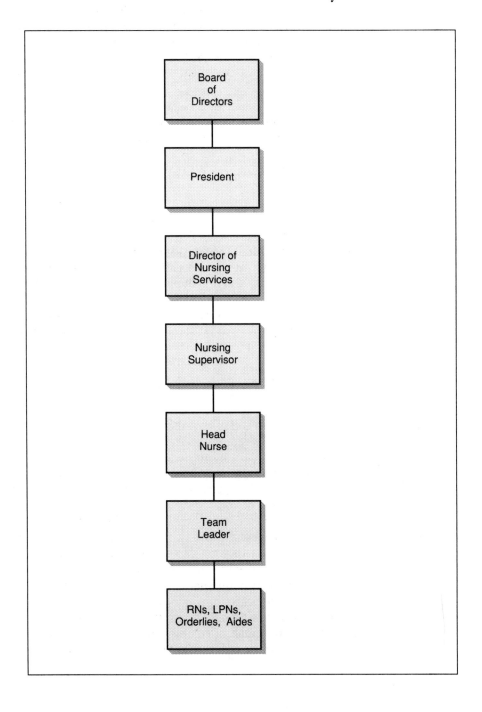

Unity of Command

The uninterrupted line of authority from the president to the team leader in Figure 12-1 ensures that each superior exercises direct command over the subordinate and that each subordinate has only one superior to whom he or she is accountable. This is known as the principle of unity of command, as discussed in Chapter 11. To repeat for this discussion, unity of command means that one person in each organizational unit has the authority to make the decisions appropriate to his or her position. Each employee has a single immediate supervisor, who in turn is responsible to his or her immediate superior, and so on up and down the chain of command. Thus, everyone in the line organization knows precisely who the boss is and who the subordinates are. The individual knows exactly where he or she stands, to whom orders can be given, and whose orders have to be fulfilled.

From what we have said thus far, it is easy to see that line authority can be defined as the authority to give orders, to command. It is the authority to direct others and require them to conform to decisions, plans, policies, and objectives. The primary purpose of this line authority is to make the organization work by evoking appropriate action from subordinates. Directness and unity of command have the great advantage of ensuring that results can be achieved precisely and quickly.

This type of direct line structure, however, does not answer all the needs of the modern organization. This structure was adequate when organizations and their environments were not as complex as they are today. In most enterprises now, activities have become so specialized and sophisticated that an executive cannot be expected to direct all his or her subordinates properly and expertly in all phases of their activities without some additional assistance. Line management today definitely needs the help of others to make the right decisions. That is, to perform the managerial functions properly, almost every line executive needs someone to lean on, someone who can give information, counsel, advice, and service. In short, a staff is needed.

Staff Organization

Staff is auxiliary in nature; it helps the line executive in many ways. Staff provides information, counsel, advice, and guidance in any number of specialized areas to all members of the organization whenever and wherever a need may exist. However, staff cannot issue orders or command line executives to take their advice. Staff can only make recommendations to the line. That advice can be accepted, ignored, rejected, or altered by the line. Because staff is an expert in its specialty, the advice is usually accepted, but it does not have to be. When the line accepts the staff's suggestion, this suggestion becomes a line order. Line authority is based on superior-subordinate relationships; it is positional and managerial. Staff's authority is based on expertise; it is advisory and not managerial. Obviously, staff is not inferior to line and line is not inferior to staff. They are just different, and both are needed to complement each other to achieve the objectives.

Although the right to command is not part of staff authority, there are two exceptions to this. First, within each staff department there exists a line of command with superior-subordinate relationships just as in any other department. Staff's own chain of command, however, does not extend over to the line organization. Rather, it exists alongside the line organization as shown in Figure 12-2. The second exception arises when staff has been given functional authority by the CEO. This important concept will be discussed fully later in the chapter.

■ **FIGURE 12-2 Staff's chain of command alongside the line organization.**

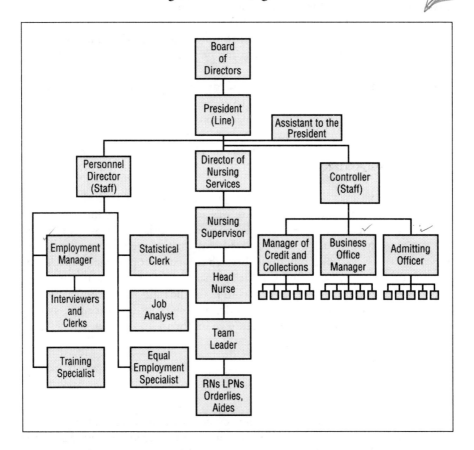

You can probably now see more clearly why all supervisors must know whether their position is attached to the organization in a line or a staff capacity. They must know this so that they will understand their function and relation to the other members of the organization. If it is staff, then the function is to provide information, guidance, counsel, advice, and service in this specialized area to whomever may ask for it. As far as the supervisor's own department is concerned, however, it will not matter whether the position is line or staff. Within every department the supervisor is the line manager. He or she is the only boss, regardless of whether the department is attached to the organization in a staff or a line capacity.

At this point, we must distinguish between *personal staff*, briefly mentioned already, and *specialized staff*. When executives find themselves in a position where they need a personal aide who will help them in the performance of duties that they cannot delegate, a personal staff position may be created. The person in this position is a staff aide to the particular executive rather than to the organization at large, for example, the assistant to the president shown in Figure 12-2. Eventually, however, a personal staff will usually become inadequate because this person normally is not sufficiently qualified and specialized; furthermore, many other members in the organization also need expert advice and guidance. At this juncture specialized staffs are introduced into the institution to provide counsel and advice in various special fields to any member of the organization who needs it. Our discussion in this chapter refers to these specialized staff positions.

■ RELATIONSHIPS BETWEEN STAFF AND LINE

Conflict over organizational and operational problems occasionally might arise between line and staff, regardless of how well the relationships were defined. This is because of the two types of authorities at work; positional and formal on one side, with the weight of expertise and knowledge on the other. In most organizations line and staff work together harmoniously. Harmonious cooperation between line and staff is especially important in a healthcare institution, since the input of so many specialists is necessary for the delivery of good healthcare. Much will depend on the sensitivity and tact of the staff people and the clarity of organizational arrangements.

It is common practice for certain activities in each organization to be undertaken as staff activities. This does not mean, however, that one can assume these activities are always staff. Line and staff, as stated before, are characteristics of authority relationships and not of functions. Thus, even a title will not offer any clue in recognizing line or staff. In industrial enterprises one typically finds a vice president of engineering, a vice president of human resources, and a vice president of production. None of these titles, however, indicates whether the position is line or staff. The little square box on the organizational chart also does not offer any help in this dilemma.

The same situation applies in hospitals and related healthcare facilities. For example, most hospital personnel managers are often known as vice president of human resources, and their departments operate in a staff capacity, although this is not obvious from their titles. The function of a staff human resources department is to provide advice and service on personnel matters to all the other departments of the institution. The human resources department is there to recruit, screen, and test applicants; keep personnel records; help provide reasonable wage and salary administration; advise line managers when difficult problems of fair employment practices or discipline arise; and so on. Whenever a line manager has a personnel problem, therefore, the specialized services of this staff department should be requested. Someone in the department of human resources certainly is best qualified to supply the current advice and information, since this is his or her background and only duty.

All the human resources manager can do, however, is submit suggestions to the line manager, who in turn can accept, alter, ignore, or reject them. If the line manager believes that the suggestions of the human resources department are not feasible, he or she is at liberty to make a different decision. Since the reason for establishing a staff in most instances is to obtain the best advice, however, it is usually in the interest of the line manager to follow staff suggestions. After all, staff members are the ones who really ought to know best. For all practical purposes the "authority" of the staff lies in their thorough knowledge of and expertise in dealing with problems in their specialized field. They will sell their ideas based on their *authority of knowledge,* not on their power to command. A person who acts in a staff relationship must know that his or her task is to advise, counsel, and guide, and not to give orders, except within his or her own department. If any of the suggestions of the staff are to be carried out, they are carried out under the name and authority of the line officer, not that of the staff person.

Functional Authority

As stated before, in most instances it is correct to say that staff provides advice and counsel to line managers but that staff lacks the right to command them. As mentioned, an important exception to this concept of staff exists: a staff office may have been given functional authority. *Functional authority* is authority restricted to a narrow area; it is a special right given to someone who normally would not have authority and therefore could not command. Although functional authority is limited to this area, it is full authority and gives this staff member the right and power to give orders outside of normal authority lines in this limited area. This right is based on expertise in the specialized field.

For example, an administrator decides that the human resources director's office should have the final word in cases of employee dismissal.[1] In recent years the laws, regulations, court decisions, and interpretations referring to fair employment practices have become an important area of managerial concern and a specialty that requires daily attention by someone in the organization. The department of human resources probably is best suited to keep up-to-date in this area. To avoid and minimize problems of this nature for the hospital, the administrator decides to confer the final decisions on separations to the human resources department. In this instance the administrator has conferred on staff (assuming that the human resources department in this institution is a staff activity) functional authority in the special area of dismissals. Now the human resources director has this authority, which no longer adheres to the line supervisors, who would normally have had the authority to do their own firing. This is an example of functional staff authority.

Functional authority undoubtedly violates the principle of unity of command. This principle, as you will recall, states that the subordinate is subject to orders from only one superior regarding all the functions. Functional authority, however, introduces a second superior for one particular function, such as the discharging of employees in our example. Functional staff orders have to be carried out by the line supervisor to whom they are directed. If the line supervisor should disagree strongly, he or she can appeal to the superior manager up the line. However, unless these orders are changed, which is unlikely, the supervisor has to comply with them.

Functional authority is advantageous because it allows for the maximum effective use of a staff specialist, leading to improved operations. It enables staff to intervene in line operations in situations designated by top-level management. The price for this intervention, violation of unity of command, is high and may cause friction in some organizations. It is up to the administrator to weigh the advantages versus the disadvantages before functional authority is assigned.

Assistants-to

The assistant-to is a personal staff position attached to a single executive, such as the assistant to the president in Figure 12-2. This person is an extension of the arms, legs, and mind of the manager; he or she does a variety of jobs, such as gather information, do research, and relieve the executive of details. This position is also often used for the training and development of junior managers to acquaint them with how higher-level executives function. The assistant-to position has no line authority. More interesting, however, is the role that individual often plays in the channels of informal communications and in the workings of the informal organization.

■ THE AUTHORITY OF ATTENDING PHYSICIANS AND SURGEONS

At this point we must discuss another line of internal authority found only in a hospital setting, the authority exercised by physicians and surgeons. Here we are not referring to those medical men and women who are full-time chiefs of the medical staff group, full-time chiefs of a medical specialty, or resident house physicians. Let us assume that all these are regular, full-time salaried employees of the hospital who do not have a private practice. Rather, our reference is to those *attending* physicians and surgeons who are in the private, fee-for-service, practice of medicine and who have been admitted to practice at the hospital. Only a staff physician, surgeon, or dentist can admit patients to the hospital.

The potential exists for tensions and misunderstandings between administration and members of the attending medical staff. This is understandable. The administration must consider the entire hospital as an organized activity, its relationships with all its employees, financial viability, its role in the community, etc., whereas the physicians' interests are likely to be geared to the patient and at times to the physicians' own economic survival. Members of the medical staff often wonder whether the administrative staff really understands their problems, and vice versa. Normally in most hospitals these frictions are minimal, since both groups strive toward the best results for the healthcare center. In most situations a natural partnership exists between administration and the physicians, the first providing the necessary facilities and personnel, and the latter providing the practice of medicine.

There is little doubt that such outside physicians are in charge of the patients they bring into the hospital. In this connection they have clinical-therapeutic-professional authority and exercise substantial influence throughout the hospital structure at many organizational levels and in many functions. These physicians admitted to practice at the hospital, usually referred to as the medical staff, are not shown on the hospital organizational chart in any direct line or staff relationship under the CEO. They are usually charted in a vague relationship to the board of directors on the chart. They practice medicine at the hospital, but they are outside of the administrative line of authority. They are "guests" who are granted practice privileges, but they have much authority over various people in the hospital.[2] Their authority is exercised over the patient and especially over the nursing staff when it comes to the medical issues. They also give orders to and expect compliance from many other employees of the hospital, for example, personnel in the radiology department, laboratories, and dietetics.

As a second line of "authority," such orders from a physician or a surgeon clearly violate the principle of unity of command. This may lead to a situation in which nursing personnel in particular are accountable to two "bosses"; that is, they must take orders from and are responsible to their supervisor and to the physician on the case. This can cause great difficulties when orders from the administrative source of authority and the medical professional source of authority are not consistent. Nevertheless, in a hospital the physician can give orders to an employee without being the line supervisor. In other words, the physician constitutes an outside source of authority who can marshal the resources of the hospital without being in the chain of command. The physician also is not responsible to the administrator, except for his or her professional responsibility to the medical world and to the hospital policies, rules, and regulations governing the medical staff. It is assumed that the physician's medical competence warrants the right and authority to remain in practice at the hospital.

This dual command obviously creates administrative and operational problems, as well as human problems. It causes difficulties in communication, discipline, and organizational coordination. Moreover, dual command can cause considerable confusion in cases when it is not clear where authority and responsibility truly reside. This can lead to frequent efforts on the physicians' part to circumvent administrative channels. By the same token, the administration may think that the physicians, through their power and authority, are interfering with administrative responsibilities. There probably will be some clarifications concerning this situation as hospitals' overall legal responsibilities are defined more clearly in the future. Regardless of all the complications inherent in this duality of command, it is an integral part of every general community hospital and exists in most other healthcare facilities as well.

■ SUMMARY

Management's organizing function is to design a structural framework that will enable the institution to achieve its objectives. First, we divided the work to be done horizontally into departments, then divided the managerial work vertically by delegating authority. Another result of specialization is the addition of staff to the organization. No manager could possibly possess all the knowledge, expertise, and information necessary to manage a modern healthcare institution, or any other organized activity, without the expertise and knowledge of specialists in many functional areas. This leads to the introduction of staff into the organization.

The CEO must decide whether a department is attached to the organization in a line or in a staff capacity. Since line and staff are quite different, it is essential for every supervisor to know in which capacity he or she serves. The supervisor in a straight direct chain of command that can be traced all the way to the top-level administrator is part of the line organization. The line organization generally follows the principle of unity of command, which means that each member of the organization has a single immediate superior. The person who is not within this line of command is attached to the organization as a staff person to provide expert counsel, service, and advice in a specialized field to whomever in the organization needs it. Staff people are not inferior to line, or vice versa; rather, they represent different types of authority relationships. The line manager has the authority to give orders, whereas the staff manager usually only has the authority to make recommendations. The advice can be accepted, ignored, rejected, or altered by the line manager who requested it. Because staff represents expertise in a specialty, however, the advice is usually accepted. Staff's authority is based on expertise; it is advisory, not managerial authority.

This situation changes in the case of functional authority. Sometimes the CEO may decide to confer functional authority on a staff office, that is, the right to give orders in a narrow area based on the staff person's expertise in a specific area. Although functional authority is limited to this area, it is full authority and the right and power to command outside of normal lines. Such functional authority violates the principle of unity of command. A similar difficult situation of duality of command is created by the attending physician's clinical-therapeutic authority. These additional channels of command result from the nature of healthcare delivery. Many areas of functional authority exist in most healthcare centers.

NOTES

1. This type of situation and the difficulties it can cause will be discussed further in Chapter 16 in connection with the supervisor's staffing function and the activities of the human resources director.
2. These remarks are necessarily general. They apply primarily to *general, private, community hospitals*. There are many ramifications in teaching hospitals or in hospitals operated by goverment agencies in which our statements would not apply or would have to be modified.

13

ORGANIZING ON THE SUPERVISORY LEVEL

Most department heads and supervisors are not likely to be involved in the major decisions concerning the overall organizational structure of their healthcare institution. However, they will be greatly concerned with the structure of their own department. Logically, we could not discuss the organizing process on the departmental level until we understood the basic principles of organizing and how they are applied in the design of the overall structure.

This is why we have discussed thus far the organizing process mainly from an overall institutional point of view. We have explored how the chief administrator establishes the formal organization structure and delegates organizational authority. With this broad understanding, we are now ready to approach the organizing function more specifically from the supervisor's point of view of the departmental goals and objectives, daily operations and activities, and existing personnel and resources. In other words, we will now look at organization on a narrow scale, zeroing in on the microcosm known as the department. We will focus attention on how a supervisor actually goes about organizing and delegating within his or her own department.

It should not be surprising to find that the organizing process is basically the same, whether it is performed by the chief executive officer (CEO) or the lowest line supervisor. Organizing involves grouping activities for purposes of departmentalization or subdepartmentalization on the supervisory level, assigning specific tasks and duties, and most importantly, delegating authority. In essence this means that the basic organizational principles must be understood and applied by supervisors when they are setting up their own department, just as they were by the chief administrator when the overall institution was structured. Let us see how a supervisor might go about applying these principles, using them on a day-to-day basis so that they are not just abstractions, but life-giving parts of a healthy departmental body.

■ IDEAL ORGANIZATION OF THE DEPARTMENT

Most supervisors are placed in charge of an existing department; only a few will ever have the opportunity to design a structure for a completely new department. When designing or rearranging the organizational structure of the department, the supervisor should conceptualize and plan for the ideal organization. The word *ideal* in this instance is not intended to mean *perfect;* rather, it is used to mean the *most desirable* organization for the achievement of stated objectives. It is the supervisor's job to design an organizational setup that will be best for this particular department. In so doing, the principles and guides of organizing must be observed. Following these is no guarantee that the department will not have any problems. A significant number of problems will be avoided, however, because the organizational network has been designed based on sound and proven principles and is likely to function smoothly in most cases.

The manager must bear in mind, however, that certain organizational concepts and arrangements that work well in a very large institution may not be applicable to a smaller institution. It is conceivable that in a 50-bed hospital a supervisor may be supervising two different activities, such as purchasing and medical records. In other words, supervisors must not blindly follow the idea that what is good for one enterprise is also good for another. Moreover, it is not essential that the manager's organizational plans for the department look pretty on paper or that the organizational chart appear symmetrical and well balanced. Rather, this ideal design should represent the most appropriate organizational arrangement for reaching the departmental objectives. It should be uniquely tailored to suit the conditions under which the manager works, instead of some abstract image of what an "ideal" department should look like.

In planning this ideal, but realistic, organization, the supervisor must consider it as something of a standard with which the present organizational setup can be compared. The ideal structure should be looked on as a guide to the short- and long-range plans of the department. Although the supervisor should carefully plan for the ideal structure on becoming the department's manager, this does not mean that the existing organization should be forced to conform to the ideal immediately. Each change in the prevailing organization, however, should bring the existing structure closer to the ideal. In other words, the ideal organization of the department represents the direction in which the supervisor will move as the organizing function is carried out.

■ INTERNAL DEPARTMENTAL STRUCTURE

At this point, you might be a bit unclear as to exactly how supervisors would go about designing the ideal departmental structure. What does this involve, how is it done, and are supervisors really equipped to do it? In most cases they are because essentially they are being asked to subdepartmentalize, to establish subdivisions or subunits within their department, just as the chief administrator established the overall divisions or units for the whole organization. Two examples of how a director of nursing services might subdepartmentalize or set up the internal departmental structure are shown in the organizational chart in Figures 13-1, 13-2, and 13-3. Additional information on this can be found in the appendix of this book.

■ **FIGURE 13-1 Internal departmental structure of a nursing service.**

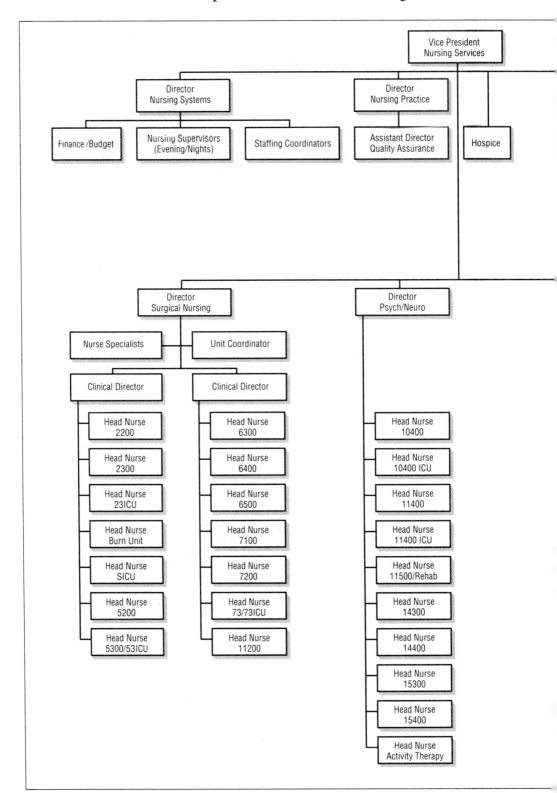

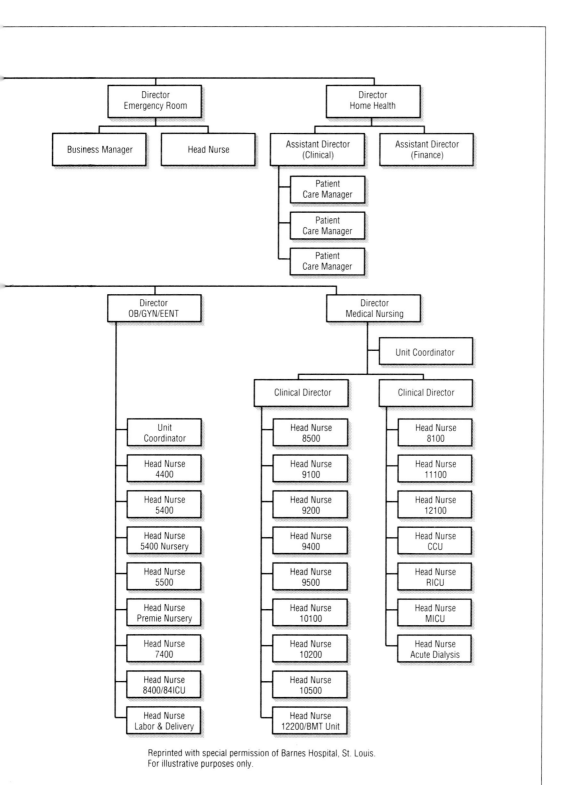

Reprinted with special permission of Barnes Hospital, St. Louis.
For illustrative purposes only.

■ FIGURE 13-2 Internal departmental structure
of a nursing service.

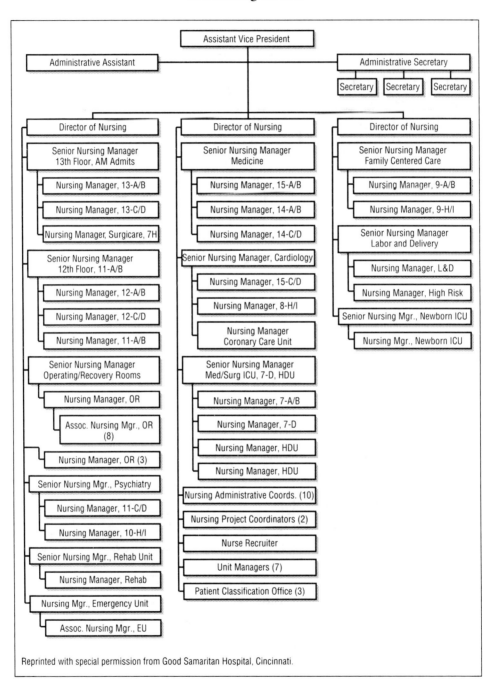

Reprinted with special permission from Good Samaritan Hospital, Cincinnati.

More specifically, what supervisors are being asked to do is to consider the groupings of activities in the department, the various existing positions, and the assignment of tasks and duties to these positions. Is what he or she finds the best possible arrangement for achieving departmental and institutional objectives? Are all the present positions necessary, or could some be eliminated or combined with others? Does each position have a fair assignment of tasks and duties, commensurate with its status and salary? Are the positions related so that there is no duplication of effort and that coordination and cooperation are facilitated? In other words, is the department well organized? Does it function in the most efficient manner? Are there any changes at all that the supervisor would like to see in the internal organizational structure of the department?

If there are any such changes, then these will become the basis for what we have been calling "the ideal organization of the department." They will become the organizational goals toward which the department head will strive when structuring the department.

If a supervisor is setting up a new department or working in a newly established institution, much of this ideal structure can probably be implemented right at the beginning. This would be the most desirable situation but is not generally the case. The supervisor is forced to implement organizational goals gradually while working within the existing departmental structure and with existing personnel.

Organization and Personnel

It is important to realize that the supervisor should design this ideal organization based on sound organizational principles, regardless of the people with whom he or she has to work. This does not mean that departments could exist without people to staff their various positions. Without people, of course, there can be no organization. The problems of organization should be handled in the right order, however; the sound structure comes first, then the people are asked to fulfill this structure.

If the organization setup is planned first around existing personnel, then existing shortcomings will be perpetuated. Because of incumbent personalities, too much emphasis may be given to certain activities and not enough to others. Moreover, if a department is structured around personalities, it is easy to imagine what would happen if a particular employee should be promoted or resign. If, on the other hand, the departmental organization is structured impersonally on the general need for personnel rather than on the incumbent personalities, it should not be difficult to find an appropriate successor for a particular position. Therefore, an organization should be designed first to serve the objectives of the department; then the various employees should be selected and fitted into departmental positions.

This, however, is easier said than done. In most instances the supervisor has been put into a managerial position in an existing and fully staffed department without having had the chance to decide on the present structure or personnel of the department. Frequently some of the available employees do not fit too well into the ideal structure, but they cannot all be overlooked or dismissed. In such

■ FIGURE 13-3 Internal departmental structure of a nursing service.

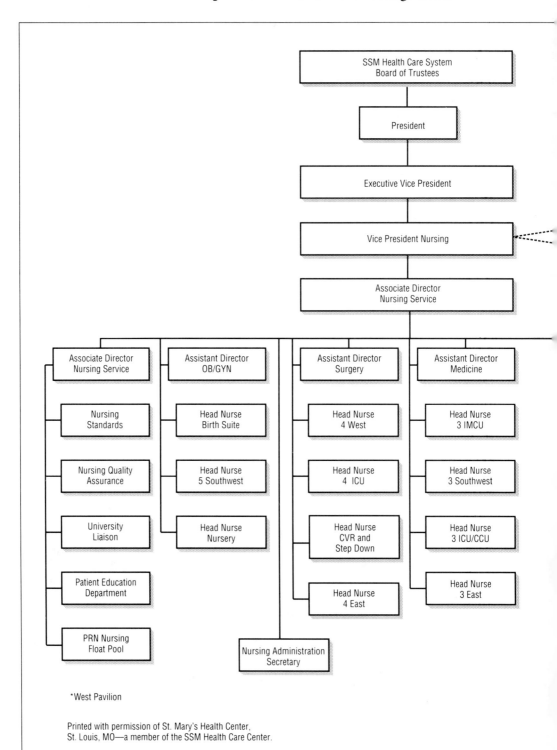

*West Pavilion

Printed with permission of St. Mary's Health Center,
St. Louis, MO—a member of the SSM Health Care Center.

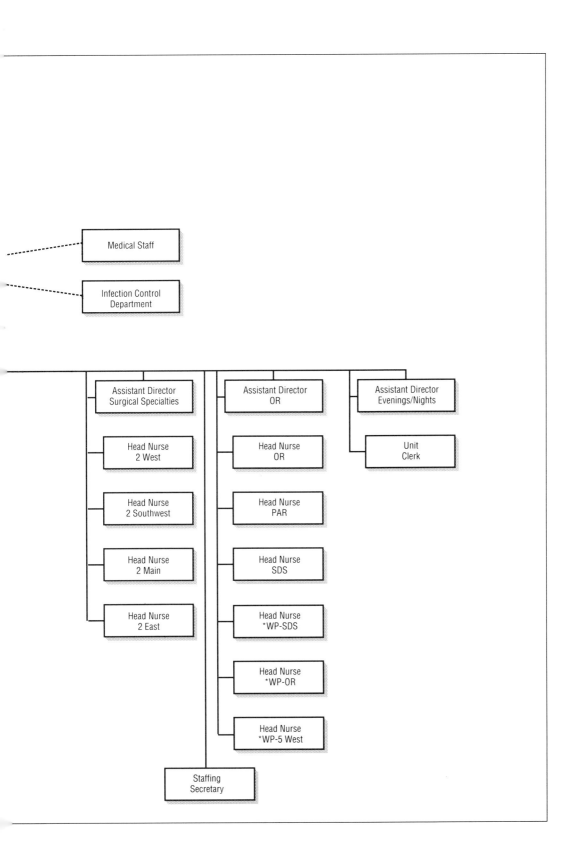

cases the best the supervisor can do for the time being is to adjust the organization to use the capacities of the employees he or she has. It should be realized that this is an accommodation of the ideal plan to fit present personalities; it should be regarded as temporary. Such personnel adjustments are sometimes necessary, but fewer of them will be required if the supervisor has already made a plan of the organization he or she would like to have if the ideal human resources were available. Then, as time goes on, the supervisor will strive to come closer and closer to the ideal departmental setup.

Reorganization

One must keep in mind that organizational structure is not static. The organization is a living institution and therefore needs a certain amount of adjustment as time goes on. For this reason, the manager's organizing function is continuous; there is a need for constantly checking, questioning, and appraising the soundness and feasibility of the departmental structure. Organization is not an end in itself, but rather a means to an end, the accomplishment of the objectives of the department. A manager must continuously watch for new developments, practices, and thinking in the field of organization. The supervisor must be willing to *reorganize* the department if developments warrant it or if it is indicated that the existing structure is too far from the ideal to permit effective functioning.

The term *reorganization* is used with all types of different connotations. In our discussion this term will refer to changes in the organizational structure, departmentalization, the assignment of activities, or authority relationships. From time to time a manager makes such changes because of scientific and technological advances, the dynamic and changing nature of the department's activities, or a shift of supervisors. As noted previously, reorganization also may be necessitated by the need to overcome existing deficiencies.

Let us look at a recent example of reorganization to overcome existing deficiencies.

As time went on, nurses found themselves burdened with a great amount of secretarial and clerical work that kept them away from actual patient care and bedside nursing. This was an undesirable situation, since the thrust of their education and purpose was the care of patients. Finally, it became apparent that many of these functions could be performed by someone else without a nursing education just as effectively; this led to the creation of positions now commonly known as unit managers, unit clerks, ward clerks, floor clerks, nursing station assistants, etc. The care of "things" was assigned to them, whereas the actual care of "people" reverted back to where it should be, the nurses.

The job of the unit clerk is to perform a variety of clerical duties, such as preparing, maintaining, and compiling records in the nursing unit. This person copies information from nurses' records, writes requisitions for laboratory tests, dispatches messages to other departments, transcribes physicians' orders, and so forth. The unit clerk also makes appointments for patient services in other departments as requested by the nursing and medical staff, maintains an established inventory of stock supplies for the unit by verifying supplies and making requisitions, and performs many other duties that the nursing personnel had to cope with previously in this situation. This was a case of reorganization where duties were reassigned and new authority relationships had to be established between unit managers, clerks, and head nurses.

Once this or any other type of reorganization has been decided on, it can be carried out either as a long-term, gradual, continued change or as a one-time change covering only a short period. The latter approach has typically been called the "earthquake" technique, indicating that the full shock of the reorganization is felt all at once. The long-range plan, on the other hand, provides for a period of more gradual adjustment to the organizational changes. No doubt this approach is less disturbing and creates fewer upsets than the earthquake approach.

One must remember that changes are always disturbing to those who are affected by them, regardless of how well intended they are. A manager who frequently changes the department's organizational structure runs the risk of damaging the morale of the subordinates. To the supervisor suggesting the reorganization, it might seem trivial, but to the subordinates it will probably appear frightening because it implies changes in their working environment, status, and security. The wise supervisor will have to learn how to strike a happy medium in the desirable amount of organizational change. In most instances the supervisor will probably find that most subordinates quickly adjust to changes if they are properly explained and if the need for them is demonstrated. A more detailed discussion of the introduction of change will be given in Chapter 19.

As stated briefly in our discussion on delegation of authority, from time to time it is necessary also to review the degree of authority that has been delegated. The supervisor may believe that he or she has lost control over certain activities and that it has become necessary to "tighten up" or to *recentralize*. In such a situation recentralization of authority is called for; that is, authority must be revoked or realigned. This is another form of reorganization that presents a difficult task for the supervisor, since feelings of suspicion, hurt, discouragement, and security on the part of the subordinate are likely to surface. To mitigate these tensions, the supervisor must explain the reasons for this action. Such an unpleasant situation can be lessened by taking great care in the choice of a subordinate when delegating authority in the first place.

Since organizing is a dynamic process, it should be emphasized that regardless of the difficulties and unpleasant aspects involved, it is necessary for a supervisor to make organizational adjustments occasionally to keep the department as viable as possible.

■ DELEGATION OF AUTHORITY ON THE SUPERVISORY LEVEL

Once a supervisor has organized or reorganized the department's internal structure, or at least planned the changes that are needed and recorded them in an ideal organizational design, the supervisor is ready to delegate or redelegate authority in accordance with the organizational structure. We assume that the supervisor has been given sufficient authority and that he or she is in charge of all the activities within this section. Just as any other manager, supervisors are faced with the necessity of delegating some of the authority that has been handed down to them. As mentioned previously, unless this is done, an organization has not been created. This is certainly the case when there are many employees. In other words, the supervisor must assign tasks, grant authority, and create responsibility within each of the subunits and for each of the positions in the department.

If a supervisor is taking over an existing department, consisting of a large and substantial number of employees, broad delegation of authority probably is in effect. It still is necessary, however, to check carefully whether all of it is consistent with the ideal organizational plans. The supervisor should check the amount and type of authority delegated to each position and whether the three essential steps in the process of delegation were followed. In other words, he or she should refer back to the specific procedure outlined in Chapter 11 to see that authority is delegated properly in the department.

Let us now turn to the situation where the number of employees in the supervisor's department is rather small. Such a department would consist merely of a supervisor and a few employees (three to six). The supervisor may wonder if in these circumstances it is necessary to delegate authority. The answer is yes. Even in a small department the supervisor will need someone who can be depended on to take over if the supervisor should have to leave either temporarily or for any length of time. Even in the smallest department there should be someone who can work as the supervisor's *backstop*. It is a sign of poor supervision when no one in a department can take over when the supervisor is sick or has to be away from the job. The supervisor also may miss a promotion because there is nobody to take charge of the unit. Thus, sooner or later every supervisor needs a backstop, understudy, assistant, or whatever this person may be called. It would be appropriate for the supervisor to discuss this intention with his or her immediate boss as well.

Availability of Trained Subordinates

The process of delegation assumes that there is someone available who is willing to accept authority. As a supervisor, you may have wanted to delegate more and more authority to some of your subordinates and to make one of them your assistant, but you had no one within your department who was willing to accept this arrangement and to take charge of an area of activities. You may not have anyone working for you who is capable of handling more authority. In such a case authority, for the moment at least, cannot be delegated and must be withheld.

On the other hand, you may find yourself in a vicious circle, complaining that without better trained subordinates you cannot delegate. Without delegating additional authority, however, your subordinates still have no opportunity to ever obtain the necessary exposure. With additional experience and training, their judgment could be improved and they could become more capable subordinates. Although this lack of trained subordinates is often used by supervisors as an excuse for not delegating authority, the supervisor must always bear in mind that unless a beginning in the delegation process is made, no subordinate capable of being a backstop and of taking over the department (if necessary) will ever be available.

It is the supervisor's duty to develop and train such a person, and in the process more authority most likely can be delegated not only to the individual selected as a backstop but to other employees as well. Moreover, this process of training for increased delegation will give the supervisor a much clearer view of his or her own duties, the workings of the department, and the various jobs to be performed. Bringing subordinates to the point where they can finally be given considerable authority is a slow and tedious process, but it is worth the effort. In the early stages the degree of authority granted will be small, but as subordinates grow in their capacities, increasingly more authority can be delegated to them.

The Supervisor's Hesitancy to Delegate

Often supervisors do not like the idea of creating a backstop; they may be reluctant to delegate authority because they know that they cannot delegate responsibility. Since in the final analysis responsibility remains with them, they may think it is best to make all decisions themselves. Thus, out of fear of their subordinates' mistakes, many supervisors are not willing to delegate authority and, as a result, continue to overburden themselves. Their indecision and delay may often be costlier than the mistakes they hoped to avoid by retaining their authority. Always remember the likelihood exists that the supervisor may make mistakes as well. Moreover, if employees are permitted to learn from some of their own mistakes, they will not resent the supervisor's authority, and they will be more willing to accept greater authority themselves.

As stated, the supervisors' reluctance in delegating such authority is understandable in view of their continued accountability for the results. The traditional picture of a good supervisor was one who rolled up the sleeves and worked right alongside the employees, thus setting an example by his or her efforts. Such a description is particularly true of a supervisor who has come up through the ranks and for whom the supervisory position is a reward for hard work and professional or technical competence. This person has been placed in a managerial position without having been equipped to be a manager and is faced with new problems that are difficult to cope with. This person therefore retreats to a pattern in which he or she feels secure and works right alongside the employees. Occasionally such participation is needed, for example, when the job to be performed is particularly difficult or when an emergency has arisen. Under these conditions the good supervisor will always be right on the job to help. Aside from such emergencies and unusual situations, however, most of the supervisor's time should be spent carrying out the supervisory job, and the employees should be doing their assigned tasks. It is the supervisor's job not to do, but to see that others get things done.

Frequently, however, supervisors will still think that if they want something done right, they have to do it themselves. Often they believe that it is easier to do the job than to correct the subordinate's mistake. Even if the supervisor lets the subordinate do it, the supervisor may feel a strong temptation to correct any mistakes rather than explain to the subordinate what should have been done. It is frequently more difficult to teach than to do a job oneself. Moreover, supervisors often believe that they can do the job better than any of their subordinates, and they are probably right. Sooner or later, however, they will have to get used to the idea that someone else can do the job almost as well as they can, and at that point they should delegate the necessary authority. In this manner they will be able to save their own time for more important managerial jobs, for thinking, planning, and more delegating. If supervisors are willing to see to it that employees become increasingly competent with every additional job, then their own belief and confidence in their employees' work will also grow. This mutually advantageous relationship will permit the supervisor to carry out the basic underlying policy of delegating more and more authority as the employees demonstrate their capability in handling it.

Despite the fact that a certain amount of authority must be delegated to create an organization, some supervisory duties cannot be delegated. The supervisor should always apply and interpret policies, give general directions for the department, take necessary disciplinary action, promote employees, and appraise them. Aside from these duties, however, their subordinates should perform most tasks by themselves.

Selecting a Backstop

As we have said, this process of delegation of authority should include making one particular subordinate into an assistant for the supervisor. The first step is to select the right person for the job. The supervisor undoubtedly knows which employees are more outstanding. These would be the ones to whom the other employees turn in case of questions and who are looked on as leaders. Outstanding employees, moreover, know how to do the job very well, seem to be able to handle problems as they arise, and do not get into arguments. They should also have shown good judgment in the way they organize and go about their own job, should be open-minded, and should be interested in further development and moving into better positions. Without such ambitions, even the best training would not achieve any results. Outstanding employees must have shown a willingness to accept responsibility and must have proven dependability. Sometimes a worker may not have had the opportunity to show all these qualities. Whatever qualities have remained latent, however, will show up rather quickly during the actual training process.

If the supervisor has two or three equally good employees in the department, training all of them for greater delegations of authority on an equal basis should begin. Sooner or later it will be obvious which one has the superior ability, and this individual will then become the major trainee for the backstop position. Once the selection of a single person is made (or in a large department there could be several backstops), it is not necessary to come out with general formal announcements in this respect. Of course, the supervisor should discuss and explain the intentions fully to the employee chosen. More importantly the supervisor must follow through by laying a thorough groundwork for good training so that the one who has been chosen will work out as an understudy.

The Reluctant Subordinate

The delegation of authority and especially the development of an understudy are two-sided relationships. Although the supervisor may be ready and willing to turn over authority, the subordinates may sometimes be reluctant to accept it. Frequently subordinates may feel unsure of themselves, unsure that they will be able to handle the job assigned to them. They may be reluctant to leave the security of their job and their co-workers. Merely ordering them to have more self-confidence will have little effect. The supervisor, as we have said, must create this self-confidence by carefully coaching and training the subordinate to undertake more and more difficult assignments. Then, and only then, will the subordinate be able to accept the increased responsibility that goes along with harder tasks and greater authority.

With increased responsibilities there should also be commensurate positive incentives. These may be in the form of pay increases, bonuses, a fancier title, recognized status within the organization, or other rewards of a tangible and intangible nature. Such rewards will include the self-satisfaction that the subordinate feels when he or she is able to handle increased responsibility and is moving up in the organizational ranks.

Training a Backstop

Although the phrase "training a subordinate" is frequently used, the term *training* is really not appropriate. It would be more fitting to speak of the development or even self-development on the subordinate's part. Understudies must be eager to improve themselves and show the initiative to be self-starters.

The supervisor should gradually let understudies in on the workings of the department, explain some of the reports to them, and show them how needed information is obtained. The supervisor should tell them what is done with these reports and why it is done. The supervisor should also introduce an understudy to other supervisors and other people in the organization with whom they must associate and contact; sooner or later the understudy should contact them himself or herself. It is advisable to take the understudy along to some of the institution's meetings after this person has had a chance to learn the major aspects of the supervisor's job. On such occasions the supervisor should show how the work of the department is related to that of the other departments in the healthcare facility.

As daily problems arise, the supervisor should let understudies participate in them and even try to solve some of them for themselves. By letting understudies come up with some solutions to problems, the supervisor will have a chance to see how well they analyze and how much they know about making decisions. In time the supervisor should give the understudy some areas of activities for which he or she will be entirely responsible. In other words, gradually more duties and authority should be assigned.

This whole process requires an atmosphere of confidence and trust. The boss must be looked on by the understudy as a coach and friend, not as a domineering superior. Supervisors should caution themselves that in their eagerness to develop the understudy as rapidly as possible, they do not overload them or pass problems that are beyond the backstop's capabilities. The supervisor must never lose sight of the fact that it takes time to be able to handle problems of any magnitude.

All of this will require much effort and patience on the supervisor's part. At some time the additional duties should result in some tangible rewards for the backstop. Conceivably, just about the time the understudy comes to the point of being truly helpful, he or she may be transferred to another job outside of the supervisor's department. This may be discouraging for the moment, but the supervisor may rest assured that the administrators will give credit for a training job well done.

■ ACHIEVING DELEGATION OF AUTHORITY

Broader delegations of authority are not always easily put into practice. To be effective, a sincere desire and willingness to delegate must permeate the entire organization. Top-level management must set the mood by not only preaching but also by practicing broad delegation of authority. Although top management's intentions may be the best, at times the desired degree of decentralization of authority may not be achieved. For instance, top management may find that authority has not been delegated as far down as it intended because somewhere along the line there is an "authority hoarder," a person who simply will not delegate authority any further. This person grasps all the authority delegated to him or her without redelegating any of it.

There are several reasons why managers might resist further decentralization of authority in this manner. To some, the delegation of authority may mean a loss of status or a loss of power and control. Others may think that by having centralized power they are in closer contact with top-level administration. Still other managers are truly concerned with the expenses involved in delegating authority. Moreover, it is difficult for many managers to part with some of their own authority and still be left with full responsibility for the decisions made by their subordinates.

There are several ways to cope with this problem and to achieve the degree of decentralization that is desired by the top-level administration. As stated before, the entire managerial group must be indoctrinated with the philosophy of decentralization of authority. They must understand that by carefully delegating authority they do not lose status, nor do they absolve themselves of their responsibilities. One way of putting this understanding into practice is to request that each manager have a fairly large number of subordinate managers reporting to him or her. By stretching the span of management, the subordinate manager has no choice but to delegate authority. Another way to achieve broader delegations of authority is for the enterprise to adopt the policy of not promoting a manager until a subordinate manager has been developed who can take over the vacated position. By doing this, as noted in the discussion of backstops, the manager is encouraged to delegate as much authority as possible at an early stage. Moreover, this process creates an ideal organizational climate in which the subordinates can find maximum satisfaction of many of their most important needs.

■ DELEGATION AND GENERAL SUPERVISION

Now that we have discussed the delegation of authority to employees within a small department who work directly below their supervisor, we have reached the lowest rung of the organizational ladder, and further delegation of authority is no longer possible. There is an end to delegation in the strict sense of the word when we reach the point of execution of daily duties, in other words, when we reach the level of employees who are actually doing the work. Since we have reached this level, the question now arises as to how a supervisor can effectively reap the benefits of delegation, that is, how the supervisor can take advantage of the motivating factors of delegation in the daily working situation. The answer to this question can be found at the point where the philosophy of delegation takes on the form of what is commonly referred to as *loose,* or *general, supervision.*

General supervision means merely giving orders in broad general terms. It means that the supervisor, instead of watching every detail of the employee's activities, is primarily interested in the results achieved. The supervisor permits the subordinates to decide how to achieve these results within accepted professional standards and organizational requirements. The supervisor sets the goals and tells the subordinates what is to be accomplished, fixing the limits within which the work has to be done, but the employees are to decide how to accomplish these goals. This gives each employee maximum freedom within the constraints of the organizational and professional standards.

The Employee's Reaction to General Supervision

Most employees accept work as a part of normal healthy life. Accordingly, most managers display the underlying managerial attitude of McGregor's Theory Y toward their employees.[1] Such managers understand that in their daily jobs employees seek a satisfaction that wages alone cannot provide. Most employees also enjoy being their own bosses. They like a degree of freedom that allows them to make their own decisions pertaining to their work. The question arises as to whether this is possible if one works for someone else, whether such a degree of freedom can be granted to employees if they are to contribute their share toward the achievement of the enterprise's objectives. This is where the ideas of delegation of authority and general supervision can help. The desire for freedom, for being one's own boss, can be enhanced and fulfilled by delegation of authority, which in a working situation means general supervision. In the daily work environment this broad, general type of supervision on the employee level has the same motivating results as the delegation of formal authority throughout the managerial hierarchy.

Advantages of General Supervision

Significant advantages result from this approach to supervision and are similar to those cited in our discussion of the process of delegation. The supervisor who learns the art of general supervision will benefit in many ways. First, the supervisor will have more time to be a manager. If the supervisor tried to practice close, detailed supervision and tried to make every decision personally, he or she would probably be exhausted physically and mentally. With delegation, however, the supervisor will be freed from many of the details of the work and will thus have time to plan, organize, and control. In so doing, the supervisor will be freed to receive and handle more authority and responsibility.

Moreover, the decisions that general supervision allows employees to make will probably be superior to those made by a harried supervisor trying to practice detailed supervision. We have already pointed out that the employee on the job is closest to the problem and therefore is in the best position to solve it. Furthermore, this will give the employees a chance to develop their own talents and abilities and become more competent. It is always difficult for a supervisor to instruct an employee on how to make decisions without letting employees make them. They can really only learn by practice.

This leads us to the third advantage of general supervision; it enables employees to take great pride in the results of their decisions. As stated before, employees enjoy being independent. Repeated surveys reveal that the one quality employees most admire in a supervisor is the ability to allow them to be independent by delegating authority. Employees want a boss who shows them how to do a job and then trusts them enough to let them do it on their own. In this way the supervisor provides on-the-job training for them and a chance for better positions. Thus, we can see that general supervision allows for the progress not only of supervisors themselves, but also of the employees, the department, and the enterprise as a whole.

Much more will be said about general supervision when we discuss the managerial function of influencing. Let us briefly state that practicing the broad, general approach to supervision, instead of an autocratic, dictatorial, detailed approach, provides many of the satisfactions employees seek on the job, which money alone does not cover. Because this approach fulfills many of their needs, employees are motivated to put forth their best efforts in achieving the enterprise's objectives.

Attitudes toward General Supervision

It seems appropriate at this stage to point out that the broad, general approach to supervision and the idea that one must provide positive motivation for employees were not always as widely accepted as they are today. In the past some managers believed that emphasis on negative authority was the best method of motivating employees. Those who depended on the force of authority as their major means of motivation—and a few may still erroneously believe in this today—believed that managing consisted of forcing people to work by threatening to fire them if they did not. Their assumptions were that the only reason people work is to earn money and that they will work only if they fear losing their jobs. This approach ignores the fact that employees want many other intrinsic satisfactions from their work besides the salary. It also assumes that people do not like work, that they try to get away with doing as little as possible. On this basis the need for close supervision is justified. The supervisor must tell the workers precisely what is to be done every minute of the day and not permit the workers any chance to use their own judgment. The older school of managerial thought was based on Theory X (see Chapters 19 and 21) as its underlying assumption.

Such reliance on the sheer weight of authority has lost most of its followers. This approach was possible in the early days of the Industrial Revolution when workers were close to starvation and would do anything to obtain food, clothing, and shelter. In recent years, however, employees have begun to expect much more from their jobs. This is particularly true when most of the employees are professionals and when times are good and employment is high. We also find that the educational process of our youth has had a significant influence on recent attitudes. Many years ago children were accustomed to strict obedience toward their elders. Now schools and homes emphasize freedom and self-expression, and it is therefore becoming more and more difficult for the young employee to accept any kind of autocratic management on the job. In addition to this, legislation, regulations, and the impact of unions have made it more difficult for a supervisor to fire an employee.

Perhaps the most important change in current attitudes is the increased awareness that the "be strong" form of "motivation" provides no incentive to work harder than the minimum required to avoid punishment and discharge. Under these conditions employees will probably dislike work, which, if workers are not unionized, can lead to slowdowns, sabotage, and spoilage. Management will probably react by watching workers even more closely. This in turn will encourage the employees to try to outsmart the administration. Thus, a vicious circle is started with new restraints and new methods of evading them. Sooner or later such a circle will produce aggression, arguments, fights, and a general devastating effect on the entire organization.

■ SUMMARY

In this chapter we considered the organizing process from the supervisor's point of view. Basically, organizing on the departmental level involves the same general steps as organizing the overall institution, that is, grouping activities or sub-departmentalizing, assigning specific tasks and duties, and delegating authority. The supervisor should supplement these steps, however, by designing an ideal organizational structure specifically for his or her particular department. Such a structure represents the way the supervisor would organize the unit if starting from scratch with ideal resources and personnel. In most cases, however, the supervisor comes into an existing department and cannot immediately implement an ideal organizational design. One reason may be that the available personnel do not fit into this model. What must be done instead is to plan changes or completely reorganize the department to make it come closer to the ideal. Such reorganization is a normal and important part of managerial life; however, it should not be done so frequently that it undermines the security and morale of employees. Organizational changes can be implemented either all at once or gradually, depending on the imminence of the need for them.

After reorganization has been accomplished or at least planned, the supervisor can proceed to delegate or redelegate authority in accordance with the departmental structure. In a large or medium department the process of delegation will be that outlined in Chapter 11: assigning duties, granting the authority to carry out these duties, and encouraging employees to accept responsibility for their duties. In a small department the delegation of authority will take the form of developing a backstop, an understudy who can take over when the supervisor is not there. This is a long and tedious process because it involves careful development and progressively increasing delegations of authority. It is well worth the effort, since it will contribute to high motivation and morale among employees. Moreover, unless the supervisor does train someone to be the backstop and does grant authority to that person, the supervisor will not have created any organization. Then the department is bound to collapse if the supervisor is absent for any length of time or leaves the scene.

This decentralization of authority is not as easily achieved as it might seem. Management frequently runs into obstacles that must be overcome to achieve broad delegation. These obstacles may be caused by an authority hoarder somewhere down the line, a subordinate's reluctance to shoulder authority and responsibility, or the unavailability of suitable subordinates to whom authority can be delegated.

At some point in the organization further delegation of authority is not possible. This is at the interface between the supervisor and the nonmanagerial employees as they go about performing their daily tasks. At this level delegation of authority expresses itself in the practice of a general, or loose, type of supervision that involves giving employees a great amount of freedom in making decisions and determining how to do their jobs. In other words, general supervision is an application of Theory Y and not Theory X (see Chapters 19 and 21). It enables the employees to use their own judgment, and, in so doing, they will receive greater satisfaction from their jobs. Such general supervision is probably also the best way to motivate employees, whereas dependence on the sheer weight of authority would normally bring about the least desirable results. Occasionally the manager must fall back on formal authority, but with the newer attitudes and expectations of our society, the general trend is toward more freedom and self-determination in management, as well as in other aspects of life.

NOTES
1. Theories X and Y will be discussed fully in Chapters 19 and 21.

14

COMMITTEES AS AN ORGANIZATIONAL TOOL

We find committees, boards, task forces, commissions, and teams everywhere—in business, government, schools, churches, and certainly in healthcare organizations. The continuous growth in size and specialization makes the administration and coordination of a large institution by the chief executive officer (CEO) and associates increasingly difficult and, at the same time, more necessary. One method to cope with this difficulty is to establish committees and turn over to them specific problems. Committees are an organizational tool that, if utilized properly, can be of great help in the smooth functioning of an enterprise. A *committee is a group of people who function collectively by working together,* whether their purpose is to make a decision, submit a recommendation, solve a problem, conduct an investigation, manage a government agency, or so forth. It differs from other units of management insofar as committee members normally have regular full-time duties in the organization and devote only part of their time to committee activities.

Yet the amount of time spent in committee activities is increasing. There is definitely a growing emphasis on committee meetings within today's organizations. This is true for several reasons. First, since most enterprise activities have become more complex and specialized, there is an increased and more urgent need for coordination and cooperation. Conferences and meetings have proved to be a good means of answering this need. Another reason for the emphasis on meetings is the growing realization that people are more enthusiastic about carrying out directives and plans that they have helped to devise than those handed down from above. Thus, committees are an additional means for effectively combining the formal and the acceptance theories of authority, giving employees more freedom, greater delegation of authority, and more motivation.

As we know, the job of a supervisor is to get things done through and with the help of the employees in the department. Skill in establishing, running, and participating in committee meetings will significantly help in achieving this objective. Although a common complaint is that there are too many meetings and that they take up too much time, committees are still a widely used device in all organizations, especially in healthcare centers. They seem to have no substitutes. Without committee meetings, it would be almost impossible for an organization of any size to operate efficiently and effectively. Of the many ways of obtaining ideas and opinions on how to handle certain problems, there is really no better way than by holding a meeting. The real criticism of meetings is probably not that there are too many, but that the results produced often do not warrant the time and effort invested.

No doubt you have sometimes been annoyed at being tied up in a meeting in which the chairperson was allowed to amble along in all directions, without any purpose whatsoever. In the meantime, more important work was accumulating on your desk. It is very likely that the chairperson had not properly prepared the meeting, and that the performance did not increase your respect for his or her managerial ability. After an experience of this type, you can quickly see how important it is for supervisors to acquaint themselves with committee meetings and with committee or conference leadership techniques. In other words, supervisors should learn how to run committees well and how to obtain effective participation. Meetings will then become increasingly interesting and stimulating because the participants will have the satisfaction of knowing that the meeting is accomplishing something.

Therefore, all supervisors must familiarize themselves with the workings of a committee. There may be occasions when the supervisor will find it necessary to establish an intradepartmental or interdepartmental committee or to chair a committee. At other times, the supervisor may only be an ordinary member of the committee. Also, there will definitely be many instances when the supervisor will have to act as a conference leader or chairperson of a committee made up only of employees of the department.

■ THE NATURE OF COMMITTEES

Definitions

A committee is a group of people to whom certain matters have been committed. They meet for the purpose of discussing those matters that have been assigned to them. As just stated, committees function collectively, and their members normally have other duties, making their committee work merely a part-time assignment. Because committees function only as a group, they differ considerably from other managerial devices.

Committees can be found at all organizational *levels*, and the chances are that at some time a committee exists or existed for every organizational activity.

Committees can be *line* or *staff*. The committee works on the problem assigned to it. When a solution is reached, a committee that has line authority will make a decision. If the committee is acting in a staff capacity, however, it will merely make a recommendation after having analyzed and debated the problem.

Committees can be classified as *standing* or *temporary*. A standing committee has a formal, permanent place in the organization. Typically it deals with the same set of recurring problems on a continuous basis; in a hospital, for instance, the quality assurance, surgical review, tissue, infection, safety, and many others would be considered standing committees. A temporary committee, on the other hand, is one that has been appointed for a particular purpose and that will be dissolved as soon as it has accomplished its task. This type is also known as an *ad hoc* committee. At times, it is called a *task force* charged with a narrow purpose and a short time frame.

Functions of Committees

The Committee as a Place to Inform or to Discuss

Most committee meetings may be described as either informational or discussional. In an *informational meeting* the leader or chairperson does most of the talking to present certain information and facts. Assume, for example, that a supervisor wants to make an announcement and a meeting is called as a substitute for posting a notice or speaking to each employee separately. It may be expensive to take the entire work force away from the job, but, on the other hand, it guarantees that everyone in the department is notified of the new directive at the same time. Such a meeting also gives subordinates a chance to ask questions and discuss the implications of the announcement. Care should be taken, however, that questions from participants are largely confined to further clarifications of the supervisor's remarks so that the meeting will not stray from its purpose.

In the *discussional meeting* the chairperson encourages more participation of the members to secure their ideas and opinions. The supervisor could ask the individuals singly for suggestions on how to solve a problem, but it is probably better to call a meeting to allow them to make recommendations. Although it is up to the supervisor to make the final decision and to determine whether or not to incorporate some of the employees' suggestions, the employees will nevertheless derive great satisfaction from knowing that their ideas have been considered and may even be used. Some good suggestions probably will be offered, and the implementation of suggestions most likely will be more enthusiastic if the employees of the department have participated in finalizing them. In this case the committee acted in a staff capacity.

The supervisor can also go beyond merely asking for suggestions. A meeting may be called for the sole purpose of having the employees of the department fully discuss and handle a problem themselves, that is, come up with their own decision. As discussed next, this involves using the committee as a sort of collective managerial decision maker.

Decision-Making Committees

In addition to committees whose purpose is to spread information or merely discuss a matter and make recommendations, other committees are delegated formal authority to make decisions. Just as a supervisor can delegate decision-making authority to an individual subordinate, so can a committee be formed and authority delegated to the group to decide on a solution to a problem. In these instances the committee has decision-making power, in other words, line authority.

Many questions in a healthcare center are of such magnitude and affect so many departments that it is far better to have the decision made by a committee consisting of representatives of several functions than by the administrator or one of the associate administrators alone. The same situation can exist within a department. For example, frequently employees are dissatisfied with the allocation of overtime, weekend work, etc., regardless of the supervisor's efforts to be fair. Naturally the supervisor can make a decision for the employees on these matters, but it would be better if they could find a solution themselves. In such a case management is not really concerned with precisely what decision is made so long as it falls within the limits set, for example, that the time allotted for overtime is not exceeded. By letting the group make this type of decision, they will come up with an acceptable solution. Even if such a solution is only adequate and not necessarily the best, it is still better if it is implemented by the group with greater enthusiasm than a perfect decision that meets with their resistance. There are many problems and areas in which management is not concerned with the details of the decision as long as it remains within certain predetermined boundaries.

Benefits of Committees

There is little doubt that a group of individuals exchanging opinions and experiences often comes up with a better answer than any one person thinking through the same problem alone. This is perhaps the major benefit of group discussion. The old saying states that "two heads are better than one." Various people will bring to a meeting a wide range of experience, background, information, perspective, and ability far beyond that of an individual; this would not be available if the subject had been committed to an individual decision maker. Indeed, many problems are so complicated that a single person could not possibly have all the necessary knowledge to come up with a wise solution. The free oral interchange of alternatives and evaluation of ideas among several persons will stimulate and clarify thinking.

Group deliberation can also be a real help in promoting coordination and cooperation. Members of the committee become more considerate of the problems of other employees, supervisors, and administration. They become more aware of the advantages of and the need for working together and seeking cooperative solutions. By being involved in the analysis, logic, rationale, and solution of a problem, individual members are more likely to accept and implement what has been decided. In reality, it matters little how much a person actually contributed to the plan, as long as this individual was a member of the committee and sat in on the meeting. Probably the most significant benefit of committees in health services organizations is the promotion of coordination and cooperation between the various units of the institution.

Committees have a number of additional benefits. They produce continuity in the organization; few committees replace all their members at the same time.

Furthermore, they are a good environment for junior managers and executives to learn how decisions are made, absorb the philosophy and thinking of the hospital, and see how it functions. Also it gives representatives from the various departments a chance to be represented, heard, and involved in the affairs of the organization.

Disadvantages of Committees

Despite all these beneficial features, the committee has often been abused. Sometimes committees are created to delay action, and many people have come to think of the committee as a debating society. Jokes about committees are numerous. They have been defined as a group "that keeps minutes but wastes hours," "where the unwilling appoint the unfit to do the unnecessary," "where the camel is a horse designed by a committee," and so forth. Remarks are often made that there are meetings all day long without leaving any time to get the work done. Indeed, one of the most often-voiced complaints about committees is that they are exceedingly *time consuming*. This is true, since each member is entitled to have his or her say, and often certain individuals use up a great amount of time trying to convince other members of the validity of their points of view.

In addition to their costliness in time, committees also cost *money*. It is clear that time spent in committee meetings is not spent otherwise. Thus, every hour taken up by a meeting costs the institution a certain amount of dollars. Furthermore, there might be travel expenses involved and additional expenses for the preparation of meetings. Obviously, a single executive could reach an answer in a much shorter time and at less expense, but the problem is whether this decision would be as good as the one reached by group deliberation.

Another shortcoming of committees is that there are limitations to the *sense of responsibility* that they evoke. When a problem is submitted to a committee, it is submitted to a group and not to individuals. Responsibility does not weigh as heavily on the group's shoulders as it would on one individual's. In other words, the committee's problems become everybody's responsibility, which in reality means they are nobody's responsibility. It is difficult to criticize the committee as a whole or any single member if the solution proves to be wrong, since each person is quick to answer that the "committee" made the decision. Members are willing to settle for less than the best solutions and blame the committee if the solution does not work out. The thinning-out of responsibility is natural, and there is no way of avoiding it.

The dangers of a *weak compromise decision* and *tyranny of the minority* are other shortcomings of committees. It has often become a tradition to reach decisions of unanimity based on politeness, cooperative spirit, mutual respect, and other considerations; however, this often leads to committee action that is a weak, watered-down, undesirable compromise solution, frequently using the lowest common denominator instead of the optimum solution. Also, in their efforts for unanimous or nearly unanimous conclusions, committees may be tyrannized by a minority or a dominant individual holding out as long as possible. Finally, the majority might allow itself to be dominated by such a minority or a dominant personality because of lack of time, interest, or sense of responsibility. This may even lead to a strain in working relationships outside of the committee.

Another danger is that committee members may become victims of the *groupthink* phenomenon.[1] This phenomenon can be characterized as a way of thinking in a group where deliberations are dominated by a desire to concur at any expense, even at the danger of overriding any realistic appraisal of alternative action and of voicing doubts and dissent. Under this influence, the group is likely to make decisions that are not in the best interest of the organization in order to avoid conflict and dissent.

■ THE EFFECTIVE OPERATION OF A COMMITTEE

After realizing the many advantages and certain shortcomings, administration has decided to establish a number of committees, since ultimately, they will contribute to the smooth functioning of today's sophisticated organizational climate. In addition to these committees, a number of committees exist in all healthcare centers to fulfill the requirements of the Joint Commission on Accreditation of Healthcare Organizations or other accrediting agencies, such as for ambulatory healthcare.

Therefore, supervisors must familiarize themselves with the means for ensuring effective committee operation and conference leadership. It is not easy to make committee meetings and conferences a success because the goals are numerous and difficult to achieve. As we have already indicated, the goals of a committee meeting are (1) to come up with the best suggestions or solutions for the problem under consideration, (2) to arrive at suggestions or solutions with a majority or ideally unanimity, and (3) to accomplish objectives in the shortest time. It is a challenge for any committee to fulfill these goals, but the task will be made easier if the following remarks are used as guides for effective committee operation and conference leadership.

Scope, Functions, and Authority of the Committee

The first thing a committee must have is a mandate; it must know its scope and functions to operate effectively. The executive establishing the committee must define the subjects to be covered and the functions that the committee is expected to fulfill; there must be a description of its job. It must also be stated how the committee relates to other units within the organization. This will prevent the committee from floundering around and will enable the manager to check on whether it is meeting the expectations.

In addition to functions and scope, the degree of authority conferred on the committee must be specified. As briefly mentioned before, it must be clearly stated whether the committee is to serve in an advisory (staff) capacity or decision-making (line) capacity. For example, in many hospitals the human research committee (sometimes known by other names) has line authority to make decisions as to whether a proposed research project should be approved or not. In reaching the decision, this committee, guided by federal rules and regulations governing human experimentation issued by the Department of Health and Human Services and the Federal Drug Administration, clearly has line authority.

On the other hand, in most hospitals the medical executive committee (sometimes known as the medical staff committee or a similar term) acts in an advisory (staff) capacity when it deals with a physician's or surgeon's application for hospital privileges. This committee simply makes a recommendation to the board of directors, and they will decide. In such an instance the medical executive committee clearly acts as a staff committee.

For a formal, standing committee, all such information should be set down in writing in the organizational manual. (See Figure 14-1.) Documents stating all this information for the various committees are also usually required by the Joint Commission on Accreditation of Healthcare Organizations. For a temporary committee, scope, functions, and authority must also be explicitly stated but perhaps not so formally. It is extremely important that temporary committees only be established for a subject worthy of group consideration. If a topic can be handled by one person or over the phone, there is no need to establish a committee.

Composition of the Committee

Since the quality of committee work is only as good as its members, care should be exercised in choosing people to serve on committees. Members should be capable of expressing and defending their views, but they should also be willing to see the other party's point of view and be able to integrate their thinking with that of the other members. They should be independent of each other so that their deliberations will not be complicated by connotations of a direct superior-subordinate relationship. If possible, members should be from approximately the same organizational rank. If committee members are chosen from different departments, the problems of rank are more easily overcome. Sometimes the composition of a committee is dictated by outside regulations.

The committee device is a good opportunity for bringing together the representatives of several different interest groups. Specialists of different departments and activities can be brought together in such a way that all concerned parties have proper representation. This will result in balanced group integration and deliberation. The various representatives will then be assured that their interests have been heard and considered. Administration should see that this concern with proper representation is not carried too far. It is more essential to appoint capable members to a committee than merely representative members. The ideal solution is to have a capable member from each pertinent activity on the committee.

Size of the Committee

No definite figure can be given as to the ideal size of a committee for effective operation. The best that can be said is that the committee should be large enough to provide for thorough group deliberation and broad resources of information. It should not be so large, however, that it will be unwieldy and unusually time consuming. Usually smaller committees with about four to ten members seem to

■ FIGURE 14-1 The functions and scope of the
Quality Assurance Committee.

The Quality Assurance Committee shall consist of active staff members who have been nominated by their clinical service chiefs to be chairpersons of the quality assurance sub-committee. Sub-committees shall be established for clinical services including but not limited to: anesthesiology, cardiothoracic surgery, dermatology, emergency department, genitourinary surgery, laboratory medicine, internal medicine, neurology, neurological surgery, obstetrics and gynecology, oral maxillofacial surgery, ophthalmology, orthopedic surgery, otolaryngology, plastic surgery, psychiatry, radiology, pathology, and general surgery. Each sub-committee shall include no less than three members of the active staff. Two representatives from medical records and administration shall serve as ex-officio members on the Quality Assurance Committee. Social services, risk management, and nursing service will have one representative each who shall serve as ex-officio members of the Quality Assurance Committee. The house staff shall have at least one representative. Reports shall be submitted at least ten times annually.

The function of the Quality Assurance Committee is concurrently and retrospectively to evaluate the quality and appropriateness of medical care throughout all clinical services and to present findings and make recommendations to the Medical Advisory Committee based on these findings. In addition, the Quality Assurance Committee will review hospital quality assurance reports relating to patient care. After review, the recommendations may be forwarded to any medical staff committee, clinical department, executive committee, or the medical advisory committee for corrective action.

Criteria used during the evaluation process shall include, but not be limited to, quality, indications for admission, appropriateness of diagnostic and therapeutic procedures and treatments as well as measures of efficiency in the management of patient care including length of stay.

The Committee shall serve as a vehicle by which concerns addressed to the services chiefs or Executive Committee can be reviewed. The Committee or an ad-hoc subgroup of the Committee shall be responsible for formulating a policy, procedure, rule, or regulation addressing each concern and submitting their recommendation for consideration by the Executive Committee.

The Quality Assurance Committee shall take action by recommendation to other medical staff committees, clinical service chiefs, the Executive Committee, or the Medical Advisory Committee to resolve concerns related to patient care identified in the risk management or screening process or through review of quality assurance reports. By subsequent reviews or follow-up reports through the quality assurance program, the Committee will monitor the effectiveness of the corrective actions.

Reprinted with special permission of Barnes Hospital. For illustrative purposes only.

work best. If the nature of the subject under consideration necessitates a very large committee, it might be wise to form subcommittees that will consider the various aspects of the problem. Then the entire committee can meet to hear subcommittee reports and decide on a final solution.

Effective Conference Leadership

Since the success of any meeting will depend largely on the chairperson's ability to handle it, he or she must be familiar with effective conference or committee leadership techniques to guide the meeting to a satisfactory conclusion.[2] The individual members of a committee undoubtedly bring to the meeting their individual patterns of behavior and points of view. The chairperson must know how to fuse the individual viewpoints and attitudes so that teamwork will develop for the benefit of the group. It will take considerable skill, time, and patience on the chairperson's part to create a closely knit group out of a diverse membership, but this is generally the best way to achieve integrated group solutions. Let us look more carefully at the chairperson's role.

Adequate Preparation

Successful committee work requires good preparation. First, the chairperson must carefully outline the strategy and an agenda before the meeting. Topics to be discussed should be listed in the proper sequence, and often it is advisable to set up a time limit as to approximately how long the meeting will last. The chairperson may even want to establish, for his or her own guidance, an approximate time limit for each item to ensure better control of the situation. If possible, the agenda should be distributed to the members before the meeting so that they can better prepare themselves for the coming discussion. Furthermore, additional background information should be gathered either by the chairperson, the committee's own staff, or by the organization's staff services. This type of factual information should be distributed to the members before the meeting for their perusal and study. Meetings should be planned far enough in advance to give the members adequate notice and time. Written minutes of the previous meeting should be sent along for review and approval. All this will enable the members of a healthcare center to avoid conflicts, since they often belong to several committees.

The Role of the Chairperson

The chairperson is the most important member of the committee. This person is expected to play and succeed in two roles: to bring about the fulfillment of the task and build and maintain successful group interaction. The committee is made up of individuals, and great skill is required to eventually fuse these individuals into a rewarding and productive interaction.

It is human nature for committee members to think first of how a new proposition would affect themselves and their own working environment. This kind of egotistical thinking can easily lead to unnecessary friction. People tend to see the same "facts" differently. Words mean different things to different people. The first necessity in a group situation, therefore, is to find agreement on the basic nature of the problem under discussion so that everybody understands the issues. The task of the chairperson is to try to find out what the participants *think* the issues are in order to learn whether or not they understand the issues as they *actually* are.

This, however, is easier said than done. A frequent comment about committees is that the issues on the conference table are really not as difficult to deal with as the people around the table. Individuals at a meeting will often react toward each other rather than toward their ideas. For instance, just because A talks too much, everything he or she suggests may be rejected; B might automatically reject whatever someone else suggests; and C may be that member of the committee who never speaks.

It is the chairperson's job to minimize these personality differences by using the legitimate tools of parliamentary procedure. The speaking time of each participant can be limited so that one person will not monopolize the entire meeting. Also, one can be especially careful to call on people who seldom speak. Sooner or later, with the help of such leadership techniques, the committee will start reacting toward the content of the meeting, the issues involved, and not the individuals around the table. For a meeting to be successful, it is necessary for the various members to forget about their personalities and outside allegiances and work together as a team in a manner that will move the meeting toward a meaningful solution of the problem at hand. In all this, the chairperson plays a critical role.

The quality of the solution will also depend to some extent on the amount of time spent in reaching it. Too much haste will probably not produce the most desirable solution. On the other hand, most meetings have a time limit. If they did not, the members would become bored and frustrated with a meeting that lasts too long. It is the chairperson's job to give every member a chance to participate and voice his or her suggestions and opinions. This is especially important when the committee members are also expected to execute the decisions they make. Then it may be necessary for the chairperson to use persuasion to induce a minority to go along with the decision of the majority. On other occasions, the majority might have to be persuaded to make concessions to the minority. All this takes time and may result in a compromise that does not necessarily represent the best possible solution. If the solution has been arrived at democratically, however, the chairperson's leadership abilities will have been demonstrated, and the major purpose of the meeting will have been accomplished.

The Chairperson and Expression of Opinions

It has often been stated that the function of a good chairperson is to help the members of the group reach their own decisions, to work as a catalyst to bring out the ideas present among the committee members. If the chairperson *expresses his or her own views,* the members of the committee may hesitate to argue further to express their opinions, especially if they disagree. This is even more likely to occur if the chairperson also happens to be their boss or high up within the hierarchy. On the other hand, in many situations it would be unwise and completely unrealistic for the chairperson not to express his or her views. This individual may have some factual knowledge or sound opinion, and the value of the deliberations would be lessened if these were left unknown to the members of the committee.

On the whole, it is best for the chairperson to express his or her opinions and, at the same time, clearly let it be known that they are subject to constructive criticism and suggestions. After all, silence on the leader's part may be interpreted to mean that he or she cannot make a decision or does not want to do so for fear of assuming responsibility. On certain occasions, however, the chairperson must use sensitive judgment as to whether or not or to what extent his or her opinions should be expressed.

The Leadership Style

There also is the question of how much of a *formal leadership role* the chairperson should display. The variations of this role can run anywhere from the one extreme of an autocratic dictator to the other extreme of a democratic moderator. At times it may be necessary for even a very permissive democratic chairperson to use tight control over the meeting, although on most occasions the loosest sort of control will be employed. Indeed, it has often been found that if the group of participants consists of mature people, no or little control and formal chairpersonship are really necessary.

Although this may be true for some higher-level committee meetings, on the lower levels the need frequently exists for a stable structure and strong leadership from a chairperson. If the group has a formally elected or appointed chairperson, the members will naturally look to that person to keep the meeting moving along so that it will come to an efficient conclusion. Under most conditions, the formal leadership of the chairperson is necessary to ensure that group decision making is effective. If the chairperson lacks leadership ability, some other member of the committee will rise to be the *de facto* chairperson. This is a natural event in group dynamics.

The Agenda and Task Control

The best means of achieving task control and keeping a meeting from wandering off into a discussion of irrelevant matters is working with a *well-prepared agenda*. Although the agenda designs the overall strategy and sequence, it must not be so rigid that there is no means for adjusting it. The chairperson should apply the agenda with a degree of flexibility so that if a particular subject requires more attention than originally anticipated, the time allotted to some other topic can be reduced. In other words, staying close to the agenda should not force the chairperson to be too quick to rule people out of order. What seems irrelevant to him or her may be important to some of the other committee members. Some irrelevancies at times actually help create a relaxed atmosphere and relieve tension that has built up.

Since it is the chairperson's job to keep the meeting moving along toward its goal, it is a good idea to pause at various points during the meeting to consult the agenda and remind the group of what has been accomplished and what still remains to be discussed. A good chairperson will learn when the opportune time has arrived to summarize one point and to move on to the next item in the agenda. If past experience tells the chairperson that meetings have a tendency to run overtime or not to complete all the agenda items, it might be advisable to schedule them shortly before the lunch break or just before quitting time. This seems to speed up meetings; the participants seem to run out of arguments around those hours of the day.

■ THE COMMITTEE MEETING

Now that we are familiar with some of the guidelines for effective committee operation, we are ready to examine how these guidelines can be applied in a typical committee meeting. In other words, we want to see how a diverse group of people can, with the help of an effective conference leader, hold a meaningful discussion and arrive at satisfactory answers to the problems under consideration.

General Participation in the Discussion

After a few introductory remarks and social pleasantries, the chairperson should make an initial statement of the problem to be discussed. This will open up an opportunity for all members of the meeting to participate freely. Any member should be able to bring out those aspects of the problem that seem important to him or her, regardless of whether or not they seem important to everyone else. Sooner or later the discussion will simmer down to those points that are relevant.

There are always some members at the meeting who talk too much and others who do not talk enough. One of the chairperson's most difficult jobs is to encourage the latter to speak up and to keep the former from holding the floor for too long. There are various ways and means to do this. For example, after a long-winded speaker has had enough opportunity to express his or her opinions, it may be wise not to recognize that member again, giving someone else the chance to speak. It might also help to ask him or her to please keep the remarks brief or to arrange the seating at the conference table so that it is easy not to recognize his or her request to have the floor. Most of the time, however, the other members of the committee will quickly find subtle ways of censoring those members who have too much to say.

This does not mean that all members of the meeting must participate equally. Some people know more about a given subject than others, and some have stronger feelings about an issue than others. The chairperson must take such factors into consideration but should still do the best possible to stimulate overall participation. In this endeavor the chairperson's general attitude with regard to participation will be extremely important. It is necessary to accept everyone's contribution without judgment and create the impression that everyone should participate. Controversial questions may have to be asked merely to get the discussion going. Once participation has started, the chairperson should continue to throw out provocative open-ended questions, which ask why, who, what, where, and when. Questions that can be answered with a simple yes or no should be avoided.

Another technique that can be used by the chairperson is to start at one side of the conference table and ask each member in turn to express thoughts on the problem. The major disadvantage of this technique is that instead of participating in the discussion spontaneously whenever they have something to say, members will tend to sit back and wait until called on. The skilled chairperson, however, will watch the facial expressions of the people in the group. This may very well provide a clue as to whether someone has an idea but is afraid to speak up. Then a special effort should be made to call on that person.

If a meeting involves many participants, it may be advisable for the chairperson to break it up into small groups, typically known as *buzz sessions*. Each of the small subgroups will hold its own discussions and report back to the meeting after a specified period. In this way those people who hesitate to say anything in a larger group will be more or less forced to participate and express their opinions. Buzz sessions are usually advisable whenever there are more than 20 or so participants.

In using all these techniques to evoke general participation in the discussion, the chairperson should try to stick to the agenda and see that the discussion is basically relevant. Sometimes a chairperson who is inexperienced at holding meetings is so anxious to have someone say something that much discussion for discussion's sake will occur. This usually is not desirable because it confuses the issues and delays the even more important decision-making phase of the meeting.

Group Decision Making

Once a problem has been considerably narrowed down and understood in generally the same sense by all members of the group, it is advisable to get to the facts in as objective a manner as possible. Only by ascertaining all the relevant facts will the group be able to suggest alternative solutions. The chairperson knows that the best solution can only be as good as the best alternative considered. Therefore, the members at the meeting should be urged to contribute as many alternatives as they can possibly think of so that no solution is overlooked.

The next step is to evaluate the alternative solutions and discuss the advantages and disadvantages of each. In so doing, the field can eventually be narrowed down to two or three alternatives on which general agreement can be reached. The other alternatives can probably be eliminated by unanimous consent. The remaining options must be discussed thoroughly to bring about a solution. The chairperson should try to play the role of a middleperson or conciliator by working out a solution that is acceptable to all members of the group.

The best procedure would probably be to arrive at a solution that is a synthesis of the desirable outcomes of integration, all important points can be incorporated into the most desirable solution. Throughout this process the chairperson has the difficult job of helping the minority to save face. It is easier to conciliate the minority if the final decision of the group incorporates something of each person's ideas so that everyone has a partial victory. This can be a long and tedious process, and as we have said, such a compromise may not always be the strongest solution.

Sometimes, however, the group may not be able to reach a compromise or to come to any decision on which the majority agrees. This will frequently happen if the chairperson of the meeting senses that the group is hostile. In such a situation it is necessary to find out what is bothering the group and bring the objections out into the open and discuss them. Participants in a committee meeting may think first of what is objectionable about a new idea rather than think of its desirable features. A discussion of such objections may dispel unwarranted fears and may allow participants to perceive the positive aspects of a certain alternative. By the same token, the objections may be strong enough to void the proposition. In any case the group must have a chance to voice negative feelings before a positive consensus can be reached.

Taking a Vote

The chairperson is often confronted with the problem of whether a vote should be taken, or whether the committee should keep on working until the group reaches a final unanimous agreement, regardless of how long this would take. Offhand, many people would say that voting is a democratic way to make decisions. Voting does accentuate the differences among the members, however, and once a person has made a public commitment to a position by voting, it is often difficult to change his or her mind and still save face. Also, if this individual is a member of the losing minority, he or she cannot be expected to carry out the majority decision with great enthusiasm. Therefore, whenever possible, it is better not to take a formal vote but to work toward a roughly unanimous agreement.

As pointed out previously, one of the disadvantages of reaching a unanimous conclusion is that it can cause serious delay in the meeting. Also, the price of unanimity is often a solution that is reduced to a lower common denominator and may not be as ingenious and bold as it would have been otherwise. The situation and the magnitude of the problem involved will determine whether or not unanimity is desirable. In most instances it is not as difficult as one might think to come up with a unanimous decision. The skilled chairperson can usually sense the feeling of the meeting, and all that is necessary is to say that such and such a solution seems to be the consensus of the group. At this point, especially in a small meeting, the group can probably dispense with parliamentary procedure and a formal vote. In a large meeting, of course, unanimity may be an impossible goal, and decisions should be based on majority rule.

Follow-Up of Committee Action

Regardless of whether a committee was acting merely to come up with a recommendation or whether it has final decision-making authority, its findings need a follow-up. After the chairperson has reported the committee's findings to the superior who originally channeled the subject to the committee, it is the superior's duty to keep the chairperson or the committee posted as to what action has been taken. The practice of good human relations and ordinary courtesy will tell the superior that he or she owes the committee some explanation. Inadequate statements or no statements will cause the committee to lose interest in its work. When the committee has had authority to make a final decision, then the problem of carrying out the decision usually belongs to the committee itself. The chairperson will generally be asked to oversee this, or the particular executive who normally deals with the subject matter may execute the decision. In any event, the committee members must be kept informed as to what has happened.

■ SUMMARY

Every supervisor probably has been involved in committees either as a member or as an organizer. Committees have become an extremely important device for augmenting the organizational structure and the functioning of an enterprise. They allow the enterprise to adapt to increasing complexity without a complete reorganization. They permit a group of people to function collectively in areas a single individual could not handle. The advantages of committees are offset to a certain extent by their limitations and shortcomings, one of the most important being that responsibility cannot be pinned to any individual members. Despite this and other criticisms leveled against committees, they can be of great value if properly organized and led.

Because the increasing complexities of today's society are making more and more committees necessary, it is essential for the supervisor to familiarize himself or herself with the workings of a committee. Committee meetings are called either to disseminate information or to discuss a topic. If discussion is involved, a distinction should be made between whether the committee is to arrive at a final decision on the question under discussion and take action based on this decision, or whether it is to merely make recommendations to the line manager who appointed the committee. A committee can be line or staff.

Regardless of the purpose of the committee, it is likely that group deliberation will produce a more satisfactory and acceptable conclusion than one formally handed down from above. Decisions will be carried out with more enthusiasm if employees have had a role in making them or in making recommendations through committees. For group decisions and recommendations to be of high quality, however, it is necessary that the committee members be carefully selected. In the composition of a committee, as many interested parties as possible must be represented. The people chosen as representatives should be capable of presenting their views and integrating their opinions with those of others. As to the size of a committee, there should be enough members to permit thorough deliberations, but not so many as to make the meetings cumbersome.

In addition to these factors, the success of committee deliberations depends largely on effective committee or conference leadership. This means that the chairperson's familiarity with effective group work will make the difference between productive and wasteful committee meetings. The chairperson's job is to produce the best possible solution in the shortest amount of time and, it is hoped, with unanimity. In trying to achieve these goals, the chairperson is constantly confronted with the problem of running the meeting either too tightly or too loosely. If control is too tight, the natural development of ideas may be frustrated, conclusions may be reached before all alternatives have been considered, and in general, resentment may be created. If the control is too loose, members of the meeting may get the feeling of aimlessness and confusion.

The chairperson will have to depend on a keen perception of the "mood of the meeting" to know exactly how to lead it and bring it to a successful conclusion. Thus, the chairperson will have to sense when there has been enough general participation in the discussion, when alternative solutions have been properly evaluated, and when and if a vote is necessary to arrive at a group decision. In all these matters the conference leadership abilities of the chairperson will be of utmost importance.

NOTES

1. For further details on and how to counteract this provocative issue, see Irving L. Janis, *Victims of Groupthink: A Psychological Study of Foreign-Policy Decisions and Fiascoes,* Boston: Houghton Mifflin Co., 1972; Philip E. Tetlock, "Identifying Victims of Groupthink From Public Statements of Decision Makers," *Journal of Personality and Social Psychology,* Vol. 37, No. 8, 1979, pp. 1314-1324; Irving L. Janis, *Groupthink: Psychological Studies of Policy Decisions and Fiascoes,* 2nd ed., Boston: Houghton Mifflin Co., 1982.
2. The term conference leadership is generally used in the literature. We have used it here to be synonymous with committee leadership.

15

INFORMAL ORGANIZATIONAL CONCEPTS

Whenever people work together, informal relationships exist and become a powerful source of influence on the formal organization. The formal task structure, goals, and functioning of the organization are affected by a social subsystem known as the *informal organization*. Early scholars maintained that an inherent conflict exists between the goals of the formal organization and informal relationships. Today we know that both formal and informal relationships are essential subsystems of a complex system and that the informal relationships help the functioning of the formal organization by providing individual satisfaction and group morale, which otherwise would be lacking.

The informal organization found in almost all enterprises is closely related to the workings of committees and to the phenomenon of group participation, but it is quite different in origin. The informal organization is a powerful source of influence that interacts with and modifies the formal organization. Although many managers would like to conveniently overlook its existence, they will readily admit that to understand the nature of organizational life fully, it is necessary to "learn the ropes" of the informal organization. In almost every institution such an informal structure will develop. It reflects the spontaneous efforts of individuals and groups to influence the conditions of their existence. Whenever people are associated, social relationships and groupings are bound to come about. The informal organization has a positive contribution to make to the smooth functioning of the enterprise, and to this extent the manager must understand its workings, respect it, and even nurture it.

To be more specific, informal organization arises from the social interaction of people as they associate with each other. Such interaction may be accidental or incidental to organized activities, or it may arise from personal desire or gregariousness. At the heart of informal organization are people and their relationships, whereas at the heart of formal organization is the organizational structure and the delegation of authority. Management can create or rescind a formal organizational structure that it has designed, but it cannot rescind the informal organization because management did not establish it. As long as people work together in a department, there will be an informal organization consisting of the informal groupings of employees.

195

■ THE INFORMAL GROUP

At the base of all informal organization is the small group, consisting of two or more people, sometimes up to ten, who interact regularly to accomplish a common goal or purpose.[1] The first question that comes to mind is why people join such groups. We may wonder what advantages they gain from groups, since they are already members of a department where their duties are specifically assigned, channels of communication exist, a line of authority has been established, and they are a significant part of a formal organizational structure. The answer to this question is that employees have certain needs that they would like to have satisfied, but apparently the formal organization leaves unsatisfied. One of the needs is for *achievement,* and the other is for *emotional satisfaction.* People have a basic need to associate with others in groups small enough to permit intimate, direct, and personal contact among individuals. The satisfactions derived from these types of relationships generally cannot be obtained from working within a large organization. Thus, the small group provides the individual with satisfactions that are uniquely different from those that can be obtained from any other source.

Benefits Derived from Groups

People join groups for various reasons, including interpersonal attraction, group goals, group activities, and social needs.

First, group participation provides a sense of *satisfaction.* An individual in a group is usually surrounded by others who share similar values. This reinforces their own value system and interest; it gives them confidence, since it is always more comfortable to be among people who think the same way. There is also the need for *friendship and companionship* that the group fulfills. The employee needs and enjoys the social contact with fellow workers, sharing experiences, joking, and finding a sympathetic listener. The group thus will fulfill the need for *belonging,* the need to associate with others who have similar attitudes, personality, economic standing, and the same purposes and goals.

Another need satisfied by belonging to a small group in many instances is the need for *balance and protection.* Social interaction may balance routine and tedious work; a small group offers protection from what the members may think of as an imposition or an encroachment by management, such as protection against increased output standards, changes in working conditions, or reduced benefits. We are all familiar with the old saying, "there is strength in unity." In this respect the small group is a source of *security and support.* Often when people enter an organization for the first time they have feelings of significant anxiety. The surroundings are unfamiliar and much uncertainty exists. When several people are in the same circumstance, a small group may arise on this basis alone, providing temporary support in an unfamiliar environment. Whenever people sense the need for protection, they can and do form small groups.

An additional need that a small group fulfills is the need for *status,* because the group enables an employee to belong to a distinct little organization that is more or less exclusive. It also gives the individual an opportunity for self-expression, a kind of audience before generally sympathetic listeners. Another reason why people join groups is to have access to the informal communications network and to secure *information* to reduce their uncertainties. The grapevine works very effectively in small groups, providing speedy, although at times inaccurate, information. Groups tend to form around an individual who seems to be the focal point in a communications network. An individual who has information is able to satisfy the communication needs of others, even though the information transmitted may be false or distorted.

In addition to these emotional needs, there exists the need for achievement, for getting things done. Groups are a means of getting a *task* accomplished by interacting, communicating, and collaborating. Informal groups help employees to accomplish tasks that may be impossible to accomplish alone. They also serve to bring the goals of these tasks more into the realm of the employee. The objectives and goals of the formal organization may appear remote and meaningless to the average employee. It is much simpler to identify with the objectives and goals of one's immediate work group. Often employees will readily forego some of their own goals and replace them with the goals of the group.

It is important for the supervisor of a department to be aware of all these needs employees want satisfied. If the supervisor understands the many reasons why employees tend to join informal groups, an attempt can be made in daily supervision to use these groups constructively rather than be suspicious or try to destroy them.

■ INFORMAL GROUPS AND THE INFORMAL ORGANIZATION

Small informal groups, as we said, are at the basis of informal organization, and all small informal groups have the potential to become informal organizations existing in the larger formal structure of the institution. In every organization, unless it consists of only a few individuals, there is an informal, also known as an invisible, organization; it does not have a printed chart, written manuals, written policies, procedures, and so forth. Also, the informal organization probably differs from the lines of the formal organization, but it is a functioning entity. (See Figure 15-1.)

The informal organization develops when small groups acquire a more or less distinct structure and a set of norms and standards, as well as a procedure to invoke sanctions to ensure conformity to the norms. The informal organizational structure is determined largely by the different status positions that people within the small group hold.

Status Positions

Generally, there are four status positions: the group's *informal leader,* the members of the *primary group,* the members who have only *fringe status,* and those who have *out status.* (See Figure 15-2.) The informal leader of the small group is the person

■ FIGURE 15-1 Informal working relationships.

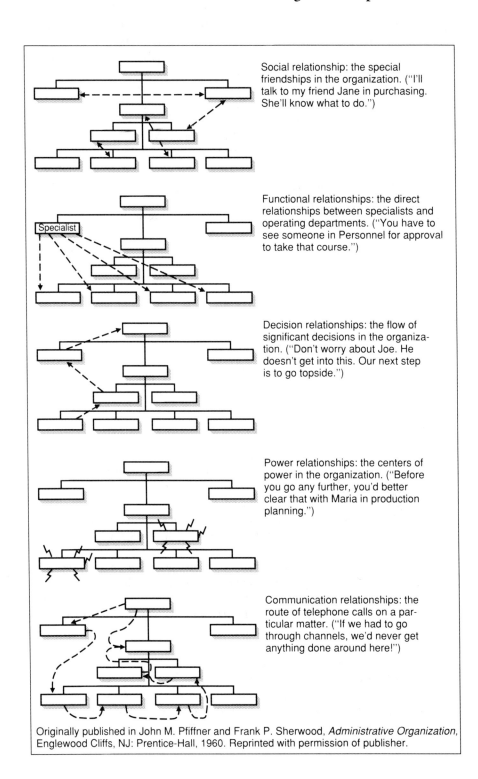

Social relationship: the special friendships in the organization. ("I'll talk to my friend Jane in purchasing. She'll know what to do.")

Functional relationships: the direct relationships between specialists and operating departments. ("You have to see someone in Personnel for approval to take that course.")

Decision relationships: the flow of significant decisions in the organization. ("Don't worry about Joe. He doesn't get into this. Our next step is to go topside.")

Power relationships: the centers of power in the organization. ("Before you go any further, you'd better clear that with Maria in production planning.")

Communication relationships: the route of telephone calls on a particular matter. ("If we had to go through channels, we'd never get anything done around here!")

Originally published in John M. Pfiffner and Frank P. Sherwood, *Administrative Organization*, Englewood Cliffs, NJ: Prentice-Hall, 1960. Reprinted with permission of publisher.

around whom the primary members of the group cluster; their association is close, and their interaction and communication are intense. This is normally considered the small nucleus group of which newcomers would like to become members.

■ **FIGURE 15-2 A model of informal relationships.**

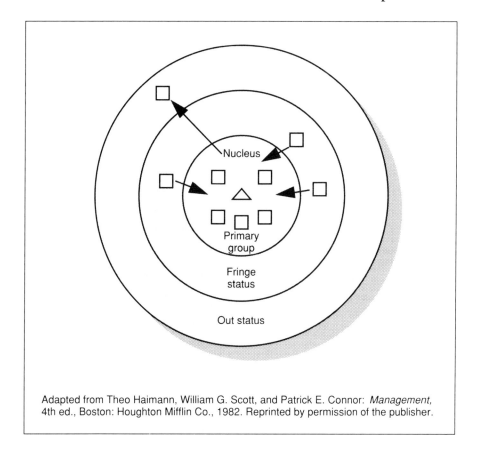

Adapted from Theo Haimann, William G. Scott, and Patrick E. Connor: *Management,* 4th ed., Boston: Houghton Mifflin Co., 1982. Reprinted by permission of the publisher.

These newcomers are usually new employees of the department. They remain on the fringe of the group while they are being evaluated by the small nucleus for acceptance or rejection. Eventually these individuals will either move into the nucleus and become a bona fide member of the small group, or they will move into the outer shell because they have been rejected.

The people in the outer shell are still a part of the department, even though they have not been accepted as members of the core group. Such rejection, however, can have serious behavioral effects, especially if a person wants badly to belong to the nucleus group. This is true because in essence the group represents a system of interaction that causes members to modify their own individual behavior and to have a significant impact on the behavior of persons in the fringe shell or the outer shell. If the rejection is mutual, the person in the outer shell can survive very well on his or her own.

Although leadership will be discussed fully in Chapter 21, a few words should be said at this time about *informal leadership*. The person who plays the role of the informal leader is usually the dynamic force of the group. As with the committee chairperson, this individual engages in leadership activities, crystallizes opinions, and sets objectives. This group leader is generally democratically chosen by the group. The leadership role is created by consensus. This leader normally is a dominant personality who functions in such a way as to facilitate the satisfaction of most of the needs of group members. This person usually possesses communicative skills, sensitivity, and intelligence, and helps the members achieve their tasks and emotive needs. Occasionally one might find small groups in which the aspects of leadership are shared, in which different leaders perform different functions, sometimes only for a brief time. For example, one leader may deal with administration, whereas another may deal with the union, and another may try to maintain internal cohesiveness and morale. Most of the time, however, there is only one informal leader with whom the supervisor will have to deal.

Norms and Standards

Besides status positions, there are norms and standards that regulate group behavior. They define the boundaries between acceptable and unacceptable behavior.[2] In addition to these standards for behavior between group members, norms will define limits for quality and quantity of work and for many other areas, such as squealing to management about a co-worker. The standards governing work output are particularly important in almost every informal organization. They tell exactly how many salad plates a worker in the food production department will fix per hour, how many records will be processed in the medical records department during a day, and so forth. These norms often are far from what the supervisor would like to have accomplished. In general, most norms are counterproductive. Norms of one group cannot be generalized to another group.

To be admitted to the group, the employee must be willing and eager to comply with such standards instead of his or her own. Since groups are capable of granting or withholding the advantages of membership, individuals must modify their behavior so that it corresponds to that of the group. This is why the informal organization has such a significant influence over the behavior and work of employees who are primary group members. In addition, the interactions between primary group members also influence the behavior of those who are in the fringe shell and even possibly someone in the outer shell, since all of them are members of the total system.

Sanctions

Along with norms, there must be an effective procedure for invoking sanctions if a group member does not conform with the standards set. These sanctions can range from being elusive and evasive on the one hand to being overt on the other. At first sanctions can be very mild; the group may try to bring the nonconformist back in line by more communication. If this does not produce the desired results, communication may stop, leading to excluding the deviant from what is going on, for example, excluding someone from social activities such as lunching together. The most powerful sanction is rejection. Employees who consistently do not comply with the group's norms will soon be on the outside. Their life can then be made miserable, their work can be sabotaged, and eventually they may want to leave the institution completely. All these sanctions of the informal organization, whether subtle or strong, serve to see that group members adhere to the group's ideas of correct on-the-job behavior.

Additional Characteristics

As stated, one of the reasons people form small groups is the need for information to reduce their uncertainties. These groups provide their own unofficial channel of communication, the *grapevine* and access to it. This manifestation of the informal organization has already been fully discussed in Chapter 5. Briefly again, the grapevine is the major connecting link of the informal organization, just as communication through regular channels serves to link the formal organizational structure. The informal organization influences the behavior of employees regardless of the status they occupy within the informal group. This is important for a supervisor to remember because one cannot hope to understand individual behavior without understanding the behavior of the organizational forces that shape it.

Another characteristic of the informal organization is inflexibility, especially *resistance to change*. It resists especially those changes that could be interpreted as a threat to the informal group. Over time, the small group has developed very satisfying social relationships, and any change that may challenge its equilibrium and stability will be greeted with resistance. This resistance can take the form of complaints, work slowdown, excessive absenteeism, reduction in the quality of the job performed, etc. It is essential for a supervisor to understand the dynamics of these types of group behavior in order to introduce change successfully. This will be discussed further in Chapter 19.

■ INTERACTION BETWEEN INFORMAL AND FORMAL ORGANIZATIONS

Often it might appear that the functioning of the informal organization makes the job of the supervisor more difficult. Because of the interdependence between informal and formal organizations, the attitudes, goals, norms, and customs of one affect the other. Informal organizations do frequently give life and vitality to the formal organization, but this is not always the case. Informal organizations can have either a constructive or hindering influence on the formal organization and on the realization of departmental objectives. In the final analysis the supervisor's basic attitude will have much to do with whether that influence is positive or negative.

The supervisor must respect the informal organization for the power it has; it cannot be ignored, and attempts to eliminate it should not be made. It is important for the supervisor to be aware that these informal groups are very strong, and they may often govern the behavior of employees to an extent that interferes with formal supervision. Sometimes it can even go so far that the pressure of the informal group frustrates the supervisor in carrying out policies that the superior manager expects the supervisor to enforce. The wise supervisor, therefore, should make all possible efforts to gain the cooperation and goodwill of the informal organization and the informal leader and to use them wherever possible to further the departmental objectives.

Both formal and informal relationships are parts of the system and they interact, each modifying the other. They may be mutually reinforcing or conflicting. The supervisor should remember that informal groups provide the satisfaction of some needs that the formal organization leaves unsatisfied. Informal relationships make a contribution to the organizational climate; they keep the organization flexible and are a means of getting the departmental job done.

The Supervisor and the Informal Organization

One way the supervisor can put the informal organization to the best possible use is to let the employees know that its existence is accepted and understood. Such an understanding will enable the supervisor to group employees so that those most likely to comprise a good team will be working with each other on the same assignments. The supervisor's understanding of how the informal organization works will also help avoid activities that would unnecessarily threaten or disrupt the informal group. The manager should do his or her utmost to integrate the interests of the informal organization with those of the formal organization.

The supervisor should exhibit this positive approach because he or she knows that there are positive attributes in a cohesive informal group. Morale is likely to be high, turnover and excessive absences tend to be low, and the members work smoothly as a team. This can make supervision much easier because the supervisor escapes a lot of bickering; it can also ease the burden of communication, since the group provides its own effective, although informal, channels. Therefore, the supervisor should emphasize the positive by "communicating" informal responsibility to the informal leader and by allowing the group, naturally within limits, to go about the job as much on their own as possible.

Group Decision Making

A supervisor can do even more to bring out the positive aspects of informal groups by sharing the decision-making authority with them, by practicing group decision making.[3] In effect, this means turning the informal group into a sort of self-contained committee. As we know, decisions arrived at by a group or committee usually turn out to the advantage of all involved. They enable the group to exercise control over their own activities and to make certain that all their interests are taken into account, with the result that no one comes out a loser. The group has a larger information base and often different and more approaches to the problem because of a variety of education, experience, and perception. The group decision-making process also produces a broader understanding of the solution, which in turn brings increased acceptance and commitment. All indications are that groups actually produce better decisions.

Group problem solving has some shortcomings as well. Often there is group pressure for conformity and consensus, possibly caused by the dominance of one individual; this at times may lower the quality of the decision, leading to undesirable compromise. Furthermore, the danger exists that the group may become a victim of groupthink, discussed in the previous chapter. Groupthink takes more time and entails greater expense. Although these are serious shortcomings, the advantages far outweigh them; supervisors can reap many advantages and benefits by using group problem solving effectively. (See Figure 15-3.)

■ **FIGURE 15-3 Assets and liabilities of group decision making.**

Assets	Liabilities
■ Groups can accumulate more knowledge and facts. ■ Groups have a broader perspective and consider more alternative solutions. ■ Individuals who participate in decisions are more satisfied with the decision and are more likely to support it. ■ Group decision processes serve an important communication function, as well as a useful political function.	■ Groups often work more slowly than individuals. ■ Group decisions involve considerable compromise that may lead to less than optimal decisions. ■ Groups are often dominated by one individual or a small clique, thereby negating many of the virtues of group processes. ■ Overreliance on group decision making can inhibit management's ability to act quickly and decisively when necessary.

From Richard M. Steers, *Introduction to Organizational Behavior,* 3rd ed., Glenview, IL: Scott, Foresman and Company, 1987, p. 418. Reprinted by permission.

However, the supervisor should establish certain ground rules for this group decision-making process. Otherwise, it could bring about opposite results. First, the supervisor must sincerely believe in group decision making and want it. Second, clear limitations to the area of deliberation must be set. For instance, if the group is to arrange its own vacation schedule, it should be stated how many employees with a special skill must always be present, what the time limits are, and so forth. Third, it must be clear whether the group is merely asked for suggestions or whether authority to find a solution and make a decision has been delegated. Finally, the supervisor should choose a problem in which the enthusiastic acceptance and execution are at least as important, if not more important, than the specifics of the decision itself. Under these conditions, group decision making can be an additional means of bringing out the positive aspects of informal organization.

The Supervisor and the Informal Group Leader

Informal leaders are powerful because of their source of authority; they can be a great help when they work in the best interest of the institution. When informal leaders work against the goals of the organization, however, they can cause great difficulties. Therefore, it is advisable for supervisors to maintain a positive attitude toward the informal group leader. Instead of viewing this person as a "ringleader," supervisors will do better to consider this individual as someone "in the know" and respect and work with him or her. In an effort to build good relations with the informal leader, supervisors can pass information on to that person before giving it to anyone else. They can ask for advice on certain problems, and, particularly if a rearrangement of duties or layouts is under consideration, they may want to discuss it with the informal leader first to get some reaction. Or supervisors may ask the informal leader to "break in" a new employee of the department, knowing full well that he or she would do it anyway.

In taking this approach, however, the supervisor must be careful not to cause the informal leader to lose status within the group because working with the supervisor means working with management. In other words, the supervisor should not extend too many favors to the informal leader, since this would ruin the latter's leadership position within the group at once. This discussion assumes that an informal group leader is easily visible in the department. Often it is difficult, however, for a supervisor, especially a new supervisor, to identify the informal leader of a group. Observation is probably the best means to find out. The supervisor should look for the person to whom the other employees turn when they need help, the person who sets the pace and who seems to have influence over them. The supervisor must continually and closely observe this because the informal group will occasionally shift from one leader to another, depending on the purposes to be pursued. Regardless of who the leader is, the supervisor should do all possible to work *with* the informal leader instead of against that person.

It would be unrealistic, however, to believe that such a positive approach is the cure for all conflicts between the informal and the formal organizations. There undoubtedly will be occasions when agreement and harmonious interaction may be impossible. Situations arise in which every supervisor must act contrary to the desires of the supervised group. In those instances the dictates of formal authority will probably be the decisive factor.

■ SUMMARY

In addition to the formal organization, there exists in every enterprise an informal organization based on informal groups. These groups satisfy certain needs and desires of their members, which apparently are left unsatisfied by the formal organization. For example, an informal group can satisfy the members' social needs. It gives them recognition and status and a sense of belonging. Informal information transmitted through the grapevine provides a channel of communication and fulfills the members' need and desire to know what is going on. The informal organization also influences the behavior of individuals within the group and requests them to conform with certain standards the group has set up. Informal organization can be found on all levels of the enterprise, from the top to the bottom. It exists in every department, regardless of the quality of supervision.

Informal organization can have either a constructive or hindering influence on the formal organization. To make the best possible use of informal organization, the supervisor must understand its workings and be able to identify its informal leaders. Then the supervisor can work with them in a way that will help accomplish the objectives of the department. For example, the informal group and its leader can be used to break in new employees or transmit messages. Instead of dwelling on the informal organization as a source of conflict, the supervisor should remember that both the formal and the informal organizations are part of a complex system interacting with each other. Instead of viewing it as something antagonistic, the supervisor should approach this group positively and emphasize its potential for the good of the enterprise. After all, informal groups are similar in many respects to formal committees and have many of the same advantages. This can be put to good use by letting the informal group act as group decision makers. The supervisor cannot ignore or try to eliminate the informal organization.

NOTES

1. George C. Homans, *The Human Group,* New York: Harcourt Brace Jovanovich, Inc., 1950.
2. Daniel C. Feldman, ''The Development and Enforcement of Group Norms,'' *Academy of Management Review,* Vol. 9, No. 1, 1984, pp. 47-53.
3. See Norman P.R. Maier, ''Assets and Liabilities in Group Problem Solving: The Need for an Integrative Function,'' in J. Richard Hackman, Edward E. Lawler, III, and Lyman W. Porter, eds., *Perspectives on Business in Organizations,* 2nd ed., New York: McGraw-Hill Book Co., 1983, pp. 385-392.

Part Five

Staffing: Human Resources Management

16

THE STAFFING PROCESS

The most valuable asset of an organization is its human resources, its people. Staffing is the managerial function concerned with the procurement and maintenance of the human resources to fulfill the institution's plans and objectives. The staffing process takes place after the managerial functions of planning and organizing. Once goals have been determined, departments set up, and duties and task relationships established, people must be found to give life to what would otherwise be only a theoretical structure. It is the manager's responsibility to vitalize the department by staffing it properly. The purpose of the staffing function is to achieve the optimum use of human resources, which is only possible when job authority and demands match the employee's capability. This balancing of capabilities with job requirements is the essence of the staffing function.

More specifically, the procurement of human resources means the planning for the present and future needs of the department. This includes the recruiting and selection, placement, development, training, and compensation of the subordinates in the department. It is every manager's job to maintain the human resources by evaluating and appraising the employees, promoting them according to effort and ability, rewarding them, transferring, and, if necessary, disciplining or even discharging them. Only if a manager performs all these duties can one say that the managerial staffing function has been truly fulfilled.

Staffing is a difficult task, and the importance of human resources management has expanded greatly in recent years. Good resource planning and maintenance have a major impact on the final performance of the organization. Poor resource planning can result in severe shortages, improper recruiting practices can lead to embarrassing situations, and so forth. Much of this is caused by the current complex legal environment affecting human resources management. Thus, the supervisor depends very much on the help of a specialized staff department to achieve the human resources goals. Most organizations with about 100 employees or more usually have a department of human resources (also still known and in this book referred to as the personnel department) to assist the line managers in their task.

In checking the previous list of activities, many supervisors may believe that some are the responsibility of the human resources department. In certain healthcare facilities some of these activities are performed by the personnel department. In such institutions this department has very broad jurisdiction. Nevertheless, good management still considers these duties as part of the supervisor's legitimate functions. Although the supervisor may be assisted by the personnel staff in the performance of these functions, they are still primarily the supervisor's responsibility. For example, the human resources department will do the recruiting and the initial screening, but the final hiring should be made by the supervisor of the department. Also, the evaluation of the employee's performance should be made by the line supervisor, although the procedures, forms, and so forth are designed by the human resources people. All this will be discussed in detail on the following pages.

■ THE STAFFING FUNCTION AND THE HUMAN RESOURCES DEPARTMENT

Throughout our text the term *human resources department* and *personnel department* will be used interchangeably. We will assume that within the organizational structure of the institution, this department is a staff department as defined in our discussion of line and staff. The usefulness and effectiveness of this department will depend largely on its ability to develop a good working and sharing relationship with line supervisors. This will be governed in part by how clearly and specifically the chief executive officer (CEO) has outlined the activities and authority of the human resources department. In determining its scope and relationship to the staffing function of line supervisors, it is necessary for line managers to understand the historical place of the personnel department in organizations. Only then will one be able to establish a structure that is meaningful in terms of current needs and environment.

Historical Patterns

The personnel department started primarily as a record-keeping department. It kept all employment records for the employees and managers, all correspondence pertaining to their hiring, application blanks, background information, various positions held within the enterprise, dates of promotions, salary changes, leaves of absence granted, disciplinary penalties imposed, and other information on the employee's relationship to the enterprise.

Proper maintenance of these clerical records is still of great importance today, especially with the growing emphasis on equal opportunity employment, pension and insurance programs, unemployment claims, seniority provisions, and promotional and developmental programs. By assigning such clerical service activities to the personnel staff, the administrator knows that they will be handled with high technical competence and efficiency because of the specialization of the department. If such a service were not provided by the personnel department, each supervisor would have to keep these records for his or her own department. This would be a cumbersome and time-consuming task to be burdened with in addition to the daily chores of getting the particular job done. Therefore, line supervisors are pleased to have the personnel staff perform these clerical services for them. The line supervisors are just not interested in doing the work themselves, and often they may not even have the ability to do so.

As time went on, mainly during the 1920s, many managers in industry believed that the threat of unionization might be thwarted if efforts were made to give employees cafeterias, better recreational facilities, bowling teams, company stores, etc. Although most of these endeavors have a strong flavor of "paternalism," management thought that they would make the employees happier and less resentful. Since none of these activities fitted into the regular line departments of the enterprise, however, the personnel department took responsibility for an increasing number of them.

During the 1930s another shift in the emphasis of the personnel department took place. With the increase of union activities, the personnel department was expected to take direct charge of all employee and union relations. It often assumed full responsibility for hiring, firing, handling union grievances, and dealing with general labor problems. In other words, management believed that by having a personnel department, all personnel questions could be handled by them, leaving the line supervisors with practically no staffing function.

This led to serious difficulties, however, because while the duties and power of the personnel department increased significantly, the standing of the supervisor as a manager decreased. The more power the personnel director acquired, the weaker the supervisor's relationship became with his or her own employees. The demoralized supervisor justifiably complained that it was impossible to manage the department effectively without having the power to select, hire, discipline, and reward the employees. The employees no longer regarded the supervisor as their boss. Because someone in the personnel department hired the employees, established their wages, and promoted, disciplined, and fired them, employees looked to someone in the personnel department as their supervisor. Since this led to a bad state of affairs in many organizations, good management had to delineate clearly between the functions of the personnel department in a staff capacity and the supervisor's role as a manager of the department.

Current Patterns

During the last decades most organizations have recognized the need for a proper balance of influence and authority between the line managers and the human resources staff. Good management dictates that supervisors and personnel people must work together and share the burden because their work is intertwined; however, their areas of authority and their roles must be clearly stated. Sound management principles advocate that the job of the human resources department most of the time is to provide the line supervisors with advice, suggestions, and counsel concerning personnel problems and to help them in every possible respect. Going beyond this could lead to a fragmentation of the supervisor's job and make it difficult for the supervisor to be an effective manager within the department. Of course, the supervisor must manage within the framework of the organization's personnel policies, procedures, and regulations. Line supervisors should take full advantage of the expertise and assistance that is available within the human resources department, but they must retain the basic responsibility for managing their department.

Since it is the supervisor's job to accomplish the work within the department, he or she must make managerial decisions that concern the department's employees. Generally, this means that the supervisor defines the specific qualifications expected from an employee who is to fill a specific position. It is the human resources department's function to develop sources of qualified applicants within the local labor market. This department must let the community know what jobs are available and in general create an image of the organization as an employer. This can be accomplished by fostering good community relations and recruiting in high schools, training schools, colleges, and other sources of employees.

The human resources department should conduct screening interviews with applicants to determine whether or not their qualifications match the requirements as defined by the supervisor. They will also perform tests if the position requires them. This department should make necessary reference checks about previous employment dates and past records and should eliminate from consideration those applicants who do not meet job requirements. Those candidates who meet the stated requirements should be referred to the supervisor.

It is up to the supervisor to interview, select, and hire from among the qualified available candidates. The supervisor normally should make the final decision, sometimes in collaboration with the direct line superior. The supervisor assigns the new employee to a specific job, and the supervisor has the responsibility to judge how this new employee's skills can best be used and developed. It is the human resources department's job to give the new employee a general indoctrination about the healthcare center's benefits, general rules, shifts, hours, etc. The supervisor, however, should introduce the employee to the specific details about the job, wages, departmental rules, hours, rest periods, etc. The supervisor instructs and trains the new employee on the job and assesses the employee's performance to determine whether he or she should be retained. The supervisor also monitors compensation within the pattern of remuneration, and, later decides whether or not this person should eventually be promoted into a better job. If the need to take disciplinary measures should arise, it is clearly the supervisor's duty to do so and, if necessary, even to fire the employee; this may have to be done with higher line management review. During the time an employee is with the organization, the complete employment record is maintained by the human resources department.

Throughout the entire staffing function the supervisor will be greatly aided by the personnel department. The latter maintains all the clerical services and keeps the records. As mentioned, this is particularly essential because of the importance of nondiscriminatory employment, insurance, pension, promotion, and other practices. The human resources department is also there to provide expertise, advice, counsel, and guidance whenever personnel problems arise. In making decisions, the supervisor can follow, ignore, reject, or alter the personnel department's advice and counsel. In today's societal and legal environment affecting the staffing function, however, the input of the human resources employees has become very important and has a strong impact on the practice of human resources management.

In some issues it is often difficult to draw such a fine line of distinction between advice, counsel, and guidance from the human resources department and the supervisor's decision making. The following example will illustrate how blurred the distinction can be between providing information and giving advice and, on the other hand, trying to make decisions for the supervisor. When the staff person merely provides information, facts are furnished that help the supervisor make a sound decision. For instance, the personnel officer might inform the nursing director that those applying for an open nursing position are expecting a starting salary that is considerably higher than the institution's starting rate. In another situation the personnel person might advise that if the director of nursing were to hire a nurse at a certain salary, the director may have some dissatisfied older employees in the department. In the second case the staff person is providing not only information but also advice. By selecting the facts and phrasing this advice carefully, the personnel officer may actually sway the line supervisor's decision one way or the other. He or she may even advise paying the new nurse a certain amount per hour. Before anyone realizes it, the information becomes advice and the advice becomes a decision. This may occur not because the personnel officer wants broader authority or wants to reduce the supervisor's authority, but because the line supervisor may have encouraged this growth of staff participation.

Sometimes supervisors will welcome the human resources department's willingness to help them out of a difficult situation. Frequently supervisors ask the personnel department to make a decision for them so that they will not become burdened with so-called personnel problems. They gladly accept the staff person's decision, believing that if the decision is wrong, they can always excuse it by saying it was the personnel department's decision. In other words, the line supervisor is only too ready to capitulate to the personnel person in many instances. In so doing, one can "pass the buck" to the human resources department.

Although it is understandable that the supervisor is reluctant to question and disregard the advice of the staff expert, the supervisor must bear in mind that the staff person sees only a small part of the entire picture. The staff person is not responsible for the performance of the department. There are usually many other factors involved in the overall picture that will affect the department, factors that staff is not as familiar with is as the line supervisor. The supervisor cannot separate his or her functions between clear areas of personnel problems and performance problems. Every situation has certain personnel implications, and it is impossible to separate the various components of each problem within the department. Only the supervisor is likely to see the broad picture.

If the supervisor capitulates and has the human resources department make the decisions, the relationship with the department's employees will sooner or later be damaged. The subordinates will decide that it is the personnel department and not the supervisor who has the real power to influence their jobs within the healthcare institution. The supervisor's leadership position will slowly deteriorate if the employees detect that the personnel staff resolves problems and determines salaries and hiring/firing practices. The workers will discover that the supervisor does not control rewards and penalties and that he or she really does not make the decisions in the department.

■ STAFFING AND LEGAL IMPLICATIONS

During recent years it has become increasingly difficult to carry out the staffing function because of numerous federal, state, and local laws; executive orders and guidelines; and court decisions. Employment practices and policies must comply with these regulations, which in general prohibit discrimination against applicants and employees on the basis of race, sex, color, religion, or national origin. Also, age cannot be used as a criterion of selection among applicants between 40 and 70 years old. Other laws might request that an organization hire handicapped persons and veterans. Affirmative-action programs might dictate that the institution give hiring preferences to minority members who are qualified or have the potential to fill available jobs.

A detailed discussion of equal employment opportunity is beyond the confines of this text; however, supervisors must be aware of this concern because it affects their staffing function. Table 16-1 is a partial listing of the major laws on equal employment opportunity requirements and the enforcement agencies. It is necessary to mention this important subject, since it clearly affects the staffing function. Equal employment will be discussed in more detail in Chapter 17.

Since the problems of equal employment opportunity, discrimination, and similar laws and court decisions are a rapidly growing special area of consideration, it would be impossible for a line supervisor to be aware of all this or to try to keep up with it. Therefore, members of the human resources department become specialists in these problems and exert a pervasive influence on the staffing function. It is imperative that the organization complies with the multitude of laws and regulations. In recent years one of the personnel department's major obligations has been to make certain that the institution is in compliance and not in violation.

■ FUNCTIONAL AUTHORITY AND THE HUMAN RESOURCES DEPARTMENT

As stated at the beginning of this chapter, this discussion refers to an organizational arrangement in which the human resources office is attached to the organization in strictly a staff position. During the last few years, however, in many healthcare institutions and in many industrial and business settings, the CEO has decided that all dismissals have to be approved by the human resources director. The top-level administrator has the authority to make such a provision, and in this instance *functional* staff authority, as discussed in Chapter 12, has been conferred on the human resources department. In other words, top-level administration wants human resources to make the final decision as to whether or not an employee who has been working in the institution longer than the customary probationary period should be dismissed. The administrator is removing this portion from the supervisor's authority and conferring it on the human resources department.

There must be strong reasons behind such a decision, since it clearly runs counter to the principle of unity of command and weakens the authority of the

■ FIGURE 16-1 Examples of current laws and regulations affecting employment policies.

Legislation	Concern or content	Administrative agency
Title VII of the Civil Rights Act of 1964†	Sex	EEOC‡
Equal Pay Act of 1963		EEOC
Title VII of the Civil Rights Act of 1964†	Color	EEOC
Title VII of the Civil Rights Act of 1964†	Race	EEOC
Title VII of the Civil Rights Act of 1964†	Religion	EEOC
Title VII of the Civil Rights Act of 1964†	National origin	EEOC
Age Discrimination in Employment Act of 1967, as amended in 1978	Age (protection for those 40 to 70 years old)	EEOC
Rehabilitation Act of 1973	Handicapped persons	U.S. Department of Labor
The Vietnam-Era Veteran Readjustment Assistance Act of 1974	Vietnam-era veterans	U.S. Department of Labor
Various executive orders, principally no. 11246 and revised order no. 4	*All* the above as part of affirmative action programs	Office of Federal Contract Compliance, U.S. Department of Labor

*Effective at the time of publication of this text. This is a partial list of the framework of laws, regulations, and administrative agencies that govern employment policies and decisions.
†As amended by the Equal Employment Opportunity Act of 1972 and the Pregnancy Discrimination Act of 1978.
‡Equal Employment Opportunity Commission.

line manager's position. The CEO's decision probably was based on the need and desire to comply with all possible fair and nondiscriminatory employment practices and regulations so as not to expose the enterprise to embarrassing situations. There may be additional reasons why the CEO may want to delegate this final authority to fire an employee to the director of human resources.

Of course, it is always desirable for the personnel director to disseminate current information regarding fair employment practices and so forth to all first-line supervisors. For example, the personnel office should familiarize the supervisors with recent government provisions. Also, the various possibilities of engaging in conscious or unconscious discriminatory practices should be brought to the attention of the supervisors. Supervisors should also understand the meaning of affirmative action. Furthermore, administration should explain the importance of documentation, and line supervisors should be urged to keep meaningful records that they and the institution can refer to if necessary. If supervisors are familiar with most of these current thoughts and considerations, it is unlikely that they would contemplate discharging an employee unless all possible ramifications have already been considered. Under these circumstances the director of human resources probably will go along with a proposed dismissal, since the supervisor has a well-documented and substantiated case that can become a valid defense. It is desirable, therefore, that the personnel director who has been given the final authority on discharges will use this authority with discretion and consult with the various supervisors and not use it as if he or she were the "supreme power."

■ THE SUPERVISOR'S STAFFING FUNCTION

The staffing function is a continuous activity for the supervisor, not something that is required only when the department is first established. It is much more realistic and more typical to think of staffing as a situation in which a supervisor is put in charge of an existing department with a certain number of employees already in it. Although there is a nucleus of employees to start with, changes in personnel probably will take place before long. Since every supervisor depends on employees for the operating results of the department, it is the supervisor's responsibility to make certain that there is a supply of well-trained employees to fill the various positions.

Determining the Need for Employees

To make certain that the department can perform the jobs required of it, the supervisor must determine both the number and type of employees who will be needed for the department. If the supervisor has set up the structure of the department, he or she has designed an organizational structure in which the functions and jobs are shown in their proper relationships. If the supervisor takes over an existing department, it is necessary to become familiar with it by drawing a picture of the existing jobs and functions. For example, the supervisor of the maintenance department may find that there are groups of painters, electricians, carpenters, and other skilled *persons* within the department. After taking this inventory of personnel, it should be determined how many skilled *positions* there are or should be within this department, considering budgetary constraints. The working relationships between these positions should be examined and defined by the supervisor.

After determining the needs of the department, the supervisor may have to adjust the ideal setup to existing necessities. Several positions may have to be combined into one if there is not enough work for one employee. Only by studying the organizational setup of the department can the supervisor determine what and how many employees are needed to perform what jobs.

Job Description

To fill the various positions with appropriate employees, it is necessary to match the available jobs in the department with the credentials of prospective employees. This can only be done with the help of job descriptions. (See Figure 16-2). The job description tells exactly what duties and responsibilities are contained within a particular job. It describes the content of the job by listing as completely as possible every duty and responsibility involved. In many instances the supervisor will find a set of job descriptions available. If none is available, the human resources director will help in establishing a set. However, no one is better equipped to describe the content of a job than the supervisor. The supervisor is responsible for the accomplishment of the department's tasks, and he or she knows or should know the content of each position. Although the final form of the job description may be prepared in the personnel office, the supervisor should determine its specific content.

Only by describing the job requirements in great detail is it possible to ascertain the skills necessary to perform the job satisfactorily. Even if the position is already in operation, it is still advisable to follow this procedure of determining the major duties and responsibilities. After this has been done, the supervisor should compare this list with the current job description and with the employee's actual duties. The older job description may no longer fit the current content of the job and should be corrected. The supervisor also may find that some of the duties assigned to the job really do not belong to it. Even if the job in question is a new position, the supervisor should proceed along similar lines. The supervisor should determine the job's duties and responsibilities, and, with the help of the personnel department, draw up a job description. Once the content of the job has been listed, the supervisor should then specify the knowledge, education, degrees, experience, and skills required of the prospective employee.

In every job an employee must know certain facts before he or she can perform the job effectively. For example, it may be necessary to be able to read simple blueprints or be familiar with mathematics. If a knowledge of mathematics is needed for a certain job, the specific type of mathematics required should be clearly defined. The word "mathematics" could imply knowledge far beyond a working knowledge of simple arithmetic, or a knowledge of simple arithmetic might be all that is required in the job. The more precisely defined the required job knowledge is, the easier it will be to select from among available applicants.

When stipulating the skills needed for a particular job, the supervisor should not ask for a higher degree of skill than is absolutely necessary. One way to avoid this is to check the requirements drawn up with the qualifications of employees who are doing the same or similar work. Such investigation may quickly reveal whether a high-school education is necessary for a certain job. The supervisor may discover that an older person without a high-school diploma can perform this work.

Equal employment opportunity laws and rulings require that job descriptions must not discriminate against certain classes and that they must be job related. Since supervisors could not possibly be aware of all the ramifications in this respect, the human resources department should be consulted. To comply

■ FIGURE 16-2 Description of nurse specialist.

Date: June 1989	Job Title: Nurse Specialist
Number of Employees Supervised: NA	Department: Nursing
Supervised by: Director of	Section: 3110
Surgical Nursing	
Approved by: _____	Job Grade: UG Job Code No.: 012

Purpose of Position
The nurse specialist provides expert nursing care in a defined clinical area to facilitate the delivery of patient care either directly or through others.

Primary Responsibilities
The nurse specialist provides direction in the management of patient care by determining the psychophysiological responses of selected patients to their illnesses. The nurse specialist performs a systematic assessment of selected patients/significant others, develops a written plan of care, assists in the implementation of identified nursing or medical interventions and evaluates the outcomes from the interventions constructed to meet identified needs.

Performs a variety of activities that meet educational needs in the clinical area of focus. These activities may include: participation in patient education subcommittees, development of teaching booklets and audiovisual materials for patients/significant others and individualized patient teaching. Participates in clinical and theoretical healthcare instruction for nursing personnel through workshops, conferences, seminars, and informal discussions.

Participates in a variety of nursing and hospital committees. Evaluates services and products based on both clinical reliability and economic feasibility.

Participates in the development and updating of policies and procedures within the specialty area.

Encourages the use of scientific investigation to resolve clinical problems in the area of focus, participates in nursing research projects, and utilizes current medical and nursing reports to recommend changes in nursing practice.

Training, Education, Experience, or Other Requirements
The nurse specialist must have graduated from an approved school of nursing and hold a Master's Degree in Nursing related to clinical specialty. RN licensure must be current in the state of Missouri. Two years of clinical practice in the specialty is required. Knowledge of teaching and learning theory, utilization of community resources, physical assessment skills and principles of both change theory and research will enhance the effectiveness of incumbent.

Physical Demands
Stands and walks most of the time. Works in a clean air-conditioned environment.

Replaces Job Description
Nurse Specialist, dated May, 1985

EXPECTATION I: Management of Patient Care
Facilitates the delivery of patient care by utilizing the nursing process to promote expert nursing care in a defined clinical area.

Nursing Process
1. Utilizes sophisticated diagnostic information in assessment of patients.
2. Identifies and evaluates realistic expected outcomes for patients/significant others.

Reprinted with permission from Barnes Hospital, St. Louis. For illustrative purposes only.

■ FIGURE 16-2 Description of nurse specialist. (cont.)

3. Plans and participates with patients/significant others interventions that assist patients to adapt to optimal level of wellness.
4. Makes rounds on patients either referred or independently identified in clinical area of focus.
5. Prepares patients and/or significant others for discharge.
6. Determines the standards for patient care related to area of clinical focus.
7. Incorporates advanced clinical skills into nursing practice relevant to clinical area of focus.
8. Serves as a resource person for complicated patients requiring specialized interventions.
9. Performs consistent ongoing assessment of learning needs and those factors which affect learning for a specific group of patients and/or their significant others.
10. Participates in development of policies and procedures by updating current policies, developing new policies that reflect changes in clinical practice and serving as a resource person during the implementation of policies.

EXPECTATION II: Financial Responsibilities
Assists in providing an atmosphere for cost-effective patient care within the specialty area.
1. Assesses the economic impact of current services and products within the specialty area.
2. Plans for services and products to meet economic needs within the specialty area.
3. Provides for services and implementation of products used which meet economic needs, within the specialty area, such as:
   a. Discharge planning.
   b. Patient referral to physicians in the hospital.
   c. Teaching and evaluation of individuals through the screening clinic.
   d. Prevention of complications through assessment and evaluation of nursing care.
4. Evaluates new services and products based on economic feasibility within the specialty area.

EXPECTATION III: Accomplishment of Goals/Objectives
Establishes and evaluates personal and professional objectives in relationship to corporate and nursing service goals.
1. Provides direction to staff related to established clinical standards.
2. Accomplishes special projects within a specific time frame.
3. Encourages use of scientific investigation of clinical problems in clinical area of focus.
4. Facilitates changes in nursing practice based on current research reports.
5. Evaluates clinical relevancy, statistical analysis, and scientific basis of research articles in the specialty area.

EXPECTATION IV: Planning/Contribution to Planning
Plans and implements programs that meet educational needs in clinical areas of focus. Forecasts changes and implements plans that impact the hospital's utilization of present and future resources.
1. Plans, develops, and evaluates strategies for educational development incorporating psychophysiological and environmental factors. (Examples include but are not restricted to those listed).
   a. Teaching booklets.
   b. Self-learning packets.
   c. Audiovisual materials.
   d. Writing nonresearch articles.

■ FIGURE 16-2 Description of nurse specialist. (cont.)

2. Participates in educational experiences directed towards the clinical area of focus within the hospital, in the community, and at a national level.
   a. Educates patients and significant other(s).
   b. Participates in educational activities of the healthcare team and students.
      • Inservice programs
      • DET planning
      • Consultation
3. Assists in assessing and planning departmental needs in specialty area for the upcoming year, such as clinical, educational, budgetary needs, committee work, and special projects.
   a. Participates in planning departmental objectives and serves as a resource person in planning nursing service objectives.
   b. Serves as a resource person during the implementation of nursing service objectives.
   c. Evaluates implementation of nursing service objectives.
   d. Serves on nursing service committees as appointed or volunteers.

EXPECTATION V: Interpersonal and Communication Skills
A. Identifies the patient and their significant other(s), staff, physicians, as consumers and demonstrates techniques for providing an open, professional, congenial atmosphere.
   1. Communicates with and listens to patient, significant others, and members of the health team in a concise, tactful, and considerate manner.
   2. Assesses consumer satisfaction within one's specialty area.
   3. Plans for methods and programs to improve consumer satisfaction.
   4. Provides services to improve consumer satisfaction, such as:
      a. Direct interventions and evaluations with patients.
      b. Formal consumer programs.
      c. Referrals to appropriate resources.
   5. Evaluates consumer satisfaction concerning services provided.
   6. Collaborates with physicians to establish programs and provide for patient care needs.
B. Utilizes effective communication methods for purposes of documentation. Identifies need for development of tools to provide optimal interdepartmental communication.
   1. Conveys written and verbal communication clearly to other members of healthcare team.
   2. Evidences through written and verbal communication the nursing process which probes beyond routine patient/significant other(s) assessment and recommends interventions individualized to patient situation.
   3. Conveys through written and verbal communication patient/significant other(s)'s response to interventions and recommendations for any needed change in therapy plan.
   4. Contributes to development of hospital forms and methods that increase clarity and efficiency of documentation.
   5. Works with nursing staff in development and utilization of effective documentation skills.

EXPECTATION VI: Teamwork and Cooperation
Demonstrates the ability to work collaboratively within nursing service and other departments. Works with peer group to promote the role of the Nurse Specialist on a local and national level.
1. Demonstrates support of nursing service and corporate goals.
2. Participates actively in assigned or volunteered committees within Nursing Service or hospital.

■ FIGURE 16-2 Description of nurse specialist. (cont.)

3. Works with members of multidisciplinary team to identify and resolve problems in patient care management.

EXPECTATION VII: Attitude/Loyalty
Demonstrates a positive manner in fulfilling responsibilities of the position.
1. Exhibits knowledge and support of Barnes' hospital and nursing philosophy, policies, and procedures as demonstrated in personal conduct and provision of nursing care.
2. Demonstrates behaviors and attitudes conducive to effective consumer relations.
3. Provides services to improve consumer satisfaction within specialty area, such as:
   a. Direct interventions and evaluations with patients.
   b. Formal consumer programs.
   c. Referrals to appropriate resources.

EXPECTATION VIII: Professional Knowledge
Assumes responsibility and accountability for personal and professional activities related to research, clinical, educational, and leadership roles.
1. Maintains membership in the professional organization which represents nurses in specialty area.
2. Attends and/or participates in one major conference in the specialty area per year.
3. Reviews journals and other publications in order to remain current within the specialty area.
4. Identifies strengths and limitations of professional practice.
5. Submits written reports of activities on a consistent basis or as required.
6. Improves professional recognition through writing and publication.
7. Increases expertise in the specialty area by attending workshops, courses, conferences, and lectures.
8. Assumes responsibility for professional communications with physicians, other disciplines, and departments.

EXPECTATION IX: Innovation/Creativity
Demonstrates ability to develop new ideas and alternate methods to improve existing conditions. Encourages use of scientific investigation of clinical problems within the specialty area.
1. Investigates researchable patient care problems relevant to the specialty area.
2. Evaluates clinical relevance, statistical analysis, and scientific basis of research articles in the specialty area.
3. Serves as resource person in specialty area for scientifically substantiating nursing practice.
4. Demonstrates the ability to design a research study.
5. Facilitates changes in nursing practice based on current research reports.
6. Develops care plans which reflect a basis in scientific methods.
7. Serves as principal or co-investigator on research studies in the specialty area.
8. Designs tools which evaluate the outcome of changes in nursing practice.
9. Publishes results of research studies as well as articles, booklets, manuals, etc.

EXPECTATION X: Development of Subordinates and Leadership
Demonstrates ability to identify potential and actual problems in patient care area. Recommends solutions and intervenes appropriately. Communicates pertinent information to appropriate manager.
1. Assesses knowledge base and skills of nursing staff in area of specialty through direct observation, conferences, and review of charting.
   a. Plans programs/conferences that help develop the knowledge base and skills of nursing staff in area of specialty.

■ FIGURE 16-2 Description of nurse specialist. (cont.)

---

   b. Participates in presenting and using appropriate resources for programs/
      conferences that will develop the knowledge base and skills of nursing staff in
      area of specialty.
   c. Contributes to evaluation of nursing staff in area of specialty concerning
      knowledge base and skills.
   d. Acts as role model in delivery of care.
2. Accepts responsibility for clinical development of assigned students as a preceptor.
3. Evaluates effects of educational intervention directed towards educational development within the clinical area of focus and provides feedback to appropriate manager
   as needed.

---

with these laws and regulations, many personnel departments have assumed responsibility for the final draft of the job descriptions.

The supervisor should realize that by setting employment standards unrealistically high, the task of finding the person to meet these specifications will become unnecessarily difficult. There is no need to specify a certain number of years of formal education and experience if all that is required is simply job know-how. This does not mean that the job specifications should ask for less than what is needed. The job description should specify the requirements realistically. If the requirements are set too high, people who are overqualified will be placed on the job. The likely result is that the particular employee may prove to be troublesome because his or her capacities are not completely utilized. By the same token, it is just as disastrous to ask for less than the necessary requirements. Once placed on the job, the employee may turn out to be unsatisfactory. Many of these difficulties can be avoided if the supervisor analyzes the job content diligently and specifies the necessary job knowledge and skills realistically.

The human resources department will prove to be of great help in drawing up these job descriptions. The supervisor should be cautioned, however, not to turn over the job of doing this to the personnel person. The content must definitely be specified by the supervisor and by no one else. Once these job descriptions have been drafted, the supervisor should consult with some of the people who are holding these jobs to compare the job descriptions with the actual positions in question. Once all difficulties have been ironed out, these job descriptions are maintained in the personnel department and also in the supervisor's file. Whenever the supervisor needs to fill a certain job, the personnel staff is informed of the opening. Personnel will recruit applicants and quickly screen out those who are obviously unsuitable because they do not have the knowledge, necessary skills, or other requirements. All who seem to fulfill the requirements will be referred to the supervisor for his or her acceptance or rejection.

Since job descriptions should be kept up-to-date, the supervisor occasionally must review the contents of the job. Without regular reviews, descriptions may become inadequate. The supervisor must continually audit the job descriptions in the department. Many activities in the healthcare field change considerably through new technology, scientific advances, and sometimes because of the creative efforts of the person occupying a position. Ambitious employees may enlarge the scope of their own activities, whereas other employees lose or forego portions of theirs. The extent and character of change must be determined so that accurate information is contained in the job description. This is necessary because the job description is constantly referred to when the personnel department recruits candidates, when the supervisor hires new employees, when their performance is appraised, and when an attempt is made to establish an equitable wage pattern within the department.

If staffing decisions are to possess any validity, they must be based on comprehensive job descriptions that are systematically revised to reflect the current job situation as accurately as possible. Furthermore, they must reflect the current situation of equal employment opportunity and nondiscrimination.

How Many to Hire

Normally the supervisor is not confronted with the situation in which many employees have to be hired at the same time. Such a situation could exist when a new department is created and the supervisor has to staff it completely from scratch. More typically the question of hiring an employee will occur infrequently. Of course, some supervisors continuously ask for additional employees to get a job done. In most of these cases their problems are not solved even if they get more help. The situation may even become worse; instead of reducing the supervisor's problems, they are actually increased.

A supervisor usually will need to hire a new worker when one of the employees leaves the department, either voluntarily quitting, being dismissed, or for some other reason. In such instances there is little doubt that the job must be filled. Occasionally changes in the technical nature of the work take place, and manual labor may be replaced by machinery or sophisticated instruments. In this case a replacement may not be needed. Normally, however, a new employee has to be hired to replace the one who left.

Other situations arise when additional employees have to be added. For example, when departmental activities have been enlarged or when new duties are to be undertaken and no one within the department possesses the required job knowledge and skill, the supervisor has to go out into the open market and recruit employees. Sometimes a supervisor is inclined to ask for additional help if the workload is increased or if the supervisor feels added pressure. Before requesting additional employees under those conditions, the supervisor should make certain that the persons currently within the department are fully utilized and that additional people are absolutely necessary. It is hoped that this can be achieved within the constraints of the budget.

If vacancies exist within the department, the supervisor should inform the human resources department, and the personnel people in turn should see that a number of suitable candidates for the jobs are made available. The personnel department accomplishes this task by consulting the various job descriptions. Again, those applicants who are obviously undesirable and unfit for the position in question can quickly be screened out. Those who seem to be generally acceptable and have the required knowledge and skills should be passed on to the supervisor.

As stated many times, the actual hiring decision is not to be made in the personnel office, but rather by the supervisor in whose department the employee is to work. Although supervisors may believe that this is not necessary in filling an unskilled job, they should not relinquish their prerogative and duty to hire their own people. Whether the job is nonskilled, semiskilled, or skilled, it is up to the supervisor to hire the employee. Since all applicants are prescreened by the personnel office, the supervisor knows that all those sent to him or her possess the minimum qualifications prescribed for the job. It is the supervisor's job to pick out the one who will probably fill the job best. This is not an easy task, but as time goes on the supervisor will gain more and more experience, and it will become easier to make the right decision. All this will be discussed in the following chapter.

■ SUMMARY

Staffing is the managerial function of procurement and maintenance of the department's human resources, a function every supervisor has to perform. Staffing means to select, place, train, evaluate, promote, discipline, and appropriately compensate the employees of the department. All this is the supervisor's line function. In fulfilling this duty, the supervisor is significantly aided by the services of the human resources department. In most enterprises the personnel department is attached to the organization in a staff capacity, and its purpose is to counsel, inform, advise, and service all other departments of the enterprise. Sometimes, to be of service to the line manager, the human resources department may be inclined to take over line functions such as hiring and disciplining. Supervisors must caution themselves not to turn over any of their line functions to the personnel department, although at times it might seem expedient to let them handle the troublesome problems.

Before the manager can undertake the staffing function, the number and types of employees needed in the department must be clarified. The organizational chart combined with job descriptions will specify what workers are needed to fill the various jobs. In addition, the supervisor must take into consideration the amount of work to be performed and the positions allocated in the budget. In all these supervisory duties the human resources department is available for assistance and service. It is the supervisor's function, however, to select, place, develop, evaluate, promote, reward, and discipline all the employees within the department.

During the last decades numerous federal, state, and local laws and regulations as well as executive orders have been enacted regarding equal employment opportunities, fair employment practices, nondiscriminatory practices, and so forth. All employment practices and policies must comply with these require-ments. This has become a rapidly growing area of special concern that is best handled by specialists in the human resources department. Because of the vast impact this has made on the activities of all managers and because of the impor-tance of compliance, the influence of the human resources department within an organization has increased substantially. The CEO has recognized and is dealing with the need for a proper balance of influence and authority between the line managers and the personnel people.

In a number of organizations functional authority has been conferred on the human resources department, especially when the problem involves dismissals and fair employment practices. The average line supervisor could not possibly be or remain aware of new laws, court decisions, and so forth. Therefore, it makes good sense that the authority of the human resources department has been greatly altered, even if this means narrowing the supervisor's line authority.

17

THE SELECTION PROCESS AND THE EMPLOYMENT INTERVIEW

The purpose of the selection process is to choose logically from among the various candidates the one who meets the job demands best and is likely to perform well and also stay with the organization. Since the selection of the right employee contributes significantly to the effectiveness of the department, the final decision should rest with the candidate's prospective superior. In so doing, the selector can be kept completely responsible for the performance of the selected candidate. Opinions of others, such as the selector's superior, those who will have working relationships with the candidates, and specialists from the human resources department, can help the supervisor. The final decision on selection, however, rests with the department supervisor.

After all the preliminary work has been performed by the human resources department, such as recruitment, preliminary screening interviews, obtaining biographical data, and relevant testing, it is the supervisor's job to see the applicants, talk to them, and select the one who will best fill the vacant job. This is a decisive step for the employee and the supervisor. This is the moment when the supervisor must match the applicant's capability with the demands of the job, the authority and responsibility inherent in the position, the working conditions, and the rewards and satisfactions it offers. The personal interview between the supervisor and applicant is an essential part of the selection process.

Although some question interviews as a reliable and valid means of selection and as a predictor of future performance, the interview is an almost universally used selection device. It involves two-way communication, enabling the interviewer to learn more about the applicant's background, interests, and values and enabling the applicant to ask questions about the institution and the job. The interview is not a precise technique, and it is difficult to interview skillfully. Since no fixed criteria exist for success or failure, prejudiced interviewers can easily evaluate an applicant's performance according to their own stereotypes. Also, job

applicants react differently to different interviewers. As a major means for deciding, however, interviews are probably more valid for accurately predicting employee behavior than decisions made on tests alone. Generally, structured
interviews are more valid than unstructured interviews. It is not an easy task to
make an appropriate appraisal of someone's potential during a brief interview.
Interviewing is much more than a technique; it is an art that can and must be
developed by every supervisor.

■ INTERVIEWS

Over a period of years the supervisor will learn that there are several types of
interviews. These include preemployment, or selection, interviews between the
supervisor and prospective employees; discussions when employees are fired; and
counseling sessions during which the abilities and deficiencies of an employee are
discussed. Other interviews occur when an employee voluntarily leaves the job, as
well as when employees want to discuss complaints, grievances, and any other
problem situations. In general, all these can be grouped into two kinds of interviews, *directive* (structured) and *nondirective* (counseling). Throughout our discussion we will separate these two approaches, but some interviews have aspects of
both categories. For example, the appraisal interview (Chapter 18) is primarily a
directive interview, but the discussion may take on some aspects of a nondirective
counseling interview.

Directive Interviews

Normally a directive interview is a discussion in which the interviewer knows
beforehand what particular facts will be discussed and what the goals, objectives,
and areas of discussion are. The directive interview is structured; the interviewer
will ask direct questions and tries to keep the discussion within predetermined
limits. The interviewer will try to obtain the necessary information by encouraging the interviewee to volunteer as much as possible, and, if necessary, by asking
the interviewee additional questions. In a structured interview the interviewer
frequently has a list of questions that is followed in all interviews, making for
consistency and asking only job-related, nondiscriminatory questions. The employment interview in which the supervisor selects one applicant over another is
an example of a directive interview.

Nondirective Interviews

Although we will be primarily concerned with the directive interview in this
chapter, the supervisor should be aware of what it means to conduct a nondirective, or counseling, interview. In a nondirective interview the interviewer encourages the interviewee to express freely his or her thoughts and feelings. This
type of interview is usually applied to problem situations in which the supervisor
is eager to learn what the interviewee thinks and feels. The nondirective interview

is employed in problem situations, such as complaints and grievances or off-the-job problems, or it may take the form of an exit interview when the employee voluntarily leaves the job. Affording your subordinates the opportunity of counseling interviews is a vital aspect of good supervision.

Supervisors must encourage subordinates to come to them with their problems. They must show that they are willing to hear employees out. Otherwise minor irritations may turn out to become major problems. The supervisor must realize that inherent in the managerial position is an invisible barrier between the supervisor and the subordinates. Some employees will have little difficulty speaking to their supervisors, but many are more timid. Therefore, the supervisor must make an effort to encourage those who are reluctant to reveal their thoughts. The supervisor should see that time is always available to listen to the subordinates and hear them out. If time is not available at the moment, then the interview, if possible, should be postponed for a few hours; the supervisor must allow enough time and not rush through the discussion.

The principal function of the nondirective interview is to give the supervisor a clue as to what the interviewee really thinks and feels and what lies at the root of a particular problem. In addition, it gives the interviewee a feeling of relief and helps the subordinate develop greater insight into his or her own problems, often finding solutions while "thinking out loud." Many sources of frustration exist within and outside the working environment, and unless frustration is relieved, it may lead to all forms of undesirable responses.

The ground rule for conducting a nondirective interview is to let the interviewee say whatever he or she wants to say and to encourage free expression of feelings and attitudes. Conducting such a nondirective interview is more difficult than conducting a directive interview. It demands the concentrated and continuous attention of the supervisor. The supervisor must exert self-control and hide his or her own ideas and emotions during the interview. The supervisor should not express approval or disapproval even though the employee may request it. This may prove exasperating, but it is essential.

In such a counseling interview the employee must feel free, perhaps for the first time in his or her life, to express feelings about everything. The fact that the troubled employee can pour out his or her troubles has therapeutic value. In all likelihood, as soon as all the negative feelings have been expressed, the employee may start to find some favorable aspects of the very same things that he or she had criticized earlier. When the employee is encouraged to verbalize problems, he or she may gain a greater insight into them or possibly may arrive at an answer or course of action that will help solve the difficulties. The employee must be permitted to work through difficulties alone, without being interrupted and advised by the counselor regarding the best course of action. If the problem concerns the job, work, and organization, however, the supervisor may have to be directive so that the solution is consistent with the needs of the institution.

The supervisor should normally exercise great care not to give advice or become burdened with the task of running the subordinate's personal life. Most of the time the interviewee wants a sympathetic and empathic listener and not an advisor. The average supervisor is not equipped to do counseling, and this is not part of the supervisor's job. If necessary, the subordinate should be helped by referral to trained specialists. This may be necessary when sensitive areas and deep-seated personality problems are involved. The patient-psychiatrist relationship is not applicable to that of subordinate and boss.

At first the nondirective interview is difficult to conduct, but as time goes on a good supervisor will learn to exercise self-control and, by concentrated listening, grasp the feelings of the employee. The counseling interviews can often be very time consuming. Although the supervisor is under many pressures and may not have much time for listening, time for such interviews must be made. The supervisor will find out that by listening, relationships with subordinates will be better and probably fewer personnel problems will arise. The supervisor must encourage subordinates to talk and must show that he or she is always willing to hear them out.

Skillful listening is an art that can be learned with training and experience. It can be learned better by practice than by reading books on the subject. The supervisor can gain this practice almost every day on the job. Eventually the supervisor will develop a system of listening that is comfortable and fits the supervisor's personality and at the same time puts the employee at ease.

A common purpose of both directive and nondirective interviews is to promote mutual understanding and confidence. It is an experience in human relations that will permit the interviewer and the interviewee to obtain greater understanding. The nondirective approach is not a cure for all human relations problems. Occasionally, as stated before, the supervisor has to be directive in the solution stage of the discussion. After fully listening to the subordinate, the supervisor may still have to overrule the employee so that the solution is in accordance with the needs and within the limits of the organization.

■ THE EMPLOYMENT INTERVIEW

The employment interview, also known as the preemployment, or selection interview, will be discussed as an example of the directive, or structured, interview. The interviewer knows ahead of time what facts will be discussed, what the objectives are, and what areas the discussion will cover. The structured interview is conducted using a set of standardized questions asked of all applicants; this produces data that can be compared and provides a basis for evaluating the applicants. The interviewer should prepare the questions in advance. This does not mean that the structured interview must be rigid. Although the questions preferably should be asked in a logical sequence, the applicant should have ample opportunity to explain the answers. At times the interviewer has to probe until a full understanding has been reached. The supervisor wants to learn as much as possible first by letting the interviewee volunteer information and then by asking direct questions.

Preparing for the Employment Interview

Since the purpose of the directive employment interview is to collect facts and reach a decision, the supervisor should prepare for it as thoroughly as possible. First, it is essential that the supervisor become acquainted with the available background information. By studying all the information assembled by the personnel director, the supervisor can sketch a general impression of the interviewee in advance.

The *application blank* is a form that seeks information about the applicant's background and present status. (See Figure 17-1.) It supplies a number of facts, such as the applicant's schooling and degrees; training; previous work experience, including nature of duties, length of stay, and salary; and other relevant data. The application blank is handed to the candidate on the first visit in the personnel department, and these data are evaluated there to decide whether the applicant merits further consideration.

■ **FIGURE 17-1 Typical employment application form used by healthcare institution.**

Employee No. _____

APPLICATION FOR EMPLOYMENT
(PLEASE PRINT OR TYPE)

P E R S O N A L   I N F O R M A T I O N

| TODAY'S DATE | POSITION APPLYING FOR |

| LAST NAME | FIRST NAME | Middle Init. | SOCIAL SECURITY NUMBER |

| STREET ADDRESS | CITY | STATE | ZIP CODE | TELEPHONE NO. |

| HOW LONG HAVE YOU LIVED AT THE ABOVE ADDRESS? | PREVIOUS ADDRESS | CITY | STATE | ZIP CODE |

| DATE OF BIRTH The Age Discrimination in Employment Act prohibits discrimination on the basis of age with respect to individuals who are at least 40 but less than 70 years of age | WHEN CAN YOU BEGIN WORK? | MINIMUM ACCEPTABLE SALARY | Have You Received Worker's Comp For Injuries? Yes No |

| SPECIFY TYPE OF WORK DESIRED FULL TIME PART TIME TEMPORARY | WILL YOU WORK OVERTIME WHEN SCHEDULED OR RE-QUESTED? Yes No | DAYS & SHIFTS YOU CAN WORK? | U.S. CITIZEN? No Yes |

| WHO SHOULD WE NOTIFY IN CASE OF EMERGENCY? NAME | ADDRESS | PHONE NO. | RELATION |

An applicant will not be denied employment due to a physical or mental handicap where reasonable accommodation can be made for such handicap.

| DO YOU HAVE A RECORD OF MENTAL OR PHYSICAL HANDICAP? | Write Yes or No | If Yes, Explain |

E D U C A T I O N

	SCHOOL	NAME	CITY	STATE	DATES ATTENDED	GRAD-UATED	DIPLOMA OR DEGREE REC'D	COURSES OR MAJOR
HIGH SCHOOL					TO			
BUSINESS SCHOOL					TO			
NURSING SCHOOL					TO			
COLLEGE					TO			
GRADUATE SCHOOL					TO			
OTHER SCHOOL OR TRAINING					TO			

LIST ANY PROFESSIONAL, TRADE REGISTRATION OR LICENSE NUMBERS AND EXPIRATION DATES:

S K I L L S

LIST SPECIFIC OFFICE OR TECHNICAL SKILLS (CLERICAL APPLICANTS, PLEASE LIST YOUR SHORTHAND AND TYPING SPEED)

M I S C E L L A N E O U S

| BY WHOM REFERRED? | Have you ever worked at BH before? No Yes, If Yes, When? | Names of friends or relatives employed at BH Relationship |

NAME OF PROFESSIONAL OR TRADE ORGANIZATIONS TO WHICH YOU BELONG (Omit any which might indicate race, religion, color or ancestry)

(1) HAVE YOU EVER BEEN CONVICTED OF A CRIME? IF YES, DESCRIBE IN FULL (Do Not Include Minor Traffic Violation)

(2) HAS ANY SURETY COMPANY EVER REFUSED TO ISSUE OR CONTINUE ANY BOND ON YOUR BEHALF? IF, YES, STATE WHEN & WHAT COMPANY

NOTE: AN ANSWER IF YES TO (1) OR (2) ABOVE DOES NOT NECESSARILY DISQUALIFY YOU FOR EMPLOYMENT AT BH.

U. S.   M I L I T A R Y

| ARE YOU A VETERAN | DATES OF SERVICE | TYPE OF DUTY | RANK AT DISCHARGE |
| | FROM   TO | | |

SERVICE SCHOOL OR SPECIAL TRAINING RECEIVED:

Reprinted with permission from Barnes Hospital, St. Louis. For illustrative purposes only.

■ **FIGURE 17-1 Typical employment application form used by healthcare institution. (cont.)**

EMPLOYMENT
(LIST LAST EMPLOYER FIRST)

DATES OF EMPLOYMENT					EMPLOYER'S NAME		Starting Salary	Ending Salary
	Month		Year		EMPLOYER'S ADDRESS/PHONE NO.		Duties:	
From					SUPERVISOR'S NAME/TITLE	YOUR JOB TITLE		
To					REASON FOR LEAVING			
DATES OF EMPLOYMENT					EMPLOYER'S NAME		Starting Salary	Ending Salary
	Month		Year		EMPLOYER'S ADDRESS/PHONE NO.		Duties:	
From					SUPERVISOR'S NAME/TITLE	YOUR JOB TITLE		
To					REASON FOR LEAVING			
DATES OF EMPLOYMENT					EMPLOYER'S NAME		Starting Salary	Ending Salary
	Month		Year		EMPLOYER'S ADDRESS/PHONE NO.		Duties:	
From					SUPERVISOR'S NAME/TITLE	YOUR JOB TITLE		
To					REASON FOR LEAVING			

MAY WE COMMUNICATE WITH YOUR EMPLOYERS? PAST: YES [ ] NO [ ] PRESENT: YES [ ] NO [ ]

PLEASE READ CAREFULLY

APPLICANT CERTIFICATION AGREEMENT

I certify that the statements made on this application are true and correct to the best of my knowledge and belief and hereby grant Barnes Hospital permission to verify such answers. I understand that any false statement on this application may be considered as sufficient cause for rejection of this application, or for dismissal if such false statement is discovered subsequent to my employment. I further understand that Barnes Hospital will perform a pre-employment investigation to determine my suitability for employment and I authorize Barnes Hospital to have written access to any records concerning education or employment background. I understand that if any inquiry is made, all information as to its nature and scope will be supplied upon written request. If this application is considered favorably, I may have to pass a physical examination as condition of employment, and I agree to abide by and comply with all of the rules of Barnes Hospital.

SIGNATURE ______________________ DATE ______________

Barnes Hospital is an equal opportunity employer, federal law prohibits discrimination in employment practices because of race, color, religion, sex, age, national origin, or handicapped status. No question on this application is asked for the purpose of limiting or excluding any applicant's consideration for employment because of his or her race, color, religion, sex, age, national origin, or handicapped status.

(APPLICANT - DO NOT WRITE IN THIS SPACE)

HUMAN RESOURCES & DEVELOPMENT DEPT. ______________________

Interviewer's Signature ______________________ Date ______________

The information contained in a completed application is somewhat limited because of laws, regulations, and court decisions regarding equal employment opportunities and discrimination. Generally, except under certain bona fide, job-related circumstances, federal regulations and guidelines prevent requiring applicants to state religion, sex, ancestry, marital status, age, birthplace of the applicant or parents, and other data. More details will be discussed later concerning what questions an interviewer can properly ask of the interviewee. Application blanks may sample the candidates' abilities to write, organize thinking, and present facts clearly. The application blank indicates whether the applicant's education has been logically patterned and whether there has been a route of progression to better jobs. Also, it gives the interviewer points of departure for the formal interview.

While studying the application blank before the interview, the supervisor should keep in mind the job for which the applicant will be interviewed. If some questions arise while studying the application blank, the supervisor should write them down so that they will not be forgotten and will be asked. For example, all previous jobs are stated in chronological sequence; however, these data reveal a gap of six months during which the applicant did not work or go to school. Careful questions about this may reveal that the candidate spent the time in a penal institution or was traveling abroad or that a car accident required a lengthy hospital stay. Some questions may concern results of skill and aptitude tests given by the personnel department, and any questions in this area should be clarified by the supervisor before the interview takes place.[1]

Some additional information can also be gained from a *reference check.* (See Figure 17-2.) Such reference checks with previous employers are best handled by the human resources department; special care is advisable because of emerging personal privacy regulations and potential exposure to damage claims. The points to be checked should be job related; all this should be done with the knowledge and permission of the applicant.

Since the purpose of the employment interview is to gather information to make a hiring decision, the supervisor should prepare a schedule or plan for the interview. The interviewer should jot down all the important items that have no available information and all those areas that need further clarification. Once all these key points have been written down, one is not likely to forget to ask the interviewee about them. Conceivably, the supervisor may be interrupted during the interview, and the applicant might be dismissed before the supervisor has had a chance to ask about certain points that still lack information. Writing them down beforehand will prevent such an occurrence. Having thought out the various questions in advance, the supervisor can devote much of the attention to listening and observing the applicant. A well-prepared plan for the employment interview is well worth the time spent on it.

In addition to obtaining background information and making out a plan for the interview, the supervisor should be concerned with the proper setting for conducting the interview. Privacy and some degree of comfort are normal requirements for a good conversation. If a private room is not available, the supervisor should create an aura of semiprivacy by speaking to the applicant in a corner or in a place where other employees are not within hearing distance. That much privacy is a necessity. If it can be arranged, precautions should be taken to avoid any interruptions during the interview by phone calls or other matters. This gives the interviewee additional assurance of how much importance the supervisor places on this interview.

Conducting the Interview

In conducting the employment interview, the supervisor should make certain that a leisurely atmosphere is created and that the applicant is put at ease. The good supervisor will think back about when he or she applied for a job and recall the stress and tension connected with it. After all, the applicant is meeting strange people who ask searching questions and is likely to be under considerable

■ FIGURE 17-2 Typical form for reference check.

REFERENCE CHECK

TO: _____

We are considering employing _____

Social Security # _____, for the position of _____

We understand that this individual was employed by you as a _____

_____ from _____ to _____

Would you kindly complete and return this form using the enclosed self-addressed envelope at your earliest convenience. Your reply will be kept confidential.

Thank you for your courtesy,

_____

Personnel Department

Reason for termination: Resigned _____ Discharged _____ Other _____

Would you rehire? Yes _____ No _____ (If no, why?) _____

Final base salary: $_____ per _____ Employed from _____

to _____

	Below average	Average	Above average
Quality of work:	_____	_____	_____
Quantity of work:	_____	_____	_____
Overall performance:	_____	_____	_____
Cooperation:	_____	_____	_____
Attendance & punctuality:	_____	_____	_____

Any additional information that will help us make our decision: _____

_____

_____

By: _____ Title _____ Date _____

I authorize the administration of this institution to investigate without liability the information requested.

I also authorize the former employer listed above to supply references without liability and to make full and complete disclosure of any other information that may be requested by the Personnel Department of this institution in connection with my application for employment.

I further certify that I have read the foregoing paragraph and knowingly make this authorization by setting forth my signature.

Signature: _____ Date: _____

Printed with permission from Saint Mary's Health Center, St. Louis, MO—a member of the SSM Health Care System. For illustrative purposes only.

strain. It is the supervisor's duty to relieve this tension, which is certain to be present in the applicant, and possibly in the supervisor as well. The applicant might be put at ease by opening the interview with brief general conversation, possibly about the weather, heavy traffic, the World Series, or some other topic of broad interest. Any topic that does not refer to the eligibility for the job will be relaxing. The interviewer may offer a cup of coffee or may employ any other social gesture that will put the applicant at ease and build rapport.

This informal "warming-up" approach should be brief, and the interviewer should move the discussion quickly to job-related matters. Excessive non-job-related informal conversation should be avoided. Studies have shown that sometimes the interviewer makes a selection decision in the first minutes of the interview, and it would be wrong to do this without having discussed job-related matters. A good starting question would be to ask how the applicant learned about this job opening.

In addition to obtaining information from the applicant, the interviewer should see to it that the job seeker learns enough about the job to help the applicant decide whether he or she is the right person for the position. The supervisor, therefore, should discuss the details of the job, such as working conditions, wages, hours, vacations, who the immediate supervisor would be, and how the job in question relates to other jobs in the department. The supervisor must describe the situation completely and honestly. In his or her eagerness to make the job look as attractive as possible, especially to professionals who are in short supply, the supervisor conceivably may state everything in terms better than they actually are. The supervisor must be careful not to oversell the job by telling the applicant what is available for exceptional employees. If the applicant turns out to be an average worker, this will lead to disappointments.

After outlining the job's details, the supervisor should ask the applicant what else he or she would like to know about the job. If the interviewee has no further questions at this time, the supervisor should proceed with questioning to find out how well qualified the applicant is. The supervisor will have some knowledge about the background from the application blank; there is no need to ask the applicant to restate information already given. However, the interviewer will need to know exactly how qualified the interviewee is in relation to the job in question. By this time the applicant has probably gotten over much of the tension and nervousness and will be ready to answer questions freely. Most of this information will be obtained by the supervisor's direct questions. The interviewer should be careful to phrase these questions clearly for the applicant. In other words, only terms that conform with the applicant's language, background, and experience should be used. Questions should be asked in a slow and deliberate form, one at a time, so as not to confuse the applicant. The interviewer should take care not to ask "leading" questions that would suggest a specific answer. For example, the supervisor should refrain from questions such as, "Do you have difficulty adjusting to authority?" or "Do you daydream frequently?" This form of questioning can only lead to antagonism.

Frequently supervisors take notes during or immediately after the interview. This can be helpful, especially if several candidates are being interviewed. It is difficult to remember in such a situation what each of the applicants said and not to get their statements confused. There is no need to take notes on everything; only the key factors should be jotted down.

All questions the supervisor asks should be pertinent and job related. This brings up the area of those questions that, although not directly related to the job itself, can become relevant to the work situation. Problems of a personal nature, although only indirectly connected with the job, may be relevant to the work situation. A supervisor will have to use good judgment and tact in this respect, since the applicant may be sensitive about some of the points to be discussed. By no means should the supervisor pry into personal affairs that are irrelevant and removed from the work situation merely to satisfy his or her own curiosity.

Equal Employment Opportunity Laws

Before the 1960s the interviewer could ask almost any question that was job related in some way. Today interviewing has become far more complicated and sophisticated because of the many laws, executive orders, and court decisions affecting equal employment opportunities, discrimination, affirmative action, etc. A number of questions are still perfectly lawful; for example, the interviewer can ask for the applicant's first and last names, current address, previous employment, educational background, etc. Questions that are for the most part unlawful include those about race or color, sex, religion, birthplace, and arrest record. Some questions are potentially unlawful to ask. For instance, it is certainly lawful to ask the applicant what other languages he or she speaks. In certain areas it is desirable, even sometimes necessary, also to speak Spanish, for example. However, this question should not lead to asking the applicant's native language and the one used at home. It would be inaccurate and presumptuous to provide a ''do and don't ask list,'' since each situation has to be judged in the local context, relatedness to the job, and the particular circumstances.

It is far better for supervisors to consult with the human resources department periodically to learn what can be asked and in which way and what should not be asked. The laws and regulations are numerous and ever changing. New decisions are made by the courts and administrative agencies almost daily, so it is a full-time job to be aware and stay abreast of them. The staff in the personnel division are usually familiar with the most recent developments and proper current practices. The interviewer should consult with them to learn which questions are appropriate, lawful if properly worded, and unlawful. The interviewer may also receive some suggestions as to how to obtain information that is necessary but cannot be asked directly. For example, the supervisor may have to resort to questions such as, ''Can you be away from home overnight if the job requires it?'' or ''Will your home responsibilities permit you to work around the clock?''

Evaluating the Applicant

The chief problem in employment interviews is how to interpret the candidate's employment and personal history and other pertinent information. It is impossible for supervisors to eliminate completely all their personal preferences and prejudices. Interviewers should face up to personal biases and make efforts to control them. It is not sufficient to claim that he or she has no biases; the supervisor should be able to clearly write down the reasons why one applicant has been selected in preference to another. It is essential that the interviewers take great care to avoid some of the more common pitfalls while sizing up a job applicant.[2]

First, the supervisor must not make *snap judgments*. It is difficult not to form an early impression and look for evidence during the rest of the interview to substantiate this first impression. The interviewer should collect all the information on the applicant before making a judgment. This will also help the interviewer not to become a victim of the halo effect.

The *halo effect* occurs when an interviewer lets one prominent characteristic overshadow other evidence. It means basing an applicant's entire potential for job performance on only one characteristic and using this impression as a guide in rating all the other factors. This may work either favorably or unfavorably for the job seeker. In any event, it would be wrong for the supervisor to form an overall opinion of the applicant on a single factor, such as the ability to express himself or herself fluently. If an applicant is articulate, there is no reason to project automatically a high rating for all other qualifications. A glance at the employees in the department will remind the supervisor that there are some very successful employees whose verbal communications are rather poor.

Another common pitfall is that of *overgeneralization*. The interviewer must not assume that because an applicant behaves in a certain manner in one situation that he or she will automatically behave the same way in all other situations. There may be a special reason why the applicant may answer a question in a rather evasive manner. It would be wrong to conclude from this evasiveness in answering one question that the applicant is underhanded and probably not trustworthy. The halo effect would be there if the interviewer lets, for example, an applicant's alma mater overshadow other aspects. People are prone to generalize quickly.

Another pitfall is that the interviewer will tend to judge the applicant by *comparisons* with current employees in the department. The interviewer may wonder how this applicant will get along with the other employees and with the supervisor and how the candidate will fit into the corporate culture. The interviewer may believe that any applicant who is considerably different from current employees is undesirable. This thinking may do great harm to the organization because it will only lead to uniformity, conformity, and thus mediocrity. This should not be interpreted to mean that the interviewer should make it a point to look for "oddballs" who obviously would not fit in the department. Just because a job applicant does not exactly resemble the other employees is no reason to conclude that the person will not make a suitable employee.

The interviewer should realize that the applicant may often give responses that are socially acceptable but not very revealing. The job seeker knows that the answer should be what the interviewer wants to hear. For example, if the interviewer asks a nurse what his or her aspirations are, the reply probably will be to be a head nurse one day. He or she settles for the head nurse's job rather than that of the director of nursing to avoid appearing conceited or presumptuous, but the applicant knows that a certain amount of ambition is socially acceptable.

Another hazard for the interviewer to avoid is *excessive qualifications*. Eager to get the best person for the job, the supervisor may look for qualifications that exceed the requirements of the job. Although the applicant should be qualified, there is no need to look for qualifications in excess of those actually required. An overqualified applicant would probably make a poor and frustrated employee for a job.

These are some of the more common pitfalls in interpreting the facts brought out during an interview. Supervisors should make an all-out effort not to fall into these traps when evaluating applicants.

■ CONCLUDING THE INTERVIEW AND MAKING THE DECISION

The decision whether or not to consider the applicant is made during or immediately after the interview. As stated before, the supervisor should have made some notes either during or after the interview so that the information can be reviewed and reevaluated. At the conclusion of the employment interview the supervisor is likely to have the choice of three possible actions: hire the applicant, defer the decision, or reject the applicant. We assume that it is within the supervisor's sole authority to decide and that checking first with the line superior or someone in personnel is not necessary. The applicant is eager to know which of these actions the supervisor is going to take and is entitled to an answer. No particular problem exists if the supervisor decides to hire this applicant; the person will be told when to report for work, and additional instructions may be given.

The supervisor also may decide to defer a decision until several other applicants for the same job have been interviewed. If this choice is made, it is necessary and appropriate for the supervisor to tell the interviewee and inform this person that he or she will be notified later. Preferably the supervisor will set a time limit within which the decision will be made.

Such a situation occurs frequently, but it is not fair to use this tactic to avoid the unpleasant task of telling the applicant that he or she is not acceptable. Under such circumstances, telling the applicant that the interviewing supervisor is deferring action raises false hopes. While waiting for an answer, the applicant may not look for another job and consequently may let some other opportunities slip by. It is unpleasant to tell an applicant that he or she is not suitable, but if the supervisor has decided that an applicant will not be hired, the applicant should be told in a clear but tactful way. Although it is much simpler to let the rejected applicant wait for a letter that never arrives, the applicant is entitled to an honest answer. If the job seeker does not fulfill the requirements of the job, it is preferable to say so.

It is better not to state the specific reasons beyond a general turn-down phrase. Supervisors may have experienced that stating reasons for not hiring someone encourages arguments and comparisons and can lead to many other problems, especially since the chances for being misquoted and misunderstood are great. It is best to turn the applicant down by stating, in a general way, that there is not sufficient match between the applicant's qualifications and the needs of the job. It is also not fair to tell the applicant that he or she will be called if something suitable opens up if the interviewer knows that no hope exists.

The supervisor should always bear in mind that the employment interview is an excellent opportunity to build a good reputation for the institution. The applicant knows that he or she is one of several candidates and that only one person can be selected. A large percentage of applicants are not hired. The way they are turned down, however, can have an effect on the applicant's impression of the institution. The only contact the applicant has with the organization is through the supervisor during the employment interview. Therefore, the supervisor should remember that the interview will leave either a good or a bad impression of the institution with the applicant. It is necessary, therefore, that an applicant leave the interview, regardless of its outcome, at least with the feeling that he or she has been courteously and fairly treated. Every supervisor should bear in mind that it is a managerial duty to build as much goodwill for the organization as possible and that the employment interview presents one of the rare opportunities to do so.

Documentation

In recent years the need for documentation has become increasingly necessary, since the supervisor's decision about a job candidate might be challenged. Therefore, the interviewer must write down the reasons for not hiring a certain applicant and/or why the one was hired in preference to the others. It is essential to have this documentation because the supervisor could not possibly remember the various reasons, and he or she may be asked to justify the decision later.

Such careful documentation is even more important now because the decision to hire or reject an applicant should be based on job-related factors and should not be discriminatory. In some cases supervisors might be pressured by the personnel department or higher management to give preferential hiring considerations to minorities or women. Supervisors should realize that the organization may have to meet certain affirmative-action goals. Again, only by careful documentation will supervisors be able to justify their decisions. Notes on a separate piece of paper attached to the application, not written on the back of the application, will serve the purpose.

Temporary Placement

Sometimes, although the applicant is not the right person for a particular job, he or she may be suitable for another position for which no current opening exists. The supervisor might be tempted to hold this desirable employee by offering temporary placement in any job that is available. The applicant should be informed about this prospect by the supervisor. At times, however, temporary placement in an unsuitable job causes misunderstanding and disturbance within the department. It is usually strenuous for an employee to mark time on a job that he or she does not care to perform while hoping for the proper job to open up. Normally such strain causes dissatisfaction after a time, and this dissatisfaction is usually communicated to other employees within the work group. Also, the expected suitable job may not open up. Therefore, interim placements are ill-advised and unsound.

■ SUMMARY

There are two ways of filling available job openings: to hire someone from the outside or promote someone from within the organization. In hiring from outside, the supervisor is aided by the human resources department, since it performs the services of recruiting and preselecting the most likely applicants. It is the supervisor's function and duty, however, to interview the various candidates appropriately and to hire those who promise to be the best ones for the jobs available. To accomplish this, the supervisor must acquire the skills needed to conduct an effective interview. The employment interview is primarily a directive, or structured, interview, in contrast to the nondirective interview often encountered in the supervisor's daily work.

During the employment interview the supervisor tries to find out whether the applicant's capability matches the demands of the job. The objective is to hire the person most suitable for the position available. To carry out a successful interview, the supervisor should become familiar with background information, list points to be covered and questions to be asked, be prepared in advance, and have the proper setting. In addition to securing information from the applicant, the interviewer should discuss with the interviewee as many aspects of the job as possible. There will be a number of additional questions and answers before the interviewer is ready to conclude the employment interview, evaluate the situation, and make a decision. All this must be accomplished while giving proper attention to the many aspects of equal and fair employment practices and other legal considerations.

In addition to conducting directive interviews, the supervisor is often called on to carry out nondirective interviews. This form of interview usually covers problem situations and gives the employees the opportunity to freely express their feelings, sentiments, and anything else on their mind. Many sources of frustration exist within and outside the working environment that can easily lead to a variety of undesirable responses. Giving subordinates the opportunity for a counseling interview is another vital duty of the supervisory position.

NOTES

1. The discussion of formal tests as a selection method goes beyond the confines of this text. More information on tests is provided in texts on personnel, personnel management, and human resources management. See Randall S. Schuler, *Personnel and Human Resource Management,* 3rd ed., St. Paul, MN: West Publishing Co., 1987, pp. 185-189; Frank L. Schmidt and John E. Hunter, "Employment Testing: Old Theories and New Research Findings," *American Psychologist,* October 1981, pp. 1128-1137.
2. W. C. Bynham, "The Ten Most Common Interviewing Mistakes," *Personnel Journal,* June 1984, pp. 10-12.

18

PERFORMANCE APPRAISALS, PROMOTIONS, AND TRANSFERS

Performance appraisals are central to organizational and management development. Their purpose is to provide a measure of the employee's job performance that leads to counseling and his or her further development. It is a formal system of measuring, evaluating, and influencing an employee's job-related activities. Performance appraisal is a control system that serves as an audit of the effectiveness of each employee. "It is the combination of performance feedback and the setting of specific goals based on this feedback that enables the performance appraisal to fulfill its two most important functions, namely the counseling (motivation) and development (training) of employees."[1] Decisions regarding an employee's continued employment, promotion, demotion, transfer, salary increase, or possible termination are made on the basis of the performance appraisal. Performance appraisals are important to maximize employee motivation and productivity and to minimize the chances of litigation suits.

In the typical organization every employee is subject to a periodic performance appraisal. Every organization needs valid information that enhances management's effectiveness in making decisions that influence the directing of human resources. The performance appraisal system is the continuous process for gathering, analyzing, and disseminating information about the performance of its members. These appraisals not only guide management in selecting certain individuals for promotion and salary increases, but also are useful for coaching employees to improve their performance. Appraisals are an important part of long-range personnel planning and the supervisor's staffing function. In addition, well-identified and described appraisal methods and procedures will contribute to a healthy organizational environment of mutual trust and understanding. This type of atmosphere is necessary if the healthcare center wants to bring about increased productivity and better patient care. A performance appraisal system helps to identify work requirements, performance standards, analysis and appraisal of job-related behaviors, and recognition of such behaviors.

■ THE PERFORMANCE APPRAISAL SYSTEM

The appraisal of an employee's performance is central to the supervisor's staffing function. It points to the need for further development, shows how effectively various subordinates contribute to departmental goals, and helps management identify those employees who have the potential to be promoted into better positions. It is important for a supervisor to be in a position to assess objectively the quality of the employees' performance in the department. Therefore, most organizations request that their supervisors carry out the provisions of the institution's formal appraisal system and periodically appraise and rate their employees. This formal appraisal system is also known as *employee evaluation, employee rating,* or *merit rating.* For our purposes it is assumed that the system has been designed so that it is legally defensible and not discriminatory in any way.[2]

Purposes of the Performance Appraisal System

The performance appraisal system serves many purposes, such as to provide a guide for possible promotion, further development, and a basis for merit increases. Another purpose is to translate into objective terms the performance, experience, and qualities of an employee and to compare these items with the requirements of the job. The formal appraisal system is designed to consider such criteria as job knowledge, ability to carry through on assignments, judgment, attitude, cooperation, dependability, output, housekeeping, safety, etc. Such a system of evaluations helps the supervisor to take all factors into account when considering merit increases or a promotion. It also provides a rational basis for decision making, since it reduces the chances for personal bias.

Such a formal appraisal system forces the supervisor to observe and scrutinize subordinates' work not only from the viewpoint of how well the employee is performing the job, but also from the standpoint of what can be done to improve the employee's performance. It is difficult to make such judgments because in most healthcare situations one is not dealing with concrete performance measures such as units produced, but with concepts of leadership, teamwork, cooperation, etc. Since an employee's poor performance and failure to improve may result from inadequate supervision, a formal appraisal system is also likely to improve supervisory qualities.

A formal evaluation system also serves another purpose. Employees have always expected security from their work. In addition to security, they seek satisfying and interesting work that enables them to grow. A well-designed appraisal system reduces ambiguity concerning job requirements and uncertainty by providing employees with information about what is expected from them and feedback on how they have performed. Every employee has the right to know how well he or she is doing and what can be done to improve the work performance.

One can assume that most employees are eager to know what their supervisors think of their work. In some instances the employee's desire to know how he or she stands with the boss can be interpreted as asking for reassurance about the employee's future in the organization. In other instances this expressed desire has different interpretations. For example, a subordinate may realize that he or she is doing a relatively poor job but hopes that the boss is not aware of it; the subordinate is anxious to be assured in this direction. On the other hand, another subordinate who knows that he or she is doing an outstanding job may wish to make certain that the boss is aware of it. This subordinate will want to receive more recognition.

The existence of regular appraisals is an important incentive to the employees of an organization. In a large, complex organization employees can easily feel that they and their contributions are forgotten and lost. Regular appraisals provide the assurance that the potential exists for improving oneself in the position and that one is not lost within the enterprise. It gives employees the assurance that supervisors and the entire organization care about them.

The appraisal program is a critical tool at the disposal of the supervisor, since it influences all personnel functions. It is a determinant in the planning, developing, and recognition of the organization's human resources. Another result of good implementation of performance appraisals is to direct employee behavior so that it benefits the employees and the organization. The supervisor will have ample opportunity to include the topics of motivation, such as Theories X and Y and hierarchy of needs (see Chapter 20), in the appraisal procedure, particularly during the postappraisal interview. These motivational theories can be incorporated into the performance appraisal, thus leading to an environment of trust.

In addition to creating a healthy organizational climate of trust, performance appraisals help management in decisions about compensation and in the area of employees' developmental and training needs. Appraisals provide an inventory of human resources suitable for promotions. They aid the supervisor because they show whether an employee is in the right job. They identify for the boss those employees who are moving ahead and those who are not progressing satisfactorily. Appraisals show whether the supervisor is succeeding in the job as a coach and teacher.

As mentioned, an appraisal program also has many advantages for employees. It reflects the quality of their work and gives them a sense of being treated fairly and not being overlooked. The employee knows what he or she can do to be promoted to a better job. Appraisals give the subordinate an opportunity to complain and criticize and express personal goals and ambitions. In this respect appraisals are motivational because they create a learning experience for subordinates that inspires them to improve.

Timing of Appraisals

Appraisals must be conducted regularly to be significant to the employee and the organization. A one-time performance measure is of little importance. Therefore, the supervisor should formally appraise all the employees within the department at regular intervals—at least once a year. This formal appraisal means the completion of special forms and a follow-up evaluation interview. One year is normally considered a sufficient period. If held more frequently, formal appraisals are likely to become mechanical and meaningless, and a supervisor with six, eight, or more employees would spend a disproportionate amount of time doing this. If an employee has just started in a new or more responsible position, however, it is advisable to make an appraisal within six months or so. These periodic appraisals will assure the employee that whatever improvement was made will be noticed and that he or she will be rewarded for this progress. As time goes on, periodic ratings and reviews will become an important determinant of an employee's morale. It reaffirms the supervisor's interest in the employees and in their continued development and improvement.

Annual formal appraisals and their review do not take the place of the feedback on performance that is part of the day-to-day coaching responsibilities of the supervisor. Employees should receive feedback daily; it is well known that performance feedback is most effective when it occurs immediately after the behavior to which it relates. This applies equally for feedback on below-par performance and for recognition of above-par performance. Without this ongoing daily feedback, formal once-a-year appraisals would not suffice.

Who Is the Appraiser?

A major difficulty in effective performance appraisal is human nature because the measurement and appraisal depend on the eye and brain of the appraiser. This creates *intellectual* and *perceptional problems,* leading to the rater's own interpretation of reality and not necessarily absolute reality. To minimize these shortcomings, some organizations devise an appraisal system in which the employee is evaluated by various appraisers. This may include self-appraisals and peer appraisals; in some systems the appraisals are subject to reviews by those higher up in the administrative hierarchy. A few organizations have assessment centers for evaluating employees for their future potential as managers. (This concept is discussed more fully toward the end of this chapter.)

Almost all organizations, however, have come to the conclusion that at lower- and middle-management levels, the appraisal is best performed by the individual's immediate supervisor. Formal authority inherent in the managerial hierarchy means, among many other aspects, the supervisor's right to make decisions in reference to the subordinate's performance. Among all other appraisers, the immediate supervisor is the person who should know the duties of the jobs within the department best. The immediate supervisor has the best opportunity to observe the appraisee on the job and provide feedback. Furthermore, most subordinates want to receive performance-related feedback from their immediate superior and feel more comfortable in discussing the appraisal with him or her.

Therefore, it is best for the immediate line supervisor to make the evaluation. Sometimes it may be necessary for the first-line boss to call on the help of the next higher supervisor. In some institutions the appraisal is made by a committee made up of the first-line supervisor, his or her boss, and possibly one or two other supervisors, as long as the appraisers have adequate knowledge of the performance of the person being rated. This also has the advantage of reducing some of the immediate supervisor's personal prejudices. Alternative sources to supervisory appraisals are particularly necessary in situations where the superior has little opportunity to observe the employee on the job.

Self-appraisal[3] or *self-rating* is an alternative source to supervisory appraisals. There are several advantages to self-ratings: they (1) often contain less halo error,

(2) show the supervisor how the employee perceives the responsibilities and problems of the position, (3) help to identify differences of opinions, and (4) are particularly useful where employees work in isolation. However, self-appraisal can often lead to a conflicting situation when the supervisor's appraisal differs significantly from an inflated self-rating of the employee. Often the appraisal system combines self-appraisals and supervisory appraisals.

At times *peers* are used as appraisers. They can provide valuable information about their colleagues because of their daily interactions if they have close contact with one another. They can observe how an employee interacts with them, the subordinates, and the boss. Peer appraisals offer independent judgment and have often proved to be good predictors of performance when used as a basis for promotion.

However, some powerful influences in organizational life may distort or cloud a peer's perception. Most employees have a strong need for security and work for present and future rewards from the employer. If someone else receives additional rewards, the chances for additional rewards become smaller for everyone else, since the resources are limited. This competition for current or future employer rewards, whether readily apparent or not, could possibly distort a peer's perception of a colleague's performance and potential. In addition, friendships and stereotyping may bias the rating. Friendship does not relate only to individuals, but also to groups. For instance, the appraiser may evaluate some peer in a group of which he or she was once a member. The appraiser may be tempted to rate members of that particular group higher than individuals in another group. Also, at times peers are not willing to evaluate each other, considering it to be an inducement to snitching on one another.

For all practical purposes, appraisal done by the immediate supervisor should suffice, and in most organizations the immediate supervisor is the primary, if not the only, appraiser of employee performance. However, the use of multiple sources of appraisals is likely to obtain a more comprehensive evaluation.

Performance appraisal consists of two distinct steps: the performance rating and the postappraisal interview that follows.

Performance Rating

To minimize and overcome the difficulties in appraising an employee, most enterprises find it advisable to use some type of appraisal form. These appraisal forms are prepared by the personnel department, often in conjunction with outside consultants and the supervisors' suggestions. As mentioned, great care must be exercised to make certain that the system used is legally defensible.

Although innumerable types of appraisal forms are available, most of them specify job-related and important criteria for measuring job performance, intelligence, and personality traits. In addition to determining criteria, standards must be clarified to determine how well employees are performing. The instrument most used in the appraisal process will be both behavior and trait based.[4] The following are qualities and characteristics that most frequently are rated. For non-supervisory personnel, typical qualities rated are quantity and quality of work, job knowledge, dependability, cooperative attitude, supervision required, housekeeping, unauthorized absenteeism, tardiness, safety, and personal appearance. For managerial and professional employees, typical factors are analytical ability, judgment, initiative, leadership, quality and quantity of work, knowledge of work, attitude, dependability, and emotional stability. For each of these factors the supervisor is supposed to select the degree of achievement attained by the employee. In some instances a point system is provided to arrive at a numerical scoring. The form is usually a "check-the-box" type and reasonably simple to fill out. (See Figures 18-1 and 18-2.)

Despite the outward simplicity of some rating blanks, the supervisor will probably run into a number of difficulties. First, not all supervisors agree on what is meant by a simple adjective rating scale, such as unsatisfactory, marginal, satisfactory, above average, and superior. It is advisable, therefore, that the form contain a descriptive sentence in addition to each of these adjectives: for unsatisfactory, "performance clearly fails to meet minimum requirements"; for marginal, "performance occasionally fails to meet minimum requirements"; for satisfactory, "performance meets or exceeds minimum requirements"; for above average, "performance consistently exceeds minimum requirements"; and for superior, "performance clearly exceeds all job requirements." Instead of the adjective, the supervisor might choose from descriptive sentences the one that most adequately describes the employee. For example, in rating the degree of emotional stability of a nurse, the appraiser may have the following choices:
1. "Unreliable in crises; goes to pieces easily; cannot take criticism"
2. "Unrealistic; emotions and moodiness periodically handicap his or her dealings; he or she personalizes issues"
3. "Usually on an even keel; has mature approach to most situations"
4. "Is realistic; generally maintains good behavior balance in handling situations"
5. "Self-possessed in high degree; has outstanding ability to adjust to circumstances, no matter how difficult"

Problems in Performance Rating

Performance rating is frequently subject to a number of errors and weaknesses because subjectivity is a part of the entire process. Appraisers are human and are subject to the same forces that influence all human behavior. Some of these errors are more common than others. The supervisor should be aware of these pitfalls in order to minimize the human weaknesses in processing, storing, and recalling observed behavior.

Some supervisors have a tendency to be overly *lenient* in their ratings, rating appraisees higher than normal. Some supervisors are afraid that they might antagonize their subordinates if they rate them low, thus making them less cooperative.

Other supervisors are overly *harsh* in rating their employees and appraise them lower than the average appraiser. This tendency of some supervisors to give consistently low ratings is equally damaging. A low rating for a subordinate may also reflect on the supervisor's own ability to encourage subordinates to improve themselves.

■ FIGURE 18-1 Example of a performance appraisal form:
weighting format.

NURSING PROFESSIONAL EVALUATION FORM

Name and title of professional being evaluated: —————————————————

Name and title of evaluator: —————————————————————

Professional's area of responsibility: ————————————————————

Time frame covered by this evaluation: ———————————————————

Reason for this evaluation: ———————————————————————

I. RATING LEVELS AND DEFINITIONS

The following definitions are to be used in evaluating the professional's performance in each criterion. Ratings must be in whole numbers.

Level 4 - Excellent performance: The professional performs within the criterion in a consistently superior manner.

Level 3 - Performance meets full expectations: The professional performs within the criterion in a fully acceptable manner. No improvement is necessary.

Level 2 - Satisfactory performance with room for improvement: The professional performs within the criterion in a satisfactory manner. However, improvement is necessary before the full expectations of the professional are realized.

Level 1 - Performance needs improvement: The professional is not performing within the criterion in a satisfactory manner. Regardless of the cause(s) of this level of performance, improvement is necessary.

Level 0 - Unacceptable performance: The professional is clearly functioning at an unacceptable level within the criterion.

II. WEIGHTING EXPLANATION

Pre-assigned weightings have been established for each position grouping within the nursing professional category. The evaluator must obtain the pre-assigned weightings from the department head to know the weight assigned to each of the ten performance criteria. These weightings should be discussed with the nurse manager at the beginning of the evaluation period in order to facilitate prioritizing.

The weight pre-assigned to each criterion may range from 1 (which equals 4% of the nurse manager's overall) to 16 (which equals 64% of the professional's overall job). HOWEVER, THE TOTAL WEIGHTS ASSIGNED TO ALL CRITERIA MUST EQUAL 25. Refer to the nursing professional performance appraisal preassigned weightings form to obtain the weightings assigned to the position you are evaluating. For example:

Criterion	Assigned Weight		Percentage of Job	Versus	Criterion	Assigned Weight		Percentage of Job
A	2	=	8%		A	16	=	64%
B	3	=	12%		B	1	=	4%
C	2	=	8%		C	1	=	4%
D	3	=	12%		D	1	=	4%
E	2	=	8%		E	1	=	4%
F	3	=	12%		F	1	=	4%
G	2	=	8%		G	1	=	4%
H	3	=	12%		H	1	=	4%
I	2	=	8%		I	1	=	4%
J	3	=	12%		J	1	=	4%
	25		100%			25		100%

NOTE: All weights must be in whole numbers.

Reprinted with permission from Barnes Hospital, St. Louis. For illustrative purposes only.

■ FIGURE 18-1 Example of a performance appraisal form:
weighting format. (cont.)

III. PERFORMANCE CRITERIA

A. Assessment/evaluation of patient care   Weight Assigned _____
As defined in the performance expectations of his/her position, the extent to which
the professional nurse:
1. Demonstrates the ability to assess the physical, psychological, and social status
   of the patients in a systematic manner
2. Demonstrates the ability to evaluate the appropriateness of patient care in
   accordance with the objectives and policies of the department
Rating Assigned _____ Why? _____

B. Planning/implementation of patient care   Weight Assigned _____
As defined by the performance expectations of his/her position, the extent to which
the professional nurse:
1. Plans patient care in accordance with nursing assessment and medical orders
2. Demonstrates competence in performance of nursing skills relative to the area of
   practice
3. Demonstrates the ability to coordinate the delivery of patient care
4. Demonstrates the ability to deliver healthcare to insure the safety of the patient
5. Demonstrates the ability to establish goals and priorities
Rating Assigned _____ Why? _____

C. Patient/significant other education   Weight Assigned _____
As defined by the performance expectations of his/her position, the extent to which
the professional nurse:
1. Assesses teaching needs and readiness to learn
2. Initiates education for the care and well-being of each patient
3. Prepares for transfer, discharge, and/or home care
4. Evaluates effectiveness of teaching and adjusts methods accordingly
5. Identifies and pursues prevention/wellness education
Rating Assigned _____ Why? _____

D. Documentation   Weight Assigned _____
As defined by the performance expectations of his/her position, the extent to which
the professional nurse:
1. Documents pertinent data in a thorough and concise manner in order to
   communicate with the healthcare team
2. Documents consistently according to the approved Barnes Hospital system of
   documentation
Rating Assigned _____ Why? _____

E. Consumer Relations   Weight Assigned _____
As defined by the performance expectations of his/her position, the extent to which
the professional nurse:
1. Represents the hospital in a professional, courteous manner
2. Interacts appropriately with patients, families, the healthcare team, and the
   general public

■ FIGURE 18-1 Example of a performance appraisal form: weighting format. (cont.)

3. Delivers quality care and/or service through proper use of resources and efficient performance to ensure patient/consumer satisfaction
4. Identifies consumer dissatisfaction and assumes responsibility for intervention

Rating Assigned _____ Why? _____

F. Leadership/Teamwork   Weight Assigned _____

As defined by the performance expectations of his/her position, the extent to which the professional nurse:

1. Utilizes judgment and perspective in problem solving, is able to identify problems and intervene appropriately; is able to anticipate patient care needs
2. Demonstrates responsibility in work commitments
3. Works in accordance with departmental goals and objectives
4. Maintains open communication with others
5. Communicates clearly
6. Solicits feedback concerning his/her performance
7. Demonstrates working knowledge and understanding of departmental policies, procedures, and duties
8. Identifies problems and/or provides input regarding problems with other departments
9. Maintains accountability for his/her own practice and other staff for whom he/she is responsible

Rating Assigned _____ Why? _____

G. Policy and Procedure   Weight Assigned _____

As defined by the performance expectations of his/her position, the extent to which the professional nurse:

1. Demonstrates knowledge and practices nursing according to the philosophy, policies, and procedures of Barnes Hospital and patient care area
2. Recommends changes to the appropriate supervisor
3. Follows appropriate channels of communication with recommendations and concerns

Rating Assigned _____ Why? _____

H. Budgetary Responsibilities   Weight Assigned _____

As defined by the performance expectations of his/her position, the extent to which the professional nurse:

1. Demonstrates appropriate use and care of equipment to aid in reducing costly repairs
2. Appropriately and judiciously utilizes supplies
3. Attempts to control costs by communicating methods for cost-effectiveness to other healthcare workers
4. Communicates the wastage of supplies and suggests methods of cost-containment to the appropriate person
5. Coordinates patient care services with other departments to decrease unnecessary costs

Rating Assigned _____ Why? _____

■ FIGURE 18-1 Example of a performance appraisal form:
weighting format. (cont.)

I. Professional Development   Weight Assigned _____
As defined by the performance expectations of his/her position, the extent to which the professional nurse:
1. Identifies strengths and limitations of professional practice
2. Remains current in the latest concepts, techniques, and methods relative to his/her area of responsibility
3. Pursues further enhancement of his/her professional knowledge

Rating Assigned _____ Why? _____

J. Problem Solving/Research   Weight Assigned _____
As defined by the performance expectations of his/her position, the extent to which the professional nurse:
1. Demonstrates ability to clearly and accurately identify problems
2. Develops new ideas and alternative methods that contribute to overall improvement of patient care and the profession of nursing
3. Evaluates suggested solutions to problems for effectiveness
4. Participates in research data collection and research as a problem-solving method

Rating Assigned _____ Why? _____

IV. OVERALL PERFORMANCE RATING
Complete the following chart to determine the nursing professional total rating points. The weight is obtained from the preassigned criteria weightings form.

Criteria	Weight	×	Rating	=	Points
A. Assessment/Evaluation of Patient Care	_____	×	_____	=	_____
B. Planning/Implementation of Patient Care	_____	×	_____	=	_____
C. Patient/Significant Other Education	_____	×	_____	=	_____
D. Documentation	_____	×	_____	=	_____
E. Consumer Relations	_____	×	_____	=	_____
F. Leadership/Teamwork	_____	×	_____	=	_____
G. Policy and Procedure	_____	×	_____	=	_____
H. Budgetary Responsibility	_____	×	_____	=	_____
I. Professional Development	_____	×	_____	=	_____
J. Problem Solving/Research	_____	×	_____	=	_____
			Total Rating Points		_____

Use the following scale to determine the professional's overall performance rating.

Total rating points		Overall performance
85–100	=	Superior overall performance
70–84	=	Performance exceeds requirements
55–69	=	Performance meets requirements
40–54	=	Performance needs improvement
Below 40	=	Unacceptable overall performance

■ **FIGURE 18-1 Example of a performance appraisal form: weighting format. (cont.)**

V. DEVELOPMENTAL SECTION

It is the goal of the hospital to integrate employee development with the performance appraisal process. A developmental plan provides the framework for identifying and documenting how improvements will be approached.

Therefore, a developmental plan must be written, attached to, and made part of this evaluation. It may cover as many or as few performance criteria as the evaluator feels are necessary and realistic.

VI. SIGNATURES AND COMMENTS

Professional's comments: _____

_____

_____

_____

_____

_____   _____
Professional's signature   Date

Professional's signature indicates this evaluation has been discussed with him/her but does not necessarily signify agreement.

_____   _____
Evaluator's signature   Date

For example, the nursing personnel on one station may be consistently appraised higher than those on the next station. Thus, it is difficult to determine whether this is because of one head nurse's strictness or the other's leniency, or whether this reflects real differences in the employees' abilities and performance.

Another common error is *central tendency;* the appraiser rates the employees average or around the midpoint, although the employees' performance would warrant a higher or lower rating. The supervisor often is reluctant to rate employees at the edges of the scale. This may be caused by a lack of knowledge on the appraiser's part and permits an easy escape from making a valid decision by neither praising nor condemning.

Another subjective error of the appraiser is to be influenced by the *halo effect,* discussed in Chapter 17. The halo effect is the tendency of most raters to let the rating they assign to one characteristic influence their rating on all subsequent characteristics. This works in two directions. Rating the appraisee excellent on one factor influences the rater to give the employee a similar high rating or higher rating on other qualities than actually deserved. On the other hand, rating the employee unsatisfactory on one factor influences the appraiser to give the appraisee a similar low rating or lower-than-deserved rating on other factors. One way to minimize the halo effect is to rate all employees on a single factor or trait before going on to the next factor. In other words, the supervisor only rates one factor of each employee at a time and then goes on to the next employee for the same factor, and so on. This enables the supervisor to consider all appraisees relative to a standard. It is not necessary that the distribution of ratings resemble a normal or bell-shaped curve; that is, it would be inappropriate to rate on a curve.

■ FIGURE 18-1 Example of a performance appraisal form: weighting format. (cont.)

NURSING PROFESSIONAL PERFORMANCE APPRAISAL PREASSIGNED WEIGHTINGS FORM

Criteria	Staff Nurse	Employee Health	Pheresis	Quality Assurance	Emergency Department	Clinics	OR	Dialysis	Clinical Specialist
A. Assessment/Evaluation of Patient Care	4	5	3	4	4	4	4	3	3
B. Planning/Implementation of Patient Care	4	5	4	1	3	4	4	3	3
C. Patient/Significant Other Education	3	2	2	2	2	3	2	3	3
D. Documentation	3	4	2	2	4	2	3	3	1
E. Consumer Relations	2	2	4	3	3	3	1	2	3
F. Leadership/Teamwork	3	3	2	3	3	3	3	3	4
G. Policy and Procedure	2	1	2	3	2	3	2	2	1
H. Budgetary Responsibilities	1	1	2	2	1	1	1	2	1
I. Professional Development	2	1	2	2	2	1	3	2	3
J. Problem Solving/Research	1	1	2	3	1	1	2	2	3

■ FIGURE 18-2 Example of a performance appraisal form: check-the-box format.

Performance Appraisal Staff Nurse—Registered Nurse

Name _____

Assignment _____

Department _____

Date of Employment _____

Patient Care Management	Needs Development	Satisfactory	Above Average	Comments
A. Collects base-line data by use of the nursing admission history, observations, input from other sources				
Uses nursing assessment skills to anticipate and recognize potentially dangerous situations and responds appropriately				
B. Defines and records patient needs, problems, concerns that need nursing intervention from the above data and records them on the care plan				
C. Establishes expected outcomes with the patient and/or family and records them on the care plan				
D. Plans nursing approaches with patient and/or family and records them on the care plan. Approaches include: 1) what other information is needed; 2) what approaches are to be used, by whom, when; 3) what patient/ family instruction/education is needed				

Printed with permission of St. Mary's Health Center, St. Louis, MO—a member of the SSM Health Care System. For illustrative purposes only.

■ FIGURE 18-2 Example of a performance appraisal form:
check-the-box format. (cont.)

	Needs Development	Satisfactory	Above Average	Comments
E. Records nursing approaches carried out and patient responses. Records reflect: 1) if the plan is working as expected; 2) new information or observations that necessitate re-evaluation				
F. Initiates appropriate nursing intervention				
G. Properly assigns priorities				
H. Anticipates work flow as evidenced by completion of work within allotted time				
I. Demonstrates flexibility by response to emergencies; schedule changes, or adverse conditions				
J. Provides skillful and safe nursing care and indicates this in charting and care plan				
K. Knowledgeable of medications, their usage and side effects, and treatments, and records accurately including the patient's response				
L. Demonstrates knowledge and proper utilization of medical equipment.				
M. Evaluates and intervenes when necessary in nursing care provided by nonprofessional personnel.				

■ FIGURE 18-2 Example of a performance appraisal form: check-the-box format. (cont.)

	Needs Development	Satisfactory	Above Average	Comments
N. Identifies and utilizes resource persons to facilitate quality care				
O. Conducts team and patient care conferences				
P. Plans, implements, and documents activities to assist patients/families in preparing for discharge				
Q. Provides patient/family teaching that will assist in maintaining health or maximum wellness within the constraints of specific disease processes				
R. Takes responsibility for own actions and decisions				
S. Daily assesses level of care and changes classification accordingly				
T. Demonstrates knowledge of infectious disease control				
U. Demonstrates knowledge of sterile technique				
V. Demonstrates knowledge of safety controls				
W. Demonstrates knowledge of disaster plan, fire drill procedure, and tornado plan				

■ FIGURE 18-2 Example of a performance appraisal form: check-the-box format. (cont.)

	Needs Development	Satisfactory	Above Average	Comments
Technical Skills				
A. Medications:				
Administers properly				
Charts appropriately				
B. Physician Orders:				
Checks for accuracy and correct signature				
Initiates orders promptly and accurately				
Communication				
A. Informs head nurse, supervisor and/or physician of unusual or difficult nursing care problems or changes in patient's condition				
B. Demonstrates a courteous respect for patients, visitors, co-workers, physicians, and hospital personnel				
C. Maintains and promotes confidentiality				
D. Communicates in a professional manner with physicians and other members of the health-care team concerning patient activities				
E. Communicates effectively in writing				
Uses acceptable and appropriate medical terminology in charting				

■ FIGURE 18-2 Example of a performance appraisal form: check-the-box format. (cont.)

	Needs Development	Satisfactory	Above Average	Comments
Accurate and timely completion of nursing service condition report				
Uses approved abbreviations in charting				
F. Communicates effectively verbally				
Gives accurate, precise, and comprehensive reports				
G. Demonstrates courteous telephone manners				
Interpersonal Relations A. Receptive and courteous to all persons				
B. Actively participates as a team member				
C. Willingly assists others				
D. Contributes toward an atmosphere of mutual trust, acceptance, and respect				
E. Conducts oneself in professional and businesslike manner				
F. Gives and accepts constructive criticism in a positive manner and in the proper setting				
G. Channels suggestions and criticism to appropriate persons				

■ FIGURE 18-2 Example of a performance appraisal form: check-the-box format. (cont.)

	Needs Development	Satisfactory	Above Average	Comments
Leadership				
A. Demonstrates leadership ability by evaluating skills and organizing personnel to accomplish established goals				
B. Guides and teaches nonprofessional staff to accomplish established goals				
C. Accurately evaluates skills of personnel and makes assignments in accordance with capabilities, and according to patient's level of care				
D. Assumes charge nurse duties as assigned				
Responsibilities to the Unit, the Nursing Service Department and Hospital Organization				
A. Understands and supports the philosophy, policies, goals, and objectives of the hospital and nursing service department				
B. Contributes to establishment and accomplishment of unit goals				
C. Participates in committees, staff level meetings or special projects and studies, or in assignments of nursing service department or the hospital				

■ **FIGURE 18-2 Example of a performance appraisal form: check-the-box format. (cont.)**

	Needs Development	Satisfactory	Above Average	Comments
D. Works on other nursing units as requested				
Personal Qualities				
A. Meets nursing service department standards for attendance and punctuality				
Complies with break and lunch time periods				
B. Meets nursing service department standards for personal appearance				
C. Demonstrates a tactful manner when dealing with delicate situations				
D. Attends hospital inservice programs and seeks out job-related programs				
E. Restricts personal telephone calls to emergencies				

■ FIGURE 18-2 Example of a performance appraisal form: check-the-box format. (cont.)

	Yes	No	Date
Mandatory Requirements			
A. Maintains current licensure in the state of Missouri			
B. Adheres to nursing service policies and procedures regarding control of narcotics and dangerous drugs			
C. Has annual physical			
D. Adheres to nursing service dress code			

Individual goals for growth

_____

_____

_____

Employee suggestions for improvement of unit and/or department

_____

_____

_____

Merit increase: _____ Annual Evaluation Only

Date _____ Employee's signature

Date _____ Head nurse's signature

Date _____ Supervisor's signature

A further distortion is caused by interpersonal relations and *bias*. The ratings will be influenced by the supervisor's likes and dislikes about each individual working in the department. This is especially apparent when objective standards of performance are difficult to determine or not available.

Another error in making appraisals is the *similar-to-me* tendency. Some raters are tempted to judge more favorably those employees whose attitudes resemble their own.

Another source of difficulty arises from *organizational influences,* the way administration uses the ratings. Often raters are lenient when they know that pay raises and promotions depend on the appraisals. If the organizational emphasis is on further employee development, appraisers are inclined to be harsh and emphasize weaknesses.

The supervisor's judgment must be based on the total performance of the employee. It would be unfair to appraise a subordinate based on only one assignment on which he or she had done particularly well or poorly. Also, instead of recognizing performance during the entire appraisal period, the supervisor may rate only the appraisee's most recent behavior. Supervisors must caution themselves not to let random or first impressions of an employee influence judgment that should be based on the employee's total record of performance, reliability, initiative, skills, resourcefulness, and capability. Supervisors also should not allow past performance appraisal ratings to influence current ratings unjustly either way. An aid to minimize these errors and biases is to document employee behavior as soon as possible after the occurrence. When the formal appraisal takes place, supervisors can refer back to the documentation, thus minimizing biases and other pitfalls in rating.

Observing all these problems in rating will help supervisors overcome human weaknesses in processing, storing, and recalling observed behavior when evaluations are made. Although the results are not perfect, many human errors can be significantly reduced and counteracted by top-level administration's continuous emphasis on training for those who do the appraising. This is necessary because appraisals that are biased, inaccurate, or distorted will not increase an employee's motivation; these errors may lead to poor decisions of promotions and retentions, even possibly to charges of discrimination. The necessity for training supervisors in observing behavior never ends. The success of the performance appraisal largely depends on the supervisor's ability to obtain accurate information and then to discuss it with the appraisee in a nonthreatening and constructive, growth-producing manner. The evaluation interview that follows the appraisal fulfills this function.

The Postappraisal Interview

The second step in the appraisal procedure, the postappraisal interview, takes place when the immediate superior who has performed the evaluation sits down with the subordinate to discuss the appraisee's performance. Some supervisors would like to shy away from the idea of having to tell their subordinates how they stand in the department and what they should do to improve. They are reluctant because, unless it is done with great sensitivity, this type of interview can lead to hostility and even greater misunderstanding. Many employees distrust anything that relates to their review, starting with the validity of the measuring instrument used, the appraiser's ability to observe, and so forth; they are often reluctant to discuss their workplace behavior. However, this discussion is absolutely essential to ensure effective appraisals.

It is of great importance that the institution provides supervisors with learning opportunities to carry on appraisals in such a way that they are effective. Therefore, many facilities provide training in conducting appraisals in the form of practice sessions, behavior modeling training programs,[5] role-playing experiences, and so forth. All this is done to increase the supervisors' effectiveness in dealing with subordinates, to improve their observer accuracy, and to aid them in carrying out appraisal interviews effectively. Some writers have classified four major formats for this interview: (1) the tell-and-sell approach, (2) the tell-and-listen format, (3) the problem-solving approach, and (4) a mixed interview combining all these formats.[6]

Although it would probably be better not to follow a formalized system, administration has often suggested that supervisors follow a standardized outline. According to this approach, the supervisor should first state the purpose of the evaluation procedure and the interview. The supervisor should proceed to a discussion of the evaluation itself, first stating the subordinate's strong points and then the weak points. Next, there should be a general discussion giving the employee an opportunity to state his or her feelings.

Another possible procedure is to let subordinates appraise themselves first. This gives the appraisees the opportunity to state their side of the story first; it is easier for many subordinates to criticize themselves than to take criticism from the supervisor. It is hoped the interview will end with a discussion of what the subordinate can and wants to do about the deficiencies and what the supervisor will do for the employee in this regard.

Although such suggested schemes will help some supervisors, it is better not to formalize this process. As supervisors gain experience, they will devise their own plan, and each subordinate probably will be approached in an individual manner.

Everything regarding general techniques of interviewing (see Chapter 17) is applicable to the postappraisal interview. Additional skills are necessary, however, since the direction of evaluation interviews cannot be predicted. At times it may be very difficult for the supervisor to carry on this interview, especially if the subordinate shows hostility when the supervisor discusses some negative evaluations. Of course, employees need to know if and where their performance is inadequate. Positive judgment can be communicated effectively, but it is difficult to communicate criticisms without generating resentment and defensiveness. It will take much practice and insight to acquire skills for handling the evaluation interview.

Some supervisors believe that no need exists for an evaluation interview because they are in daily contact with their employees. These supervisors claim that their door is open at all times, but this is not enough. The employee knows that he or she has been formally appraised, and the subordinate understandably might be eager to have a firsthand report on how he or she made out. Also, employees may have some things on their mind that they do not want to discuss in the everyday contacts with the supervisor.

The supervisor must be well prepared for this review session. The appraiser must know what should be covered and achieved in this meeting and gather all the information that has any meaning for the discussion. The various events that occurred during the entire evaluation period must be clear in the interviewer's mind. It may be advisable to prepare an agenda for this meeting. Thorough preparation enables the appraiser to be ready for any direction the discussion will take. It is difficult to predict what will happen in this review session. It may be an exceedingly dull meeting, and the appraisee's responses may be minimal—an occasional yes or no or nod of the head. Another meeting, however, may end up as a major bitter confrontation.

Because of the importance and sensitivity of the performance review, the appraiser must not only be well prepared for this session, but also skilled in interviewing and counseling. The reviewer must ask the right question at the right time and be a constructive listener. In the review session information must be shared. The appraisee must feel that his or her concerns are important. Success of this review session can be improved if the appraiser has empathy, listens constructively, asks the right questions at the proper time, and observes keenly. Last, the appraiser must allow enough time to conduct the interview.

The appraisal interview should be held shortly after the appraisal has been performed, and, as stated before, supervisors should refresh their memories regarding the reasons for the opinions expressed in the appraisal. Appraisees should be given enough notice so that they can prepare themselves for the interview as well. At the outset the supervisor should state that the main purpose of the interview is to be a constructive and positive experience for both the appraisee and the appraiser and for the benefit of the employee, the supervisor, and the institution. Some suggest that the supervisor ask the employee to appraise his or her own performance. This will give the supervisor a chance to refer to the progress the worker has made since the preceding counseling interview, compliment the subordinate on achievements, and then discuss areas that need improvement.

The formula of starting with praise, following it up with criticism, and ending the interview with another compliment is not necessarily the best method. Good and bad may cancel each other out, and the worker may forget about the criticism. A mature employee is able to take deserved criticism when it is appropriate. By the same token, when praise is merited, it should be expressed. It is not always possible to mix praise and criticism effectively.

Since the idea of being rated imposes some extra tensions and strains, feelings of friendliness and privacy in the interview are probably more important than at any other time. Since personal feelings and points of view most likely will be brought out in the discussion, the appraisee must be assured of privacy and confidentiality. No distractions or interruptions should occur.

The supervisor should stress that everybody in the same job in the department is rated according to the same standards and that the employee has not been singled out for special scrutiny. The supervisor should be in a position to document the rating by citing specific instances of good and poor performance. The supervisor should be careful to relate the measured factors to the actual demands of the job. The rating must be geared to the present qualities of the employee's performance. This is particularly important if an employee is already doing good work and the supervisor is tempted to leave well enough alone. These are probably the very employees who are likely to make further progress, and to tell them simply to keep up the good work is not sufficient. These employees may not have major problems, but nevertheless they deserve thoughtful counseling. Such an employee is likely to continue to develop, and the supervisor should be specific as far as future development plans are concerned. The appraiser must be familiar, therefore, with the opportunities available to the employee, requirements of the job, and the employee's qualifications. Whenever discussing a subordinate's future, however, the supervisor should not make promises for promotion that may not be possible to keep.

The interview should also give the employee an opportunity to ask questions so that the supervisor can answer them fully. Any misunderstanding cleared up at this time may avoid future difficulty. The appraiser should also clarify that further performance ratings and interviews are regular procedures with the enterprise. The supervisor should always remember that the purpose of the appraisal interview is to help employees to see their shortcomings and aid them in finding solutions. The real success of the interview lies in the employees' ability to see the need for their own improvement, stimulating in them a desire to change.

Since the postappraisal interview is the most important part of the evaluation procedure, the supervisor should make certain that at its termination, the employees have a good objective view of their performance and the ways in which they can improve. They also should have a desire to improve. It is hoped that employees will establish goals that are mutually satisfying to both themselves and the supervisor. An employee's commitment will provide some measurable goals against which future performance can be judged. At the end of the next period, both supervisor and subordinate will meet to evaluate how well the goals have been achieved and what the next objectives will be. This will give the subordinate a custom-made standard for evaluation. It provides him or her with a specified goal within a specified period. The employee will be that much more motivated, since the goal was a commitment on his or her part.

Management by objectives (MBO) has been discussed on several occasions in this text. The underlying concept of MBO is that identified, measurable, and workable objectives are agreed on by the supervisor and the employee; this leads to improved performance and a motivating environment. MBO creates a participative climate because it involves the subordinates in the identification of required performance. Although MBO is primarily a planning tool and a process that goes beyond performance appraisals, it can be logically and conveniently linked with performance evaluation and postappraisal interviews. The review lends itself well to measuring the quality of an employee's on-the-job performance, achievements, and participation in setting new objectives. These new goals are to be achieved during the next period and appraised and reviewed at the end of the period. Thus, the subordinate is judged by standards he or she helped determine.

Some experts strongly advocate that the annual performance appraisal review be separate from *salary review*. They suggest that discussions of the past, future potential, coaching inputs, counseling inputs regarding desired behavior changes, further education, and development should not be tainted by discussions of pay and compensation. Whether a salary adjustment will be made does not depend only on the performance but also on the financial condition of the enterprise, wages paid elsewhere, the economic conditions, and many other factors. Most likely, however, the appraisee listens to everything that is said, figuring out what all this means in terms of future reward opportunities and possible promotions. A proposed solution is to have two separate review sessions. The first would be concerned with the review and employee development, and the second session, four to eight weeks later, would cover the compensation issue.[7]

Appraisal forms customarily require the appraisee to *sign* the evaluation form on completion of the review. Usually a statement above the signature line says that the employee's signature merely confirms that the interview occurred and that the appraisee in no way approves or disapproves of the statements contained in the evaluation.

With this understanding the subordinate will probably sign. If, however, the appraisee would like to state personal views, no harm is done in letting him or her do so. Many employees will not verbalize their disagreement with the rating; signing the forms with such feelings can create resentment against the organization. The real purpose of the signature is to document for the supervisor's boss that the evaluation interview took place. As stated, many supervisors have mixed reactions about the postappraisal interview. Since it is essential as feedback in the entire evaluation procedure, administration must make certain that it occurs, and the signature is the simplest way to ascertain this.

Proper Wages and Salaries

Although people want more from their jobs than just a wage or salary, these are basic necessities. Pay provides more than the means of satisfying physical needs; it provides a sense of accomplishment and recognition. Most people at work consider relative pay as very important, and real or imagined wage and salary inequities are frequent causes for dissatisfaction, friction, and low morale. It is top-level management's duty[8] to pursue a sound policy of wage and salary administration throughout the entire organization; the goal is to have a sound and non-discriminatory compensation structure. By setting wages high enough, the healthcare center will be able to recruit satisfactory employees and motivate their present employees to work toward pay increases and promotions. Reducing inequities among employee's earnings will raise morale and reduce friction.

In most healthcare centers and most other organizations wage rates and schedules are set by top-level administration, and the supervisor's authority in this respect is severely limited and handicapped. Nevertheless, it is a part of the supervisor's staffing function to make certain that the employees of the department are properly and equitably compensated. It is every manager's job to offer the amount of compensation that will retain competent employees in the department and, if necessary, attract good workers from the outside. Monetary rewards are an exceedingly important factor for all employees. However, many employees are much more concerned about how their salaries compare to the earnings of others than they are about their absolute earnings. No doubt many wage rates and schedules follow historical patterns, whereas others are often accidental. For instance, the problem of personalities has frequently distorted certain wage rates. In the long run such a situation cannot be tolerated.

It is the supervisor's duty to see that the wages paid within the department are properly aligned *internally* and *externally*. *Internal alignment* means that the jobs within the department and institution are paid according to what they are worth. Internal consistency based on internal equity provides a system of compensation that is acceptable to the employees involved, resulting in satisfaction and a desire to be promoted and to remain with the present employer. *External alignment* means that the wages offered for the work to be performed in the department compare favorably with the going rate in the community and area. "External competitiveness refers to the pay relationships *among* organizations and the *competitive positions* reflected in these relationships."[9] If wages do not compare favorably, the supervisor knows that some of the most experienced workers will leave and that it will be difficult to attract new ones from the outside.

Internal Alignment

To pay the various jobs within the department according to what they are worth, the supervisor should call on the help of the human resources department to conduct a job evaluation. Job evaluation is a method of determining the relationships between pay rates and the relative monetary value of jobs within a department. In such a procedure the jobs are evaluated according to various factors, and an appropriate wage rate can be devised based on the worth of each job. Based on the results of what the jobs are worth, an appropriate wage schedule can be instituted. Of course, some questions will arise about what to do with exceptional cases, that is, those employees who are receiving either excessively high or exceedingly low salaries in relation to others. Once a plan has been designed, however, it is necessary to maintain it properly so that no new inequities arise.

The job evaluation program is usually administered by a committee under the general guidance of the personnel department. The human resources department is familiar with this procedure, and if it has not been performed recently, the supervisor might request a job evaluation for his or her department. Sometimes the help of an outside consultant is used. There are several methods of job evaluation. Although they are systematic, they are not totally precise because they involve questions of human judgment. In addition to the most widely used point system, other methods such as ranking, factor comparison, and job classification methods are typically used.[10]

External Alignment

If the wage and salary policy of the institution is to be externally competitive,[11] pay rates must be approximately the same as those prevailing in the community. Thus, accurate wage and salary data must be collected through surveys. Job evaluations establish differentials between jobs based on different job content; wage surveys provide management with information on whether the organization's wage level is competitive externally and aligned. A wage survey involves collecting data on wages paid in the community for similar key jobs in similar or related enterprises. Without proper external alignment, the supervisor cannot recruit competent employees or prevent present employees from leaving for better-paying jobs.

To conduct such a survey is a rather costly and sophisticated procedure; performing one's own survey will probably produce the most meaningful results. Many other sources publish reliable surveys, including government agencies such as the Bureau of Labor Statistics, professional healthcare associations, and metropolitan hospital associations. The area usually considered in the survey is the geographical region within which workers seek employment and employers recruit workers without necessitating a change of residence.

Most enterprises also provide fringe benefits for employees, such as vacations with pay, retirement plans, insurance and health services, and low-cost meals. In general these are incentives to do a better job. Most of these additional benefits are established by top-level administration as institution-wide measures. The supervisor has little to do with such benefits other than to make sure that the subordinates understand how they operate and that each subordinate receives his or her fair share. It is advisable to include information along these lines in any wage survey.

To determine whether or not the rates offered by the department are competitive, the supervisor should request that the human resources department undertake such a wage and salary survey unless recent reliable information is available. Then, by comparing this information with the wage patterns, the supervisor can determine whether or not wages are properly aligned externally. A sound wage and salary pattern should always be of great concern to the chief executive officer (CEO). Although the supervisor has very little direct authority in this area, his or her awareness of inadequacies and inconsistencies will often cause the administrator to investigate.

In most instances supervisors will not have enough authority to make wage and salary adjustments except within the framework of the departmental wage scale. However, they should definitely plead their case with top-level administration. To make an intelligent presentation, the supervisor must know the value of the various jobs within the department and also the going rates within the community. As every supervisor knows, proper compensation of employees is a significant aspect of the employee's continuing satisfaction and motivation. Without a sound wage and salary pattern, it is almost impossible for a supervisor to recruit competent employees or keep the subordinates motivated.

■ PROMOTIONS

Promotions provide an internal source of potential applicants. A promotion is a transfer involving the reassignment of an individual to a position of higher rank. This higher-level job will entail more demands on the individual but also results in higher pay, more authority and responsibility, more privileges, higher status, increased benefits, greater potential, etc. A promotion also carries symbols of higher status, such as a more important job title, a larger office, a bigger desk, and a secretary. Although some people do not want to advance, promotions are sought by most people who have a high level of aspiration. It is part of our culture to start at the bottom of the ladder and rise in status and income as one grows older. Since most persons in our society look on promotions in this way, it is essential that organizations develop and pursue sound promotion policies.

Promotion from Within

Organizations depend heavily on promoting their own employees into better and more promising positions. The policy of promoting from within the organization is one of the most widely practiced personnel policies today. This policy will help achieve the organizational objective of being a good employer and a good place to work. The latter is undoubtedly one of the many goals of all healthcare centers.

The policy of promotion from within versus recruitment from without is important to the enterprise and the individual employee. For the enterprise it ensures a constant source of trained people for the better positions; for the employees it provides a powerful incentive to perform better. After an employee has worked for an enterprise for a time, much more is known about that person than even the best potential candidate from outside the organization. Internal promotion often is less expensive to the institution in time and money than luring applicants from the outside. Additional job satisfaction will result when employees know that with proper efforts they can work up to more interesting and more challenging work, higher pay, and more desirable working conditions. Most employees like to know that they can get ahead in the enterprise in which they are working and feel more secure in a setting that provides future job opportunities. All this provides strong motivation. Little motivation exists for employees to do a better job if they know that the better and higher-paying jobs are always reserved for outsiders.

The internal promotion policy should be applied whenever possible and feasible. Most organizations are aware that under special circumstances outside people must be hired; sometimes strict adherence to internal promotion would do harm to the organization. For example, if there are no qualified candidates for the job, the internal promotion policy cannot be followed. If no one with the necessary skill is available, then someone from the outside has to be recruited for the position. Also, an organization may be forced to go outside because employees with inadequate potential for promotion have been hired in the past.

At times the injection of "new blood" into an organization may be very important because it prevents inbreeding and will keep the members of the enterprise from becoming conformist and repetitious. Such threats are important primarily in high-level managerial jobs and for highly trained professionals but are less important in hourly paid jobs. Another reason the enterprise may have to recruit employees from the outside is that the organization cannot afford the expense of training and schooling current employees. A particular position may require a long period of expensive and sophisticated schooling, and the institution simply cannot afford this type of upgrading program. Only large organizations can afford such expenses. Another problem with promotion from within is that the organization must continue to live amicably with those who were bypassed. Such a problem does not exist with an applicant from the outside who was rejected. In all this, considerations of equal employment opportunity and possibly affirmative action must be included.

On the other hand, the supervisor should remember that not every employee wants advancement; many people know their limitations. Some employees are quite content with what they are doing and where they are within the enterprise. They prefer to remain with employees whom they know and responsibilities with which they are familiar. These employees should not be pressured into better positions by the supervisor. The supervisor should also bear in mind that what he or she may consider a promotion may not seem like a promotion to the employee. A nurse may believe that a "promotion" to administrative work is a hardship and not an advancement. The nurse may find the administrative activities less interesting than the professional duties and may be concerned about his or her professional future. The supervisor will have to provide promotional opportunities that do not entail compromises of professional feelings.

Sometimes a supervisor does not want to release an employee because this employee is viewed as indispensable and the supervisor does not want to release him or her to take a better job in another department. This could occur because that supervisor is extremely good in developing subordinates; for example, as soon as a head nurse has developed a number of outstanding nurses, they are promoted out of that unit. The head nurse may believe that the unit suffers because of it. In such a situation administration should give credit to this head nurse for developing promotable employees and show him or her that there will also be good employees entering the unit from other head nurses' units.

At times the supervisor may be inclined to bypass someone for promotion because the promotion would cause the supervisor some extra work in replacing the promoted employee and training a new employee. The supervisor may fear that the productivity of the department will suffer. This is shortsighted, since promotion from within is one of the prime motivators. Supervisors who are tempted to think this way should ask themselves where they would be today if their former superiors had had this attitude.

Basis of Promotion

Despite the objections just stated, there are usually more applicants for promotions than there are openings within the organization. Because of this, it is important for the organization and supervisors to formulate a sound basis on which employees are chosen for promotion. Since promotions are considered an incentive for employees to do a better job, it follows that the employee who has the best record of quality, productivity, and skill should be promoted. In many situations, however, it is difficult to measure objectively some employees' productivity, although supervisors continually attempt this through merit ratings and performance appraisals. The most important criteria for choice are *merit* (current performance), *ability* (potential future performance), and *seniority* (experience).

Merit and Ability

Since promotion is an incentive for good performance, the best-performing employees should be promoted. Our discussion of performance appraisals emphasized the difficulty in measuring performance. The differences in *merit* between different employees in healthcare jobs are also often difficult to measure precisely. The person who was not promoted may feel that bias and favoritism were involved. Nevertheless, performance in one's present job is one of the criteria.

Ability and *potential* to assume the responsibilities of a higher-level position are another input. The performance appraisal process is a major source of information. As stated repeatedly, performance appraisals are central to all organizational and management development. Generally, performance appraisals are used as a means of measuring performance focused on the past, but just as important is appraisal of *potential,* or looking to the future. The appraisal of potential is based on the process and personal resources the employee uses to achieve results, that is, the ability to lead, intellect, maturity, and so forth. Some of the factors for appraising potential and future performance are oral and written communication, flexibility, decision making, leadership, and planning.

Since it has been recognized that traditional methods of selecting managers are fraught with many shortcomings and subjectivity, thousands of industrial, utility, and some healthcare organizations have adopted an *assessment center* approach for evaluating and selecting managers.[12] An assessment center is a process where current employees or job applicants are evaluated as to how well they might perform in a managerial or higher-level position. Individual and group exercises are administered to a group of candidates who are seeking promotions to managerial jobs. The candidates are evaluated for their potential for success in management. The exercises and activities include job-related simulations such as interviews, in baskets, tests, questionnaires, videotape exercises, group problems, and so forth. These exercises are designed to bring forth skills the organization considers critical to success. As the candidates go through these exercises, they are being observed by a group of specially trained observers (assessors, evaluators) who are members of the institution's management group. After the session the candidates are evaluated by these assessors to make selections and placement decisions or to determine a candidate's future promotability. Generally the composite performance evaluation is communicated to the candidate.

Seniority

The exclusive use of merit and ability, which are to a great degree subjective criteria, often gives employees the feeling that promotions are not made fairly. Also, since many factors beyond an employee's control may affect productivity and performance, it would be unfair to base a promotion solely on these factors. Frequent charges of favoritism, bias, and possible discrimination caused managers to search for more automatic decision criteria that would not create morale problems. Since it is difficult to find objective criteria that completely eliminate favoritism and possible discrimination, it has been stated that the only objective criterion is length of service. Supervisors generally believe that their relations with their employees will be easier if they promote on the basis of seniority. Therefore, all organizations give some weight to seniority, whether they have a union or not. Unions have put the greatest stress on seniority; this thinking is now regularly accepted even by those enterprises that do not deal with unions and is applied to those jobs not covered by union agreements. Regardless of unions, managers have come to depend heavily on this concept of seniority as a basis for promotion.

Basing promotion on the length of service assumes that the employee's ability increases with service. Although this may be questionable, with continued service the ability to perform and the knowledge about the organization probably are increasing. If management is committed to promotion based on length of service, it is likely that the initial selection procedure of a new employee will be more careful and that the employee will get as much training as possible in the various positions. Most managers believe that an employee's loyalty is expressed by the length of service and that consequently this loyalty deserves the reward of promotion. On the other hand, some good employees may become discouraged and leave the organization, realizing that their chances for promotion are slim because of many long-service employees ahead of them.

Balancing the Criteria

Good supervisory practice will attempt to draw a happy medium between the criteria of merit and ability on the one hand and length of service on the other. When the supervisor selects from among almost equally capable subordinates, the one with the longest service will no doubt be chosen. Then again, the supervisor may decide to promote an employee who is more capable but has less seniority than another employee because the first stands ''head and shoulders'' above the one with longer service. If this is not the case, the one with more seniority will be promoted. These decisions become increasingly difficult, and it is easy to see why some supervisors have finally resolved the matter by making length of service the sole determinant of selection for promotion. The ideal solution is to combine both factors. Rarely will a supervisor choose a person with the greatest merit and ability from all eligible candidates without giving any weight to length of service.

Selection for promotion will also depend on the type of work involved, demands of the position to be filled, degree requirements prescribed by accrediting and professional associations, and many other factors. Most likely, increasingly more emphasis will be placed on merit and ability when the position to be filled is a demanding and sophisticated job on a higher level, whereas more weight can be given to seniority for promotion into a lower-level position. Every organization must decide on the relative weight of these factors in each case when deciding who is to be promoted.

■ TRANSFERS

Transfers are another internal source of recruitment. A transfer is a reassignment of an employee to another job of similar pay, status, and responsibility. A transfer is not a promotion; it is a horizontal move, whereas a promotion is a vertical move in rank and responsibility. Transfers take place either because the organization makes it necessary or because the employee requests a transfer. Employees may want a transfer for various reasons, for example, to gain broader experience or to avoid some friction in a department. If an employee has problems causing friction, a transfer is not always the right solution unless these problems are resolved.

Sometimes technological changes in one department free a number of employees for transfer into a unit where needs for employees are expanding.

Transferring an employee from one position to another within the healthcare institution often results in greater job satisfaction. For example, a nurse's aide may consider a job as an aide in the operating room to be more prestigious than being an aide on the nursing floor. The pay is the same and one cannot call it a promotion, but to the aide such a transfer means greater job satisfaction and constitutes an achievement. Transfers also provide employees with the opportunity to gain a broader knowledge of the institution's activities. It is necessary, therefore, that a healthcare institution have sound transfer policies and procedures so that those who desire a lateral transfer will be given the possibility of doing so, always considering equal employment opportunity provisions. The director of human resources, together with the various line managers, should design these policies and procedures and see to it that employees are prepared to make successful transfers.

It is probably best for the human resources department to act as a clearance center for interdepartmental transfers. If the responsibility is given to supervisors, the subordinate may be reluctant to request interdepartmental transfers. Some supervisors may be understanding in these matters, whereas others may be resentful and not give their consent. Whatever procedure is instituted must have provisions that the employee inform the immediate supervisor of the desire to transfer. It is only fair that the present supervisor should be aware of the employee's intent. In the event the immediate supervisor does not recommend the transfer, if this is necessary, the employee should be able to appeal this decision to a higher line officer or possibly to the personnel director.

There also must be provisions as to whether transfers are to be made only within departments or between departments. The procedure must state whether the employee carries previous seniority credits with him or her and must make provisions for the situation when two or more persons want to transfer to the same job. For example, should length of service be the sole determinant, or should capacity to handle the job be taken into consideration also? Good transfer policies and procedures must cover many additional aspects, such as equal employment opportunities. In any event, the opportunity must exist for employees to be transferred, since this will provide more job satisfaction and will motivate employees in much the same way as a promotion.

■ SUMMARY

Performance appraisals are central to organizational and management development. Performance appraisals are formal evaluations of employees' job-related activities. Such a system not only guides management in the process of gathering and analyzing information, but also provides guidance for merit increases, promotions, and coaching of employees. The purpose of the appraisal system is to provide a measure of the employee's job performance that leads to counseling and further development. An evaluation system consists of the process of rating the employee and the appraisal interview, which usually occurs later. Although the appraisal interview between the supervisor and the employee may prove to be a difficult situation, the entire performance appraisal system is of no use if this aspect is ignored or not carried out appropriately.

An important source of candidates for job openings is the reservoir of employees who are currently with the institution. Whenever possible, promotion from within is one of the most rewarding personnel policies any enterprise can practice. It is of great benefit to the enterprise and to the morale of the employees. Although it is difficult to specify clearly the various criteria for promotion, it is normally acknowledged that a good balance between merit and ability on the one side and length of service on the other should be used. To be able to assess the ability, merit, and future potential of the employee, however, supervisors must remain continuously aware of the employee's performance. Therefore, the supervisor must regularly appraise the performance of the employees in the department. A further internal source of recruitment is available from transfers.

In addition to all these duties, the staffing function includes making certain that the employees of the department are properly compensated. Although much of this is out of the supervisor's domain, it is a supervisory duty to make certain that good internal wage alignment exists within the department, meaning that each job is paid in accordance with its worth and difficulties. To achieve this, a job evaluation is necessary. In addition to good internal alignment, the compensation pattern must also be competitive externally. This means that the wages paid must be high enough to attract people from outside the organization, if necessary, and to prevent present employees from leaving for higher wages. To do this, the supervisor must be familiar with the going rates being paid in similar occupations in the community. Such information can be obtained by wage and salary surveys conducted by the human resources department.

NOTES

1. Gary P. Latham and Kenneth N. Wexley, *Increasing Productivity Through Performance Appraisal,* Reading, MA: Addison-Wesley Publishing Co., 1981, p. 4. See also H.J. Bernardin and L.A. Klatt, "Managerial Appraisal Systems: Has Practice Caught Up to the State of the Art?" *Personnel Administrator,* November 1985, pp. 79-86.
2. For a method to develop a legally defensible appraisal system, see H. John Bernardin and Wayne F. Cascio, "Performance Appraisal and the Law," in Randall S. Schuler, Stuart A. Youngblood, and Vandra L. Huber, eds., *Readings in Personnel and Human Resource Management,* 3rd ed., St. Paul, MN: West Publishing Co., 1987, pp. 235-247. See also Wayne F. Cascio and H. John Bernardin, "Implications of Performance Appraisal Litigation for Personnel Decisions," *Personnel Psychology,* Vol. 34, 1981, pp. 211-226.
3. For a thorough discussion of self-appraisal and peer appraisal, see Latham and Wexley, pp. 84-89.
4. It is beyond the scope of this text to discuss BARS (behavioral anchored rating scale) and BOS (behavioral observation scale), which are recent approaches to reduce the errors and shortcomings of conventional appraisal forms. These concepts are discussed in most texts on personnel management. See Randall S. Schuler, *Personnel and Human Resource Management,* 3rd ed., St. Paul, MN: West Publishing Co., 1987, pp. 228-230.

5. See Latham and Wexley, pp. 155-161.

6. For a detailed discussion of the pros and cons of these types of interviews, see Latham and Wexley, pp. 152-154; and C. Hymowitz, "Bosses: Don't Be Nasty (and Other Tips For Reviewing a Worker's Performance)," *Wall Street Journal,* Jan. 17, 1985, p. 35.

7. Other opinions advocate linking money with performance appraisals; see Latham and Wexley, pp. 138-142.

8. The human resources department or a special division within it is concerned with the administration of the wage and salary program, but top-level administration has the continuing responsibility and overall authority regarding wage and salary policies. Managers at all levels often become involved in these problems. For a good reference on the subject, see George T. Milkovich and Jerry M. Newman, *Compensation,* 2nd ed., Plano, TX: Business Publications, Inc., 1987.

9. Milkovich and Newman, p. 191.

10. For more information on job evaluation, see Milkovich and Newman, pp. 99-171; and Stephen E. Bemis, Ann Holt Belenky, and Dee Ann Soder, *Job Analysis,* Washington, DC: The Bureau of National Affairs, 1983.

11. Milkovich and Newman, pp. 190-260.

12. Eleanor J. Sullivan, Phillip J. Decker, and Sherlyn Hailstone, "Assessment Center Technology: Selecting Head Nurses," *The Journal of Nursing Administration,* May 1985, pp. 13-18.

· *Part Six* ·

INFLUENCING

19

GIVING DIRECTIVES AND MANAGING CHANGE

motivating

Influencing is the managerial function by which the supervisor evokes action from others to accomplish organizational objectives. It is the process that management uses to achieve goal-directed action from subordinates and colleagues in the organization. Influencing is a human resources function that is particularly concerned with behavioral responses.

The influencing function is also known as *leading, motivating, directing,* and *actuating.* Regardless of the terminology, however, it is that managerial function the supervisor exercises to get the best and most out of the subordinates. At the same time the supervisor strives to create a climate in which the subordinates find as much satisfaction of their needs as possible. In the past managers depended largely on negative persuasion, disciplinary action, and a few incentive programs to influence their employees. The notion of organizational hierarchy dominated managerial thinking until the behavioral sciences brought about new understanding of human motivation and taught us better methods of influencing. Today every manager must be aware of the human activities of which the supervisor is an essential part and of the potential for influencing them. That is, the manager must understand some of the psychology involved in interpersonal relations.

As stated before, it is the role of every manager, of every supervisor, to influence in order to get the work done through and with the help of employees. Influencing is the managerial function that *initiates* action. Without it, nothing, or at best very little, is likely to be accomplished. Influencing includes the issuance of directives, instructions, assignments, and orders, as well as the guidance and overseeing of employees. It also encompasses the problems of motivation.

Moreover, the manager should consider the influencing function as a means not only for getting the work done and motivating the employees, but also for *developing* them. The most effective way to achieve such development of employees is diligent coaching and teaching by their immediate superior. Thus, influencing is more than just giving orders or supervising the employees to make certain that they follow directives. Influencing means building an effective work force and inspiring its members to perform their best. Influencing is the function

274

of getting the employees to work in a large enterprise as effectively as possible and with the same enthusiasm that they would display if they were working for themselves, either in their own enterprise or at a hobby. Only by appropriately influencing and supervising the employees will the manager be able to instill in them this motivation to work energetically on the job and at the same time to find personal satisfaction.

Influencing is the job of every manager, whether the chief executive officer (CEO) of a healthcare facility or the supervisor of one of its many departments. Every manager performs the influencing function, regardless of the position held. The amount of time and effort a manager spends in this function will vary, however, depending on the level, number of employees supervised, and other duties. The supervisor of a department will spend most of the time influencing and supervising, more so than the administrator of the institution. Influencing is an ever-present continuous function of the supervisor that covers the day-to-day activities within the department.

The supervisor's influencing function is interconnected with the other managerial functions. Planning, organizing, and staffing can be considered preparatory managerial functions; the purpose of controlling is to find out whether or not the goals are being achieved. The connecting and actuating link between these functions, however, is the managerial function of influencing. Influencing is largely affected by the type of employee the supervisor has selected while performing the staffing function. The plans that the supervisor has made and the organization drawn up also have a bearing on the influencing function. The controlling function is likewise affected by influencing, inasmuch as control often involves human problems.

To get the job done, every supervisor spends much time and effort in giving directives to subordinates. In this regard, recall the principle of *unity of command* referred to earlier in this text. Unity of command means that in each department only one person has the authority to make decisions appropriate to his or her station. Each employee has a single immediate supervisor, who is in turn responsible to his or her immediate superior, and so on up and down the chain of command. This also means that a subordinate is responsible to only one supervisor.

The principle of unity of command further states that the supervisor is the only one who can give directives to the employees. All directives can come only from the immediate supervisor, and no one else should interfere in the guiding and overseeing of the employees. In other words, there is a direct line of authority from the supervisor to the subordinate, just as there is one from the CEO to the director of a service and from there to the supervisor of a department. The administrator's line, however, extends only to the director of a service and not to the supervisors and employees under these supervisors. Thus, all supervision of the employees in a department rests with the supervisor or the head of that department and must not be exercised by anyone else, except in emergencies. Otherwise, the principle of unity of command is violated; no person can serve two bosses.

■ CHARACTERISTICS OF GOOD DIRECTIVES

Because issuing directives is such a basic and integral part of the supervisor's daily routine, it has often been taken for granted that every supervisor knows how to give orders. The frequent assumption is that anybody can give orders. This is probably not true, but even if it were, there is general agreement that some ways of issuing directives are much more effective than others. The experienced supervisor knows that faulty or bad order giving can easily upset even the best-laid plans, and, instead of coordination of efforts, a general state of chaos is created.

To the uninitiated outsider, it may seem that some supervisors can get excellent results even though they appear to break every rule in the book. Other supervisors may use all the best techniques of order giving and phrase their requests in the most courteous ways and still get only grudging compliance. The question of what is the most appropriate method of order giving depends on the employees concerned, work situation, supervisors and how they view their job, their attitude toward people, and many other factors. There are definite techniques for giving orders, however, and since the supervisor's own success depends largely on how the subordinates carry out the orders, the manager must possess the knowledge and skill for good directing. In other words, since directing is the fundamental tool employed by supervisors to start, stop, or modify activities, it is necessary for every supervisor to become familiar with the basic characteristics that distinguish good and accomplishable directives from those that are not. These characteristics are fulfilled when directives are reasonable, intelligible, worded appropriately, compatible with the objectives, and within reasonable time limits.

Reasonable Directives

The first essential characteristic of a good directive is that it must be reasonable; that is, compliance can reasonably be expected by the supervisor. Unreasonable orders will not only undermine morale, but will also make controlling impossible. The requirement of reasonableness immediately excludes orders pertaining to activities that physically cannot be done or are dangerous. In judging whether or not a directive can be reasonably accomplished, supervisors should not only appraise it from their own point of view, but should also try to place themselves in the position of the employee. The supervisor should not issue a directive if the capacity or experience of the employee is not sufficient to comply with the order. This becomes particularly important in the case of recent graduates, who may have had an excellent education in many areas, but lack experience and even some of the basic knowledge required. Supervisors should not forget the value of their own on-the-job training.

It can easily happen that a supervisor issues unreasonable instructions. For instance, to please the superior, a supervisor promises the completion of a job at a particular early time, and then issues such an order without considering whether the employee who is to carry out the order can actually do so. In this situation the supervisor should make it clear that he or she will try to get the job done in time, but unreasonable pressure should not be put on the subordinate. The supervisor should place himself or herself in the position of the subordinate and ask if compliance reasonably can be expected under these limits. The decision will depend on many factors prevailing at the time. In some cases the directive may actually be intended to stretch the subordinate's capabilities a little beyond what had previously been requested. Then the question of reasonableness becomes a question of degree. Generally, however, a prime requirement of a good directive is that it can be accomplished by the employee to whom it is assigned without undue difficulty.

Intelligibility

Another requirement is that a good directive should be intelligible to the employee; that is, the employee should be able to understand it. The subordinate cannot be expected to carry out an order that he or she does not understand. For example, a directive in a language not intelligible to the subordinate cannot be considered an order. The same also applies if both speak English, and the supervisor uses words that the employee does not comprehend. This, then, becomes a matter of communication. (See Chapter 5.) The supervisor must make certain that the employee understands, and it is the supervisor's duty to communicate in words and forms that the employee actually understands and not merely *should* understand. Instructions must be clear but not necessarily lengthy. What is clear and complete to the supervisor, however, is not always clear and complete to the employee. Also, sometimes the supervisor has not made up his or her mind as to exactly what he or she wants done. A supervisor simply cannot expect subordinates to carry out directives that have not been made clear and intelligible.

Appropriate Wording

Every good supervisor knows that the tone and words used in issuing directives significantly affect the subordinates' acceptance and performance of them. A considerate tone is likely to stimulate willing and enthusiastic acceptance, which is preferable to routine or grudging acceptance or outright rejection. In the patient care field the word "order" in connection with the attending physician's directives is normally used without unpleasant connotations. However, most supervisors should refrain from using the term *order* as much as possible and instead use such terms as *directives, assignments, instructions, suggestions,* and *requests.*

Requests

Phrasing orders more as requests does not reduce their character as a directive, but there is a major difference in the reaction a request will inspire as compared to a command. With most subordinates, a request is all that is usually needed and used. It is a pleasant and easy way of asking an employee to get the job done, particularly with those employees who have been working for the supervisor for some time and who are familiar with the personality of the supervisor, and vice versa. A request works best with this type of employee, and it usually does not rub anyone the wrong way.

Suggestions

In other instances it might be advisable to place the directive in the form of a suggestion, which is an even milder form than a request. For example, the supervisor might say, "Mary, we are supposed to get all of this work done before noon and we seem to be a bit behind. Do you think we can make up for it?" Suggestions of this type will accomplish a great deal for the supervisor because they will be understood and accepted by responsible and ambitious employees. Such employees like the feeling of not being ordered around and of being on their own to get the job accomplished. This suggestive type of order, however, would not be advisable in dealing with new employees. New employees simply do not have the background of the department and have not been around long enough to have received sufficient training and familiarity with its activities. Suggestion is also not the proper way of giving orders to those employees who are less competent and less dependable.

However, some subordinates must be told what to do simply because a request or suggestion might invite an argument as to why they should not do it. Sometimes the *command* type of order is the only way to get things done. Everyone remembers commands from parents and schoolteachers as part of growing up. Most people, however, think that once they are adults, commands are no longer necessary. Thus, the best rule for a supervisor is to avoid commands whenever possible but to use them when necessary.

Compatibility with Objectives

A good directive must be compatible with the purposes and objectives of the organization. If the instructions are not in accord with these objectives, chances are the subordinate may not execute them adequately or may not execute them at all. Thus, when issuing directives that appear to conflict with the organizational objectives, the supervisor must explain to the employee why such action is necessary, or the supervisor should explain that the directive merely appears to be but actually is not contrary to the institution's objectives. Instructions must also be consistent; they must not be in opposition to orders or directives previously given unless there is a good explanation for the discrepancy.

Time Limit

An additional characteristic of a good directive is that it specify the time within which the instructions should be carried out and completed. The supervisor should allow a reasonable amount of time and, if this is not feasible, must realize that the quality of performance will only be as good as can be produced under the time limit. In many directives the time factor is not stated, although it is probably implied that the assignment should be carried out within a reasonable length of time.

These are some of the major characteristics that should be incorporated in a good directive. Because the performance of the employee depends to a great extent on the format and content of directives given, the supervisor should make certain that the directive is in accord with these most essential characteristics.

■ MAJOR TECHNIQUES OF DIRECTING

In previous chapters we have mentioned various theories describing the supervisor's underlying managerial attitudes, such as Theories X and Y,[1] autocratic and democratic leadership, participation in decision making, and broad or narrow delegation of authority. The following is a more detailed discussion of how these managerial attitudes manifest themselves in the daily working environment, in which the supervisor depends on the subordinates to get the job done.

Generally the supervisor may choose from two basic techniques of direction: *autocratic,* or *close, supervision* on the one hand and *consultative,* or *participative, general supervision* on the other. In our discussion we can clearly distinguish between these two extremes, but in practice the supervisor usually combines and blends the techniques. For example, the manager might use the autocratic technique for one situation and the democratic technique for another. For some employees the supervisor might consider it more advisable to use one method and for other employees another technique. No one form of supervision is equally good in all situations. Whether it is better to apply a more autocratic or a more democratic type of supervision will depend on many factors: the type of work, current situation, attitude of the employee toward the supervisor, personality and ability of the employee, and personality, experience, and ability of the supervisor. A good supervisor is sensitive to all these factors and to the needs of each situation, and the style of supervision will be adjusted accordingly.

Autocratic, Close Supervision

When the autocratic technique of directing—close supervision—is employed, the supervisor gives direct, clear, and precise orders to the subordinates with detailed instructions as to exactly how and in what sequence things are to be done. This, as we know, allows little room for the initiative of the subordinate. The supervisor who normally uses the autocratic technique will delegate as little authority as possible and believes that he or she probably can do the job better than any of the subordinates. The supervisor relies on command and detailed instructions, followed by close supervision. An autocratic supervisor believes that subordinates are "not paid to think"; they are expected to follow instructions. The boss alone is to do the planning and decision making; this is what he or she is trained and paid for. This type of supervisor does not necessarily distrust the subordinate but believes that without detailed instruction the subordinate could not properly carry out the directive. This person believes that only he or she can specify the best method and that there is only one way, the supervisor's way, to get the job done. In other words, Theory X management is practiced.

With most people the consequences of autocratic supervision can be fatal. Employees lose interest and initiative; they stop thinking for themselves because no need or occasion arises for independent thought. They are obedient but silent and lack initiative, sparkle, and ingenuity. It becomes difficult to remain loyal to the organization and to the supervisor; the subordinates secretly rejoice when the boss makes a mistake. This form of supervision tends to make the employees somewhat like automatons. Freedom is curtailed, and it is difficult for them to learn even by making mistakes. They justly conclude that they are not expected to do any thinking about their job, and, although they perfunctorily perform their duties, they find little involvement in the work. They are certainly not motivated.

Shortcomings of the autocratic technique of supervision are obvious. Generally, young men and women who have been brought up in a democratic and permissive society from their earliest days resent autocratic order giving. It is contrary to our traditional democratic way of life in America. No ambitious employee will remain in a position where the supervisor is not willing to delegate some degree of freedom and authority. Any subordinate who is eager to learn and progress will resent being constantly given detailed instructions that leave no room for his or her own thinking and initiative. The employee will be stifled and sooner or later will leave the enterprise if at all possible. This method of supervision does not produce good employees and will only chase away those who have potential.

On the other hand, one must not forget that under certain circumstances and with certain people a degree of close supervision may be necessary. This is the exception, however, not the rule. Suppose, for example, that the subordinate is the type of person who does not want to think for himself or herself and prefers to receive clear orders. Firm guidance gives reassurance, whereas loose and general supervision may be frustrating. Some employees lack ambition and imagination and do not want to become at all involved in their daily job. Other employees have been brought up in an authoritarian manner by their families in the United States or a foreign country, and their previous work experience leads them to believe that general supervision is no supervision at all. Moreover, a work situation sometimes is so chaotic that only autocratic techniques can bring order. Aside from these rather unusual situations, however, it can generally be assumed that autocratic, or close, supervision is the least desirable and effective method.

Also, the autocratic supervisor usually makes the basic Theory X assumption that the average employee does not want to do the job and that close supervision and threats of loss of the job are needed to get people to work. Such a supervisor believes that if he or she were not on the job and "breathing down their necks," all the subordinates would stop working. Under these conditions, they probably would. On the other hand, the supervisor who follows Theory Y and believes in general supervision assumes that the average employee is eager to do a good job, wants to do the right thing, and must have motivation to perform his or her best. Autocratic, or close, supervision is not conducive to motivating employees to perform their best; general supervision, however, is conducive.

Consultative, General Supervision

The opposite of autocratic supervision is consultative. Consultative supervision is also known as *participative, democratic,* or *permissive supervision.* This is similar to the concept of *general supervision* referred to earlier. Its basic assumption is that employees are eager to do a good job and are capable of doing so. The supervisor behaves toward them with this basic assumption in mind, and the employees in turn tend to react in a manner that justifies the expectation of their supervisors.

This democratic approach to the directing function manifests itself in the practice of general supervision when it comes to routine assignments within the department. When new jobs have to be performed and new assignments made, the democratic method of supervising will appear in the consultative, or participative, technique of directing. Both have the underlying assumption that employees will be more motivated if they are left to themselves as much as possible. *motivate* We will first discuss situations that require consultation, then explore the meaning of general supervision for routine assignments.

Consultation

The essential characteristic of consultation is that the supervisor consults with employees concerning the extent, nature, and alternative solution to a problem before the supervisor makes a decision and issues a directive. The supervisor who uses the consultative approach before issuing directives is earnestly seeking help and ideas from the employees and approaches the subject with an open mind. More important than the procedure is the attitude of the supervisor. A subordinate will easily sense superficiality and is quick to perceive whether or not the boss genuinely intends to consult on the problem or only intends to give the impression of doing so.

Some supervisors are inclined to use such pseudoconsultation merely to give employees the feeling that they have been consulted. In many instances supervisors ask for participation only after they have already decided on the directive. Here the supervisor is using the consultative technique as a trick, a device for manipulating people to do what he or she wants them to do. The subordinate will quickly realize that he or she is not being taken seriously and that this participation is not real. The results achieved will be much worse than if the superior had used the most autocratic method. To practice actual consultative management when issuing new directives and assignments, the supervisor must be ready to take it seriously and be willing to be swayed by the employee's opinions and suggestions. If the manager is not sincere, it would be better not to apply this technique in the first place.

If the subject matter concerns only the supervisor and one employee, the consultative, or participative, method can be carried out informally. Numerous occasions arise during the day to hold such private consultations; however, if this approach is used all the time, the subordinates may begin to doubt whether the supervisors have any opinions of their own and are able to make any decisions. Although some supervisors are incapable of making a decision, many go too far in using this philosophy of direction, and while implementing the technique of participation, they cannot retain the atmosphere of managing.

To reinstate the atmosphere of managing, one should recall that consultative direction does not lessen or weaken formal authority, since the right of decision making still remains with the supervisor. Moreover, the supervisor using this approach is just as concerned with getting the job done economically and expeditiously as the manager who uses another approach. Although the supervisor must not dominate the situation to the exclusion of any employee participation, this does not mean the supervisor cannot express an opinion. It must be expressed in a manner that indicates to the employee that even the supervisor's opinions are subject to critical appraisal. Similarly, participative consultation does not mean that the suggestions of the employee cannot also be criticized or even rejected. True consultation implies a sharing of information between the supervisor and employee and a thorough and impartial discussion of alternate solutions, regardless of who originated them. Only then can it be said that the manager really consulted the subordinate.

For such consultative practices to be successful, it is not only necessary that the supervisor be in favor of them, but the employee must also want them. If the employee believes that "the boss knows best" and that making decisions and giving directives is none of his or her concern, then little likelihood exists that the opportunity to participate will induce better motivation or morale. The supervisor must also keep in mind that an employee should have certain pertinent knowledge about and should be capable of contributing to the area of consultation. The problems involved must be consistent with the subordinate's ability. Asking participation in areas that are outside their scope of experience will make the employees feel inadequate and frustrated instead of motivating them.

In using consultation, the danger exists that at the end of an extended discussion the employee may not have a clear idea of the solution. It is therefore desirable and even necessary for the supervisor or subordinate to summarize the conclusions to avoid such a pitfall. This is even more essential if several employees participated in the consultation.

One of the obvious advantages of summarizing the results of the consultation is that the emerging directive does not appear to the employee as an order, but rather as a solution in which he or she participated. This ensures the subordinate's best cooperation and enthusiasm in carrying out the directive. It imparts a feeling of importance, since the ideas evidently were desired and valued. Active participation also provides an outlet for reasoning power and imagination and an opportunity for the employee to make a worthwhile contribution to the organization. Since there is considerable talent among employees, their ideas often prove to be valuable in improving the quality of directives.

An additional advantage of consultation is that it will bring the employee closer to the supervisor, which will make for better communication and understanding between them. Looking at these impressive advantages, it becomes apparent that consultation is by far the best method to use whenever the supervisor has to issue new assignments, directives, and instructions.

General Supervision

This democratic, participative approach to directing subordinates leads to what we have already referred to as general, or loose, supervision when it comes to *routine assignments* and carrying out the daily chores involved in each employee's job. General supervision, as we know, means allowing the subordinate to work out the details of the job and make decisions on how best to do it. Through this process workers will gain great satisfaction from being on their own and from having a chance to express themselves and make decisions. Instead of having a specified detailed list of orders to comply with, the supervisor will just generally indicate what needs to be done and might make a few suggestions as to how to go about it. In so doing, the supervisor assumes that given the proper opportunity, the average employee wants to do a good job. The supervisor is primarily interested in the results. Once the subordinate is told what is to be accomplished and goals are established and limits defined, the employee is left on his or her own. This form of thinking and supervision can only lead to higher motivation and morale and ultimately better job performance. It gives employees the opportunity to satisfy their needs for self-expression and being their own boss.

Explaining Directives. The supervisor who practices general supervision creates an atmosphere of understanding and mutual confidence in which the employee will always feel free to call on the boss whenever the need arises without fear that this would indicate incompetence. By the same token, the supervisor takes the necessary time to explain to the workers the reasons for general directives and why certain things have to be done. By explaining the purpose behind the directives, the employee will be able to understand the environment of the activities. This will make the employee better informed; the better informed the subordinate is, the better he or she will be able to perform the job.

In many enterprises a common complaint is that subordinates are kept in the dark most of the time and that supervisors hoard knowledge and information that they ought to pass on. In most instances it is exceedingly difficult to issue directives so completely as to cover all particulars. If the person who receives the directive knows the purpose behind it, however, he or she is in a better position to carry it out than one who does not know. This will enable the worker to put the environment in total perspective and make sense out of it so that he or she can take firm and secure action. Without such knowledge, employees might find themselves in an anxiety-producing situation. Also, subordinates may run into unforeseen circumstances; if they know why the directive was given, they will probably be able to use their own good judgment and carry out the directive in a manner that will bring about proper results. They could not possibly do this if they were not well informed.

Sometimes a supervisor can overdo a good thing, however, and instead of clarifying the situation, provide so much information that the subordinate is utterly confused. Explanations should include only enough information to get the job done. If the directive involves a very minor activity and not much time is available, the explanation will probably be brief. Supervisors must use their own judgment in deciding how far they will go in explaining their directives. They will take into consideration such factors as the capacity of the subordinates to understand, the training they have had, the content of the directive, the underlying managerial attitude, and the time available. After evaluating these factors, the supervisor will be in a better position to decide what constitutes an adequate explanation.

General Supervision Compared with "No Supervision." As mentioned, general supervision is not the same as no supervision at all. General supervision requires that the employee be given a definite assignment, but this assignment is definite only to the extent that the employee understands the results expected. It is not definite regarding the specific instructions that state precisely how the results are to be achieved. General supervision does not mean that subordinates can set their own standards. Rather, the supervisor will set the standards and will make them realistic, high enough to be a challenge, but not higher than possibly can be achieved. Although general supervision excludes direct pressure, employees know that their efforts are being measured against these standards, and this knowledge alone should lead them to work harder. By setting the standards reasonably high, the supervisor does apply a degree of pressure, but this pressure is quite different from that exerted by "breathing down someone's neck."

General supervision requires a continuous effort from the supervisor to develop the potential of the employees. Everyone knows that active learning is more effective than passive learning. Employees learn more easily when they work out a solution for themselves than if they are given the solution. It is also known that employees learn best from their own mistakes. In general supervision continuous training of employees is an absolute necessity; the supervisor spends considerable time teaching employees how to solve problems and make decisions as problems arise in the work situation. The better trained the employees become in basic problem-solving methods, the less need there will be for supervision. One way to judge the effectiveness of a supervisor is to see how the employees in the department function when the boss is away from the job.

General supervision, however, is a way of life that must be practiced over time, and the supervisor cannot expect instantaneous results if general supervision is introduced into a situation where the employees have been accustomed to close supervision. It will take time before the results can be seen. The "general" supervisor is just as much interested in results as any other supervisor, but he or she is also interested in the employee's individual development, which differentiates him or her from the "autocratic" supervisor.

Although the supervisor may be a firm believer in general supervision and will practice it whenever possible, under certain conditions firmness, fortitude, and decisiveness must be shown. Certain employees simply may not thrive under loose supervision. This, however, is the exception and not the rule. Although general supervision is not a cure-all for every problem, all research studies seem to indicate that it is more effective than close supervision in terms of productivity, morale, and achievements. General supervision permits the employee to acquire pride in the work and in the results achieved. It helps develop the employee's talent and capabilities and permits the supervisor to spend less time with the employees and more time on overall management of the department. General supervision provides the motivation for the employees to work on their jobs with enthusiasm and energy, thus deriving full satisfaction from their work.

■ QUALITY CIRCLES

The quality circle, sometimes called *quality control circle*, is one form of increasing employee participation in the daily work routine. Although the underlying ideas came from the work of McGregor, Maslow, Herzberg, Deming, Drucker, and others, the first practical applications were made in Japanese industry. This Japanese management technique claims much credit for high levels of productivity, quality, and worker satisfaction. Lately the idea has been introduced into American industry and a number of healthcare settings.[2]

A quality circle is a group of approximately 8 to 12 employees (workers) and a supervisor from the same work area. These members strictly volunteer to meet regularly about once a week, during regular working hours, after hours, or both, to discuss work, and quantity- and quality-related problems and to stimulate innovation. They try to identify problems, isolate the causes, and develop practical solutions; the supervisor acts as facilitator and leader of the circle. Usually the team leader is first exposed to some basic training course in group dynamics, problem-solving, and similar techniques. The members are often given some training in problem-solving techniques, establishing priorities, brainstorming, and so forth.

The underlying thought is to tap an organization's own work force, realizing that the employees doing the job often know best why productivity is low and quality poor; often they have excellent ideas and answers. These circle solutions are then presented to management. The quality circle idea fits into the existing organizational structures, following the existing channels of communication and authority. Since quality circles are an application of participative management, the concept can be introduced with success into any organization where administration's philosophy has been democratic, open, and participative. It is unlikely that quality circles would produce results in an environment that practices autocratic and highly centralized management. Many organizations found the adoption of quality circles to be successful, whereas others found them disappointing.[3]

■ CHANGE AND INFLUENCING

All organized activities are under continuous pressure for change. There are various reasons for change; the most common are scientific and technological developments, people, competition, and communication.[4]

Supervisors' effectiveness in the influencing function is extremely important whenever they are faced with change. Since every enterprise operates in a larger context and a dynamic environment, change is inevitable and a part of everyday life. In fact, the growth of most undertakings depends largely on the concept of change and the accommodation of changes.

Although all organized activities are subject to change, the degree and complexity of change vary considerably from one activity to another. This is particularly so in the field of healthcare, in which the speed and complexity of changes have continuously increased in the last few decades and will continue to do so in the future. There is little doubt that most of these changes have been beneficial. Hospital floors are filled with patients benefiting from one new breakthrough or another. The healthcare center as a social system produces an ever-shifting equilibrium of forces because of the amazing changes in medical sciences and technologies and the social and economic environment. The supervisor's own department is a small social subsystem, interdependent with the larger system of the healthcare center. Any change imposed from outside is likely to shift the equilibrium of forces within each individual department, as well as within the organization as a whole.

The departmental supervisor is in the forefront of change, since he or she is the one in the daily working situation who has to make it a reality. The supervisor must "sell" the idea of change to the subordinates. Most often the supervisor has had little to do with the decision to make the change or with its timing;

it originated higher up in the administration or somewhere else. However, the supervisor should understand and accept the change because now his or her duty is to introduce it, explain it to the subordinates, and report their reactions to the superiors. The supervisor will encounter reactions from the employees that range from ready acceptance to outright rejection and hostility.

Most people pride themselves on being modern and up-to-date, and most gladly accept and welcome changes in material things. When it comes to jobs and interpersonal relations, however, there is a tendency to resist change. This is unfortunate because if an enterprise, especially in healthcare, is to survive, it must be able to react to the prevailing forces. Since resistance to change is a common phenomenon, the supervisor must recognize and understand this and be familiar with ways and means to overcome it.

Resistance to Change

Many reasons exist for resistance to change; they are mainly uncertainty, perception, loss, self-interests, insecurity, and so forth. One of the important factors of internal inflexibilities is psychological. Supervisors and employees may develop patterns of thought and behavior that are resistant to change. Supervisors are often frustrated in instituting a change by the unwillingness or inability of people to accept change. To overcome these inflexibilities, the supervisor must realize that it requires patient selling of the idea, education, careful dissemination of information, good leadership, and development of a tradition of change among the department's members. The supervisor must not fail to realize that even a trifling change may cause deep reactions within some of the employees.

This difficulty is further complicated because of *different perceptions*. For example, employees may believe that a new organizational arrangement will result in loss of control or influence. This belief will cause resistance to change. The fact that the new structure will in no way reduce their influence does not diminish their resistance as long as they perceive a threat and feel threatened or attacked.

To a large degree these sources of resistance to change center around a major consideration, *uncertainty* about the effects of change. An impending change is likely to cause anxiety and nervousness. The employees may worry about their being able to fulfill the new job demands. Also, the change may be fraught with weaknesses that have been overlooked or brushed aside.

Another reason for resisting change is that it disturbs the *equilibrium* of the current state of affairs. The assumption is that before the change, the employee exists within an environment where his or her *need satisfaction* has reached a high degree of stability; the change may threaten, prevent, or decrease the satisfaction of these needs. Therefore, it is natural for the employee to do whatever possible to thwart the introduction of the change.

A further reason for resisting change is that any change is seen as a potential threat to the employee's *security and self-interests*. The subordinate must give up the known familiar routine for something new and unpredictable. For example, new apparatus in the laboratory could make some of the technologists' previous skills superfluous. This could undermine their sense of occupational and professional identity. The change may require the technologists to upgrade their skills, and they are not sure that they can master the new responsibilities. At the outset, any new ideas and methods almost always present a threat to the security of the individuals involved in the change. Usually people fear change because they cannot assess or predict what it will bring in terms of their own position, activity, and future. It makes no difference whether the change is actually threatening or not. What matters is that the subordinate believes or assumes this.

Another reason for resistance to change is that the change may threaten the employee's *status* within the organization and the existing social networks. The employee may fear that his or her status will be lowered and someone else's raised. Such feelings of loss have, for example, caused many new computer installations to be used less effectively than anticipated or to be slowed down in their effects on the overall organization. This was because employees in the controller's office, where the computer might be housed, started to gain a different status in the organization once the computer became their domain. Its introduction caused what appeared to be threatening changes in the reporting relationships and status of numerous employees.

Often threats of an *economic* nature provide an additional reason for resistance to change. The subordinate may fear that the change will affect his or her job economically. The employee is not willing to give up existing benefits because the costs of change will probably not be made up by the rewards. Many years ago hand-weavers in the Low Countries of Europe tried to destroy mechanical looms by throwing their wooden clogs (sabots) into the machinery (sabotage) because they feared that the machines would destroy their jobs and income. The same fears of loss still prevail today when it comes to the size of the paycheck.

In general one may say that the changes affect different people in different ways. A change that causes great disturbance to one person may create little disequilibrium for another. The severity of the reaction that occurs in a particular situation will depend on the nature of the change and the person concerned.

The important thing for the supervisor to recognize is that changes do disturb the equilibrium of the employee and that, when individuals become threatened, they develop behaviors that serve as barriers to the threat. Therefore, it is the supervisor's duty to facilitate the inevitable process of adjustment when changes are necessary. Let us see how this can be done.

Overcoming Resistance to Change

Fortunately there are several useful ways to overcome these difficulties.[5] The supervisor should always remember that employees seldom resist change just to be stubborn. From the previous discussion we learned that there are valid reasons for resistance. Subordinates resist because the change affects their equilibrium socially, psychologically, and possibly economically. One of the factors that is particularly important in gaining acceptance of change is the relationship that exists between the supervisor who is trying to introduce the change and the employee who is subject to the change. If a relationship of mutual confidence and trust exists between the two, the employee is much more likely to go along with the change.

The supervisor should assume that a considerable amount of time is necessary to implement a change; a rigid timetable for change is unrealistic. The change must be planned far in advance, and its impact on each position and job should be anticipated. Even if the change is well thought out and carefully planned, some ramifications will probably be overlooked. The supervisor must leave room to discuss and accommodate them. With the proper attitude and the right techniques, however, the supervisor can facilitate the introduction of change. Involving subordinates in change discussions and decisions will help to overcome the various types of resistance.

Explanation and Communication

The most important aspect in facilitating the introduction of change is the supervisor's duty to *explain* the change to the employees in advance. This should begin long before the change is to be initiated. There should be ample time before the changeover to familiarize the employees with the idea, allow them to think through the implications and ramifications, and ask questions for more clarification. In other words, there must be sufficient time for feedback and additional *communication*.

In explaining the change, the supervisor should put himself or herself into the subordinate's position and discuss its pros and cons from their point of view. This discussion should explain what will happen and why. It should clarify the way in which the change will affect the employee and what it means to that person. It should show that the change will not adversely affect the employee or will even improve the present situation. In this process of communication the manager might want to interject what is often referred to as the *force-field analysis,* an approach to overcome resistance to change. In every change process there are forces acting for and forces acting against the change. The supervisor should comment on the pluses and minuses connected with the change from the employee's point of view, then try to tip the balance so that the forces for the change outweigh the forces against the change, thus tipping the scales toward acceptance. All this information should be communicated to the entire department, those employees who are directly involved as well as those who are indirectly involved. Overstatements are ill-advised, however, and it is essential to be absolutely truthful. The supervisor cannot afford a credibility gap.

The supervisor must also try to communicate, explaining to the employees what they consciously and subconsciously want and need to know in order to resolve prevailing fears. Only then can employees assess and understand what the change proposal would mean in terms of their positions and activities. The supervisor must help the subordinate understand the need for the change. This will be easier if the supervisor has always been concerned with setting the proper stage and giving the proper background information for all the directives. In such a case the employee is thoroughly acquainted with the underlying factors and is more likely to view the change as a necessary adjustment in a dynamic environment. The subordinate might ask a few additional questions about it, but then can quickly adapt to it and resume his or her previous behavior. The subordinate who has been informed of the reasons for change knows what to expect and why. Instead of blind resistance, there will be intelligent adaptation to the instructions;

instead of insecurity, a feeling of security. In the final analysis it is not the change itself that leads to so much misunderstanding, but more the manner in which the supervisor introduces the change. In other words, resistance to change that comes from fear of the unknown can be minimized by supplying appropriate explanation.

Participation

Another effective way of reducing resistance to change is to permit participation in planning and implementing the change. Playing a part in planning the change will reduce uncertainty and remove some of the fears and threats to social relationships and self-interests. Furthermore, those who are affected by the change may have something to contribute, since they are close to the situation and may see some weaknesses in the change proposal that management might have overlooked.

This participation may be in the form of *consultation,* whereby criticism and suggestions are sincerely solicited from the employees in relation to the contemplated change. In face-to-face conversations the supervisor discusses problems, asks questions, and tries to get the employees' ideas and reactions. One hopes management will then incorporate as much of this into the change as possible, and the employees will consider themselves partners in the change. A change imposed from above without participation is likely to generate resentment.

A more advanced stage of participation occurs when the supervisor lets the employees make the decision themselves. The supervisor defines the problem and sets the limits, but allows the subordinates to develop the alternatives and choose between them. *Group decision making* could also produce a better decision because pooled expertise is likely to identify and evaluate more alternatives than an individual could; those who are involved in this process are probably more deeply committed to the alternative selected. Therefore, group decision making is an effective means for overcoming resistance to change. Such an approach recognizes that if the employees threatened by a change have the opportunity to work through the new ideas and methods from the beginning and can be assured that their needs will be satisfied in the future, they will accept the new ideas and methods as something of their own making and will support the changes. Group decision making also makes it easier for each member to carry out the decision once it is agreed on, and the group will put strong pressure on those who have reservations or who do not want to go along.

Both types of participation should be encouraged because they help to facilitate the introduction of change. Of course, in trying to implement change in the department, the supervisor will make use of all means available—persuasion, discussion, participation, and group decision making. Participation is not always possible, however; in extreme situations, it may be necessary to make unpleasant changes unilaterally, impose them, and then help the subordinates understand and accept them.

■ SUMMARY

The influencing function of the manager forms the connecting link between planning, organizing, and staffing on one side and controlling on the other.

Issuing directives is perhaps the most important part of the influencing function because without them, nothing or at best very little would be achieved. Certain prerequisites ensure that a directive will be properly carried out. A good directive must encompass the formula of who, what, where, when, how, and why. The directive should be accomplishable, intelligible, properly phrased, and compatible with the objectives of the enterprise. In addition, a reasonable amount of time should be permitted for its completion.

In issuing directives, the supervisor may employ two major techniques: the autocratic technique, which brings about close supervision, and the consultative technique, characterized by general supervision. For certain occasions, employees, and conditions the autocratic technique is probably more effective, but for most situations it is far better for a supervisor to apply consultative techniques to produce the highest motivation and morale among employees. This means that in the case of new assignments the supervisor will consult with the employees as to how the job should best be done. Their contributions to the decision are elicited.

In directives primarily concerned with routine assignments and the daily performance of the job, the supervisor will employ a form of general supervision instead of close supervision. In so doing, the supervisor gives the employees the freedom to make their own decisions on how the job is to be done, after he or she has set the goals and standards to be achieved. This also gives employees the freedom to use their own ingenuity and judgment; experiences of this type offer continuous room for further training and improvement. In addition, general supervision motivates employees to the extent that they find satisfaction in their jobs. All indications are that general supervision produces better results than close supervision.

Since the healthcare field is dynamic, necessitating constant and often substantial changes, the supervisor is confronted with the problem of how to introduce change. To cope successfully with the average employees' normal resistance to change, the supervisor must realize that there are social, psychological, and possibly economic reasons for this resistance. By involving employees in change discussions and decisions, much of the resistance can be overcome. In the final analysis, the supervisor is in the front line, and it is his or her responsibility to accommodate change and make it become reality.

NOTES

1. Douglas McGregor, *The Human Side of Enterprise,* New York: McGraw-Hill Book Co., 25th anniversary printing, 1985, Chapters 3 and 4.
2. George Munchus, III, "Employer-Employee Based Quality Circles in Japan: Human Resource Policy Implications for American Firms," *Academy of Management Review,* April 1983, pp. 255-261; Sandy J. Wayne, Ricky W. Griffin, and Thomas S. Bateman, "Improving the Effectiveness of Quality Circles," *Personnel Administration,* March 1986, pp. 79-90; Charles N. Greene and Timothy A. Matherly, "Quality Circles: A Need for Caution and Evaluation of Alternatives," in Randall S. Schuler, Stuart A. Youngblood, and Vandra L. Huber, eds., *Readings in Personnel and Human Resource Management,* 3rd ed., St. Paul, MN: West Publishing Co., 1987, pp. 509-517.

3. Berkeley Rice, "Square Holes for Quality Circles," *Psychology Today,* February 1984, p. 17.
4. Two popular books dealing with the broad nature and impact of change are Alvin Toffler, *Future Shock,* New York: Random House, 1970; and John Naisbitt, *Megatrends: Ten New Directions Transforming Our Lives,* New York: Warner Books, 1982.
5. A model for facilitating change that is frequently cited was developed by Kurt Lewin. This model is concerned with changing the attitudes, skills, and knowledge of individuals and suggests three elements: a period of unfreezing old attitudes; changing, or moving to a new attitude; and refreezing. Kurt Lewin, "Frontiers in Group Dynamics: Concept, Method, and Reality in Social Science; Social Equilibria and Social Change," *Human Relations,* June 1947; pp. 5-42. See also Edgar H. Schein, "Management Development as a Process of Influence," *Industrial Management Review,* May 1961, pp. 59-77; and James Brian Quinn, "Managing Innovation: Controlled Chaos," *Harvard Business Review,* May-June 1985, pp. 73-84.

MOTIVATION

Motivation of employees is of great importance to managers because of its impact on performance. Motivation is closely related to the crucial managerial function of influencing because it deals most intimately with the human being. Thus, we must understand something about what makes the human being tick, what motivates a person, and more basically what underlies a person's motivations.

Motivation is the process affecting the inner needs or drives that arouses, moves, energizes, directs, channels, and sustains human behavior. It is important for contemporary managers to understand this basic motivational process. Generally the motivational process begins with inner needs and drives that impel the individual to work toward certain goals he or she believes will satisfy these inner needs and drives. Once these goals are attained, the individual judges whether these efforts were worthwhile. If so, this works as reinforcement, and the individual will continue in the pursuit of these and/or other needs and drives. All this will be discussed in great detail later in this chapter. Understanding motivation will enable managers to help their employees achieve higher levels of job satisfaction and job performance.

■ THEORIES OF MOTIVATION

Managers have been aware of the importance of motivation for a long time. It has been a major concern for managers and psychologists, and many theories have been developed explaining how people are motivated.[1] There are several different ways to interpret the concept of motivation; two of the major categories of contemporary motivational theories are the *content* theory and the *process* theory.

Content theory focuses on the question of what factor or set of factors moves, energizes, and starts the behavior of an individual. This theory discusses the concept of needs or motives that drive people and the incentives that cause people to behave in a particular manner. Three of the most publicized content theories of motivation are Maslow's hierarchy of needs, Herzberg's two-factor approach of satisfiers and dissatisfiers, and McClelland's needs for achievement, affiliation, and power. Each of these three content theories tries to explain individual behavior from a slightly different perspective.

Process theory examines how and why people choose a particular behavior to accomplish a goal and how they evaluate their satisfaction after reaching the goal.

Equity and expectancy are the two major process perspectives on motivation.[2] The first approach stresses the equity of effort in relation to the results; the other emphasizes the importance of the likelihood of success of the expected results.

■ MODEL OF MOTIVATIONAL PROCESSES

Although the complete set of processes is very complex, a generalized and over-simplified model of basic motivational processes is presented in Figure 20-1. This model shows four basic parts of the process: (1) needs; (2) desires, expectations, perceptions, values, and attitudes; (3) behavior; (4) goals; and (5) feedback. At any point in time individuals are likely to have a mixture of needs, desires, and expectations. For instance, one subordinate may have a strong need for achievement and a desire to earn more money; this person expects that doing the job well will lead to the desired rewards. This expectation is likely to cause behavior that is directed toward specific goals. Achieving the goals serves as feedback on the impact of this behavior and reassures this individual that the behavior is correct; it satisfies the needs and expectations. On the other hand, it may tell the person that the present course of action is incorrect and should be altered.

■ FIGURE 20-1 Model of the motivational process.

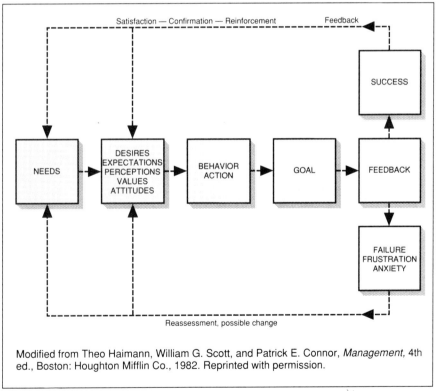

Modified from Theo Haimann, William G. Scott, and Patrick E. Connor, *Management,* 4th ed., Boston: Houghton Mifflin Co., 1982. Reprinted with permission.

This model of motivation obviously is oversimplified because it does not take into account all influences on motivation; however, it shows the basic cyclical nature of the process. People are forever restlessly striving to satisfy a variety of needs and expectations, and the success of one effort triggers the pursuit of another need and desire. Once one need has been met, another need or desire emerges and stimulates further action.

Maslow's Hierarchy of Human Needs

One of the approaches to employee motivation is based on individual human needs. Every action is motivated by unsatisfied needs. These unsatisfied needs cause human beings to behave in a certain manner and to try to achieve certain goals in hopes of reducing the tensions that arise from unmet needs. A person eats because hunger creates the need for food. Someone else has a strong need for achievement and strives for advancement within his or her field of work. In other words, there is a reason for everything that people do. People are always striving to attain something that has meaning to them in terms of their own particular needs. It is often observed that human beings never seem satisfied; they are continuously fulfilling needs. After the successful fulfillment of one need, they will start on another round of pursuits. Indeed, we can say that life is a process in which needs constantly arise and demand satisfaction.

Probably the most widely known and accepted theory of needs and motivation is the model designed by Abraham H. Maslow.[3] He developed a model consisting of *deficiency needs* and *growth needs*. Deficiency needs are those needs that must be satisfied if the individual is to be healthy and secure. These are the physiological needs for food, water, clothing, shelter, etc.; needs for safety; and the feeling of belonging, love, and respect from others. Growth needs refer to development and achievement of one's potential. We should not think, however, that all needs are of the same order of importance. Many different kinds of needs exist, and some produce stronger motivation or demand more immediate satisfaction than others. Maslow suggests that these needs are arranged in a hierarchy. (See Figure 20-2.)

■ FIGURE 20-2 Hierarchy of needs.

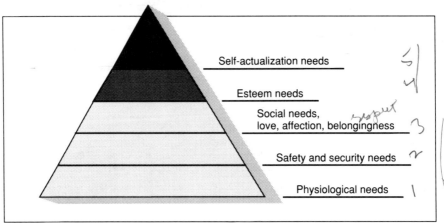

Maslow's model contains five levels of needs that can be visualized as forming a pyramid. The most basic needs are *physiological needs*. These are the biological needs that everyone has for survival and biological function, food, shelter, rest, recreation, etc. Normally, in organizational settings, adequate wages and the work environment itself enable an individual to obtain the necessities and comforts of life that are vital to fulfilling these physiological needs.

When the physiological needs are reasonably satisfied, needs at the next higher level begin to dominate. These are usually called *safety needs*. The second level stresses the needs for a safe physical and emotional environment. They are the needs we have for protection against danger and threat. Such needs are natural reactions to insecurity. We all desire more control over and protection from the uncertainties of life. In a work environment these uncertainties would produce safety needs caused by fear of arbitrary management action, loss of job, favoritism, discrimination, unpredictable administration of policy, etc. Most enterprises today offer various programs that are designed to satisfy and fulfill these safety or security needs. For example, most enterprises have grievance systems, adequate medical and other insurance plans, provisions for retirement benefits, provisions for unemployment compensation, seniority, etc.

Once the physiological and safety needs are satisfied, *social and belongingness needs* become important motivators. Social needs consist of belonging, association, acceptance by one's peers, and giving and receiving friendship and love. These needs are often identical with the needs people have for a feeling of group identity, being part of a group or team, and being accepted and respected by their peers. A supervisor must be aware of the existence of these needs, which can be fulfilled in organizational settings by informal groups. As we know, tightly knit, cohesive work groups will generally enable employees to gain greater on-the-job satisfaction and produce a better climate for motivation. This is why the supervisor should look at the positive aspects and strengths of informal groups. Often supervisors go to great trouble to control and interfere with the natural "grouping" tendency of human beings. This is ill-advised. When a person's social needs are thwarted and frustrated, this individual will behave in ways that are likely to hurt organizational objectives. The manager should always realize that social needs are fulfilled to a large extent by informal groups and informal organization, as discussed in Chapter 15.

Once the first three needs, also known as *deficiency needs*, have been satisfied, people will generally attempt to satisfy *growth needs*. These are the needs for esteem and self-actualization.

Esteem needs focus on one's desire to have a worthy self-image and receive recognition from others. The needs for *esteem* are both self-esteem and esteem from others. Self-esteem includes the need for self-confidence, a positive self-image, self-respect, independence, achievement, competence, and knowledge. These needs are often fulfilled by mastery over part of the environment, for example, by knowing that you can accomplish a certain task. However, a person also needs the esteem and recognition of others for his or her accomplishments. These needs relate to reputation, need for status, recognition, appreciation, and the deserved respect of colleagues. Many jobs in industrial settings offer little opportunity for satisfaction of such needs. Many positions in the healthcare field are much more conducive to the achievement of these needs because of their challenging nature. The manager can facilitate the situation by providing external symbols of esteem such as appropriate titles and offices. Of course, it is desirable that both aspects of the need for esteem are fulfilled. Frequently, however, the esteem of self comes before esteem from others.

The highest level of needs is the need for *self-actualization, self-fulfillment,* or *self-realization.* These are the needs for realizing one's own potential, for continued self-development, for being creative in the broadest sense of the term. It has often been said that this is the need "to become what one is capable of becoming." Unlike the other four needs, which probably will be satisfied, self-actualization is seldom fully achieved. It is a process of becoming, and as one gradually approaches self-fulfillment, this process is intensified and sustained. Since this need probably can be met only from within, there is little the manager can do, except to provide an organizational climate conducive to self-actualization. Conditions of modern life give many people little opportunity to fulfill this need. Most employees are continuously struggling to satisfy the lower needs; they must divert most of their energy to satisfy them. Therefore, the need for self-fulfillment frequently remains dormant and unfulfilled.

It is interesting that there seems to be a relationship between the hierarchy of needs and age. Physiological and safety needs are paramount in the life of an infant. As a child grows up, love needs become more important. When the adolescent reaches young adulthood, needs for esteem seem to dominate the field. If the person is successful in life, then the move to self-actualization later in life is likely. Such a step does not necessarily follow because pressing circumstances may arrest the route of progress at the esteem level or at lower levels. Also, as we shall see later, this situation is often the basis of conflict between organizational and individual goals.

Maslow's hierarchy of needs has been and still is popular among and appealing to managers. Since it is the supervisor's job to create a climate in which employees can satisfy the multitude of needs, this theory makes clear recommendations to management. Some of the specific dynamics of Maslow's theory may still be in question and have been challenged.[4] Nevertheless, Maslow's hierarchy was the first clear statement urging managers to recognize the importance of higher-order needs. It caused a shift from the traditional lower-order motivators to higher motivators. Most healthy and normal employees probably have satisfied the lower-order deficiency needs (they are not hungry, feel reasonably secure, and have sufficient social relationships); therefore, supervisors should emphasize a working climate conducive to satisfying the higher-order growth needs. This means supervisors should stress some variety of duties, delegation of authority, autonomy, and responsibility so that employees can more fully realize their potential, their growth needs.

Two-Factor Motivation-Hygiene Theory

Another approach to the content perspective to motivation seen as a need classification system was developed by Frederick Herzberg.[5] Herzberg, a psychologist, has done much research on job satisfaction and developed a number of conditions on which satisfaction is based. He distinguishes between those factors in the work situation that are unlikely to motivate employees (hygiene factors) and those that tend to motivate employees (motivators). In essence he states that the hygiene rewards satisfy what are commonly known as lower-order needs, whereas the motivators satisfy higher-order needs. Herzberg identified the following groups as hygiene factors and as motivators:

Hygiene Factors	*Motivation Factors*
The organization's policy and administration	Achievement
Technical supervision	Recognition
Salary	The work itself
Interpersonal relations	Responsibility
Working conditions	Advancement

Herzberg measures satisfiers and dissatisfiers in terms of the frequency with which they appear and the duration during which they produce either a significant improvement or reduction in job satisfaction. (See Figure 20-3.) The five hygiene factors are environmental. When they are at an unacceptable level, dissatisfaction will occur. When they are at an acceptable level, satisfaction results. The factors most frequently involved in events causing job dissatisfaction (dissatisfiers) are company policy and administration, supervision, salary, interpersonal relations, and working conditions. When these factors are negative or lacking, they are considered to be dissatisfiers. Even when they are positive and appropriate, these factors do not tend to motivate people; it is almost as if they are expected. When positive, they are *satisfiers*.

This, however, does not mean that these factors are unimportant. They are essential because their fulfillment or absence is either satisfying or dissatisfying. Therefore, the manager must make certain that administration and policies are fair and suitable, that pay and benefits are appropriate, that technical supervision is acceptable, that working conditions are safe and healthy, and so forth. By providing these factors at the proper level, the manager does not give the employees the opportunity to experience motivation, but does keep them from being dissatisfied.

If managers really want motivated employees, however, they should use *motivators*. Herzberg's study indicates that the most frequently mentioned factors in improved job satisfaction are achievement, recognition, the work itself, responsibility, and advancement. These are the factors that, if present, truly motivate people. It is the opportunity for advancement, greater responsibility, the possibility of promotion, growth, achievement, and interesting work that make a job challenging, meaningful, and really motivating to subordinates. The manager, therefore, should give the employees an environment and the opportunity to experience these motivational factors. Such motivational factors are obviously associated with the higher-order needs of people; they are related to the work content, whereas the hygiene factors relate to the work environment.

Herzberg's findings have important implications for the supervisor.[6] Although management strives for good organizational "hygiene" through sound wage administration, enlightened supervision, pleasant working conditions, appropriate fringe benefits, and so forth, these factors alone normally do not

■ **FIGURE 20-3 Factors affecting job satisfaction.**

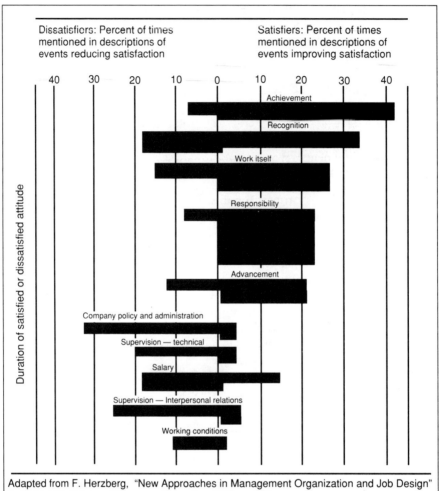

Dissatisfiers: Percent of times mentioned in descriptions of events reducing satisfaction

Satisfiers: Percent of times mentioned in descriptions of events improving satisfaction

Duration of satisfied or dissatisfied attitude

Achievement

Recognition

Work itself

Responsibility

Advancement

Company policy and administration

Supervision — technical

Salary

Supervision — Interpersonal relations

Working conditions

Adapted from F. Herzberg, "New Approaches in Management Organization and Job Design" *Industrial Medicine and Surgery,* November 1962, p. 480.

produce a motivational climate. If properly fulfilled, we merely minimize dissatisfaction; however, these factors are not motivators. What is actually required, therefore, is a two-way effort that is directed first at the hygiene factors and then at the development of motivation. In addition to the need to avoid unpleasantness that comes from largely dissatisfying conditions, the supervisor must produce positive motivation through a more sophisticated set of factors, which is closely related to the concept of self-actualization. Although it is difficult to apply these motivators in some situations, most positions in the healthcare setting provide ample opportunity to stress them.

Other Needs

Another approach to the content view of motivation is concerned with other important needs themselves. David McClelland's research in organizational behavior led to what he has termed and is now commonly known as *need for achievement* (n Ach), *need for affiliation* (n Aff), and the *need for power* (n Pow).[7]

The need for achievement is a need for personal challenge and accomplishment. It involves the desire to assume personal responsibility and pursue reasonably difficult goals, a preoccupation with the task, and specific and quick feedback as to accomplishment. This n Ach is obviously essential for a successful manager; it can be learned from early childhood on and can be taught to adults. McClelland defines it as behavior toward competition with a standard of excellence.

The need for affiliation is the need for human companionship, support, and reassurance. People with a strong n Aff look for approval and reassurance from others, are willing to conform to the norms and wishes of others, and are sincerely interested in the feelings of others. They are likely to do well in situations that include a lot of social interaction.

The third need is the need for power, or need for dominance. It is a need to influence others and to lead and control them. One of McClelland's studies concluded that all managers tend to have a stronger power motive than the general population and that successful managers tend to have stronger power motives than less successful managers.[8]

Levels of Aspiration

A person's level of aspiration is closely related to the order of needs. Level of aspiration causes an individual's goals to shift as various needs are satisfied. That is, once the needs on one level are satisfied, the individual tends to aspire to higher levels.

For example, suppose an individual is highly motivated by the need for achievement, and attitudes and personality cause this person to look for satisfaction of this need by working as a nurse in a healthcare center. Such a person will not be satisfied for any length of time by a low-level supervisory position. Once the position has been attained, this individual is likely to strive for the next higher position, such as assistant director of nursing. After achieving the top position within the service, the objectives may shift to higher positions within the overall administration of the hospital; for instance, this person may seek to become an associate administrator or even the chief administrator. The objectives also may shift to something outside the hospital, such as governmental activities that present possibilities for the satisfaction of the achievement needs.

This endless search for alternatives to satisfy increasing aspirations is an important aspect of human motivation. If an organization can provide an individual with a wider range of need satisfactions, this person's commitment to the organization will be greater.

■ PERCEPTIONS, VALUES AND ATTITUDES

As we have said, all human behavior is motivated by unsatisfied needs. These needs spring from causes that are deep within the person and, together with other motives, attitudes, and behaviors, form the configuration usually called the *personality*. From this point of view, motivations that contribute to personality can be defined as a potential to act in order to satisfy those needs that are not met. The term *potential to act* implies that some motives are stronger than others and thus more likely to produce action. The strength of motivation is determined by the strength of a particular need, the probability that the act required to satisfy that need will be successful, and the rewards forthcoming. An individual is more likely to act if the motive is stronger, the probability for success is high, and the reward is significant.

Other factors are also involved in producing human behavior or action. Motives do not stand alone. Closely related to them and significantly affecting their strength are *perceptions, values,* and *attitudes*.

We are constantly subjected to many stimuli from our environment; all of them compete for our attention. In our daily working environment there are noises, sights, sounds, smells, supervisors' instructions, memos, reports, physicians' directives, co-workers' remarks, people walking by, paging over the loudspeaker, phones ringing, posted signs, etc. All these and many more vie for our attention. The individual therefore has the problem of how to make sense out of all of them, how to interpret and organize the more important stimuli, and how to respond to them.[9]

Perception is the process by which this is done. With perception the individual screens, selects, organizes, and interprets stimuli so that an appropriate behavioral response can be made. This does not necessarily lead to an accurate portrayal of the environment, but to a unique picture, influenced by the perceiver's needs, desires, values, disposition, and frame of reference. It is a personal construction for which the individual has selected certain objects for a major role perceived in an individual manner. Through the process of *perceptual selectivity* certain stimuli catch our attention and are selected, whereas others that a person does not want to bother with or that make the person uncomfortable are screened out.

Perception and the perceptual process plays an important role in all managerial activities, including decision making, appraising employees, communicating orally, and writing. It is important for the manager to understand the perceptual process and to realize that people perceive things differently.

Once individuals notice a particular object, they then attempt to make sense out of it by organizing it according to their frame of reference and needs. This is known as the process of *perceptual organization* by categorizing, grouping, and filling in information systematically. Once meaning has been attached to a certain stimulus, the individual can reach an appropriate response. *Several barriers* to accurate perception, however, can enter into these perceptual processes. Examples of barriers are the frame of reference, stereotyping, the halo effect, biases, perceptual defense, etc. (See Chapters 5 and 17.) All the perceptual processes affect a person's attitudes and behavior at work.

Attitudes and values also play a role in all behavior. Attitudes are different from values. Values are closely held normative standards; the individual chooses them based on personal preference. "Values carry with them an 'oughtness' component. They are frequently defined as ideas about how everyone *should* feel or behave."[10] *Values* are broader, general, more encompassing concepts than attitudes; for example, most of us value freedom and equality. Our values of equality can be translated into our attitude toward minority groups.

Attitudes can be seen as *"a predisposition to respond in a favorable or unfavorable way to objects, persons, concepts, or whatever."*[11] They are how an individual tends to interpret, understand, or define a situation or relationship with others. Attitudes constitute one's feelings about something, an individual's likes and dislikes directed toward persons, things, situations, or a combination of all three. Attitudes are more than casual opinions, since they are heavily charged with emotional overtones. Attitudes may include feelings as well as intellectual elements. They also include evaluations and value judgments. Attitudes differ in type, strength, and the extent to which they are open or hidden. Basically they are revealed in two ways: either by the individual's expressed statements or behavior. An individual may express dislike for the hospital he or she works for or may merely demonstrate this attitude by being absent excessively. Although we cannot see perceptions, values, and attitudes, their consequences can be observed in behavior.

Factors Determining Attitudes

Attitudes are learned from prior experiences. An infinite number of factors determine and influence an individual's attitudes. A major influence is a person's *biological,* or *physiological, makeup.* Such factors as sex, age, height, race, weight, and physique are important in determining the attitudes that contribute to overall personality structure. In addition, many psychologists believe that the very early years of life are crucial to attitudinal development. Freudian psychologists, in particular, believe that early childhood is the most critical period of all in what a person actually becomes. This theory is often referred to as *childhood determinism;* it maintains that such factors as feeding patterns, training patterns, and home conditions in early childhood are the primary determinants of personality structure.

Another area that influences a person's attitudes and personality is the *immediate environment.* Education, employment, income, and many other experiences that confront an individual as he or she goes through life will influence what this person is and eventually becomes. Furthermore, one should never forget that the *broader culture* of society also influences a person's attitudes. In the United States people believe in competition, reward for accomplishment, equal opportunities, and other values that are part of the democratic capitalistic society. Individuals learn from their early years to strive for achievement, think for themselves, and work hard; they learn these are roads for success. All such cultural influences affect a person's attitudes and thus behavior. Countless other factors also influence attitudes and personality. We have only touched on the more obvious ones.

Attitudes and Behavior

No matter what factors have caused their development, however, attitudes become deep-seated attributes of the individual's makeup. They are learned and acquired through all life's experiences. As stated, they do not have to be rational or logical. Attitudes tend to last for a long time. We hold firmly to our attitudes and resist forces that attempt to interfere with them. Attitudes can change, but they change very slowly. Attitudes do not exist only within individuals, but are also generated within groups. The discussion of informal organizations stated that often individuals gladly accept as their own the attitudes of the group to which they belong.

As shown in Figure 20-1, needs and motives do not stand alone as determinants of behavior. They are also influenced by the underlying attitudes and values of a person. Indeed, we can say that *values and attitudes will determine the route a person takes for the satisfaction of his or her needs.* Although basically the same needs appear in every person, an individual's attitudes will vary greatly and will affect his or her unique responses to his or her needs. In other words, attitudes help determine what motivates a person to take a certain action in order to fulfill a certain need. For example, many people may have a strong need for achievement. However, differing attitudes and values will motivate one individual to seek fulfillment of need by working in a hospital, another by working in a government agency, another by working in industry, and a fourth person may seek fulfillment by teaching in a university or going into politics.

■ MOTIVATION VERSUS FRUSTRATION

If the individual's chosen route results in goal accomplishment, the need will be satisfied and the attitudes reinforced. In other words, accomplishment of the goal works as "feedback" to let the individual know that the needs are satisfied and the attitudes are reinforced. What happens, however, if the chosen course of action does not result in goal accomplishment? What happens when an individual wishes to pursue a certain course of action, but is prevented from doing so? This obstruction may be caused externally or internally.

Generally, actions that do not succeed in obtaining goals result in blocked satisfaction, frustration, and anxiety. As shown in Figure 20-1, feedback notifies the individual that his or her needs are not being fulfilled. In other words, there is stress: frustration and anxiety instead of need satisfaction. Basically there are five ways in which people usually resolve the problems of conflict and frustration. The best way is (1) problem-solving behavior, but other methods include (2) resignation, (3) detour behavior, (4) retreat, or (5) aggression.

Problem-solving behavior is usually the most desirable way of meeting frustration. It is advantageous if a person can look at personal problems objectively and base his or her decisions on reasoned analysis of the situation. Unfortunately many people are not capable of doing this, and it is the supervisor's duty to help the employees learn problem-solving behavior. Suppose, for instance, that an LPN is eager to advance to a better position, but all better positions demand the RN degree as a prerequisite. The LPN is frustrated because she is beating her head against a wall. In this case reasoned analysis of the situation and a thorough discussion with her supervisor could encourage the LPN to go to school and obtain the RN degree, which will enable her to move up within the hierarchy of nursing services. Such a route would constitute intelligent problem-solving behavior.

Another way to solve a conflict situation is by *resignation*. Suppose the same LPN were to say to herself, "What else can I do? I have to stick it out." She seems resigned to her lot. She will keep on working for the healthcare institution but may no longer consider herself a part of it. Once an employee has given up in the face of obstacles, it is difficult to build up morale to the point where institutional and departmental goals are really important. Some employees simply stay on the job listlessly until they are able to retire. Such employees who have resigned themselves to their lot are usually passive and resistant to change. They are difficult for the supervisor to deal with because new ideas do not excite or stimulate them. It is hoped that the supervisor can help such subordinates use problem-solving methods of reasoned analysis and objective evaluation. If, however, the supervisor does not succeed in this respect, he or she may try to restimulate the employee to strive either for past goals or toward some new and desirable goals. The supervisor knows that the result of resignation is usually inferior performance on the job, lowering of morale, and a climate that is not conducive to the best performance of the department.

A third way to solve a frustrating situation is to resort to *detour behavior.* Since the direct way of reaching the goal is barred, the employee will try to find another way to get there. Such detours, however, are often obscure and sometimes devious. For example, one kind of detour behavior is self-induced illness. Children learn early in life that being sick gives them an acceptable excuse for getting out of doing an unpleasant task. Similarly, employees will often have painful and real physical disorders to evade a conflict situation. Some people can stand conflict and frustration better than others, but sooner or later the strain begins to tell, and some sort of conflict resolution is necessary.

Retreat (leaving the field) is a fourth way to meet the problems of conflict and frustration. Most people at one time or another have looked at their jobs and have wished that they could quit right there and then. They may believe that they are not getting the satisfaction they thought the position would bring, that no one realizes the difficulties involved in the job, that their supervisor does not appreciate all the things they are doing, and so on. Most people have such feelings prevail sometime in their lives. In many instances an employee finds it necessary to leave the organization and find alternative employment, possibly in another town. Whether this reaction to frustration is good or bad, however, will depend on the major source of the conflict and frustration. If the major source is in the employee's personality and the conflict does not stem from the working situation, then leaving the field would not be the right answer. In other words, if the frustration is caused by the person's own peculiar psychological makeup, such a change probably will not bring about the desired result. If, however, the conflict is because of an unfavorable work situation, then leaving the field, quitting, or even leaving the city may represent a real solution to the problem. Often it is difficult for the individual to determine whether or not this is the case. Of course, it is not always necessary to quit the job or move to another city in order to "leave the field." Leaving the field may show itself simply by daydreaming, spending a lot of time in the washroom, developing a high rate of absenteeism, resorting to alcoholism and drug abuse, or using some other form of symbolic escape. All these forms of retreat will cause the supervisor additional problems.

Aggression is the fifth way in which people may meet the problem of severe frustration. The individual feels frustrated and cannot find an acceptable, legitimate remedy. Sabotage, for example, is one common form of aggressive behavior. By aggression we mean not only overt hostile behavior aimed at harming other people or inanimate objects, but also merely the tendency to commit acts of aggression. This tendency may manifest itself in thoughts or words or even in feelings that have not as yet been put into words. The supervisor should always remember that frustration and aggression are closely tied together and that all aggressions stem from some form of frustration. As we have said, some individuals can stand more frustration than others and are not as easily moved into aggressive behavior. Moreover, many minor frustrations that could lead to aggressive behavior do not because people hold back and inhibit them. The job of the supervisor is to see that frustration is minimized and to provide constructive outlets for frustration. The supervisor should try to anticipate the sources of frustration and attempt to eliminate them. If this cannot be done, however, then the best the supervisor can do is see that the causes of frustration are not aggravated. Often patient listening will help to ease employee tensions, and it may enable the subordinate to seek the real source of the frustration.

■ CONFLICTS BETWEEN INDIVIDUAL AND ORGANIZATIONAL GOALS

Although many causes of frustration exist, a major cause arises when individual needs and goals conflict rather than coincide with those of the organization or, to be more specific, with those of the department. Much has been written about the conflict between the individual who seeks activity and independence and the climate in a bureaucratic, formalized organization that stifles a person's natural desire for freedom and self-determination. The consequences of such a climate manifest themselves in high turnover, waste, lower productivity, slowdown, lack of innovative and creative behavior, nonacceptance of leadership, and so on. The most serious consequence of a bureaucratic organization, however, is that it blocks the individual from attaining satisfaction of his or her needs.

Managers today are becoming more aware of these consequences and of the necessity for an organization to provide a climate that will enable its employees to find personal satisfaction. In fact, the need for an appropriate organizational climate is increasing because of the rising expectations of employees. This is especially true in the healthcare field, where organizations are confronted with an ever-advancing and more sophisticated area of activity. The highly skilled and educated employees are primarily professionals who expect to fulfill many of their needs right on the job. Since such employees tend to take high wages and appropriate fringe benefits for granted, it should be apparent that the key to long-term motivation for them rests in the satisfaction of the higher-level needs, that is, their esteem and self-fulfillment needs. It is management's duty to develop an organizational climate that will produce effective motivation and satisfaction of these needs, thereby helping to resolve the conflict between individual and organizational goals. Therefore, the supervisor's knowledge of the basic motivational processes is necessary because it will facilitate high levels of job satisfaction and minimize conflicts.

■ SUMMARY

Influencing is the managerial function in which the supervisor creates a climate that enables subordinates to find as much satisfaction as possible while getting the job done. The influencing function is particularly concerned with behavioral responses and interpersonal relations. Only by appropriately influencing will the supervisor instill in the department's employees the motivation to go about their jobs with enthusiasm and also to find personal fulfillment of their needs. Therefore, it is necessary for supervisors to understand basic motivational processes.

Motivation is the force that arouses, energizes, directs, and sustains human behavior. All human behavior is caused by unsatisfied needs. These needs eventually stimulate the formation of goals that motivate people to take certain actions. Motivation, however, not only is caused by unmet needs, but also is largely influenced by an individual's perceptions, values, attitudes, and entire personality.

An individual's attitudes are formed beginning in early childhood. They affect and are affected by an infinite number of factors in the person's life. Attitudes will determine the individual route a person takes for the satisfaction of those needs. Although they vary in strength, most needs are basically the same in all people. Thus, Maslow speaks of a hierarchy of needs; in ascending order they are physiological, safety, social, esteem, and self-fulfillment. A person's level of aspiration is closely related to this hierarchy of needs.

People generally move from one level to the next in Maslow's hierarchy. McClelland focuses on describing various other important human needs: achievement, affiliation, and power. Herzberg, in his two-factor approach, stresses the importance of motivators versus hygiene factors. He shows that the more important forces of employee motivation lie in factors related to work content and not work environment, or hygiene factors.

A person who is able to understand his or her needs and attitudes fairly well will be able to choose courses of action that result in achievement of goals. Goal accomplishment serves as a feedback to the individual; the need is satisfied and the underlying attitudes are confirmed. If a goal is not attained, however, conflict often sets in. This is because action that does not succeed results in blocked satisfaction, frustration, and anxiety. Most people usually react to conflict and frustration in one of the five following ways: problem-solving behavior, resignation, detour behavior, retreat, or aggression.

It is the supervisor's duty to minimize frustrating situations, especially if these result from a conflict between individual and organizational goals. One way to minimize such conflict situations is to realize that in the work environment various factors influence the realization of an employee's expectations. Some of these factors are merely satisfiers and dissatisfiers (Herzberg's hygiene factors), whereas others are motivators and are able to fulfill the higher-level needs and goals of people. These motivators include opportunity for advancement, greater responsibility, chance for promotion, growth and achievement, and an interesting and challenging job. Supervisors, in their desire to create a good organizational climate, must make sure that in addition to satisfying hygiene factors, as many of these motivators as possible exist within the healthcare institution.

NOTES

1. For more details, see Richard M. Steers, *Introduction to Organizational Behavior,* Glenview, IL: Scott, Foresman & Co., 3rd ed., 1988, pp. 151-176; Kae H. Chung, *Motivational Theories and Practices,* Columbus, OH: Grid, Inc., 1977; Terence R. Mitchell, *People in Organizations,* 2nd ed., New York: McGraw-Hill Book Co., 1982; Richard M. Steers and Lyman W. Porter, *Motivation and Work Behavior, 3rd ed., New York: McGraw-Hill Book Co., 1983;* Craig Pinder, *Work Motivation,* Glenview, IL: Scott, Foresman & Co., 1984; and Keith Davis and John W. Newstrom, *Human Behavior at Work: Organizational Behavior,* 7th ed., New York: McGraw-Hill Book Co., 1985.
2. Victor H. Vroom, *Work and Motivation,* New York: John Wiley & Sons, Inc., 1964. See also Burt Scanlan and J. Bernard Keys, *Management and Organizational Behavior,* 2nd ed., New York: John Wiley & Sons, Inc., 1983, pp. 229-232.
3. Abraham H. Maslow, "Theory of Human Motivation," *Psychological Review,* Vol. 50, 1943, pp. 370-396; *Toward a Psychology of Being,* 2nd ed., New York: Van Nostrand, 1968; *Motivation and Personality,* 2nd ed., New York: Harper & Row, Publishers, Inc., 1970, Chapter 4.
4. Mahmoud A. Wahba and Lawrence G. Bridwell, "Maslow Reconsidered: A Review of Research on the Need Hierarchy Theory," *Organizational Behavior and Human Performance,* Vol. 15, 1976, pp. 212-240; Clayton P. Alderfer, *Existence, Relatedness, and Growth,* New York: The Free Press, 1972.
5. Frederick Herzberg, "New Approaches in Management Organization and Job Design," *Industrial Medicine and Surgery,* November 1962, pp. 477-481; "One More Time: How Do You Motivate Employees?" *Harvard Business Review,* January-February 1968, pp. 53-62.
6. For a criticism of Herzberg's theory, see Robert J. House and Lawrence A. Wigdor, "Herzberg's Dual-Factor Theory of Job Satisfaction and Motivation: A Review of the Evidence and Criticism," *Personnel Psychology,* Winter 1967, pp. 369-389.
7. D.C. McClelland, J.W. Atkinson, R.A. Clark, and E.L. Lowell, *The Achievement Motive,* New York: Appleton-Century-Crofts, 1953; D.C. McClelland, *The Achieving Society,* Princeton, NJ: Van Nostrand, 1961; D.C. McClelland, "Toward a Theory of Motive Acquisition," *American Psychologist,* Vol. 20, 1965, pp. 321-325; D.C. McClelland, *Power: The Inner Experience,* New York: Irvington Publishers, Inc., 1979; D.C. McClelland and D. H. Burnham, "Power Is the Great Motivator," *Harvard Business Review,* March-April 1976, pp. 100-110.
8. D.C. McClelland and D.H. Burnham, "Power Is the Great Motivator," *Harvard Business Review,* March-April 1976, pp. 100-110.

9. Much of this is based on Richard M. Steers, *Introduction to Organizational Behavior,* Glenview, IL: Scott, Foresman & Co., 3rd ed., 1988, pp. 92-118.
10. Terence R. Mitchell, *People in Organizations,* 2nd ed., New York: McGraw-Hill Book Co., 1982, pp. 127-128; see also Steers, pp. 283-293.
11. Mitchell, pp. 127-128; see also Steers, pp. 283-293.

21

LEADERSHIP

Because leaders can have a substantial impact on performance, leadership is one of the most popular and important topics in the field of management. It is a key process in any organization, and an organization's success or failure is largely attributed to leadership. It is an essential component of the organizational climate; we have mentioned the term *leadership* repeatedly throughout this text, but merely in passing. Ultimately management leadership is responsible for establishing the type of climate that facilitates motivation and the successful performance of the institution.

The concept of leadership is still being widely researched and investigated. It is of great importance because every organization is concerned with attracting and developing people who will be effective leaders. Leadership plays an important role in organizational life. It fills in many areas not covered by organizational design or manuals. Leadership provides greater organizational flexibility, facilitates coordination and personal need satisfaction, and ultimately makes the difference between an effective and an ineffective organization.

We can define leadership as a process by which people are imaginatively directed, guided, and influenced in choosing and attaining goals. It is helpful to look at leadership in an organizational setting as a behavior, as something one person does to influence others.[1] Leadership can also be defined as "the influential increment over and above mechanical compliance with routine directives of the organization."[2] Leadership is the process by which one person influences others to do something of their own free will, rather than of fear of the consequences if they do not do it or because they are forced to do it. This voluntary aspect is different from other processes, such as influence by authority or power.

In any organized activity a leader mediates between organizational and individual goals so that the degree of satisfaction to both is maximized. A manager also plays this mediating role but not necessarily in the same manner that a leader does. Although the terms *manager* and *leader* are often used interchangeably, they are not synonymous. A person can be the manager but not the leader, and vice versa. A person who has formal positional authority may use formal legitimate authority and power to get things done; this individual certainly is a manager but may not be the leader. On the other hand, the individual who has no position of formal authority, such as the informal leader, may use the leadership influence but is not the manager. Therefore, a manager can do a reasonably good job of managing without being a leader. From the view of organizational effectiveness, however, it is desirable for the manager to also be the leader. Thus, it is essential to learn what other qualities and what other prerequisites must prevail to be a leader as well as a manager.

■ LEADERSHIP THEORIES

Much has been written and said about leadership ever since the days of antiquity, when emphasis was focused on the person as a leader often to the exclusion of everything else. Many theories have been formulated as to what constitutes a good leader and what enables some people to be a leader and not others. We will look at a few of these theories briefly.

The Early Genetic Theory

For hundreds of years observers recognized leadership as the ability to influence people in such a manner that they willingly strove toward an objective. It was believed that this ability was something apart from official position. This view held that certain people were born to be leaders, having inherited a set of unique traits, characteristics, or attributes that could not be acquired in any other way. This position, also known as the "great man" theory of leadership, concluded that leadership qualities were inherited simply because the leadership phenomenon emerged frequently within the same prominent families. In reality, however, strong class barriers made it impossible for anyone outside these families to acquire the skills and knowledge required to become a leader. With the beginning of the twentieth century this belief in inherited leadership characteristics lost ground, although the belief in the significance of leadership attributes remained in the picture.

The Trait or Attribute Theory

As social and economic class barriers were broken down and leaders began to emerge from the so-called lower classes of society, the early genetic theory was modified. This modification primarily occurred because in the first half of this century behavioral scientists began to contribute to the literature on leadership. The first contribution was made by writers who, rather than considering leadership only a function of inherited characteristics, held that it could also be acquired through experience, education, and training. Efforts were made to identify the traits great leaders throughout the ages had in common. These writers tried to focus on all the traits, whether inherited or acquired, that were found in individuals regarded as leaders. Lists of qualities that recognized leaders had in common were compiled.[3] These traits frequently included physical and nervous energy, above-average height, a sense of purpose and direction, willingness to accept the consequences, enthusiasm, friendliness and affection, integrity, technical mastery, decisiveness, verbal fluency, assertiveness, initiative, originality, intelligence, teaching skill, faith, ambition, and persistence.

The inadequacy of this approach soon became obvious, however; seldom, if ever, did any two lists agree on the essential leadership characteristics. Furthermore, the lists were confusing because they used different terminology and had different numbers of characteristics. Nevertheless, the trait approach was widely accepted for a long time. It was extremely plausible because studies of various successful leaders almost always indicated many similar personality and character traits; however, the intensity and degree of the traits varied. Moreover, no satisfactory answer could be reached about which traits were most essential for leadership, or whether a person could be a leader if certain traits were lacking. Also, there was no suggestion about how to isolate and identify all the specific traits common to leaders. A further weakness of the trait approach was that it did not distinguish between those characteristics needed for acquiring leadership and those necessary for maintaining it.

Although the trait approach is partially discredited today, a considerable body of research shows that leaders *do* have in common certain general characteristics. Some of these are intelligence, communication ability, sensitivity to group needs, and many of those previously mentioned. Such traits are interwoven in the personality of the leader.

All this led researchers to question the validity of the trait approach as the predictor of leadership. Subsequent research resulted in new approaches pointing out that the situation had some impact on the profile of the leader and that different groups also called for a different profile of the leader.

The Situational Approach

In their search for other variables, behavioral scientists discovered the importance of situational factors that make it easier for certain persons to acquire positions of leadership. This theory makes the assumption that leadership behavior varies in accordance with the situation.[4] This approach, also known as the *contingency model* of leadership effectiveness, points out the interdependence between leadership style and the demands of the situation.

The proponents of the situational approach do not deny that the characteristics of individuals play an important part in leadership, but they point out that leadership is also the product of situational factors. Leadership in one group will differ from leadership in another group; in one situation a certain person might evolve as the leader, whereas under different environmental conditions someone else would emerge as the leader. For example, in a political meeting someone with good public speaking ability may rise to the top. In other words, the leadership characteristics and leadership behavior needed are a function of the specific situation.

In their desire to de-emphasize the traits approach, however, some behavioral scientists may have gone overboard in emphasizing the situation. In so doing, they may have ruled out the possibility that at least some characteristics *predispose* people to attain leadership positions or at least increase their chances of becoming leaders. Both characteristics and the situation are involved in the concept of leadership.

The Follower Approach

A still better understanding of leadership incorporates the input contributed by groups and followers. This approach maintains that the followers and the makeup of the group must also be studied because essentially it is the follower who perceives the leader and the situation and accepts or rejects leadership. Proponents of this approach further maintain that followers' persistent motives, points of view, and frames of reference will determine what they perceive and how they react to it. The follower approach emphasizes the importance of the group at a particular point in time, but it also acknowledges that certain characteristics will help one person emerge as the leader rather than another person. The satisfaction of the followers' needs, however, is an important aspect.

More specifically, the group and follower approach stresses the idea that the leadership function must be analyzed and understood in terms of a dynamic relationship, a social exchange process between the leader and the followers. They bring to the situation their personalities, needs, motivations, and expectations. The leader appears to the followers as the best means available for the satisfaction of their needs, whether those needs are emotive or task oriented. The group members will follow the leader because they see in that person the means for personal fulfillment. A leader is essential for influencing a group to act as a unit to move toward task accomplishment. The members look at this individual as their leader not only because he or she possesses certain characteristics, such as intelligence, skill, drive, and ambition, but also because of his or her functional relationship to the members of the group.

Leadership Roles

Most of us have had the occasion to observe individuals and the different roles they play in groups. One person may organize the group to achieve goals, whereas another plays the "devil's advocate," raising a stream of objections, and yet someone else is a "synthesizer" who puts together the ideas of all group members. These roles and many others are essential for group life. They fulfill the needs of the individual members of the group and are vital to the group's accomplishment. The group's leader is not necessarily expected to assume all these roles, but he or she is expected to fulfill some of them. Generally, leadership roles fall into two broad classifications, task-oriented roles and emotive leadership roles, in order to satisfy the followers' task and emotive needs.

Task-oriented roles are those used by the leader to organize and influence the group to achieve specified objectives. Usually in an organized activity these objectives are imposed on the group from above. In groups that arise spontaneously, however, tasks and objectives are generated from within the group itself. In both instances the leader must facilitate the accomplishment of the group's goals. That is, the leader plays the role of getting the group to fulfill its tasks.

Emotive leadership roles are just as important as task roles. They are employee centered and provide satisfaction for the individual needs of the group's members. The emotional needs of people are of a social and psychological nature. A leader in the emotive role helps members of the group to gain satisfaction of these needs and at the same time prepares the way for task performance.

Frequently the ideal leader is one who plays both roles effectively. In some instances, however, leadership of a group can be shared without diminishing the group's performance or morale. In such a case, one person plays the task role and another takes the emotive role. This would not be an unusual situation in a large healthcare institution. The formal organization of such an institution often forces a supervisor to be primarily concerned with getting the job done. He or she must concentrate largely on task leadership. Under these conditions, however, the groups will probably select another individual, the informal leader, who will function in the emotive role. The supervisor should not object to the informal leader's role. Rather, the supervisor should realize that it is a necessary part of the leadership process, one that fulfills important human needs and is an essential component of high employee morale. (See Chapter 22.)

Conclusions

All three variables play a role in the leadership process: personal characteristics, the situation, and the followers. The leader is an individual perceived in harmony with the needs of the group and responsive to the group situation. However, because leaders must always be recognized as such by group consensus and because managers who are appointed do not necessarily reflect subordinate group choice, they are not generally regarded as leaders at the outset. They may become true leaders of the group, but they do not start out as such. It is desirable from an influencing standpoint that subordinates accept the manager as a leader and not merely as the head of their department.

■ LEADERSHIP STYLE

Leadership style is of great importance because it influences acceptance of managers by subordinates. Generally, leadership styles can be classified into three broad categories: autocratic, democratic, and free rein.

Autocratic Leadership (Theory X)

Autocratic leadership usually reflects tight supervision, a high degree of centralization, and a narrow span of supervision. The autocratic style is repressive and normally withholds communication other than what is absolutely necessary for doing the job. Autocratic management makes decisions unilaterally and does not consult with the members of the department. Therefore, the autocratic style of leadership minimizes the degree of involvement by subordinates.

In more specific terms, autocratic leadership is described by Douglas McGregor as Theory X.[5] According to McGregor, a manager who fits into Theory X leans toward an organizational climate of close control, centralized authority, authoritarian practices, and minimum participation of the subordinates in the decision-making process. As we already know, the reason why a

Theory X manager accepts this combination is that he or she makes certain assumptions about human behavior. McGregor's Theory X assumptions are as follows:

1. The average person dislikes work and will avoid it to the extent he or she can.
2. Most people have to be forced or threatened by punishment to make the effort necessary to accomplish organizational goals.
3. The average individual is basically passive and therefore prefers to be directed rather than take any risk or responsibility. Above all else, he or she prefers security.

Democratic Leadership (Theory Y)

The democratic style emphasizes a looser type of supervision and greater individual participation in the decision-making process. Authority is delegated as far down as possible, and a wide span of management is advocated. A free flow of communication is encouraged among all members of the department so that a climate of trust and confidence can be established.

In McGregor's terms, the democratic style is represented by Theory Y. The Theory Y manager operates with a completely different set of assumptions regarding human motivation. He maintains that an effective organizational climate uses more general supervision, greater decentralization of authority, democratic techniques, consultation with subordinates on departmental decisions, and little reliance on coercion and control. The assumptions on which this type of organizational climate is based include the following:

1. Work is as natural to people as play or rest, and therefore it is not avoided.
2. Self-motivation and inherent satisfaction in work will be forthcoming when the individual is committed to organizational goals; thus, coercion is not the only form of influence that can be used to motivate.
3. Commitment is a crucial factor in motivation, and it is a function of the rewards coming from it.
4. The average individual learns to accept and even seek responsibility given the proper environment.
5. The ability to be creative and innovative in the solution of organizational problems is widely, not narrowly, distributed in the population.
6. In modern businesses and organizations the intellectual potentials of employees are only partially utilized.

McGregor underscores the notion that Theories X and Y are beliefs held by management about the nature of human beings. As such, they constitute the foundation on which the organizational climate is built. The supervisor who follows Theory X has a basically limited view of people and their capabilities. He or she believes that individuals must be controlled, closely supervised, and motivated on the basis of money, discipline, and authority. Thus, the autocratic manager believes that the key to motivation is in the proper implementation of approaches designed to satisfy the lower-level needs of people.

The Theory Y supervisor, however, has a much different opinion of the capabilities and possibilities of people. He or she believes that if the proper approach and conditions can be presented, people will exercise self-direction and self-control toward the accomplishment of objectives. The Theory Y manager recognizes that the supervisor's activities must fit into the scheme of each employee's own set of needs. He or she also believes that the higher-level needs of people are more important in terms of personality and self-development.[6] Thus, the supervisory skills are used to try to enable employees to achieve on the job at least partial satisfaction of their needs for esteem and self-actualization.

This confronts the supervisor with the question as to which management philosophy and organizational climate will produce the best results. On the surface one is inclined to say that Theory Y would be more desirable than Theory X because it appears humanistic and less harsh. Also, it is more optimistic about human motives at work.

Theory Z Approach

A different managerial approach that has been widely discussed recently is the Theory Z approach, influenced by practices in Japanese industry. The success of Japanese industry in respect to productivity and quality has been attributed to a managerial philosophy about people and organizations that is different from ours.[7] The Japanese organizational climate is based on lifetime employment, slow evaluation and promotion paths, nonspecialized careers, consensual decision making, collective responsibility, informal controls, and a holistic concern toward the firm. This is contrary to many current practices in the United States, such as short-run employment expectations, rapid evaluation and promotions, specialized careers, individual decision making and responsibility, and explicit controls. Theory Z is an approach that would incorporate some of the Japanese ideas into our present system as a possibility for increasing productivity and job satisfaction. Quality circles, discussed in Chapter 19, are an outgrowth of the Japanese approach to management.

Free-Rein Leadership

The free-rein style goes beyond democratic leadership and Theory Y. It is often called laissez-faire leadership because the climate of the organization is such that people are left almost entirely alone to do their jobs. On the assumption that individuals are self-motivated, a minimum amount of supervision is imposed. Although the manager is available as a consultant to help out if necessary, the individuals have enough authority to provide their own solutions.

Making a Choice

Obviously, no single leadership style is appropriate for all situations. A leader must be able to call on a whole range of responses. A good manager knows when to use one or another style of leadership. Each of these three styles has a place in the practice of management. Free-rein is probably the most useful in an organization of professional people who desire and have shown the capacity for independent work. This would apply, for example, to research scientists and professors. The democratic style seems to be appropriate when a relatively unfettered environment is necessary, under which skilled and educated people seem to thrive. This would probably include most activities performed in any healthcare center. It would be wrong to state, however, that a democratic leadership style is beneficial for all organizations, regardless of the nature of their activities and skill levels of their employees. In some situations even the autocratic leadership style will produce good results, especially among unskilled subordinates who are poorly prepared to participate in decision making and who might be uncomfortable if urged to do so.

In conclusion, it is proper to state that leadership style must be adapted to each specific situation. It seems that in general a more democratic, open style achieves greater leader acceptance than an autocratic one. Such a style is more humanistic and more optimistic, which also makes it more acceptable to most employees. In addition, much of the research evidence indicates that the Theory Y democratic leadership approach is more likely to achieve better results.

Nevertheless, it is a sign of a good manager and a good leader to be able to use any one of these three techniques or a mixture of one or more whenever the need or occasion arises. Employing the appropriate style will largely determine the degree to which the leader can influence others in the performance of a task. This is what leading is all about.

■ SUMMARY

Leadership is a process by which one person tries to influence others in the performance of a common task. Through leadership subordinates are imaginatively directed, guided, and influenced in choosing and attaining goals. One cannot equate the terms *leadership* and *management;* a person does not have to be a leader to be an adequate manager, but it would be far more desirable if the supervisor of the department were also the leader.

Much research has been directed to the leadership phenomenon. The early genetic theory maintained that leadership was a function of specific characteristics with which a leader was born. Later the genetic approach was altered to state that leadership was a function of numerous personal traits that could be acquired as well as inherited. More recent studies point out that the situation has significant bearing on who emerges as a leader. Furthermore, the follower approach adds to the concept of leadership the importance of the perception of the followers and the group that they constitute. A person usually must be accepted by the group as a leader before he or she can actually function as one. Thus, each manager must adopt a leadership style that facilitates such acceptance.

Three broad categories of leadership style exist: autocratic (Theory X), democratic (Theory Y), and free-rein styles. Managers will use these styles in their efforts to emerge as a leader. A manager who is appointed to a position of organizational authority is not generally perceived as a leader at the outset. It is hoped, however, that this person will emerge as a leader of the subordinates, thus becoming a much more effective manager as well.

In the leadership process it is necessary to fulfill both the task role, that is, influencing the group to achieve its goals, and the emotive role of satisfying the emotional needs of group members. If it is impossible for the leader to fulfill the emotive role, however, one should not object if an informal leader is chosen by the group to substitute for the leader in this role.

Although much about leadership remains to be studied, the research into this concept has given us a better understanding of the types of behavior needed in different settings and the importance of leadership for organizational effectiveness.

NOTES

1. Richard M. Steers, *Introduction to Organizational Behavior,* Glenview, IL: Scott, Foresman & Co., 3rd ed., 1988, pp. 460-486.
2. D. Katz and R.L. Kahn, *The Social Psychology of Organizations,* 2nd ed., New York: John Wiley & Sons, Inc., 1978, p. 528.
3. See Ralph M. Stogdill, "Personal Factors Associated With Leadership: A Survey of the Literature," *Journal of Psychology,* Vol. 25, 1948, pp. 35-71.
4. Fred Edward Fiedler, *A Theory of Leadership Effectiveness,* New York: McGraw-Hill Book Co., 1967. See also Victor H. Vroom and Philip W. Yetton, *Leadership and Decision Making,* Pittsburgh: University of Pittsburgh Press, 1973.
5. Douglas McGregor, *The Human Side of Enterprise,* New York: McGraw-Hill Book Co., 25th anniversary printing, 1985, Chapters 3 and 4.
6. For more about theories of changing organizational climates, see Rensis Likert, *The Human Organization,* New York: McGraw-Hill Book Co., 1967, pp. 14-24 and 120-121; and Robert R. Blake and Jane Srygley Mouton, *The New Managerial Grid,* Houston: Gulf Publishing Co., 1978.
7. William G. Ouchi and Alfred M. Jaeger, "Type Z Organization: Stability in the Midst of Mobility," *Academy of Management Review,* April 1978, pp. 305-314; William G. Ouchi, *Theory Z: How American Business Can Meet the Japanese Challenge,* Reading, MA: Addison-Wesley Publishing Co., 1981.

22

MORALE

Understanding the supervisor's role in motivation and leadership has a great bearing on the morale of the subordinates. Some writers do not speak of morale of the individual but refer to job satisfaction, emphasizing the satisfaction of needs. Others stress the social aspects of groups and friendships, and some are particularly concerned with attitudes toward co-workers, the organization, and supervision. Many writers link satisfaction with the needs and attitudes of an *individual*, whereas morale pertains to the spirit of a *group*. Although this distinction is precise, it is largely academic, since the factors and methods used in measuring group morale are usually the same as those used in measuring an individual's satisfaction.

Although there are many definitions for morale, a particularly useful one is to describe it as a state of mind and emotion affecting the attitudes, feelings, and sentiments of individuals and groups toward their work, environment, administration, and colleagues. Morale is not a single feeling. It is a composite of feelings, satisfaction, sentiments, and attitudes. It is the total satisfaction a person derives from the job, work group, boss, the institution, and the environment. "Morale pertains to the general feeling of well-being, satisfaction, and happiness of people."[1] When morale is high, the employees are likely to strive hard to accomplish the objectives of the enterprise; conversely, low morale is likely to prevent or deter them from doing this.

■ THE NATURE OF MORALE

Supervisors often make the mistake of speaking of morale as something that is either present or absent among their employees. Morale is always present, however, and by itself has neither a favorable nor unfavorable meaning. Morale can range from excellent and positive through many intermediate degrees to poor and completely negative. If the attitude of the subordinates is poor, then the morale is also poor. If the subordinates' state of mind and emotion affecting their willingness and dedication to strive hard for the best possible patient care is high, then we speak of high morale. Employees with high morale find satisfaction in their position in the enterprise, have confidence in their own and associates' ability, and show enthusiasm and a strong desire for voluntary cooperation in achieving the healthcare center's objectives to the fullest extent of their ability.

High morale of this type cannot be ordered, however; it can only be created by introducing certain conditions into the work situation that are favorable to its development. High morale is not the cause of good supervision and human relations. Rather, it is the result of good motivation, respect and dignity of the individual, realization of individual differences, good leadership, effective communication, participation, counseling, and many other human resources practices. In other words, the state of morale will reflect how appropriately and effectively the administration practices good human relations and good supervision.

■ THE LEVEL OF MORALE

Every manager, from the chief executive officer (CEO) down to the supervisor, should be concerned with the level of morale in the organization. A good supervisor is aware that it is a supervisory function to elicit and maintain the morale of the subordinates at as high a level as possible. The immediate supervisor, in the day-to-day contact with the employees, is the one who influences and determines the level of morale more than anyone else. Raising morale to a high level and maintaining it there is a long-term project and cannot be achieved solely on the basis of short-term devices such as pep talks or contests. The supervisor will also find that although good morale is slow to develop and difficult to maintain, it can change quickly from good to bad. The level of morale varies considerably from day to day and is far more changeable than the weather. Morale, moreover, is contagious. The higher the degree of individual satisfaction of group members, the higher is the morale of the entire group. This in turn tends to raise the overall level of morale even higher, since individuals get personal satisfaction from being in a high-morale group. Although favorable attitudes spread, unfavorable attitudes among employees spread even more quickly. It seems to be human nature to forget the good quickly and remember the bad.

Management is not alone in its desire for a satisfactory level of morale. Each employee of the institution is likewise concerned because bad morale is simply not as satisfying as good morale. A state of bad morale creates an unpleasant environment for the employees of the healthcare center, and they have as much at stake as the administration. Good morale, on the other hand, will make the employee's day at work a pleasurable and satisfying experience and not a misery. The employee will find satisfaction in working with the supervisors and associates. High morale is also important to the patient and the patient's family. They will quickly sense whether the employees of the institution are operating on a high or low level of morale, and they will respond accordingly. But what, we may ask, determines the level of morale?

■ FACTORS INFLUENCING MORALE

Since morale is a composite of feelings, sentiments, attitudes, satisfaction, well-being, and happiness, almost anything can influence the morale of the employees. Some of these factors are within the control of the supervisor, whereas others are not. Although there are countless morale determinants, they can generally be classified into two broad groups: (1) those factors that arise primarily from situations external to the institution and (2) those factors that originate mainly within the realm of the supervisor's activities.

External Factors

External factors affecting morale, those connected with events and influences outside the work environment and institution, are generally beyond the scope of the supervisor's control. Although they are external in origin, these factors nevertheless concern the supervisor, since everyone takes his or her problems to work and does not check them in the morning at the hospital door or leave them in the car on the parking lot. Examples of external factors are family problems, financial worries, associations with friends, a breakdown of the car, or a sickness in the family. What happens away from the job may change the employee's feelings quickly; an argument before leaving home may set the emotional tone for the rest of the day. The morning news may be depressing, or it may be conducive to high morale.

These external factors can generally be dealt with only indirectly, primarily in the form of a nondirective counseling interview, as discussed in Chapter 17. The supervisor should try to sense such factors; often they are reflected in the work behavior of the subordinates. If something has happened to lower an employee's morale and if the supervisor is familiar with the cause, he or she should try to get the employee to forget the incident as quickly as possible by supplying an antidote. One of the best ways to erase the effects of an occurrence that depresses morale is to encourage the employee to talk about it freely. Aside from a nondirective counseling interview, however, a supervisor can do little else to cope with outside factors affecting morale. The supervisor must remember that he or she or the institution is not the sole cause of shifts in the level of morale.

Internal Factors

Many important factors that affect the morale of employees are within the realm of the supervisor's activities. These include incentives, working conditions, and, above all, the quality of supervision. When considering incentives, the first thing that comes to mind is pay. Wages are exceedingly important, but aside from wages and fringe benefits, many other aspects are essential to the employee. Considerations such as job security, interesting work, good working conditions, appreciation of a job well done, chance for advancement, recognition, and prompt and fair treatment of grievances are all necessary components of a high-morale environment. (See Chapter 20.) None of these will take the place of appropriate compensation in dollars and cents, but assuming that the pay properly reflects the job, these additional factors play a significant role. Although reasonable monetary incentives may be provided and the quality of supervision is high, morale can still sink quickly if, for example, working conditions are neglected. The important factor is that an honest attempt is made to improve working conditions whenever possible. In many cases employees work under undesirable conditions and still maintain high morale, as long as the supervisor has made a serious effort to correct the conditions.

The Supervisor's Role

Aside from these on-the-job factors influencing morale, the most significant influence is exercised by supervisors in their immediate, day-to-day relationship with employees. The supervisor's overall manner of supervision, directing, leadership, interpersonal skills, and general attitude will, more than anything else, make for good or bad morale. Employees will put forth their best efforts when given an opportunity to obtain their need satisfactions through work they enjoy and that at the same time achieves the department's objectives. Such job satisfaction will raise and keep morale at a high level. It can only be maintained if the supervisor lets the employees know how significantly they contribute to the overall goals of the healthcare institution and how their work fits into the overall effort. Morale can also be maintained if the boss gives them a feeling of accomplishment in their work and allows them to be on their own as much as possible. The supervisor who practices democratic supervision, as discussed in previous chapters, is likely to reduce the undesirable features of a job and create an environment in which the employees derive genuine satisfaction from the work they do every day. In addition, the supervisor should not forget the importance of social satisfaction on the job. The employees should have an opportunity to develop friendships and work as a team. In other words, one must not forget the positive contributions that informal groups and informal organization make.

The supervisor should bear in mind that the employees' morale is affected not only by what the supervisor does, but also by how it is done. If the supervisor's behavior indicates a feeling of superiority to the employees or the supervisor is suspicious of the employees' motives and actions, only a low level of morale can result. The supervisor should not forget how little it takes to make one's own spirits rise or fall. A word of appreciation from the boss or administrator can change the supervisor's outlook toward the whole work situation. He or she will become more cheerful, and in all likelihood so will the employees.

Supervisors also know that a frown or quizzical expression on their superior's face can have the opposite effect. The supervisor will begin to wonder what he or she did wrong, and morale will sink. Supervisors should remember that employees react the same way to them as they do to their bosses. Attitudes beget like attitudes. If the supervisor shows worry, the employees tend to follow suit. If he or she becomes angry, others become angry. When the supervisor appears confident in the operation of the department, employees will react accordingly and believe that things are going well. This does not mean that the supervisor should only see the good side of departmental operations and refuse to acknowledge difficulties and troubles. The supervisor should show the employees that as a leader he or she has the situation well in hand and that if anything goes wrong, he or she will give them an opportunity to correct the situation and prevent it from happening again.

The supervisor can never relax his or her efforts to build and maintain a high degree of morale among the employees. The supervisor also should not be discouraged if the morale occasionally drops. Many factors can cause such a change, some of which are beyond the supervisor's control. The supervisor can be reasonably satisfied when the employees' morale is high most of the time. As stated before, the supervisor will make it possible for the employee showing signs of low morale to sit down for counseling interviews. As discussed in Chapter 17, such a nondirective counseling interview can have great therapeutic value.

In addition to this remedy, in recent years many organizations have developed what is called *employee assistance programs*. These are staffed by professionals, such as social workers and medical and counseling personnel, who are trained in providing confidential, professional assistance to employees and their families. Some programs may also regularly use the services of an outside clinic. The purpose of the employee assistance program is to help employees who have personal problems that may interfere with attendance and job performance; whether this counterproductive behavior is the result of work, home, or outside pressures is unimportant. Some of the more common problems are caused by alcoholism, drug dependency, financial worries, marriage or family difficulties, stress, and poor health. An employee can seek out this support on his or her own. However, most often the supervisor refers an employee to this program, or the referral might come from a medical person, or from the union. All visits and discussions must be handled in the strictest confidence. The objective of an employee assistance program is to help employees to help themselves for humanitarian as well as for economic reasons. In addition to the human rewards, such a program makes good economic sense for the institution because the cost of excessive absenteeism, reduced productivity, accidents, and other incidents can be substantial.

■ THE EFFECTS OF MORALE

The question arises as to how high or low morale affects other variables, such as turnover, absenteeism, the rate of accidents, teamwork, and productivity. Much research has been done in this area, and some general conclusions can be drawn; for example, high morale is moderately related to lower employee turnover. Probably the same holds true for a lowered rate of absenteeism. Furthermore, higher morale most likely also leads to other desirable consequences, such as fewer grievances, better mental and physical health, faster learning of new tasks, and possibly a lowered rate of accidents, although some apparent results have no relation whatsoever to high or low morale. Let us look at some other consequences.

Morale and Teamwork

The term *teamwork* is often associated with morale, but the two terms do not have the same meaning. Morale applies to the *attitudes* of the employees in the department, whereas teamwork is the smoothly coordinated and synchronized *activity* achieved by a small, closely knit group of employees. Although good morale is usually helpful in achieving teamwork, it is possible for teamwork to be high, yet morale low. Such a situation could exist in times when jobs are scarce and when the employees will put up with close and tight supervision for fear of losing their jobs. Also, teamwork may be absent even though morale is high; in such a case the employee, a solo performer, probably prefers individual effort and finds satisfaction in his or her own job performance.

Morale and Productivity

It is generally assumed that high morale is automatically accompanied by high productivity. Supervisors believe that as long as the morale of employees is high, their output will be correspondingly high. They are aware that the willing cooperation of employees is almost always necessary to get continuous superior performance. Moreover, some research evidence backs up the contention that there is a small but positive relationship between overall morale or job satisfaction and productivity.[2] Every supervisor also believes, based on personal experience, that a highly motivated, self-disciplined group of employees will consistently do a more satisfactory job than a group where morale is low. Therefore, supervisors will do everything possible to keep morale high so that the department's performance remains high.

However, many studies show that this general statement does not hold true in all situations. There is proof that the morale-productivity relationships can appear in many forms: low morale and high productivity, high morale and low productivity, as well as high morale and high productivity and low morale and low productivity. Much depends on other factors, such as the economic situation, the rewards, the job market, and the mechanical pace of the job. Thus, a supervisor cannot automatically depend on the positive relationship between morale and productivity; this is still a controversial issue.

■ ASSESSING CURRENT MORALE

It is important for management to be familiar with the extent of job satisfaction or dissatisfaction of the employees. Much of the foregoing discussion has assumed that the level of morale can be measured, but one should realize that morale cannot be measured directly. Nevertheless, suitable indirect ways and means exist for determining the prevailing level of morale and its trends. Although some supervisors pride themselves on their ability to detect intuitively low or high morale, the wise supervisor would do better to approach this problem more systematically in either of two ways. One approach is through observation of activities, events, trends, and changes; the other method is to use what is usually referred to as attitude, opinion, or morale surveys.

Observation

Observation is a tool that involves watching people and their reactions. Although this tool is available to every supervisor, it is often not fully utilized. If the supervisor does observe the employees consciously and systematically, however, their level of morale and major changes in it can be appraised. The manager should watch the subordinates' behavior and listen to what they have to say; he or she should observe their actions and notice any changes in their willingness to cooperate. The supervisor will probably find it fairly easy to recognize through observation the extremes of high and low morale. Finer means of measurement, however, may be required to differentiate among the intermediate degrees. Personal observation can be used for obvious manifestations of morale, such as a facial expression or a shrug of the shoulder, but often these signs are difficult to interpret. It is also difficult to determine how far from normal the behavior must be in order to indicate a shift in morale. Thus, it takes an extremely sensitive supervisor to conclude correctly from such indicators that a change in morale has occurred or is taking place.

Moreover, the supervisor may not be able to make the detailed observations necessary for accurate morale appraisal. Although the closeness of the day-to-day working relationship usually offers much opportunity for supervisors to become aware of morale changes, they are often so burdened with work that they do not have time to look, or if they do look, they do not actually see. At times they may even be afraid to look for fear of what they might find. Although some supervisors may realize that changes are taking place, they are frequently inclined to ignore them. Only later, after a change in the level of morale is openly manifested, will they recall the first indications and admit to noticing them but not giving them much thought at the time.

To avoid such situations, the supervisor must take care not to brush any indicators conveniently aside. The most serious shortcoming of observation as a yardstick for measuring current morale is that when the activities and events causing an observable lowering of morale are recognized, the change has probably already occurred. The supervisor, therefore, should be extremely keen in his or her observation in order to do as much as possible to prevent such changes before they take place or to counteract them quickly if they have already begun. The closer the supervisor's relationship with the employees, the more sensitive he or she will be to these changes and the shorter will be the reaction time.

Attitude Surveys

The other approach to assessing current morale is the use of attitude surveys, also called opinion or morale surveys. Many institutions use attitude surveys as a way of finding out how employees view their jobs, co-workers, benefits, wages, working conditions, quality of services, supervisors, the institution as a whole, specific policies, etc. Such a survey is a valuable diagnostic tool for management to assess employee problems. It is like taking the pulse of the organization.[3] Surveys provide the most accurate indicators of the organization's human resources, as well as valuable upward communication because they allow employees to express their feelings about their jobs. As a result, administration will know the general level of satisfaction in the institution and which specific areas cause dissatisfaction. The attitude survey shows employees that management is truly concerned and at the same time gives the employees an opportunity to vent their opinions. This in itself will improve morale.

For surveys to be meaningful, however, administration must be committed to this undertaking. This means that management must be willing to invest efforts, time, and money. Administration must be willing to follow through with action based on the results of the survey and be ready to communicate the major findings of the survey to the employees. Such a survey requires careful planning and professional development. Unless the institution's human resources department is large and has in-house professionals trained and experienced in attitude surveys, it is advisable to hire an outside consultant. This will ensure a well-designed instrument with appropriate validity, reliability, sampling, and statistical methods. The employees probably have more confidence in an outside consultant's work than in their own personnel department doing the job. An outside consultant could also help in deciding whether a standardized survey, customized one, or a combination would be more appropriate.

Taking the Survey

Expressions of employees' opinions are requested in the form of answers to written questionnaires. These questionnaires must be prepared with great care and much thought. A good attitude survey measures the major variables of organizational life, such as leadership, supervision, administration, job satisfaction, job conditions and work environment, co-workers, pay, benefits and rewards, job security, advancement, and stress. The questionnaire should be written at a level appropriate for most of the employees. A cover letter from the CEO should accompany the questionnaire, encouraging the employee's participation; at the same time the confidential and anonymous nature of the employees' involvement must be stressed.

In a healthcare center attitude surveys can cover the entire organization. At times it is feasible to limit the survey to only one large department, such as nursing services, which usually accounts for half of all the employees. This, however, must be cleared with top-level administration, since too many surveys at frequent intervals would not be advisable. Full-scale attitude surveys should not be given in less than approximately three-year intervals; this allows enough time to indicate significant attitude changes.

Once an institution-wide survey is decided on, the administrator and all other managers must be prepared to endure criticisms because many dissatisfactions will probably be expressed. More importantly, however, management must be prepared and willing to act on the complaints once they are revealed. Until the survey is taken, management can always plead complete ignorance, but after a survey, everyone knows that the administration has heard about the problems causing dissatisfaction. It is hoped that some of the complaints can be adjusted; at least a serious and honest effort must now be made. If the administration is not prepared or willing to act, it is far better not to take surveys. Once management asks the employees for their input and ideas and fails to take action, the employees will avoid expressing themselves in the future.

Questionnaires submitted to employees come in a variety of types. (See Figures 22-1 and 22-2 for example.) Two general forms are used most often.

■ FIGURE 22-1 Employee opinion survey.

X Y Z Health Center_____   Dept._____
                                              Unit_____

Each question may be answered in several ways, any one of which will give us the information we need. Check only *one* answer that most closely expresses your true feelings. DO NOT sign the form. Seal your questionnaire in the accompanying envelope and drop it in the box in the Department of Human Resources tomorrow or any day on or before Sept. 15.

1. How would you rate the hospital as a place to work?
   ☐ Poor   ☐ Not so good   ☐ Better than most   ☐ Good
2. Are you kept informed on the policies of the hospital and changes in them?
   ☐ Never   ☐ Sometimes   ☐ Usually   ☐ Always
3. Do you feel that the policies of the hospital are fair to you?
   ☐ Never   ☐ Sometimes   ☐ Usually   ☐ Always
4. Are you kept informed about what is going on at the hospital?
   ☐ Never   ☐ Sometimes   ☐ Usually   ☐ Always
5. Where do you get most of your information about what is going on?
   ☐ Grapevine   ☐ Local newspapers   ☐ Bulletin boards   ☐ Supervisor
6. Were you given a satisfactory introduction to and explanation of your new job before you started to work?
   ☐ No explanation   ☐ Very little   ☐ Fair amount   ☐ Sufficient
7. Were you made to feel at home and at ease by your supervisor and fellow workers?
   ☐ Never   ☐ Sometimes   ☐ Usually   ☐ Always
8. Do you like your job?
   ☐ Not at all   ☐ Neither like it or dislike it   ☐ Fairly well   ☐ Very much
9. How well do you feel your experience and abilities are used in your job?
   ☐ Poorly   ☐ Not so well   ☐ Fairly well   ☐ Very well
10. What do you think of your department head and supervisor?
    Department Head
    ☐ Poor   ☐ Below average   ☐ Above average   ☐ Very good
    Why?
    Immediate Supervisor
    ☐ Poor   ☐ Below average   ☐ Above average   ☐ Very good
    Why?
11. Are your duties and responsibilities clear to you?
    ☐ Never   ☐ Sometimes   ☐ Usually   ☐ Always
12. Can you depend on your department head's and supervisor's promises?
    ☐ Never   ☐ Sometimes   ☐ Usually   ☐ Always
13. Do your supervisor and department head give you full credit for suggestions you make about your job or department?
    ☐ Does not   ☐ Seldom does   ☐ Almost always does   ☐ Always does
14. Do you get conflicting orders because of too many "supervisors"?
    ☐ Never   ☐ Sometimes   ☐ Usually   ☐ Always
15. When your department head and supervisor criticize you or your work, is it done in a friendly and helpful way?
    Department Head
    ☐ Never   ☐ Sometimes   ☐ Usually   ☐ Always
    Supervisor
    ☐ Never   ☐ Sometimes   ☐ Usually   ☐ Always

■ **FIGURE 22-1 Employee opinion survey. (cont.)**

16. Do your department head and supervisor give clear, exact, and easily understood instructions about your work?
    Department Head
    □ Never   □ Sometimes   □ Usually   □ Always
    Supervisor
    □ Never   □ Sometimes   □ Usually   □ Always

17. Does your department head or supervisor have a tendency to show favoritism?
    Department Head
    □ Does   □ Usually does   □ Seldom does   □ Never does
    Supervisor
    □ Does   □ Usually does   □ Seldom does   □ Never does

18. When changes are made in your work, are you usually given a reason for them?
    □ Never   □ Sometimes   □ Usually   □ Always

19. Does your department head or supervisor take an understanding attitude toward your difficulties?
    Department Head
    □ Never   □ Seldom does   □ Usually does   □ Does
    Supervisor
    □ Never   □ Seldom does   □ Usually does   □ Does

20. If you are in trouble whether it is your fault or not, what are your chances of a fair hearing and getting a "square deal"?
    □ No chance   □ Very little chance   □ Fair chance   □ Good chance
    Why?

21. Do you feel that you can appeal to a higher authority if your immediate supervisor decides a point against you?
    □ I do not   □ Reasonably so   □ Almost always   □ Always can
    If not, why?

22. Is your job and future secure if you do good work?
    □ No   □ Fairly secure   □ To a large extent   □ Very secure

23. Are your associations with your fellow workers and superiors as pleasant as they should be?
    □ Not pleasant   □ Fairly pleasant   □ Almost always pleasant
    □ Most pleasant
    If not, why?

24. Do you feel that your fellow workers in your department are doing their fair share of the work?
    □ Very few   □ About half of them   □ Most of them   □ All or almost all

25. Please list by number (1-10) items in the order of importance to you.
    □ Physical working conditions   □ Doing something worthwhile
    □ Opportunity for advancement   □ Liking of job   □ Job security
    □ Satisfactory relations with co-workers   □ Wages
    □ Knowing what is going on   □ Fair supervision   □ Credit for work done

26. What do you like best about your job?

27. What do you like least about your job?

28. Length of service at X Y Z Health Center (check one)
    □ One month or less   □ 1 - 3 months   □ 3 - 6 months   □ 6 - 12 months
    □ 1 - 5 years   □ 5 - 10 years   □ 11 years or more

29. Age (check one)
    □ 16 - 20 years   □ 21 - 25 years   □ 26 - 34 years   □ 35 - 45 years
    □ 46 - 50 years   □ 51 - 70 years

■ **FIGURE 22-1** Employee opinion survey. (cont.)

30. Employed   □ Part-time   □ Full-time
    Please add any additional information that you feel would make the hospital a better place in which to work.

    _____

    _____

    _____

    _____

    _____

    _____

    _____

According to the format of the question asked, one can distinguish between *objective* surveys and *descriptive* surveys. An objective questionnaire asks the question and offers a choice of answers; there can be "multiple choice" questions or "true and false" questions. In objective surveys the employees mark the one answer that comes closest to their feelings. In a descriptive survey the question is asked, but the employees answer freely in their own words and ways. Since many employees have difficulty stating their opinions in complete sentences or even completing a started sentence, the best results are usually obtained on a form that enables the employees to check the box that seems to provide the most appropriate answer for them.

The survey forms may be filled out on the job or at home. Although there are many advantages to filling out questionnaires at home, a high percentage of those questionnaires are never returned. It is better to have more meaningful answers, however, even if the number of replies is smaller. Some organizations are concerned that the rate of returned surveys might be low and prefer to distribute and collect the surveys the same day during working hours. The employees complete the survey forms on the premises and on company time. This procedure is likely to maximize the number of completed surveys.

Regardless of whether they are filled out on the job or at home, care must be taken that the questionnaires remain unsigned and that the replies be kept secret and cannot be personally identified. Respondents must be assured that the replies will be kept confidential. Employees are sometimes suspicious of the institution's motives; they may respond in ways they believe the institution wants to hear. Therefore, it is essential that no individual identification information appear on the survey; otherwise the employees believe that such numbers would identify them.

■ **FIGURE 22-2 Employee opinion survey.**

	Agree	Don't Know	Disagree	Importance of this item to me		
				Very Important	Important	Not so Important
1. My relationship with my immediate supervisor is clearly spelled out.	□	□	□	□	□	□
2. The deductions from my paycheck are adequately explained.	□	□	□	□	□	□
3. I am in favor of a no smoking area in the cafeteria.	□	□	□	□	□	□
4. The employees' lockers are conveniently located and easy to use.	□	□	□	□	□	□
5. The staff physicians are pleasant to work with.	□	□	□	□	□	□
6. My supervisor knows whether or not I am doing a good job.	□	□	□	□	□	□
7. I would be willing to rotate shifts more often.	□	□	□	□	□	□
8. I will accept the first chance to leave my job.	□	□	□	□	□	□
9. The hallways and stairways are spacious and clean.	□	□	□	□	□	□
10. My co-workers are usually friendly and courteous to other employees.	□	□	□	□	□	□
11. Compared to other cafeterias SMHC's meal costs are reasonable.	□	□	□	□	□	□
12. As long as I do a good job I will have a job at SMHC.	□	□	□	□	□	□
13. Do you think the employee who "yells the loudest" gets the "better pay."	□	□	□	□	□	□
14. I find the in-service training and education sufficient.	□	□	□	□	□	□
15. My work area is too small.	□	□	□	□	□	□
16. The pay at SMHC is competitive with other places for which I could work.	□	□	□	□	□	□
17. I consider the fringe benefits at SMHC to be good.	□	□	□	□	□	□
18. Considering the job I do, my pay is good.	□	□	□	□	□	□
19. The personnel policies have been clearly explained to me.	□	□	□	□	□	□
20. I know what responsibility I have should there be a disaster or fire.	⊓	□	□	□	□	□
21. My supervisor could have been more helpful in orienting me to my job.	□	□	□	□	□	□
22. I get a salary increase only when my supervisor feels like it.	□	□	□	□	□	□
23. There are many employees who abuse the sick leave policy.	□	□	□	□	□	□
24. More often than not I am criticized for the job I do rather than given credit for a job well done.	□	□	□	□	□	□
25. My job orientation was adequate.	□	□	□	□	□	□
26. I feel that administration is concerned about me and my fellow employees.	□	□	□	□	□	□

Modified from a form developed several years ago by Saint Mary's Health Center, St. Louis, MO—a member of the SSM Health Care System, and printed with their permission.

■ FIGURE 22-2 Employee opinion survey. (cont.)

	Agree	Don't Know	Disagree	Very Important	Important	Not so Important
				Importance of this item to me		
27. I find it more convenient to go to the canteen or bring my lunch rather than go to the cafeteria.	☐	☐	☐	☐	☐	☐
28. My work area is the cleanest area in which I have ever worked.	☐	☐	☐	☐	☐	☐
29. Whenever a complaint is filed it takes too long to get it settled.	☐	☐	☐	☐	☐	☐
30. The patients at SMHC are getting the best care available.	☐	☐	☐	☐	☐	☐
31. My supervisor encourages and assists me in improving my skills so I may have the opportunity to advance.	☐	☐	☐	☐	☐	☐
32. Many of my co-workers love to gossip.	☐	☐	☐	☐	☐	☐
33. The people I work with help each other get the job done.	☐	☐	☐	☐	☐	☐
34. My job is a challenge.	☐	☐	☐	☐	☐	☐
35. The cafeteria has a wide selection of food from which to choose.	☐	☐	☐	☐	☐	☐
36. SMHC should provide a day care center where young children would be taken care of during the working hours of the parent.	☐	☐	☐	☐	☐	☐
37. My supervisor is vague on instructions given me.	☐	☐	☐	☐	☐	☐
38. I think the Department of Human Resources is doing a good job.	☐	☐	☐	☐	☐	☐
39. My supervisor really tries to explain new policy changes or new ideas.	☐	☐	☐	☐	☐	☐
40. Visitors are treated courteously.	☐	☐	☐	☐	☐	☐
41. The parking lots are secure.	☐	☐	☐	☐	☐	☐
42. I find that the noise in my work area is distracting.	☐	☐	☐	☐	☐	☐
43. My supervisor is an asset to SMHC and knows his/her job well.	☐	☐	☐	☐	☐	☐
44. My work area is well lighted and ventilated.	☐	☐	☐	☐	☐	☐
45. I am interested in extracurricular activities such as team sports, social outings, baseball and football games, etc.	☐	☐	☐	☐	☐	☐
46. My job description clearly spells out the work I am doing.	☐	☐	☐	☐	☐	☐
47. I would recommend SMHC to my friends and relatives if hospitalization is needed.	☐	☐	☐	☐	☐	☐
48. There exists some jealousy between my co-workers.	☐	☐	☐	☐	☐	☐
49. My work is tiring—I am exhausted at the day's end.	☐	☐	☐	☐	☐	☐
50. If an employee is dismissed at SMHC there is always just cause.	☐	☐	☐	☐	☐	☐
51. My supervisor treats me with respect and listens to my suggestions.	☐	☐	☐	☐	☐	☐
52. I would rather "time in" and "time out" with a time clock than with a time sheet.	☐	☐	☐	☐	☐	☐
53. No one ever has a chance for promotion from within the ranks.	☐	☐	☐	☐	☐	☐

■ FIGURE 22-2 Employee opinion survey. (cont.)

	Agree	Don't Know	Disagree	Very Important	Important	Not so Important
				Importance of this item to me		
54. My supervisor doesn't have enough time to spend with me when I have a problem.	☐	☐	☐	☐	☐	☐
55. Safety is stressed in my work area.	☐	☐	☐	☐	☐	☐
56. My work group always has all the supplies it needs to get the job done.	☐	☐	☐	☐	☐	☐
57. Parking facilities at SMHC are adequate.	☐	☐	☐	☐	☐	☐
58. My supervisor is fair in any disciplinary action that is taken.	☐	☐	☐	☐	☐	☐
59. Most news reaches me through the grapevine and not through the regular channels.	☐	☐	☐	☐	☐	☐

60. *Do not sign* the opinionnaire. However, please check one of the following boxes so that the results of this opinion survey will be more meaningful.

I am a member of the:

Nursing Services   ☐

Professional Care Division
(Pharmacy, clinical labs, medical records, dietary, rehabilitation, therapy, radiology, nuclear medicine, social service, central supplies)   ☐

Administrative Services
(Executive offices, data processing, general clerical, admitting, public relations, purchasing, switchboard, volunteer services, accounting, personnel, etc.)   ☐

Plant Operation and Maintenance Services
(Engineering, maintenance, housekeeping, laundry, dispatch, security, grounds, etc.)   ☐

61. I have been employed by SMHC:

For 1 year or less	From 1-3 yrs.	From 3-5 yrs.	From 5-10 yrs.	For 10 yrs. or more.
☐	☐	☐	☐	☐

Please return this form to the Department of Human Resources in one week.
Please do not sign.

Analyzing the Results

Once the forms have been filled out, the results must be analyzed. Even if the survey is well designed, organized, and properly conducted, it can lead to a failure if it is improperly or superficially analyzed. The manner in which the data are analyzed is critical for the success of the survey. Only proper analysis will ensure that management will get a clear picture of the results so that the real problems will be addressed by action and appropriate solutions. A misdiagnosis of the survey results will lead to ineffective solutions.

A discussion of statistical approaches and concepts such as segmenting the survey, cluster analysis, and so forth are beyond the scope of this text.[4] Briefly, the analysis must be thorough and instead of simple straight-run statistics, it should produce more meaningful interpretations. For example, the interaction of organizational and demographic variables must be examined in relation to attitudes. Instead of simply stating that 65 percent of the subordinates have frequent communication with their boss and 35 percent do not, or that 75 percent of the respondents like their jobs and 25 percent do not, it would be better to state that of the 75 percent who like their jobs, 85 percent have frequent contact with their boss and 15 percent do not. At the same time, one can learn that among the 25 percent who do not care for their jobs, 55 percent claim that they have infrequent communication with their superiors. Also, for example, the results may determine whether females are more or less satisfied than males, young more than older employees, and so forth.

After a meaningful analysis and interpretation of the survey have been done, the results are presented to the top-level executive team. Then each executive will meet with his or her line managers to analyze and evaluate the survey results. Plans for action to correct the problems that surfaced should be formulated in these meetings. This process then moves downward throughout the hierarchy, first to all supervisors. Then the results of attitude surveys are used as discussion material with the rank-and-file employees in workshop meetings.

Besides this feedback of results to those who filled out the questionnaires, attitude surveys provide top-level administration, department heads, and supervisors with information to guide them in their overall efforts to improve morale. The surveys will reveal certain deficiencies, and specific actions should be taken. For example, the questionnaire may show an overwhelming interest in and need for a child care center where young children would be cared for during the working hours of the parent. This obviously is an area of dissatisfaction, and administration should take immediate and specific action. Occasionally, however, the results of initial surveys are not so clear. They may raise many questions, and sometimes additional surveys are required to probe deeper. Survey techniques and analyses are becoming more and more sophisticated, and with their help management should be able to arrive at a solution to almost any morale problem that arises.

■ SUMMARY

Morale is a composite and not a single feeling. It is a state of mind and emotion affecting the attitudes, feelings, and sentiments of groups of employees and individuals toward their work environment, colleagues, supervision, and the enterprise as a whole. Morale is always present, and it can range from high to low. The level of morale varies considerably from day to day. Morale is contagious; that is, favorable attitudes spread, and unfavorable attitudes spread even more quickly. High morale is not only the concern of the supervisor; the employees are just as interested in a satisfactory level of morale. Moreover, the effect of high or low morale is felt not only by insiders, but also by outsiders such as patients and visitors.

Morale can be influenced by many factors, which can be classified into two broad groups: those factors affecting the employee's activities that arise outside the enterprise and those factors originating within the job environment. The supervisor can do little to change directly the effects of outside factors on the subordinates' morale, but many internal factors, such as incentives, working conditions, and quality of work life, are within the supervisor's power to control. These factors can be used to raise significantly the level of subordinates' morale. If the supervisor succeeds in maintaining high morale, good teamwork and increased productivity probably will result. Recent research indicates that some interesting correlations exist between morale and productivity, turnover, absenteeism, and so forth.

An astute supervisor can sense changes in the level of morale by keenly observing the subordinates, but this is difficult. Often supervisors do not realize that a change has taken place until it is too late. Attitude surveys are primarily used as a way of finding out how employees view their jobs, co-workers, wages, benefits, supervisors, working conditions, etc. Surveys, once requested by management, often are instituted by outside consultants or by the institution's human resources department. Surveys take the form of questionnaires submitted to the employees. Once a morale survey has been performed and properly analyzed, it is absolutely necessary that management do something about those areas of dissatisfaction that appear to contribute to a lowering of morale. It is also advisable to report the results to all those who participated and to discuss these in workshops throughout the organization in order to find solutions to the problems.

NOTES

1. Dale S. Beach, *Personnel: The Management of People at Work,* New York: Macmillan Publishing Co., 5th ed., 1985, p. 307.
2. Beach, pp. 307-308.
3. David R. York, "Attitude Surveying," *Personnel Journal,* May 1985, pp. 70-73.
4. Robert C. Ernest and Leonard B. Baenen, "Analysis of Attitude Survey Results: Getting the Most from the Data," *Personnel Administrator,* May 1985, pp. 71-80.

23

POSITIVE DISCIPLINE

The term discipline is used to express many different ideas and is understood in several different ways. To many, discipline carries the disagreeable connotation of punishing wrongdoers. When one hears the word "discipline," one is often inclined to think immediately of authority enforcing obedience. There is a positive way of considering discipline, however, a way that is far more in keeping with good supervisory practices. Maintaining positive, sometimes also known as constructive, discipline and good influencing go hand in hand.

■ ORGANIZATIONAL DISCIPLINE

For our purposes, discipline can be defined as a state of affairs, as a condition of orderliness, in which the members of the enterprise behave sensibly and conduct themselves according to the standards of acceptable behavior as expressed by the needs of the organization. Discipline is said to be good when the employees willingly follow the rules of the enterprise, live up to or exceed standards, and practice self-discipline. Discipline is said to be poor when subordinates either do this reluctantly or actually refuse to follow regulations, violate the standards of acceptable behavior, and require constant surveillance by their supervisors. Positive discipline thrives in an organizational climate where management applies positive motivation, sound leadership, and efficient management.

Discipline and Morale

Discipline is not the same as morale. As discussed in Chapter 22, morale is an attitude, a state of mind, whereas discipline is a state of affairs. The level of morale, however, significantly influences the problems of discipline. Normally, fewer problems of a disciplinary nature can be expected when morale is high. By the same token, low morale brings about increased problems of discipline. A high degree of discipline could also exist despite a low level of morale. Under these conditions discipline would probably be controlled by fear and sheer force. On the other hand, however, it is usually not possible to maintain a high level of morale unless there is also a high degree of positive discipline.

Self-Discipline

The best discipline is self-discipline. By this we mean the normal human tendency to do what needs to be done; in the healthcare setting this means doing one's share and subordinating some of one's own needs and desires to the standards of acceptable behavior set for the enterprise as a whole. From early childhood on, people have been trained to respect rules, accept orders from those legitimately entitled to issue them, and realize that all organized activities set limits on the behavior of their members.

Experience shows that most employees want to do the right thing. Even before they start to work, most mature persons accept the idea that following instructions and fair rules of conduct is a normal responsibility that goes with any job. Thus, most employees can be counted on to exercise a considerable degree of self-discipline. They believe in coming to work on time, following the supervisor's instructions, signing the time sheet, and refraining from fights, drinking at work, stealing, etc. In other words, self-imposed discipline is based on the commitment of employees to conform with the rules, regulations, and orders that are necessary for the proper conduct of the institution.

Once the employees know what is expected of them and believe that the rules by which they are governed are reasonable, they usually will observe them without problems. The supervisor occasionally must check whether some of these rules and regulations are still reasonable. Times are changing, and certain rules that were once reasonable are no longer considered to be so. For example, the dress codes and codes of general appearance have most certainly undergone changes in the past decade. It would be unreasonable to request subordinates to comply with a dress and appearance code set up years ago.

When new rules are introduced, however, the supervisor must show their current reasonableness and need to the employees. For instance, women's fashion may dictate a style such as very short skirts, which is not conducive to a nurse's appearance on the job. Instead of simply outlawing short skirts, however, a rule giving nurses their choice between wearing a certain length of hemline or uniforms with long pants might be considered a more reasonable dress code. Rules regarding hair length are relevant in some job settings, as in the surgical suite, but irrelevant in others. Therefore, since hair is a danger to asepsis, the supervisor and possibly the chief of surgery, infection committee, and director of nursing work out rules that will make a hood or helmut-type covering mandatory for operating room personnel. No need existed for such a device previously, but past rules do not provide the necessary protection any longer. In other words, the supervisor must be alert to changing styles and mores and must make certain that the rules and regulations truly respect them. Otherwise rules are not enforceable, and many unnecessary disciplinary problems will arise.

If present, employees' strong sense of self-imposed discipline will exert group pressure on any possible wrongdoer, thus further reducing the need for the supervisor's disciplinary action. Work groups also set standards for conduct and performance; for example, fellow employees are expected by the group to carry their fair share of work, be at work on time, and so on. Group discipline reinforces self-discipline and will exert pressure on those who do not comply with group norms and standards.

Employees must also know that they will have the supervisor's unqualified support as long as they stay within the ordinary rules of conduct and their activities are consistent with what is expected of them. Proper discipline makes it necessary for the supervisor to give positive support to the right action and criticize and punish the wrong action. The subordinate must know that failure to live up to what is expected will result in "punishment."[1]

The administration cannot expect employees to practice self-discipline unless self-discipline starts at the top. Similar restrictions must be imposed on all managerial personnel to remain within the acceptable patterns of behavior. For example, workers cannot be expected to impose self-discipline if supervisors do not show it. Proper conduct with respect to the needs of the organization requires the supervisor also to comply with the necessity to be on time, observe "no smoking" and "no drinking" rules, and dress and behave in a manner commensurate with the organizational and departmental activities.

Maintaining Positive Discipline

Although the vast majority of employees will exercise considerable self-discipline, a few employees in every large organization occasionally fail to abide by established rules and standards even after having been informed of them. Some employees simply will not accept the responsibility of self-discipline. Also, a few unruly employees, probably because of their personality, background, and development, find it difficult to function within policies, rules, and regulations.

Since the job must go on, the supervisor cannot afford to let those few "get away with" violations. Firm action is called for to correct the situation. Unless such action is taken, the morale of the other employees in the work group will be seriously weakened. This is when the supervisor has to rely on the power and force inherent in the managerial position, even though the supervisor may dislike doing so. In this situation the supervisor must clearly realize that he or she is in charge of the department and is therefore responsible for discipline within it. If the supervisor does not correct the situation, some individuals who are merely on the borderline of being undisciplined may follow the bad example. When a defect in discipline becomes apparent, it is the supervisor's responsibility to take proper action firmly and to resolve this employee-management conflict properly.

The Purpose of Positive Discipline

When administering positive discipline, managers should remember that the purpose is to preserve the interests of the organization and to protect the rights of the employees. Discipline is not for the purpose of punishment or "getting even" with an employee. Rather, its purpose is to improve the employee's future behavior, to correct and rehabilitate, but not to injure. Discipline corrects the subordinate's breach of the rules and carries the notice of more serious consequences in the future. Discipline also serves as a warning for other people in the department. It reminds the disciplined individual's co-workers that rules exist and that violating them does not go unnoticed or without any action from the supervisor. Moreover, discipline reassures all those employees who respect the rules out of their desire to do the right thing. Discipline's primary purpose most certainly is not punishment or retribution.

The supervisor should administer discipline so that it motivates rather than demotivates. In other words, the boss must exercise positive discipline. This is not an easy task, since inherently the act of punishing a subordinate for violating a rule always presupposes that the subordinate was caught violating it. Yet many others who may have done the same thing go free, so to speak, because the supervisor did not catch them. This invariably injects a note of unfairness into the disciplinary process. Another reason that it is difficult to administer positive discipline is because any discipline is normally resented, and it places a strain on the supervisor-subordinate relationship. Sometimes all discipline does is make the subordinate double his or her efforts not to be caught again. Nevertheless, positive discipline will generally be successful and accepted if the supervisor follows a few simple rules when taking disciplinary action.

■ TAKING DISCIPLINARY ACTION

Taking Responsibility

Normally few occasions will arise that force a good supervisor to take disciplinary action. When it becomes necessary, however, it is the supervisor's job to do so.[2] The supervisor is best qualified to know the employee, alleged violations, and circumstances. By being in charge of the department, the supervisor has the authority and responsibility to take appropriate action. Although it may be expedient for the moment to let someone in the human resources department handle such unpleasant problems, the supervisor would be shirking responsibility and abdicating and undermining his or her own position if this were allowed.

The same result would occur if the supervisor were to ignore or conveniently overlook for any length of time a subordinate's failure to meet the prescribed standards of conduct. If such breaches are condoned, the supervisor is merely communicating to the rest of the employees that he or she does not intend to enforce the rules and regulations. Thus, the supervisor must not procrastinate in administering discipline. On the other hand, the supervisor must take caution against haste or unwarranted action. The first step is to obtain all pertinent facts. Before the supervisor does anything, it is necessary to investigate what has happened and why the employee violated the rule. In addition, the employee's past record should be checked, and all other pertinent information should be obtained before any action is taken.

Maintaining Control of Emotions

Whenever taking disciplinary action, the supervisor must not lose his or her temper. Regardless of the severity of the violation, the supervisor must not lose control of the situation, thus running the risk of losing the employees' respect.

This does not mean that the supervisor should face the situation halfheartedly or haphazardly. If the supervisor is in danger of losing control, however, action should be avoided until tempers have cooled down. Even if the violation is significant, the supervisor cannot afford to lose his or her temper. Moreover, the supervisor should follow the general rule of never laying a hand on an employee in any way. Except for emergencies, when an employee has been injured or becomes ill or when employees who are fighting need to be separated, such a gesture could easily make matters worse.

Discipline in Private

The supervisor must make certain that all disciplinary action takes place in private, never in public. A public reprimand builds up resentment in the employee, and it may permit unrelated factors to enter the situation. For instance, if in the opinion of the other workers, a disciplinary action is too severe for the violation, the disciplined employee would appear as a martyr to the rest of them. A supervisor who is disciplining in public is bound to have his or her performance judged by every employee in the department. Also, the employees may not agree with the facts on which the disciplinary action is based, and the supervisor may end up arguing with the other employees over what happened. Varying eyewitness reports probably will only confuse the situation. In addition, public discipline would humiliate the disciplined employee in the eyes of the co-workers and would cause considerable damage to the entire department. Therefore, privacy in taking disciplinary action must be the rule.

■ PROGRESSIVE DISCIPLINARY ACTION

The question of which type of disciplinary action to use is answered differently in different enterprises. In recent years, however, most enterprises have accepted the idea of progressive discipline which provides for an increase in the "penalty" with each "offense." First offenders get less severe penalties than repeat offenders; more serious infractions receive more severe penalties than lesser offenses. Unless a serious wrong has been committed, the employee would rarely be discharged for the first offense. Rather, a series of progressive steps of disciplinary action would be taken. The following steps, presented in ascending order of severity, are merely suggested; they are not the only means of disciplinary action, nor are they all necessary. Many enterprises, however, have found the progression of these disciplinary steps to be a viable approach: (1) informal talk, (2) oral warning or reprimand, (3) written warning, (4) disciplinary layoff, (5) demotional downgrading, and (6) discharge.

The Informal Talk

If the incident is minor and the employee has no previous record of disciplinary action, an informal friendly talk, also referred to as *counseling,* will clear up the situation in many cases. In such a talk the supervisor will discuss with the employee his or her behavior in relation to the standards that prevail within the enterprise. The supervisor will try to get to the underlying reason for the undesirable behavior. If the institution has an employee assistance program, as discussed in Chapter 22, the supervisor may refer the employee to it if indications show this program can help him or her. At the same time the boss will try to reaffirm the employee's sense of responsibility and reestablish the previous cooperative relationship within the department. It may also be advisable to repeat once more why the action of the employee is undesirable and what it may possibly lead to. If the supervisor later finds that this friendly talk was not sufficient to bring about the desired results, then it will become necessary to take the next step, an oral warning.

Oral Warning or Reprimand

In the reprimand interview the supervisor should again point out how undesirable the subordinate's violation is and how it could ultimately lead to more severe disciplinary action. Such an interview will have emotional overtones, since the employee most likely is resentful for having been caught again and the supervisor may also be angry. The violation should be discussed in a straightforward statement of fact, however, and the supervisor should not begin with a recital of how the fine reputation of the employee has now been "tarnished." The supervisor also should not be apologetic but should state the case in specific terms and then give the subordinate a chance to tell his or her side of the story.

The supervisor should stress the preventive purpose of discipline by manners and words, but the employee must be advised that such conduct cannot be tolerated. In some enterprises a record is made on the employee's papers that this oral warning has taken place. The purpose of the warning is to help the employee correct the behavior and prevent the need for further disciplinary action. The warning should leave the employee with the confidence that he or she can do better and will improve in the future. Some supervisors believe that such an oral reprimand is not very effective. If it is carried out skillfully, however, many employees will be straightened out at this stage.

Written Warning

A written warning is formal insofar as it becomes a part of the employee's record. Written warnings are particularly necessary in unionized situations so that the document can serve as evidence in case of grievance procedures. The written warning, of which the employee received a duplicate, must contain a statement of the violation and the potential consequences. Another duplicate of the warning is sent to the human resource department so that it can be inserted in the permanent record.

Disciplinary Layoff

A disciplinary layoff is the next step when the employee has continued the offense and all previous steps were of no avail. Under such conditions the supervisor must determine what length of penalty would be appropriate. This will depend on how serious the offense is and how many times it has been repeated. Usually disciplinary layoffs extend over several days or weeks and are seldom longer than a few weeks.

Some employees may not be impressed with oral or written warnings, but they will find a disciplinary layoff without pay a rude awakening and probably will be convinced that the institution is really serious. A disciplinary layoff may bring back a sense of compliance with rules and regulations.

There are, however, several disadvantages to invoking a disciplinary layoff. Some enterprises do not apply this measure at all because it hurts their own productivity, especially in times of labor shortages when the employee cannot be replaced with someone who is just as skilled. Also, the employee might return from the layoff in a much more unpleasant frame of mind than when he or she left. Although most managers consider disciplinary layoff as a serious measure, some employees who frequently violate the rules may not regard it as such; they may even view a few days of disciplinary layoff as a welcome break from their daily routine. Although most institutions use it effectively, a number of institutions no longer use disciplinary layoffs. Instead, they move right on to discharge, or they practice the newer concept of discipline without punishment discussed later in this chapter.

Demotional Downgrading

The usefulness of demotional downgrading is seriously questioned; therefore, this disciplinary measure is seldom invoked. To demote for disciplinary reasons to a lower-level, less desirable, and lower paying job is likely to bring about dissatisfaction and discouragement. Over an extended period demotional downgrading is a form of constant punishment. The dissatisfaction, humiliation, and ill will that result may easily spread to other employees in the department. Sometimes this measure can be viewed as an invitation for the employee to quit, rather than be discharged. Many enterprises avoid downgrading as a disciplinary measure just as they avoid disciplinary layoffs or the withholding of a scheduled pay increase.[3] If so, they will have to use termination of employment as the ultimate solution.

Discharge

Discharge—corporate capital punishment—is the most drastic form of disciplinary action, and it should be reserved exclusively for the most serious offenses. Supervisors should resort to it infrequently and only after some of the preliminary steps have been taken. Discharge is the ultimate penalty and is costly to the organization and causes real hardships to the person who has been discharged.

When a serious wrong has been committed, however, discharge should be invoked at once. For instance, when an employee brandishes a loaded gun and threatens to shoot, immediate discharge would be in order. Even for lesser offenses, in some healthcare institutions the supervisor goes through the earlier steps of friendly and more formal oral and written reprimands and then points out that the next measure would be discharge without any further discussion. In these institutions there is no intermediate penalty such as a several-day disciplinary layoff, which could hurt the superior-subordinate relationship. Discharge is the only step left in this progression. It is hoped that this severe penalty is invoked infrequently.

For the employee, discharge means hardship because it eliminates the seniority standing, possibly some pension rights, substantial vacation benefits, a high pay scale, and other benefits that the employee has accumulated in many years of service. Discharge also makes it difficult for the worker to obtain new employment. In regard to the enterprise, discharges involve serious losses and waste, including the expense of training a new employee and the disruption caused by changing the makeup of the work team. Discharge may also cause damage to the morale of the group. If the discharged employee is a member of a legally protected group, such as minorities or women, administration has to be concerned about nondiscrimination and quotas.

Therefore, because of these possibly serious consequences of discharge, many organizations have removed from the supervisor the right to fire. This has been reserved for higher levels in administration, or in some institutions the supervisor's recommendation to discharge must be reviewed and approved by higher administration and/or by the human resource director. With unions, management is concerned with possible prolonged arbitration procedures, knowing full well that arbitrators have become increasingly unwilling to permit discharge except for the most severe violations. Although situations may arise where there is no other answer but to fire the employee for "just cause," these cases will be the rare exception and not the rule.

■ TIME ELEMENT

In all the disciplinary steps just discussed, the time element is significant. There is no reason to hold an indiscretion of past years against a person forever. Current practice is inclined to disregard offenses that have been committed more than a year previously if the person has reformed. For example, an employee with a poor record because of tardiness would start a new life if he or she maintained a good record for one year or maybe only for six months. This time element will vary, depending on the nature of the violation.

■ DOCUMENTATION

It is essential for the supervisor to keep detailed records of all disciplinary actions, since such actions have the potential of becoming the subject of further discussions, disputes, and even litigation. The burden of proof is on the employer. The written record should cover the time of the event, details of the offense, the supervisor's decision, and action taken. It should also include the reasoning involved. If at some future time the supervisor or the institution is asked to substantiate the action taken, it is not sufficient to depend on memory alone.

At present it is more important than ever to keep accurate detailed records because the aggrieved employee may file a lawsuit for wrongful discharge, based on discrimination, harassment, or similar reasons. If a union is involved, documentation is a must to justify a disciplinary measure if it is challenged by a formal grievance procedure. Regardless of any potential consequences, written documentation at the time of the event is essential for the institution and the supervisor's own records.

■ THE SUPERVISOR'S DILEMMA

Throughout this book we have stressed the importance of the relationship of trust, confidence, and help between the supervisor and the employee. Disciplinary action is by nature painful. Therefore, despite all the restraint and wisdom with which the supervisor takes disciplinary action, it still puts a strain on the supervisor-subordinate relationships. It is difficult to impose discipline without generating resentment because disciplinary action is an unpleasant experience and puts a barrier between the supervisor and the employee. The question therefore arises as to how the supervisor can apply the necessary disciplinary action so that it will be the least resented and most acceptable.

The "Red-Hot-Stove" Approach

McGregor refers to what he calls "the red-hot-stove rule" and draws a comparison between touching a red-hot stove and experiencing discipline.[4] When one touches a hot stove, the resulting discipline has four characteristics: it is *immediate*, with *warning, consistent,* and *impersonal*. First, the burn is immediate, and there is no question of the cause and effect. Second, there is a warning; everyone knows what happens if one touches a hot stove, especially if the stove is red hot. Third, the discipline is consistent; every time one touches a hot stove, one is burned. Fourth, the discipline is impersonal; whoever touches the hot stove is burned. A person is burned for touching the hot stove, not because of who he or she is.

This comparison illustrates that the act and the discipline seem almost as one. The discipline takes place because the person did something, because he or she committed a particular act. The discipline is directed against the act and not against the person. Following the four basic rules expressed in this "hot-stove" approach will help the supervisor take the sting out of many disciplinary actions. It enables the manager to achieve positive discipline and at the same time generate in the employee the least amount of resentment.

Immediacy

The supervisor must not procrastinate; a prompt beginning of the disciplinary process is necessary as soon as possible after the supervisor notices the violation. The sooner the discipline is invoked, the more automatic it will seem and the closer will be the connection with the offensive act. As already stated, the supervisor should refrain from taking hasty action, and enough time should elapse for tempers to cool and for assembling all the necessary facts.

In some instances it is apparent that the employee is guilty of a violation, although the full circumstances may not be known. Here the need for disciplinary action is unquestionable, but some doubt exists as to the amount of penalty. In such cases the supervisor should tell the employee that he or she realizes what went on, but that some time will be needed to reach a conclusion. In other cases, however, the nature of the incident makes it necessary to get the offender off the premises quickly. Some immediate action is required even if there is not yet enough evidence to make a final decision in the case.

Temporary Suspension. To solve this dilemma, many enterprises invoke what is called "temporary suspension." The employee is suspended, pending a final decision in the case. This device of suspension protects management as well as the employee. Suspension gives management a chance to make the necessary investigation and consult higher levels of administration or the human resources department, and it provides an opportunity for tempers to cool off. In cases of temporary suspension the employee is told that he or she is "suspended" and will be informed as soon as possible of the disciplinary action that will be taken.

The suspension in itself is not a punishment. If the investigation shows that there is no cause for disciplinary action, the employee has no grievance, since he or she is recalled and will not have suffered any loss of pay. If, on the other hand, the penalty is a disciplinary layoff, then the time during which the employee was suspended will constitute all or part of the layoff assessed. The obvious advantage of this device of temporary suspension is that the supervisor can act promptly without any prejudice to the employee. Nevertheless, temporary suspension should not be used indiscriminately; it should be invoked primarily when the offense is likely to call at least for a layoff.

Advance Warning

To have good discipline and have the employees accept disciplinary action as fair, it is absolutely essential that all employees be clearly informed in advance as to what is expected of them and what the rules are. There must be warning that a certain offense will lead to disciplinary action. Some enterprises rely on bulletin board announcements to make such warnings. These cannot be as effective, however, as a section in the handbook that all new employees receive when they start working for the institution. Along with the written statements in the handbook, it is advisable to include oral clarification of the rules. During the induction process shortly after new employees are hired, they should be orally informed of what is expected of them and of the consequences of not living up to behavioral expectations.

In addition to the forewarning about general rules, it is essential to let the employees know in advance about the type of disciplinary action that will be taken. The various steps of disciplinary action should be clarified *before* employees could possibly become involved in an offense. There are considerable doubts, however, as to whether or not a standard penalty should be provided and stated for each offense. In other words, should there be, for example, a clear statement that falsifying attendance records will carry a one-week disciplinary layoff? Those in favor of such a list suggest that it would be an effective warning device and that it would provide greater disciplinary consistency. On the other hand, such a list would not permit management to take into consideration the various degrees of guilt and mitigating circumstances. In general it is probably best not to provide a schedule of penalties for specific violations, but merely to state the progressive steps of disciplinary action that will be taken. It should be clearly understood that continued violations will bring about more severe penalties. Some enterprises do specify that certain serious offenses will bring the penalty of immediate discharge. For most violations, however, it is unwise to spell out a rigid set of disciplinary measures.

The practice of forewarning before taking disciplinary measures also applies to rules that have not been enforced recently. If the supervisor has not disciplined anyone who violated them for a long time, the employees do not expect these rules to be enforced in the future. Suddenly the supervisor may decide that to make a rule valid, he or she is going to make "an example of one of the employees" and take disciplinary action. Disciplinary action should not be used in this manner. Because a certain rule has not been enforced in the past does not mean that it cannot ever be enforced. What it does mean is that the supervisor must take certain steps before beginning to enforce such a rule. Instead of acting tough suddenly, the supervisor should give the employees some warning that this rule, previous enforcement of which has been lax, will be strictly enforced in the future. In such cases it is not enough to put the enforcement notice on the bulletin board. It is essential that, in addition to a clear written warning, supplemental oral communication be given. The supervisor must explain to the subordinates, perhaps in a departmental meeting, that from the present time on he or she intends to enforce this rule.

Consistency

A further requirement of good discipline is consistency of treatment. The supervisor must be consistent in the enforcement of discipline and in the type of disciplinary action taken. By being consistent, the supervisor sets the limit for acceptable behavior, and every individual wants to know what the limits are. Inconsistency, on the other hand, is one of the fastest ways for a supervisor to lower the morale of the employees and lose their respect. If the supervisor is inconsistent, then the employees find themselves in an environment where they cannot feel secure. Inconsistency will only lead to anxiety, creating doubts in the employees' minds as to what they can and cannot do. At times the supervisor may be lenient and overlook an infringement. In reality, however, the supervisor is not doing the employee any favor, but only making it harder for the employee and for the others.

Mason Haire, a well-known psychologist, compares this situation to the relations between a motorist and a traffic police officer.[5] He says that whenever we are exceeding the speed limit on the highway, we must feel some sort of anxiety, since we are breaking the rule. On the other hand, the rule is often not enforced. We think that perhaps this is a place where the police department does not take the rule seriously, and we can speed a little. There is always a lurking insecurity, however, because the motorist knows that at any time the police officer may decide to enforce the rule. Many motorists probably think that it would be easier to operate in an environment where the police would at least be consistent one way or the other. The same holds true for most employees who have to work in an environment where the supervisor is not consistent in disciplinary matters.

In addition, the supervisor faces another problem in trying to be consistent. On one hand, the supervisor has been continuously cautioned to treat all employees alike and to avoid favoritism, whereas on the other hand it has been stated again and again to treat people as individuals in accordance with their special needs and circumstances. On the surface these two requirements appear to contradict each other. The supervisor must realize, however, that treating people fairly does not mean treating everyone exactly the same. What it does mean is that when an exception is made, it must be considered as a valid exception by the other members of the department. The rest of the employees will regard an exception as fair if they know why it was made and if they consider the reason to be justified. Moreover, the other employees must be confident that if any other employee were in the same situation, he or she would receive the same treatment. If these conditions are fulfilled, the supervisor has been able to exercise fair play, be consistent in discipline, and still treat people as individuals.

The extent to which a supervisor can be consistent and still consider the circumstances is illustrated as follows. Assume that three employees were engaged in horseplay at work. Conceivably the supervisor may simply have a friendly informal talk with one of the employees, who just started work a few days ago. The second employee may receive a formal or written warning, since he had been warned about horseplay before. The third employee might receive a three-day disciplinary layoff, since he had been involved in many previous cases of horseplay. All three situations must be handled with equal gravity. In deciding the penalty, however, the supervisor must take into consideration all circumstances.

Being Impersonal

Another way that a supervisor can reduce the amount of resentment and keep the damage to the future relations with the subordinates at a minimum is to take disciplinary action on as impersonal a basis as possible. In recalling the "hot-stove" rule, it is worth repeating that whoever touches the stove is burned, regardless of who he or she is. The penalty is connected with the act and not with the person. Looking at disciplinary action in this way reduces the danger to the personal relationship between the supervisor and the employee. It is the specific act that brings about the disciplinary measure, not the personality.

Keeping this in mind, the supervisor will be able to discuss the violation objectively, excluding the personal element as far as possible. The supervisor should take disciplinary action without being apologetic about the rule or what he or she has to do to enforce it and without a sign of anger. Once the disciplinary action has been taken, the supervisor must let bygones be bygones. The supervisor must treat the employee as before and try to forget what happened. Understandably the person who has been disciplined harbors some resentment; the supervisor who meted out the discipline probably found doing it distasteful as well. Therefore, the supervisor and the employee may feel like avoiding each other for a few days. Such feelings are understandable, but it would be far more advisable for the boss to find some opportunity to show his or her previous friendly feelings toward the disciplined employee as a person. This is easier said than done. Only the mature person can handle discipline without hostility or guilt. As we have said, these feelings can be minimized by following the "hot-stove" approach in practicing positive discipline.

■ DISCIPLINE WITHOUT PUNISHMENT

Recently a number of organizations have tried to remove some of the shortcomings and resentment created by even the most sensitive way of following progressive disciplinary action, for example, unpaid suspension. It has frequently been observed that no employee comes back from an unpaid suspension feeling better about himself or herself, about the supervisor, or about the institution. Despite our discussion on how to reduce the supervisor's dilemma, many supervisors are not satisfied with a system of discipline in which they often suffer more pain than the employee who was disciplined. Frequently the supervisor is faced with hostility, apathy, martyrdom, reduced output, a decline in trust, and an uncomfortable personal relationship with a subordinate. Organizations such as healthcare institutions, with mostly white-collar professionals and highly educated technological employees, have often searched for a more palatable approach to discipline. An unpaid suspension for an operating room nurse, for example, somehow has been deemed inappropriate by many supervisors. The same concern was expressed in industrial or office settings, such as an unpaid suspension for a programmer.

For all these and other reasons, many organizations have resorted to a nonpunitive approach that is a more adult, more positive, and a better way to encourage a disciplined work force. This approach is known as *discipline without punishment*. The important feature of this concept is the *decision-making leave*. When counseling discussions have not produced the desired changes, management places the person on a one-day "decision-making leave."[6] The institution pays the individual for the day to show the employer's desire to have him or her remain a member of the organization; this removes resentment and hostility usually produced by punitive action. The employee is instructed to return the day following the leave with a decision either to change and stay or to quit the job. Remaining with the institution is conditional on the individual's decision to solve the immediate problem and make a "total performance commitment" to good performance.[7] When the employee returns to the job to announce the decision to stay, his or her supervisor expresses confidence in the individual's ability to live up to the requirements but also makes it clear that failure to do so will lead to dismissal.

The decision-making leave with pay shows the individual the seriousness of the situation and offers an opportunity for cool reflection. It puts the burden on the employee and clearly represents the institution's refusal to make the employee's career decision. This nonpunitive approach forces the individual to take responsibility for future performance and behavior. The employee also realizes that he or she is confronted with a tougher employer's response in case of failure to meet standards. The costs connected with paying the employee for the day are far less than those associated with disciplinary suspension without pay.

The use of decision-making leave has proved as powerful in the executive suite as on the nursing floor or in the clinical laboratories. The organizations that have adopted this nonpunitive approach show good results, since the responsibility for action is shifted from the supervisor to the employee. Also, the time frame changes from the past to the future. Nonpunitive discipline forces the problem employee to choose: "Become either a committed employee or a former employee."[8]

■ RIGHT OF APPEAL

In our society and legal environment an individual's wrongdoing is not judged by the accuser. The judge is not a party to the dispute between the accused and the wrongdoer. In industrial and healthcare settings, however, this is not the case. The line superior decides whether a violation has occurred, how severe it is, and what the penalty should be. If there is a union, the employee can appeal the case through a formal grievance procedure leading to binding arbitration. Non-union organizations should also have a formal way for appealing a manager's decision because it is always possible that an individual in a position of authority might treat a subordinate unjustly. Thus, there must be a system to right such wrongs. Every enterprise must have a system of corrective justice that is concerned with maintaining a healthy organizational climate. A system for grievances must exist that will enable employees to obtain satisfaction for unjust treatment and to resolve such a conflict.

This right of appeal to higher authority should also exist in an enterprise that does not have a union. It must be possible for any employee to appeal the supervisor's decision in regard to disciplinary action. Following the chain of command, the immediate supervisor's boss would be the one to whom such an appeal would first be directed. From there, the complaining employee can usually carry the appeal procedure through various levels, ultimately to the chief executive officer of the organization as the final court of appeal. Unfortunately, in the contemporary organization, there is no system to separate the executive functions from a judicial review.

Probably all healthcare centers have provided for such an appeal procedure. However, great care must be taken that the right of appeal is a real right and not merely a formality. Some supervisors will gladly tell their subordinates that they can go to the next higher boss but will never forgive them if they do. Such statements and thinking merely indicate the supervisor's own insecurity in the managerial position. As a superior, he or she must permit the employee to take an appeal to the boss without any resentment. Sometimes the appealing employee may bring along a co-worker or an ombudsman to plead his or her case.[9] It is management's obligation to provide such an appeal procedure, and the supervisor must not feel slighted in the role as manager or leader of the department when it is used. Management's failure to provide an appeal procedure may even be a chief reason why employees take recourse to local, state, or federal agencies or unionization.

Undoubtedly, however, it requires a mature supervisor not to see some threat from appeals that go over his or her head. Such a situation should be handled tactfully by the supervisor's boss. In the course of an appeal the disciplinary penalty imposed by the supervisor possibly may be reduced or completely removed. Under these circumstances the supervisor understandably may become discouraged and frustrated, since the boss has not backed him or her up. This usually happens in situations where doubt remains as to the actual events and where the boss cannot get two stories to coincide. In such cases the "guilty" employee normally goes free. Although this is unfortunate, it is preferable that in a few instances a guilty employee goes free instead of an innocent employee being punished. In our legal system the "accused" is assumed innocent until proven guilty, and the burden of proof is on management.

Another reason for the reversal of a decision by higher-level management is that the supervisor may have been inconsistent in the exercise of discipline or that not all the necessary facts were obtained before disciplinary action was imposed. To avoid such an unpleasant situation, the supervisor must adhere closely to all that has been said in this chapter about the exercise of positive discipline. If a supervisor is a good disciplinarian, the verdict will normally be upheld by the boss. Even if it should be reversed, this is still not too high a price to pay to guarantee justice for every employee. Without justice, a good organizational climate cannot exist.

■ SUMMARY

Discipline is a state of affairs. If morale is high, discipline probably will be good, and less need will exist for the supervisor to take disciplinary action. A supervisor is entitled to assume that most of the employees want to do the right thing and that much of the discipline will be self-imposed by the employees. If the occasion should arise, however, the supervisor must know how to take disciplinary action. There is usually a progressive list of disciplinary measures, ranging from an informal talk or an oral warning to "capital punishment," namely, discharge. The supervisor should bear in mind that the purpose of such disciplinary measures is not retribution or humiliation of employees. Rather, the goal of disciplinary action is improvement of the future behavior of the subordinate in question and of the department's other members. The idea is to avoid similar violations in the future.

Nevertheless, taking disciplinary action is a painful experience for the employee, as well as the supervisor. To do the best possible job, the supervisor must ensure that all disciplinary action fulfills the requirements of immediacy, forewarning, consistency, and impersonality. Moreover, the need for a good organizational climate makes it mandatory that a system of corrective justice exists, whereby any disciplinary action that an employee feels is unfair can be appealed.

NOTES

1. For reasons of semantics and simplicity, the words "penalty," punishment," offense," etc., are used occasionally in this text.

2. In all of our discussions we assume that the employees of the department do not belong to a union, and therefore no contractual obligations restrict the supervisor's authority in the realm of disciplinary action.

3. Although monetary fines are employed in professional team sports, they are not used in other employment situations.

4. As cited in Leonard R. Sayles and George Strauss, *Managing Human Resources,* 2nd ed., Englewood Cliffs, NJ: Prentice-Hall, Inc., 1981, p. 129; and George Strauss and Leonard R. Sayles, *Personnel, The Human Problems of Management,* 4th ed. Englewood Cliffs, NJ: Prentice-Hall, Inc., 1980, p. 221.

5. Mason Haire, *Psychology in Management,* 2nd ed., New York: McGraw-Hill Book Co., 1964, p. 74.

6. David N. Campbell, R.L. Fleming, and Richard C. Grote, "Discipline Without Punishment—At Last," *Harvard Business Review,* July-August 1985, pp. 162-178.

7. Campbell, Fleming, and Grote, "Discipline Without Punishment—At Last," p. 170.

8. Campbell, Fleming, and Grote, "Discipline Without Punishment—At Last," p. 178.

9. An ombudsman in a work environment is a full-time employee whose job is to facilitate the resolution of conflicts, for example, between a supervisor and a subordinate. That person listens to the problems the employee has and acts as his or her spokesperson to higher-level management. The ombudsman does not have the right to make a decision but will bring the matter to the attention of higher management to resolve the conflict.

Part Seven

CONTROLLING

24

FUNDAMENTALS OF CONTROL

Controls, a term that often arouses negative connotations if it is not used properly, play an active part in everyone's life whether they are at work, at home, or anywhere else. Everyone is affected by many controls, such as thermostats in the home, alarm clocks, coffeemakers, toasters, door openers, fuel gauges in the car, traffic lights, traffic police officers, elevators, timers, and bells. Controls also play an important role in the life of any organization; everyone active in an organized activity depends on controls to make certain that the organization functions effectively.

Controlling is an essential managerial function for all managers at all levels in the organization. It is the function of monitoring performance and taking corrective action when needed. Controlling is the process that checks performance against standards. Its purpose is to make certain that performance is consistent with plans; controlling ensures that the organizational and departmental goals and objectives are achieved. - *guides action towards predetermined target.*

The controlling function is closely related to the other four managerial functions, but it is most closely related to the planning function. When the manager performs the planning function, the direction, goals, objectives, and policies are set and become standards against which performance is checked and appraised. If deviations are found, the manager has to take corrective action, and such action may entail new plans and standards. This is how planning decisions affect controls and how control decisions affect plans, illustrating the circular nature of the management process. The controlling function is directly tied to planning.

■ THE NATURE OF CONTROLLING

Control and the Other Managerial Functions

Because the discussion of controlling comes last in this book, many readers may conclude that controlling is something that the manager does only *after* everything else has been done. In other words, it conveys the general impression that controlling is concerned only with events after the fact. This impression is reinforced by practical considerations; for example, faulty workmanship in a product is usually not discovered until after the mistake is made. However, it is much more appropriate to look at controlling as something that goes on *simultaneously* with the other functions. Although the relationship between planning and controlling is particularly close, controlling is interwoven with *all* managerial functions. The better the manager plans, organizes, staffs, and influences, the better the supervisor can perform the controlling function, and vice versa. As stated earlier, a circular relationship exists among all these functions, and their interrelatedness does not permanently place any one function first or last.

A supervisor cannot expect to have good control over the department unless sound managerial principles in pursuing the other duties are followed. Well-made plans, workable policies and procedures, a properly planned organization, appropriate delegation of authority, continuous training of employees, good instructions, and good supervision all play a significant role in the department's results. The better these requirements are fulfilled, the more effective will be the supervisor's function of controlling, and there will be less need for taking corrective action.

The Human Reactions to Control

Another important aspect of control is the *response of people* to it. As stated before, the word "control" often arouses negative connotations. In previous chapters we said much about work and human satisfaction; we spoke about tight versus loose supervision, delegation of authority, and on-the-job freedom in connection with motivation. Although controls are an absolute requirement in any organized activity, one must keep in mind that in behavioral terms control means placing constraints on behavior so that what people do in organizations is more or less predictable. Control systems are designed to regulate behavior, and this implies loss of freedom. People react negatively to loss of freedom. The amount of control will determine how much freedom of action an individual has in performing the job. Complete absence of control, however, does not maximize an individual's perception of freedom. Some controls are needed to maximize the human perception of freedom. The reason for this is that controls not only restrict a person's behavior, but also the behavior of others toward him or her.

A certain amount of control, therefore, is essential for any organizational freedom. Neither the extremes of tight control nor complete lack of control, however, will bring about the desired organizational effectiveness. What is needed is a mixture between the two extremes that will take into consideration the amount of decentralization in the organization, management styles, motivational factors, the situation, the professional competence of the employees, etc. In other words, to arrive at the most desirable mixture of freedom and control, the manager must try to balance the goals of organizational effectiveness and individual satisfaction. These goals must be kept in mind whenever a manager is determining the degree of control.

The Supervisor and Control

The purpose of the controlling process is making certain that performance is consistent with plans, that plans and standards are being adhered to, and that proper progress is being made toward objectives. Also, if necessary, controlling means correcting any deviations. The essence of control for a supervisor is mainly the action that adjusts performance to predetermined standards if deviations from these standards occur. The supervisor is responsible for the results of the department. The manager must make certain that all functions within the department adhere to the established standards, and, if they do not, corrective action must be taken. At times the supervisor may enlist experts within the organization for assistance in obtaining control information data and counsel. It would be inappropriate, however, for the supervisor to expect anyone else to perform the controlling function for him or her.

Planning, organizing, staffing, and influencing are the preparatory steps for getting the work done. Controlling is concerned with making certain that the work is properly executed. Without controlling, supervisors are not doing a complete job of managing. Control remains necessary whenever supervisors assign duties to subordinates, since the supervisors cannot shift the responsibility they have accepted from their own superiors. A supervisor can and must assign tasks and delegate authority, but, as stated throughout this text, responsibility cannot be delegated. Rather, the supervisor must exercise control to see that the responsibility is properly carried out.

The supervisor knows that the eventual success of the department depends on the degree of difference between what should be done and what is done. Having set up the standards of performance, the supervisor must stay informed of the actual performance through observation, reports, discussion, control charts, and other devices. The supervisor's job is to use these tools to evaluate the difference between what should be done and what is accomplished. Only then can the corrections necessary to bring about full compliance between the standards and the actual performance be prescribed.

Anticipatory Aspect of Control

To a large degree controlling is a forward-looking function; it has *anticipatory* aspects. Management is concerned with controls that anticipate potential sources of deviation from standards. Past experience and the study of past events tell the supervisor what has taken place, where, when, and why certain standards were not met. This enables management to make provisions so that future activities will not lead to these deviations. Unfortunately the anticipatory aspect of controlling is not always sufficiently stressed, and often supervisors are primarily concerned with its *corrective* and *reactive* aspects. Deviations from standards are detected after they have occurred and are corrected at the point of performance, rather than anticipated.

Even if this is the case, however, the corrections will have an effect on the future. Normally the supervisor can do little about the past. For example, if the work assigned to a subordinate for the day has not been accomplished, the controlling process cannot correct that. Some supervisors are inclined to scold the person responsible and assume that he or she was negligent and deliberate because something went wrong, but there is no use "crying over spilled milk." The good supervisor will look forward rather than backward. The supervisor must study the past, however, to learn what has taken place and why. This will enable the supervisor to take the proper steps to ensure corrective and ideally preventive action for the future.

Since control is forward looking, the supervisor must discover deviations from the established standards as quickly as possible. Therefore, the supervisor's duty is to minimize the time lag between results and corrective action. For example, instead of waiting until the day is over, it is more advisable for a house-keeping supervisor to check at midday to see whether or not the work is progressing satisfactorily. Even then, the morning is already past and nothing can be done about it any longer. Although this is a painful thought to the supervisor, one cannot alter that sometimes effective control must take place after the event has occurred. Such control is often unavoidable. Minimizing the time lag between results and doing something about them, however, will enable the supervisor to institute corrective action before the damage has gone too far.

Types of Control Systems

These considerations are the basis for three different types of control systems in relation to the time factor: controls that are in place before (preliminary), during (concurrent), and after (feedback) the job is being done. Therefore we will distinguish between anticipatory (preventive or preemptive, preliminary or ahead of time), concurrent (in process, during the event, or steering), and feedback (reactive, postaction, after-the-process, or after-the-event) controls.

Anticipatory Controls

Anticipatory controls are in place before the service activity or production starts. These controls include the statement of the appropriate specifications; they anticipate potential problems and prevent their occurrence. Anticipatory control is a proactive, not a reactive, approach.

The supervisor should think through the entire process and task ahead of time and anticipate potential problems. In doing this, forward-looking control mechanisms will be built into the system, and mistakes are likely to be avoided. The purpose of preliminary controls is to anticipate and prevent mistakes by taking care of a possible malfunctioning in advance. For example, the supervisor will plan and arrange for a regular preventive maintenance program so that the equipment will not break down when needed. Another example of a preventive control is the sign on the curb of the street informing drivers that there is a two-hour parking limit.

Other examples of anticipatory controls are policies, procedures, standard practices, and rules. These are designed so that a predetermined course of action is prescribed to prevent mistakes or malfunctioning. For example, every hospital has established, detailed plans and precise procedures in case of an emergency such as a fire. Disciplinary rules dealing with the problem of carrying a weapon on hospital premises constitute an anticipatory control mechanism because it serves as a deterrent. Other examples of preventive control mechanisms are warning signals on a piece of equipment or checklists before starting a test; consider the extensive checklist a pilot goes through before takeoff. Using this anticipatory approach to control will enable the supervisor to eliminate many of the daily crises.

Concurrent Controls

Another group of control mechanisms are concurrent controls, which are capable of spotting problems as they occur. The purpose is to apply controls while the operations are in progress instead of waiting for the outcome. In these situations the supervisor does not anticipate problems but monitors operations in process. For example, concurrent controls enable the supervisor to keep the quality and quantity of output standardized. There are numerous examples of concurrent control mechanisms all around the supervisor, such as simple numerical counters, automatic switches, warning signals, or even a sophisticated on-line computer system. Whenever the supervisor does not have such aids available, he or she will monitor the activities by observation and instruction and possibly by being helped by several other employees. Other examples of familiar concurrent control mechanisms are the fuel gauge in the car and the parking meter. As stated before, the purpose of concurrent controls covers a middle ground between anticipatory controls at the one end and feedback controls, after the event, on the other end.

Feedback Controls

A third group of control mechanisms, feedback controls, alert the supervisor after the event is completed, such as the police officer writing a parking ticket after the time on a meter expires. The feedback control system is the most widely used category. It takes place after the process is finished and the mistake or damage is done. Feedback control is the least desirable of the three alternatives. The purpose of this type of control is to improve *from* the point of damage and to prevent any future deviation and recurrence. Feedback controls are most helpful in planning similar future activities. Examples of feedback controls are quality control, quantity of output, statistical information, and accounting reports. The feedback and information should go to the supervisor who is responsible for it and who will have to take action to improve future performances; the supervisor in turn will give as much information to the employees as possible.

Since control after the fact is the least desirable mechanism, the supervisor should make every effort to devise as many as possible anticipatory and concurrent control mechanisms. The supervisor should be able to convert many of the after-the-fact controls into on-line, during-the-process mechanisms or even to anticipatory controls with the help of up-to-date information systems.

The Closeness of Control

Knowing how closely to control or follow-up the work of a subordinate is a real test of any supervisor's talents. The closeness of follow-up from the subordinate's point of view is based on such factors as the experience, initiative, dependability, and resourcefulness of the employee who is given the assignment. Giving an employee an assignment and allowing that person to do the job is part of the process of delegation. This does not mean, however, that the supervisor should leave the employee completely alone until it is time to inspect the final results. Delegation also does not mean that the supervisor should be "breathing down the subordinate's neck" and watching every detail. Rather, the supervisor must be familiar enough with the ability of the subordinate to determine accurately how much leeway to give and how closely to follow through with the control measures.

■ BASIC REQUIREMENTS OF A CONTROL SYSTEM

For any control system to be workable and effective, it must fulfill certain basic requirements. Controls should (1) be understandable; (2) register deviations quickly and be timely; (3) be appropriate, adequate, and economical; (4) be somewhat flexible; and (5) indicate where corrective action should be applied. These requirements are applicable to all services in all organized activities and to all levels within the management hierarchy. We will discuss them only in a general sense, since it would be impossible to spell out the specific characteristics of controls used in each department or service of a healthcare enterprise.

Understanding of Controls

The first requirement of a workable control system is that the control mechanisms must be understandable and fit the people involved, the tasks, and the environment. Both the manager and the subordinates must understand the data and what type of control is to be exercised. This is necessary on all managerial levels. The farther down the hierarchy the system is to be applied, the less complicated it should be. Thus, the top-level administrator may use a complicated system of controls based on mathematical formulas, statistical analysis, and complex computer printouts that are understandable to top-level administration. The control system for the lower supervisory level, however, should be less sophisticated. It must be designed to the level of the user. If the control system is too complicated, the supervisor will frequently have to devise his or her own control system that will fulfill the same need and is understood by the employees as well.

Prompt Indication of Deviations

To have a workable control system, controls must indicate deviations quickly so that trends can be corrected without delay. As pointed out, controls are forward looking, and the supervisor cannot control the past. The sooner the supervisor is aware of such deviations, however, the sooner he or she can take corrective action. It is more desirable to have deviations reported quickly, even if substantiated only by partial information, approximate figures, and estimates. In other words, it is far better for the supervisor to have prompt approximate information than highly accurate information that is too late to be of much value. This does not mean that the supervisor should jump to conclusions or take corrective action hastily. The supervisor's familiarity with the job to be done, knowledge, and past experience will help him or her quickly sense when something is not progressing as planned and requires prompt supervisory action. *as correction*

Appropriateness and Adequacy

Controls must always be appropriate and significant for the activity they are to monitor. Control tools that are suitable for the dietary department are different from those used in nursing. Even within nursing, the tools used by the director of nursing services are different from those the head nurse uses on the floor. An elaborate control system required in a large undertaking would not be needed in a small department; however, the need for control still exists, only the magnitude of the control system will be different. Whatever controls are applied, it is essential that they be appropriate for the job involved. They must be consistent with the organizational structure so that the person with authority to act will obtain the data.

Economics of Controls

Controls must be worth the expense involved; that is, they must be economical. At times, however, it may be difficult for management to ascertain how much a particular control system is worth and how much it really costs. One of the important criteria might be the consequences that would follow if the controls did not exist. Thus, the nurses' control of narcotics is stringent and exact, for example, whereas no one is too concerned with close control of bandages or aspirin.

Flexibility

Since all undertakings work in a dynamic situation, unforeseen circumstances could play havoc even with the best-laid plans and standards. The control system must be built so that it will remain flexible. It must be designed to keep pace with the continuously changing pattern of a dynamic setting. The control system must permit change as soon as the change is required, or else it is bound to fail. If the employee seems to run into unexpected conditions early in the assignment—through no fault on the employee's part—the supervisor must recognize this and adjust the plans and standards accordingly. The control system must leave room for individual judgment and changing circumstances.

Corrective Action

A final requirement of effective controls is that they must point the way to corrective action. It is not enough to show deviations as they have occurred. The system must also indicate *where* they have occurred and *who* is responsible for them. Supervisors must make it their business to know precisely where the standards were not met and who is responsible for not achieving the standard. If successive operations are involved, it may be necessary for the supervisor to check the performance after each step has been accomplished and before the work is passed on to the next employee or to another department.

■ SUMMARY

Controlling is the managerial function of monitoring performance; the manager checks performance against standards and takes corrective action if deviations exist. Control is most closely related to the planning function, but it is interwoven with all the other managerial functions as well. Control is essential in every organized activity, although in behavioral terms control means placing constraints on people. A good control system must be designed so that it will bring about organizational effectiveness without infringing on individual satisfaction.

In relation to the time factor, one can distinguish between anticipatory, concurrent, and feedback control mechanisms. There are several basic requirements for a control system to be effective. The supervisor must make sure that the subordinates fully understand the controls and that the controls established are appropriate for the situation. Since control is anticipatory, a control system should be designed to report deviations as promptly as possible. Controls must also be worth the expense involved; they must be worth the effort put forth. A good control system also must provide for sufficient flexibility to cope with new situations and circumstances in a dynamic setting. Finally, a viable control system must clearly indicate where and why deviations have occurred so that the supervisor can take appropriate corrective action at the proper place.

25

THE CONTROL PROCESS

■ THE FEEDBACK MODEL OF CONTROLS

The organizational control system can be viewed as a feedback model. Information on how the system is doing is obtained by the supervisor; the supervisor, the sensor, then monitors the system by comparing the actual results with the desired performance. Whenever the actual performance deviates from the standards set, the system triggers corrective action in the form of an input. (See Figure 25-1.) This closed-loop feedback system works the same way a thermostat in the home functions. The thermostat is set at the desired degree of temperature. Whenever the room temperature falls below or rises above that temperature, the thermostat, continuously comparing room temperature to the desired temperature, corrects the variation by turning on or shutting off the furnace or air conditioner. This latter type of control is known as *cybernetic* because it monitors and manages a process with the help of a self-regulating mechanism.

■ FIGURE 25-1 Closed-loop system of feedback.

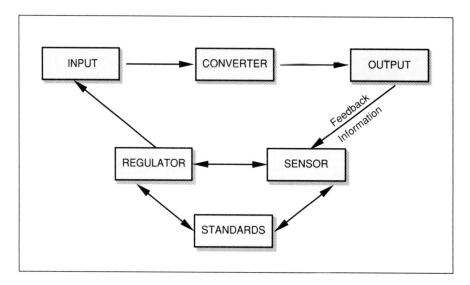

■ STEPS IN THE CONTROL PROCESS

In performing the controlling function, the supervisor must follow three basic steps. First, the supervisor sets the standards. Next, the supervisor must check and measure performance and compare it against these standards to determine whether the performance meets the expected standards or not. If not, the supervisor must take corrective action, which is the third step in the controlling process. (See Figure 25-2). This sequence of steps is necessary for effective control. The supervisor could not possibly check and report on deviations without having set the standards in advance, and corrective action cannot be taken unless deviations from these standards are discovered.

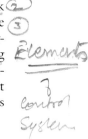

■ FIGURE 25-2 Steps in the controlling process.

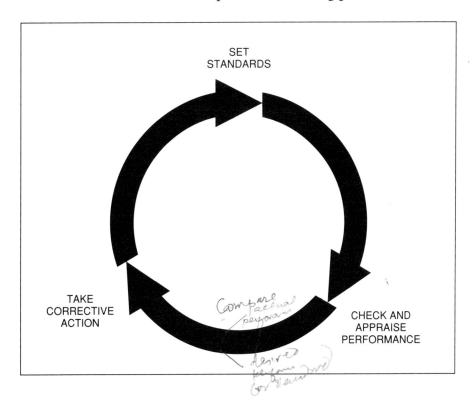

■ ESTABLISHING STANDARDS

The establishment of standards is the first step in the control process. Standards are criteria against which to judge subsequent performance or results. Standards state what should be done. They are derived from organizational goals and objectives; they should be expressed in measurable terms. Control standards can be as broad or as narrow as the level to which they apply. In planning, the chief executive officer (CEO) sets the overall objectives and goals that the healthcare center is to achieve. These overall objectives are then broken down into narrower objectives for the individual divisions and departments. The supervisor of a department establishes even more specific goals that relate to quality, quantity, costs, time standards, quotas, schedules, budgets, etc. These goals become the criteria, the standards, for exercising control. The examples just mentioned are tangible; however, many standards are intangible. Although the latter are much more difficult to set and work with, a healthcare institution has to consider many intangible standards, especially concerning patient care. Let us look at both types of standards in more detail.

Tangible Standards

The most common tangible standards are physical standards that pertain to the actual operation of a department in which goods are produced (e.g., the dietary department) or services are rendered (e.g., nursing services, laboratories, and laundry). Physical standards define the amount of work to be produced within a given time span. Cost standards define direct and indirect labor costs, costs of the materials and supplies used, overhead, and many other items.

These standards are quantitative and qualitative. Not only do they define, for example, how much money can be spent per patient on food, supplies, and materials for three meals a day, but they also state what quality these meals are to have as far as nutritional values, taste, and aesthetic appeal are concerned. Likewise, there are standards on how much one pound of laundry should cost and how many pounds are to be processed in a certain time, taking into consideration the state of mechanization and automation of the laundry. Furthermore, the laundry will have qualitative standards as to sanitation and sterilization, cleanliness of the linens, color, absence of stains, etc. In another example, standards specify the number of nursing personnel on a floor in relation to the number of patients to be cared for. Such standards vary depending on the time of day, the nursing unit in question (e.g., an intensive care unit versus a regular floor unit), and many other factors. Standards also exist for the patient's comfort, physical needs, and safety and for the room's cleanliness and orderliness.

In setting standards, the supervisor is aided by experience and knowledge of the various jobs to be done within the department. A supervisor has a general idea of how much time it takes to perform a certain job, what resources are required, what constitutes a good quality of performance, and what is a poor job. Job knowledge and experience will be resources the supervisor uses to establish the standards against which to judge the performance and results of the department.

Motion and Time Studies

There are also better, more scientific and systematic ways of establishing objective standards. In some activities the supervisor can call on industrial engineers who will use work-measurement techniques to help determine the amount of work an average employee should turn out within a given time period. There are many departments in a healthcare center, such as housekeeping, laundry, laboratories, dispatch office, dietary service, and possibly nursing services, where this approach is worth the effort and cost. Standards arrived at through work-measurement techniques help the supervisor distribute the work more evenly and judge fairly whether an employee is performing satisfactorily.

The supervisor, however, rarely conducts work-measurement analyses. They are usually assigned to an industrial engineer or perhaps to an outside consultant trained in doing motion and time studies. *Motion study* involves an analysis of the elements of the job and of how the job is currently performed with a view to changing, eliminating, or combining certain steps and devising a method that will be quicker and easier. Often flowcharts are drawn up that analyze the steps taken in performing the jobs; the workplace layout may be redesigned and hand-motions revamped. After a thorough analysis of the motions and work-flow arrangements, the engineer will come up with what is considered the ''best method'' for doing the job in question.

Once the best method has been designed, *time studies* are performed to find out the standard time required to do the job using this method. One or more qualified workers are timed with a stopwatch as they perform the prescribed work methods. Time studies are done scientifically and systematically by selecting an average employee for observation, measuring the times used for the various elements of the job, applying leveling and other corrective factors, and making allowances for fatigue, personal needs, contingencies, delays, etc. The combined result then leads to a standard time necessary to perform the job. Although this method is rather scientific, one must keep in mind that considerable judgment and many approximations will be used to arrive at the standard time.[1] There is still the need for decisions involving judgment and discretion. Standard times, however, are a sound basis on which to determine objective standards. They also enable the supervisor to predict the number of employees required and the probable cost of the job to be done. In many activities outside the healthcare field, standards of this type serve as a basis for cost estimates and incentive plans.

If industrial engineers are not available, the supervisor can perform some of the studies simply by observing and timing the various operations and making the necessary adjustments previously stated. If the job to be performed in the department has never been done there before, the supervisor should try to base tentative standards on similar operations. If the new job has no similarity to any previous function, then the best the supervisor can do—unless the help of industrial engineers is available—is to observe the operation while it is being performed for the first few times. The supervisor will have to make approximate time and motion studies to arrive at a standard for the new function. Sometimes the manufacturer of a new piece of equipment can be helpful to the supervisor in providing standard data, for example, how long it will take an apparatus to perform a certain task.

Although they may not be absolutely scientific, standards are more likely to be effective if they are set with the participation of the supervisor and the subordinates instead of being handed down by a staff engineer, a manager, or an outside consultant. The purpose of any standard is to establish a specific goal for the employees to strive toward, and, as with all directives, employees are likely to be more motivated to achieve those standards in which they have had some part.

Intangible Standards

In addition to tangible standards that can be expressed in physical terms, there are also standards of an intangible nature. In a hospital or related healthcare facility, some intangible standards are the institution's reputation in the community, the quality of medicine practiced, the excellence of patient care, and the degree of "tender loving care," including attention to the patients' psychological needs, and the level of morale of the employees. It is exceedingly difficult, if not impossible, to express the criteria for such intangible standards in precise and numerical terms. It is much simpler to measure performance against tangible standards, such as number of nursing personnel in relation to the number of patients.

Nevertheless, a supervisor should not overlook the intangible achievements even if it is difficult to set standards for them and measure their performance. Tools for appraising some of these intangible standards are being developed in the form of attitude surveys, questionnaires, and interviews. Although these tools are not exact, they should be helpful in determining to what extent certain intangible standards are being achieved.

How to Select Strategic Standards

The number of standards that can be used to ascertain the quality and quantity of performance within a department is very large and increases rapidly as the department expands. As the operations within the department become more sophisticated and complex and the functions of the department increase, it will become more difficult and time consuming for supervisors to check against all the conceivable standards. Therefore, they will need to concentrate on certain standards by selecting some of them as the *strategic* ones, that is, namely those that best reflect the goals and that best indicate whether the goals are being met.

For example, a head nurse making the rounds knows which strategic points to check first. She probably checks with the Kardex and makes certain that the tests and treatments are being done on time, the physical setup of the room is in order, and the patient is safe, clean, and comfortable and understands what is being done on that day. She also observes where the other nursing personnel are and what they are doing. Each of these areas constitutes a strategic point of control for the head nurse.

Unfortunately there are no specific guidelines on how to select these strategic control points. The peculiarities of each departmental function and the makeup of the supervisor and employees will be different in each situation. Thus, only general guidelines can be suggested for selecting strategic standards.

One of the first considerations in choosing one standard as more strategic than another is *timeliness*. Since time is essential in control and controls are anticipatory, the earlier the deviation can be discovered, the better. This will help to correct problems early before errors begin to compound. Keeping this in mind, the supervisor can determine at what point in time and in the process activities should be checked. For example, in the maintenance department, the strategic control point may be after a crack has been repaired, but before it has been repainted.

Another consideration in choosing strategic control points is that they should permit *economic observations*. In Chapter 24 we pointed out that a control system must be worth the expense involved; it must be economical. The same applies to the strategic control points. A further consideration is that the strategic standards should provide for *comprehensive and balanced control*. The supervisor must be aware that the selection of one strategic control point might have an adverse effect on another. Excessive control on the quantity of achievements often has an adverse effect on the quality. On the other hand, if expenses are selected as a strategic control point, the quality or quantity of the output may suffer. For example, the executive housekeeper must not sacrifice quality standards that have been designed to prevent infections in order to cut expenses. All these decisions will depend on the nature of the work within the department. What serves well as a strategic control point in one activity will not necessarily apply in another.

Standards and Individual Responsibility

For control to have an effective influence on performance, the supervisor must make certain that the goals and standards are known to all the employees within the department. The supervisor must clarify who is responsible for the achievement of standards so that the supervisor knows who to blame for deviations if the results are not achieved and who to praise if they are exceeded. After all, the supervisor is interested in having the standards and objectives reached. Only if each employee knows exactly what is expected concerning his or her own work can the subordinate try to achieve it. This is why the supervisor must link the standards with the individual responsibilities of each employee.

■ CHECKING ON PERFORMANCE

Measuring and Comparing

The second step in the process of control is to check on actual performance and compare measured performance against the standards. Observing and measuring performance is an ongoing activity for every manager. Work is observed, output is measured, and reports are compiled. Such checking activities are usually carried on by the supervisor after the subordinate has completed the function. Since the supervisor does not shift responsibility when assigning a duty to a subordinate and when delegating authority, he or she must make certain that enough controls are available to take corrective action in case the performance does not meet the standards.

There are several ways for a supervisor to *check on performance and measure:* (1) comparing performance with standards, (2) directly observing the work, and personally checking on the employees, or (3) studying various summaries of reports and figures that are submitted to the supervisor.

Comparing

As the manager observes and measures performance, the measured performance must be *compared* with the standards developed in the beginning of the control process. Such comparisons are an ongoing activity of the supervisor daily, weekly, and monthly. The observed performance may be higher, the same, or lower than the standards. In the first two situations the supervisor obviously does not have any problems. If the performance does not meet standards, however, corrective action is required.

Since some deviation is expected in some activities, the question is how much deviation is acceptable before taking remedial action. This will depend on the activity; in some activities minor deviations may be acceptable. In other activities, such as nursing, deviations can be critical, and even a small one may not be tolerated. Furthermore, in some activities it is easy to measure performance, as in controlling sales and production; in other activities, as in many healthcare activities, measuring performance is not easy and comparisons are sometimes less clear-cut. (See the discussion on performance appraisal in Chapter 18.) However, it is the supervisor's job to develop valid performance measures to control effectively and take corrective action when necessary.

Direct Personal Observation

Observation is probably the most widely used technique for measurement. There is no better way for a supervisor to check performance than by direct observation and personal contact. Unfortunately personal observation is time consuming, but every manager should spend part of each day away from the desk observing the performance of the employees. For example, regular rounds are not only necessary for the head nurse; they are just as important for the director of nursing. The director may make the rounds less frequently, but even he or she should make some personal observations.

For the supervisor direct observations are the most effective way of maintaining close contact with employees as a part of their continuous training and development. This opportunity for close personal observation is one of the great advantages of the supervisor's job; it is something that the top-level administrator cannot do to any great extent. The farther removed a manager is from the firing line, the less he or she will be able to observe personally and the more he or she will have to depend on reports.

Whenever supervisors observe their employees at work, they should assume a questioning attitude and not necessarily a fault-finding one. Supervisors should not ignore mistakes, but the manner in which they question is essential. They should ask themselves whether or not there is any way in which they could help the employees do the job better, more easily, safely, or efficiently. They should notice the way the employee is going about the job, whether it is good or bad. Such observations can check specific areas, such as inadequate patient care, lack of orderliness, not meeting the physical needs of the patient, sloppy work, or poorly performed jobs. At times it may be difficult to convince an employee that his or her work is unsatisfactory. If reference can be made to concrete cases, however, it is not easy for the subordinate to deny that they exist. It is essential for the supervisor to make specific observations because without being specific, one cannot realistically appraise performance and take appropriate corrective action.

As stated, measuring performance through direct personal observation has some shortcomings; it is time consuming and means being away from the desk and office. Some other limitations exist. The employee may perform well while the boss is around but drop back to a lower-level performance shortly after the boss is out of sight. Furthermore, it may be difficult to observe some of the activities at a critical time. Also, the supervisor should make an effort to see what is really happening and not only what he or she wants to see. Still, direct observation is practiced widely and is probably the best way of checking performance.

Reports

Written reports, with or without oral presentation, and oral reports are a good means of checking on performance if a department operates 24 hours a day, 7 days a week, or if it is large or operates in different locations. When a department operates around the clock and one supervisor is responsible for it 24 hours each day of the week, this person depends on reports to cover those shifts during which he or she is absent. Even with reports the supervisor should get to work a little earlier and stay a little later in the day so that there is some overlap with the night supervisor in the morning and with the afternoon supervisor later in the day. This gives the supervisors a chance to add some oral explanations to their written reports. Reports should be clear, complete, concise, and correct. They must be brief but still include all the important aspects.

As the departmental supervisor checks these reports, he or she probably will find many activities that have been performed up to standard. The supervisor should concentrate on the *exceptions,* namely, those areas where the performance significantly deviates from the standard. Only the exceptions require the supervisor's attention. In fact, if the supervisor depends on reports from the various shifts, the subordinates may have been requested not to send data on those activities that have reached the preestablished standards, but to report only on those items that do not meet the standards or exceed them. In this way the supervisor can concentrate all efforts on the problem areas. This is known as practicing the *exception principle.* In such situations, however, a climate of trust must exist between the supervisor and subordinates so that they can freely report the deviations. Subordinates should know that the boss has full confidence in the rest of their activities even though there is no report on them.

If the supervisor does depend on reports for information, it is essential that they are reviewed immediately after they are received and that action is taken without delay when needed. It is demoralizing to send reports to a supervisor who does not even read them.

The nature of healthcare activities calls for reports that are accurate, complete, and correct, especially when patient care is involved. In all other areas as well, most employees will submit truthful reports, even if they are unfavorable to the employee. Much will depend on their relationships and the supervisor's reaction. The supervisor must check into the matter and correct any shortcomings. As long as the supervisor handles these reports constructively, stressing their honesty, the employees will continue to submit reliable reports instead of "stretching the truth." The supervisor must remember the importance of upward communication, and this is one opportunity to keep the channel open and flowing. (See Chapter 5.)

■ TAKING CORRECTIVE ACTION

The third stage in the control model is taking corrective action. If there are no deviations of performance from the established standards, then the supervisor's process of controlling is fulfilled by the first two steps—setting standards and checking performance. If a significant and worthwhile discrepancy or variation is found, however, the controlling function is not fulfilled until and unless the third step, appropriate corrective action, is taken. If the deviation is minor and acceptable and within a noncritical activity, it may be appropriate to do nothing except call it to the employee's attention and maintain the status quo. As always, data must be examined as quickly as possible after the observations are made so that timely corrective action can be taken to curb undesirable results and bring performance back into line.

The supervisor must first make a careful analysis of the facts and look for the reasons behind the deviations. This must be done before any specific corrective action can be prescribed. The supervisor must bear in mind that the performance standards were based on certain prerequisites, forecasts, and assumptions and that some of these may have been faulty or may not have materialized. A check on the discrepancy may also point out that the trouble was not caused by the employee in whose work it showed up, but in some preceding activity. For instance, a patient's infection might not be caused by the nursing activities or conditions on the nursing floor, but rather by conditions or actions in the recovery room or the surgical suite. In such a situation the corrective action must be directed toward the real source. In this case the corrective action would emanate from the nursing director's office, assuming that the latter is the common line superior to all the departments concerned.

The supervisor might also discover that a deviation may be caused by an employee who is not qualified or who has not been given the proper directions and instructions. If the employee is not qualified, additional training and supervision might help, but in other cases finding a replacement might be in order. In a situation where directions have not been given properly and the employee was not well enough informed of what was expected of him or her, it is the supervisor's duty to explain again the standards required.

Only after a thorough analysis of the reasons for a deviation has been made will the supervisor be in a position to take appropriate corrective action concerning the employee in question. Again, it is not sufficient merely to find the deviation; controlling means to correct the situation. The supervisor must decide what remedial action is necessary to secure improved results in the future. Corrective action may require revising the standards, a simple discussion, a reprimand or other disciplinary action, transferring or even replacing certain employees, or devising better work methods.

Corrective action, however, is not the final step. The supervisor must follow up and study the effect of each corrective action on future control. With further study and analysis the supervisor may find that additional or different measures may be required to produce the desired results, keep operations on line, or get them back on track.

■ SUMMARY

In performing the controlling function, the manager should follow three basic steps: (1) standards must be set, (2) performance must be measured and compared with standards, and (3) corrective action must be taken if necessary. In setting standards, the supervisor must be aware of both the tangible and intangible aspects. Many of the tangible standards can be established with the help of motion and time studies. It is much more difficult, however, to establish standards for intangible aspects of performance. Moreover, since the number of both types of standards is so large, the supervisor is the most qualified person in the department to determine which are the strategic control points. After establishing the strategic standards, the supervisor's function is to check and measure performance against them. In some instances the supervisor will have to depend on reports, but in most cases direct personal observation is the best means for appraising performance. If discrepancies from standards are revealed, the supervisor must take corrective action to bring matters back into line.

NOTES

1. For additional information, see George Strauss and Leonard R. Sayles, *Personnel: The Human Problems of Management,* 4th ed., Englewood Cliffs, NJ: Prentice-Hall, Inc., 1980, pp. 622-628; and Dale S. Beach, *Personnel: The Management of People at Work,* 5th ed., New York: Macmillan Publishing Co., 1985, pp. 494-497.

26

BUDGETARY AND OTHER CONTROL TECHNIQUES

A budget is a written plan expressed in figures and numerical terms, primarily in dollars and cents, that extends for a specific time; it sets the standards to be met. The budget is the most widely used control device not only in healthcare centers, but for all phases of all other organized activities. Budgetary control is an extremely effective managerial tool, whether the manager is the chief executive officer (CEO) of a hospital or the supervisor of a department. For this reason it is essential that every manager learn how to plan budgets, live within their boundaries, and use them properly for control purposes. Of all available control devices, the budget, especially the expense budget, is probably the one the supervisor is most familiar with and has been coping with for the longest time.

As pointed out in Chapter 7, budget making is a planning function, but its administration is part of the controlling function. Budgets are preestablished standards to which operations are compared and, if necessary, adjusted by the exercise of control. In other words, a budget is a means of control insofar as it reflects the progress of the actual performance against the plan. In so doing, the budget provides information that enables the supervisor to take action, if needed, to make results conform with the plan.

■ THE NATURE OF BUDGETING AND BUDGETARY CONTROL

When all aspects of the institution's operations are covered with budgets and when all departmental budgets are consolidated into an overall budget, the enterprise practices *comprehensive* budgeting. When there is a budget only for specific activities, such as nursing or laboratories, we are using *partial* budgeting. Most enterprises practice comprehensive budgeting, including the overall budget for the organization and many subordinate budgets for the various divisions and departments. Whereas the overall budget is of great concern to the CEO and the board of directors, the supervisor is mainly involved with the departmental

368

budget, although overall budget considerations do have their effects on every departmental budget. The term *budgetary control* refers to the use of budgets to control the department's daily operations so that they will conform with the goals and standards set by the institution. Budgetary control goes beyond merely evaluating results in relation to established goals. Such control also involves taking corrective action where and when needed.

Numerical Terms

The budget states the anticipated results in specific numerical terms. Although the terms are ultimately monetary, at first not all budgets are expressed in dollars and cents. Many budgets are stated in nonfinancial numerical terms, such as nursing hours, worker hours, quantities of supplies, and raw materials. Personnel budgets indicate the number of workers needed for each type of skill required, the number of hours allocated to perform certain activities, and so on. Although budgets may start out with numerical terms other than monetary values, ultimately every nonfinancial budget must be translated into dollars and cents. This is the common denominator for all activities of an organization, which is why one normally thinks of a budget as a plan expressed in monetary terms.

Improved Planning

Making a budget, whether it is financial or otherwise, leads to improved planning. For budgetary purposes, it is not sufficient just to make a general statement. One must quantify, date, and state specific plans in a budget. A considerable difference exists between making a general forecast on one hand and attaching numerical values to specific plans on the other. The figures in the budget are the actual plans that will become the standard of achievement. The plans are then no longer merely predictions. Rather, they are the basis for daily operations and are viewed as standards to be met.

■ MAKING THE BUDGET

A complete budgetary program requires the involvement of all levels of management; it requires serious and honest considerations. Rigorous budgetary thinking is certain to improve the quality of organizational planning. Indeed, participation by all the managers and supervisors who will be affected by the various budgets is a prerequisite for their successful administration. Again, this is important because it is natural for people to resent arbitrary orders. Thus, it is imperative that all budget allowances and objectives are determined with the full cooperation of those who are responsible for executing them. In all the following remarks we assume that the institution practices what is typically known as traditional budgeting; later in this chapter zero base budgeting will be discussed.

Participation in Traditional Budgeting

As stated, the supervisor who must function under the departmental budget should play a significant role in preparing it. This increases the reliability, accuracy, and acceptance of the budget; the supervisor is closest to the activity, understanding all the elements going into the budget. The supervisor should be requested to submit a proposed budget and participate in what is commonly known as *grass-roots budgeting*.

For example, as the fiscal year draws to a close, the supervisor of the operating rooms should sit down and gather together those figures that will make up next year's budget. In this endeavor the supervisor might need the help and assistance of his or her immediate line superior, in this case most likely the director of nursing services. The supervisor must gather all available information on past performance, expenses, salaries of nursing personnel, other wages, supplies, maintenance, etc. Then the supervisor should think of new developments, such as increases in wages, the increased costs of supplies, and additional personnel, before he or she can prepare an intelligent and realistic budget.

The full responsibility for preparing the budget does not lie with the supervisor alone. It is the administrator's and every upper-level manager's duty to work on budgets. They in turn, together with the controller's and accounting department's printouts and further help, will give the departmental supervisor much information on past performance and figures. The supervisor will use such information to substantiate future estimates and proposals in a free exchange of opinions with the line superior. After both reach a certain level of agreement, the line boss will carry the overall departmental budget to higher administration.

For example, let us assume that the director of nursing services supervises three different areas of activity: the regular floor nursing function, the operating rooms, and in-service nursing education. The supervisors of each of these three activities work out their departmental budgets and discuss and substantiate them fully with the director of nursing services. Then the director combines all three inputs and comes up with a proposed budget for the entire nursing services division. This budget is submitted and discussed with top-level administration or whoever is the immediate line superior. Ultimately the final budget is adjusted and set by top-level administration. Its effectiveness is ensured, however, since true grass roots participation has taken place.

Such participation does not mean that the suggestions of the supervisors should or will always prevail. A careful and thorough analysis and study of the figures will be necessary. There should be a full discussion between the supervisor and the line superior, and the supervisor should have ample opportunity to be heard and to substantiate his or her case. The budget suggestions of subordinate supervisors will not be accepted if the superior believes the figures are unrealistic, incorrect, or inadequate. One of the shortcomings of broad participation is that the budget is loose.

Some subordinates are inclined to suggest budgets at levels that they hope to achieve without too much effort. This is obviously done for self-protection and because the supervisor wants to play it safe. The supervisor rationalizes that by setting the estimates of expenses high enough, he or she can be sure to stay within the allocated amount and will be praised if he or she stays well below the budget.

This defeats the purpose of grass-roots budgeting. The line superior should remind the supervisor that the purpose of budget participation is to arrive at realistic budgets. The superior should explain that favorable and unfavorable variances will be carefully scrutinized and that the supervisor's managerial rating will depend, among other factors, on how realistic a budget proposal he or she submits. Many discussions will be needed before the budget is completed and brought to top-level administration for final approval.

Zero Base Budgeting

As stated before, so far this discussion on budgeting has referred to traditional, or conventional, budgeting. As demonstrated, under traditional budgeting management's attention is primarily focused on planned changes from the previous year's level of expenditures. Conventional budgeting involves projections for the following year based on current expenditures and the previous annual budget. This is often referred to as *incremental budgeting*. Although considerable effort goes into the development of these budgets, the most critical and analytical attention by top-level management is devoted to the year-over-year increment; the base is treated as though it were already authorized and requires no review.

This method assumes that the activities making up the historical base (1) are essential, (2) must be continued, (3) are being performed effectively in a cost-efficient manner, (4) are more needed than new programs, and (5) will continue to be necessary and effective next year. Although some activities meet all these criteria, it is unrealistic to assume that for the new year all of them will. Furthermore, another potential problem exists in real life—wasteful expenditures. If the department incurs less costs than budgeted, conceivably efforts are made to spend the money even if there is no real need. Although this is reprehensible and not excusable, the fear of "losing" the money is great if the new budget is influenced by the current level of expenditures. Another potential shortcoming arises when a department that is currently operating efficiently is faced with an across-the-board edict to cut budget requests by a certain percentage. This penalizes the efficient supervisor, whereas it rewards the inefficiently run department.

Because of these limitations and the recent emphasis on cost containment, a need for better budgeting techniques has become more important. *Zero base budgeting* is a new approach to budgeting. It was developed in early 1970 in industrial settings and then quickly introduced into state and federal government agencies. Today many major corporations are using zero base budgeting, and more and more healthcare institutions are introducing it. Changing healthcare priorities, constrained financial resources, changing technologies, available computer capabilities, and particularly emphasis on cost containment have fostered the application of zero base budgeting in an increasing number of healthcare settings.

Under zero base budgeting nothing is taken for granted; the budget for the new period ignores the previous budget. Every activity submitted for funding must be justified. This approach requires substantiation and justification of each budget item from the ground up, "from scratch." Zero base budgeting gives administration an excellent opportunity to reassess all activities, departments, and projects in terms of their benefits and costs to the organization. The great advantage is that each "package" has to be planned anew and costs are calculated from scratch; this avoids the tendency to look only at changes from the previous period. Ongoing programs are reviewed and have to be justified in their entirety.

Without going into the details of zero base budgeting, in general terms the process involves four steps. The first step is to break the general activity into specific activities called *decision units,* such as ICU/CCU inpatient care. The second step is to analyze the unit and develop *decision packages,* specifying the cost-and-benefit information of the package. Then in the third step, the decision packages are *ranked* in order of importance, the third step. This is done considering the activity's importance relative to the goals of the organization. The ranked decision packages are forwarded to the higher organizational level. They are reviewed and possibly reranked, and the final ranking leads to the fourth step of *funding* and *determining the budget.* After the final funding decisions are made, the approved decision packages are handed back to each manager. Through such a process all activities are identified, evaluated, and justified, and the resources are allocated effectively.

All budgeting systems have some limitations, and zero base budgeting is no exception. The additional time necessary for budget preparation and the large amount of paperwork, especially in the initial implementation year may be viewed as offsetting the benefits. In subsequent years, however, the process will take much less time as managers become familiar with it. In the long run the benefits of zero base budgeting seem to far outweigh the additional work and expenditures involved. Just as each item in the budget has been examined and justified by the benefits projected, the new procedure will be fully justified and worth its costs and efforts.

Budget Director and Budget Committee

Although the authority and responsibility for the budget rest with the line officers and ultimately with the CEO and the board of directors, they will be helped in some cases by a staff unit headed by a budget director or the controller. This staff will provide the line managers with advice and technical assistance but should not attempt to prepare the budgets for them. The staff will be particularly helpful, however, in putting the various budget estimates together in final form so that top-level administration can submit it to the board.

Some institutions also have established a budget committee which serves in an advisory and supportive capacity in coordinating the various budgets. In this instance the budget committee clearly performs a staff function. This must be distinguished, however, from those budget committees to which the board has delegated the line function of setting, rather than just coordinating, the budget. In this situation the budget committee considers all departmental budget estimates and makes the final decisions. This form of budget committee has ultimate line authority and responsibility for determining the budget instead of the institution's top-level administrator or executive director. The budget is approved by the committee, and nothing can be done without its approval. If budget revisions and changes are requested, it is also up to the budget committee to allow or disallow them. Several arrangements are possible within these two extremes as to where the final authority for the overall budget rests. Usually it has to pass the CEO, the finance committee of the board, and eventually the board of directors.

Length of the Budget Period

Although the length of the budget period may vary, most healthcare enterprises choose one year. This period is then broken down into quarters, and many institutions will even divide it by months at the time of the original budget preparation. This is usually referred to as *periodic budgeting*.

Besides the annual budgets, healthcare institutions also typically have budgets extending over a longer term, such as three, five, ten, or even more years. These budgets usually cover such items as capital expenditures, research programs, and expansions. Long-term budgets of this nature are not direct operating budgets and are of no direct concern to the supervisor. Rather, they involve the chief administrator and the board of directors; they are planning, not controlling, tools.

Flexibility of the Budgetary Process

The supervisor should keep in mind that budgets are merely a tool for management and not a substitute for good judgment. Also, care should be taken not to make budgets so detailed that they become cumbersome. Budgets should always allow the supervisor enough freedom to accomplish the best objectives of the department. There must be a reasonable degree of latitude and flexibility. In fact, one of the most serious shortcomings of budgeting is the danger of inflexibility. Although budgets are plans expressed in numerical terms, the supervisor must not be led to believe that these figures are absolutely final and unalterable.[1] Realizing that a budget should not become a strait jacket, enlightened management builds into the budgetary program a degree of flexibility and adaptability. This is necessary so that the institution can cope with changing conditions, new developments, and even possible mistakes in the budget because of human errors and miscalculations. Flexibility should not be interpreted to mean, however, that the budget can be changed with every whim, or that it should be taken lightly.

Nevertheless, if operating conditions have appreciably changed and there are valid indications that the budget cannot be followed in the future, a revision of the budgetary program is in order. Such circumstances may be caused by unexpected events, new legislation, unanticipated wage increases, or large fluctuations in demand. Consider, for example, the budget of the department of respiratory therapy, in which activities have been and are increasing constantly because of new applications, ideas, technology, etc. Revenues derived from this service are increasing rapidly at the same time. It would be absurd to expect the supervisor of this department to stay within the budgeted figures for salaries and supplies. If the department is expected to respond and supply the increased demand, this budget must be altered. In such a case the old budget has become obsolete; unless provisions are available to make the budget flexible, it will lose its usefulness altogether.

Budget Review and Budget Revision

Because of the potential to become obsolete, increasing attention has been given to ways of ensuring budget flexibility to avoid the danger of rigidity.[2] Most enterprises are achieving this by means of periodic budget reviews and revisions. At regular intervals of one, two, or three months the budget is reviewed. In meetings between the departmental supervisor and the line superior, actual performance will be checked and compared with the budgeted figures and the supervisor will be called on to explain the causes for any variations or inadequacies. A thorough analysis must then be made to discover the reasons for the deviation from the budgeted amount; this may lead to budget revisions or other corrective measures.

An unfavorable variation by itself does not necessarily require a budget change; it must be checked into and explained. In the example just cited, however, the supervisor of the respiratory therapy department will not have any difficulties in proving the need for an upward budget revision. In some organizations such a revision can be made on the departmental level, whereas in other institutions it must be carried up to the CEO or even the budget committee. If the deviations are of sufficient magnitude, it is advisable to make the necessary revisions no matter how high up in the hierarchy they have to go or how much work they may involve. If the variation is minor, it may be more expedient to let it go instead of revising the entire budget, since it has been explained and justified.

No matter what decision is made, regular budget reviews and revisions seem to be the best way of ensuring the flexibility of the budgetary process. They prevent the budget from being viewed as a strait jacket and allow the supervisor to consider it a living document and a valuable tool for control purposes.

■ BUDGETS AND HUMAN PROBLEMS

Budgets necessarily represent restrictions, and for this reason subordinates generally resent budgets. Often subordinates have a defensive approach to budgets, an approach they acquire through painful experience. Many times the subordinates become acquainted with budgets only as a barrier to spending, or the budget is blamed for failure to get or give a raise in salary. Moreover, in the minds of many subordinates the word "budget" has often become associated with penurious behavior rather than with planning and direction.

The line manager's job is to correct this erroneous impression by pointing out that budgeting is a trained and disciplined approach to many problems and is necessary to maintain standards of performance. The budget must be presented to the supervisor as a planning tool and not as a pressure device. Most of the problems arise at the point of budgetary control. In other words, when deviations from the budget occur, subordinates are often censured for exceeding the budget. Such budget deviations necessitate explanations, discussions, and decisions. As stated before, the budget should not be looked on lightly. The subordinate should also know that in most enterprises enough flexibility is built into the budget system to permit good common-sense departures necessary for the best functioning of the institution.

Avoiding unnecessary pressures over the budget presupposes that a good working relationship exists between the supervisor and the immediate superior. This in turn rests on clear-cut organizational lines and a thorough understanding that the line managers are responsible for control. Staff people are excluded from the process of controlling. They cannot take operating personnel to task for deviations in the budget; they can merely report the situation to the administrative officer. In the final analysis effective use of budgetary procedures depends on the administration's attitudes toward the entire budgetary process, whether it will be an effective planning tool or a pressure device. Only with the planning-tool view will a supervisor believe that whatever can be done without a budget can be done much more effectively with a budget.

■ COST CONTROLS

Cost Containment and Cost Awareness

Healthcare providers have been and still are under continuous unrelenting pressure to keep healthcare expenditures from spiraling. It is safe to predict that the drive to control costs will increase even more because of pressures from government agencies, legislators, insurors, and purchasers of healthcare, such as large corporations, HMOs, PPOs, and even enlightened individuals. In such an environment control of costs is a ongoing problem for everyone from the president down to the lowest line supervisor; it is a problem that will never go away.

Cost control, better referred to as *cost awareness, cost consciousness,* or *cost containment,* should be viewed as a significant part of the supervisor's daily job. Supervisors must continuously strive for cost consciousness with even emphasis. Sporadic efforts, crash programs, economy drives, etc., seldom have lasting results. Since cost awareness is an ongoing problem, the supervisor must set definite numerical objectives and make plans for achieving cost containment by a given date. Priorities must be clarified without infringing on the quality of healthcare; this is difficult to achieve, especially if there is more sophistication in patient care accompanied by general escalation of prices and wages.

To succeed in cost containment, it is essential to involve the employees of the department and make them realize that ultimately their actions will bring about results. All employees should consider cost consciousness as a part of their job. Most employees will normally try to do the right thing and will help save costs and reduce waste; most workers are not deliberately wasteful. Many employees can make valuable suggestions and contributions to cost-effectiveness. The supervisor should welcome employees' suggestions and not fault them for not having thought of these changes before. Cost awareness should be an ongoing challenge in everyone's daily job.

Allocation of Costs

Every supervisor must see that his or her department contributes effectively to the operation of the institution. In this context of overall controls we are not referring to the qualitative aspect, but to the financial operation of a department. At times a supervisor is told that the department is operating in the red and that it is losing money each year instead of contributing to a financial surplus. Consider, for example, an operating room supervisor who has been confronted with such a statement. The supervisor may be at a complete loss to understand this. Everyone is working as effectively as possible, the utilization of the operating rooms is high, there is no surplus of employees or waste of materials or supplies, and the supervisor is staying within the expense figures set out in the budget. The patient charges for using the operating room have been arrived at by the accounting department in conjunction with the administration. Still the overall figures at the end of the year indicate that the operating rooms are "costing" the hospital a great deal of money because this division ends up as a deficit activity.

The supervisor must realize that in a healthcare center, just as in all other organized activities, some departments are revenue producing, whereas others are not. Clearly the operating rooms and nursing services produce revenue. These patient care departments could not function, however, without the facilities provided by the other departments, such as housekeeping, dietary services, medical records, laundry, and administration. Admitting, credit and collections, the executive offices, the human resources department, public relations, purchasing, and the telephone system are additional services without which no other department in the hospital could function. Although these are not revenue-producing departments, their costs must be carried if the hospital is to function on a fiscally sound basis. Hospitals must allocate such costs to those patient care departments that do produce revenue. The question arises as to *how* the costs of the many non-revenue-producing departments are *allocated* to the revenue-producing departments. The supervisor has no control over this portion of a department's expenses, which can make the difference between ending up with a departmental surplus or with a deficit.

It is beyond the scope of this text to go into a detailed discussion of the various methods of cost analysis, contribution margin approach, and other bases for allocations. However, the supervisor should have a general understanding of the bases on which a department is being charged for these various expenditures. This is merely for the supervisor's own information, since in reality this person is powerless to influence the costs allocated to the department. The supervisor can readily understand the direct expenses (e.g., wages, salaries, supplies, materials), as well as some of the indirect expenses (e.g., Social Security), charged to the department. The supervisor also probably understands that departments are charged with housekeeping based on the hours of service provided, maintenance figures on the basis of work orders, linen based on pounds of laundry, and so forth. When it comes to the allocation of many other charges, however, the supervisor should find out what the basis is. The healthcare institution will try to select a basis of distribution that is fair to all departments and feasible from an accounting point of view.

The overall financial performance of a department will be greatly affected by how these allocations for other expenditures are made, for example, administrative expenses, operation of the plant, depreciation, intern and resident service costs, in-service education, and interest expenses. Although all this is determined higher up in the administrative hierarchy, the supervisor is well advised to obtain some information and explanation on how it is done. Then the supervisor will understand how a department operates in the red, despite the effective work of the manager and its employees.

■ ADDITIONAL CONTROLS

We have stated many times that the supervisor's controlling function is closely related to and goes on simultaneously with all other managerial functions. Throughout this text many subjects were discussed as part of a particular function at the time, and now their meaning as an aid in the system of control can also be shown.

In Chapter 7 standing plans such as *policies, procedures, methods,* and *rules* as basic tools for planning were discussed. At this point in the text, however, they can be viewed as anticipatory control devices. These tools are established with the hope and intention that they will be followed and that they work out as preventive controls. If they are violated, the supervisor, using feedback control, must take the necessary corrective action to get things back on track; in some cases disciplinary measures may be necessary.

We discussed *positive discipline* and *disciplinary measures* in Chapter 23 as a component of the influencing function. In the controlling context, this topic can be viewed as a preventive and reactive control technique. If a rule has been violated, the supervisor must invoke disciplinary measures, which is synonymous with taking corrective action and sending a message to the employees about proper behavior on the job.

On various occasions *management by objectives* (MBO) was discussed. As mentioned, this is an agreement between the subordinate and the supervisor concerning a measurable performance objective to be achieved and reviewed within a given time period. This concept includes aspects of control. After mutually agreed-on objectives have been set, results are evaluated in the light of these standards, and, if necessary, shortcomings are corrected. This is another example of a control model mechanism.

Performance appraisal systems, the process of formally evaluating performance and providing feedback for performance adjustments, as discussed in Chapter 18, can also be viewed as part of the organizational control system. Although performance evaluation measures were presented with the staffing function, they can now be regarded as a feedback control technique in the managerial control system.

These are just a few examples taken from previous discussions of the various managerial functions; they show how closely related controlling is to all the other functions. This confirms the statement that the better the supervisor plans, organizes, staffs, and influences, the better he or she will also perform the controlling function.

■ SUMMARY

Budget making is planning, whereas living with the budget and budget administration falls into the manager's controlling function. Budgets are plans expressed in numerical terms that ultimately will be reduced to dollars and cents, since this is the common denominator used in the final analysis. Budgets are also pre-established standards to which the operations of the department are compared and, if necessary, adjusted by the exercise of control. Of all control devices, the budget, (primarily the expense budget) is the one most widely used and thus the one with which most supervisors should be familiar.

Since the supervisor is responsible for living up to the departmental budget, he or she must play a significant role in its preparation. Budget making is a line responsibility shared by the supervisor and the direct line superior. Ultimately all budgets are submitted to and approved by top-level administration, but it is essential that lower-level management participate in making their own budgets and have sufficient opportunity to be heard and substantiate their cases.

Zero base budgeting is a new approach to budgeting; under traditional budgeting management's attention is primarily focused on planned changes from the previous year. Under zero base budgeting nothing is taken for granted and every activity and budget item must be substantiated and justified from "scratch."

For a budget to be a live document and not a strait jacket, the budgetary process must be flexible. There must be frequent periodic budget reviews within the normal one-year budgeting period and provisions for budget revision. Such provisions will lessen the human problems that budgetary controls often cause.

In addition to budgetary controls, the supervisor should be aware of other costs that will influence the overall performance of the department. Here the supervisor will be concerned with how the expenditures of the nonrevenue-producing departments in a healthcare institution are allocated to those departments that do produce revenues. The bases of these allocations can often make the difference between showing a departmental surplus and operating at a loss. Supervisors also play an important role in cost containment. Cost awareness and cost consciousness should be an ongoing consideration and part of the supervisor's daily activities.

Throughout this text we stressed the close relationship between the controlling function and the other managerial functions. Many of the managerial duties and activities discussed previously can now be viewed as additional controls, including policies, procedures, etc.; disciplinary measures; management by objectives; and performance appraisals. The most widely used control device, however, remains the budget and budgetary procedures.

NOTES
1. Much of this is different in public sector organizations, such as those run by the Veterans Administration or federal, state, and local governments.
2. In the world of commerce some organizations, in order to ensure some flexibility, resort to "alternative" budgets, "variable expense" budgets, or "supplemental monthly" budgets, concepts that are not normally used in healthcare facilities.

Part Eight

LABOR
RELATIONS

27

THE LABOR UNION AND THE SUPERVISOR

Although labor unions have lost membership since the late 1970s, they are still an influential part of the work force. At this time about 15 to 20 percent of the labor force in the United States are members of a labor union or some employee association. Therefore, it is essential for supervisors to be familiar with the role labor unions play in the workplace in order to be able to work with them properly.

Collective bargaining gained its major legal basis in 1935 with the enactment of the National Labor Relations Act, also known as the Wagner Act, which guaranteed workers the right to bargain collectively with their employers. In 1947 the Wagner Act was amended by the Labor-Management Relations Act, also known as the Taft-Hartley Act. In 1959 the Labor-Management Reporting and Disclosure Act, sometimes referred to as the Landrum-Griffin Act, was added. In 1974 these laws were extended to cover most healthcare institutions.

The union movement was primarily a blue-collar movement because there were more blue-collar workers in the United States' labor force than white-collar workers. Since the middle 1950s, however, the number of people in white-collar occupational categories and in service industries has been on the increase and has surpassed the blue-collar sector. With this change, labor unions have made inroads in representing business services (e.g., computers), retail trade, finance, healthcare, government, and other sectors. A number of unions or employee associations have become the bargaining agents for teachers, college professors, nurses, airline pilots, nursing home employees, and various other white-collar workers. It is beyond the confines of this text to discuss the details of labor laws or give a history of the union movement in the United States.

Union-organizing efforts usually are resisted by employers and create a period fraught with controversies. The issues, claims, and counterclaims are on everyone's mind and are present in the workplace, on the parking lot, and even in the local news media. The verbal battle may even accelerate into work slowdowns or stoppages. If the employees vote to join a union, managers are likely to believe that they have lost a battle and that their employees and union representatives have been victorious. It will take time for the ill feelings created during the organizing campaign to disappear.

There is little doubt that the introduction of a union or an employee association into a hospital or related healthcare facility may be a trying experience for the supervisors, as well as for the chief executive officer (CEO). It may bring a time of tension during which constructive solutions to problems may be difficult. Gradually, however, both the union and the administration must learn to accommodate and live with each other. Every manager must accept the fact that the labor union is a permanent force in our society. Every manager must realize that the union, just as any other organization, has in it the potential for either advancing or disrupting the common effort of the institution. It is in the self-interest of the administration to create a labor-management climate that directs this potential toward constructive ends. There is no simple or magic formula, however, for overnight cultivation of a favorable climate that will result in cooperation and mutual understanding between the union and management. It takes wisdom and sensitivity from every manager of the organization, from the administrator down to the supervisor, to demonstrate in the day-to-day relations that the union is respected as a responsible part of the institution.

In this effort to create and maintain a constructive pattern of cooperation between the healthcare institution and the union, the most significant factor usually is the supervisor of a department. Supervisors, more than anyone else, feel the strongest impact of the new situation because they make the most decisions concerning unionized employees. The supervisor is the person in day-to-day employee relations who makes the labor agreement a living document, for better or for worse. Supervisors are often confused as to how they should behave during an organizing campaign and after the election when the union arrives on the scene. The supervisor should realize that the subordinates usually decide for a union not because they were gullible or naive or because the union used deceit or strong-arm methods, but primarily because some of their major needs were not satisfied on the job. The supervisor should approach the union professionally and try to build a satisfactory relationship.

The supervisor should have received information and training in the fundamentals of collective bargaining and in the nature of labor agreements. This is essential for the development of good labor relations. The supervisor is involved in two distinct phases of labor relations: (1) the inception of unionization and the phase of negotiations and (2) the day-to-day administration of the union agreement, which includes handling complaints and grievances. Although the supervisor is primarily concerned with the second phase of relations with the union, he or she also plays a role in the first.

■ UNIONIZATION AND LABOR NEGOTIATIONS

As soon as supervisors learn that union-organizing activities are starting, this information should be passed on to higher administration and/or the director of human resources. Often administration has already learned of such a campaign through other channels. This will enable the organization to plan its strategy, usually with the help of legal counsel. Supervisors should be aware of a number of legal restrictions that must be observed during the union-organizing efforts. The following remarks are only of a very general nature; supervisors will probably receive more detailed instruction from their administrators and lawyers.

Labor laws restrict what managers, including supervisors, are permitted to say and do during this critical period without the danger of their being involved in unfair labor practices. First, supervisors should continue to do the best possible job of supervision during this critical period. Administration should provide supervisors with information of the dos and don'ts. Generally supervisors should not make any statements in reference to unionization that could be construed as a promise if the union fails or as a threat if the union is successful. Supervisors should not question their employees privately or publicly about organizing activities. When asked, supervisors can express their opinions about unionization in a neutral manner, if this is possible, without running into the danger of having the answer interpreted as a threat or promise.

These are only a few guidelines that the supervisor should keep in mind; there certainly are additional guidelines. Usually an election conducted by the National Labor Relations Board will determine the outcome of the organizing campaign. If the union loses the election, the employees will not have a union for the immediate future. If the union wins, management has to recognize the union as the bargaining agent and begin negotiations in good faith.

On the surface it might not seem as if the supervisor is significantly involved in the negotiations of a labor agreement. As stated earlier, the period when a union first enters a department of a healthcare organization is usually trying and filled with tensions. Emotions run high, and considerable disturbance can result. Under such conditions, it is understandable that the delicate negotiations of a union contract are carried on primarily by members of top-level administration, probably assisted by legal counsel. There is usually an air of secrecy surrounding the negotiations, which often take place in a hotel or a lawyer's office.

Since a committee of employees may be participating in these negotiations, a fast line of communication exists with the other employees of the healthcare institution, but not necessarily with the supervisor. The supervisor often runs the danger of being less well informed about the course of negotiations than the employees. Therefore, the administrator must see to it that the supervisor is fully advised as to the progress and direction the negotiations are taking. In addition, the supervisor should be given an opportunity to express opinions on matters brought up during the negotiations. In other words, even though top-level management is representing the institution at the negotiating sessions, supervisors should be able to express their views through them, because ultimately it is the supervisor who bears the major responsibility for fulfilling the contract provisions.

The same necessity exists whenever renegotiations of the labor agreement take place. At that time top-level administration should consult with the supervisors as to how specific provisions in the contract have worked out and what changes in the contract the supervisors would like to have made. Both the administrator and the supervisors must realize that although the supervisors do not actually sit at the negotiating table, they have much to do with the nature of the negotiations. Many of the demands that the union brings up during the negotiations have their origin in the day-to-day operations of the department. Many of the difficult questions to be solved in the bargaining process stem from the relationship that the supervisors have with their employees.

Therefore, a great amount of checking must occur back and forth between the administrator and the supervisor before and during the negotiation of a labor agreement. To supply valuable information, the supervisor must know what has been going on in the department and have facts to substantiate his or her statements. This points to the value of documentation, keeping good records of disciplinary incidents, productivity, leaves, promotions, etc. The supervisor should also be alert to problems that should be called to the administration's attention so that in the next set of negotiations these matters may be worked out more satisfactorily. It is in the interest of both the union and the institution to have as small a number of unresolved problems as possible. If problems do arise, however, it is the supervisor's responsibility to see that administration is aware of them at the time of contract negotiations.

■ CONTENT OF THE AGREEMENT

Once administration and the union have agreed on a labor contract, this agreement will be the basis on which both parties must operate. Since the supervisor is now obligated to manage the department within the overall framework of the labor agreement, the supervisor must have complete knowledge of its provisions and how they are to be interpreted. The supervisor is the one who can cause disagreements between the union and the healthcare institution by failing to live up to the terms of the agreement. Thus, the content of the union contract must be fully explained to and understood by the supervisor.

A good way to present such explanations is at a meeting arranged for top administration and all the supervisors, which is usually chaired by the human resources or labor relations director. The purpose of the meeting is to brief the supervisors on the content of the labor contract, giving them an opportunity to ask questions about any part they do not understand. Copies of the contract and clarification of the various clauses may be furnished to the supervisors so that they may study them in advance. Since no two contracts are alike, however, it is impossible to pinpoint specific provisions that the supervisor should explore. Normally all contracts deal with matters such as union recognition, management's rights, union security, wages, bonus rates, conditions and hours of work, overtime, vacations, holidays, leaves of absence, seniority, promotions, and similar details. Almost certainly there will also be provisions concerning complaint and grievance procedures and arbitration. In addition, there are likely to be many other provisions that are peculiar to each institution in question.

Besides the need to familiarize the supervisors with the exact provisions of the contract, it is just as important for the administrator to explain to them the philosophy of top-level administration in reference to general relations with the union. The supervisors should understand that the intention of the administration is to maintain good working relations with the union so that organizational objectives can be achieved in a mutually satisfactory fashion. The CEO should clarify that the best way to achieve good union-management relations in a hospital or any other institution is by effective contract administration. The experts in the personnel or the labor relations department will have a great deal to do with effective contract administration, but much will still depend on how the supervisor handles the contract on a day-to-day basis.

The supervisors must bear in mind that the negotiated contract was carefully and thoughtfully debated and finally agreed on by both parties. Thus, it is not in the interest of successful contract administration for the supervisors to try to "beat the contract," even though they may think they are doing the institution a favor. The administrator must make it clear that to achieve satisfactory cooperation, supervisors may not construct their own contractual clauses, nor can they reinterpret clauses in their own way. Once the agreement has been reached, supervisors should not attempt to change or circumvent it.

If the administrator fails to familiarize the supervisors with the provisions and spirit of the agreement, they should insist on briefing sessions and explanations before they apply the clauses of the contract in the daily working situation of the department. The advent of the labor contract does not change the supervisor's job as a manager. The supervisor must still perform the managerial functions of planning, organizing, staffing, influencing, and controlling. There is no change in the authority delegated to the department head by the administrator or in the responsibility the supervisor has accepted. The significant change is that the supervisor must now perform the managerial duties within the framework of the union agreement. The supervisor still has the right to require the subordinates to carry out orders and the obligation to get the job done within the department. Certain provisions within the union agreement, however, are likely to influence and even limit some activities, especially within the areas of job assignments, disciplinary action, and dismissal. In many instances these provisions of the contract undoubtedly will make it more challenging for the supervisor to be a good manager. The only way to meet the challenge is for the supervisor to improve his or her own managerial ability, as well as improve his or her knowledge and techniques of good labor relations.

■ APPLYING THE AGREEMENT

It is in the daily application of the labor agreement that the real importance of the supervisor's contribution appears. The manner in which the day-to-day problems are handled within the framework of the union contract will make the difference between positive labor-management relations and a situation filled with unnecessary tensions and bad feelings. At best, a union contract can only set forth the broad outline of labor-management relations. To make it a positive instrument of constructive relations, the contract must be filled in with appropriate and intelligent supervisory decisions. It is the supervisor who interprets management's intent by everyday actions. In the final analysis the supervisor, through decisions, actions, and attitudes, really gives the contract meaning and life.

In many instances the supervisor may expand on some of the provisions of the contract when interpreting and applying them to specific situations. In so doing, the supervisor sets precedents that arbitrators pay heed to when deciding grievances that come before them. Almost all labor agreements have a grievance procedure leading to arbitration. An *arbitrator* is a person called on by the union and management to make a final and binding decision in a grievance that the parties involved are unable to settle themselves.

It is impossible for the administrator and the union to draw up a contract that anticipates every possible situation in employee relations and specifies exact directives for dealing with them. Therefore, the individual judgment of the supervisor becomes very important in deciding each particular situation. This again illustrates the significance of the supervisor's influence on the interpretation of the labor agreement.

As a representative of administration, any error in the supervisor's decisions is the administration's error. The immediate supervisor has the greatest responsibility for seeing that the clauses of the agreement are carried out appropriately. This includes the supervisor's duty to ensure that the employees comply with the provisions, just as supervisors have to operate within them. Therefore, the administrator must realize how significant a role the supervisor plays in the contract administration. Likewise, it is just as essential for the supervisor to realize how far reaching his or her decisions and actions can become.

Problem Areas

There are usually two broad areas where the supervisor is likely to run into difficulties in the administration of a labor agreement. The first covers the vast number of complaints that are concerned with single issues. These would include grievances involving a particular disciplinary action, assignment of work, distribution of overtime, as well as questions of promotion, transfer, downgrading, etc. In each situation the personal judgment of the supervisor is of great importance. As long as the contract provisions are met, the supervisor should feel free to deal with grievances as he or she sees fit. The supervisor must make certain, however, that the actions are consistent and logical even though they are made on the basis of personal judgment rather than hard and fast rules.

The second area of difficulty in contract administration covers those grievances and problems in which the supervisor is called on to interpret a clause of the contract. The supervisor is placed in a situation where an attempt must be made to carry out the generalized statement of the contract but finds that it is subject to varying interpretations. In such instances the supervisor would be wrong to handle the problem without consulting higher management first. Whenever an interpretation of the contract is at issue, any decision is likely to be long lasting. Such a decision may set a precedent that the institution, union, or even an arbitrator would want to make use of in the future.

Therefore, if interpretation of a clause is in doubt, the question should be brought to the attention of higher management, the administrator, and possibly the human resources director. Although the supervisor may have been well indoctrinated in the meaning, philosophy, and clauses of the contract, his or her perspective is probably not broad enough to make a potentially precedent-setting interpretation. Since the supervisor did not attend the bargaining meetings, he or she cannot know the intent of the parties nor the background of this provision. For these and other reasons the supervisor should consult with superiors.

The Supervisor's Right to Make Decisions

In non-precedent-setting situations and in the daily administration of the labor agreement, the supervisor must bear in mind that as a member of management, he or she has the right and even the duty to make a decision. The supervisor must realize that the union contract does not abrogate management's right to decide; it is still management's prerogative to do so. The union, however, has a right to protest the decision.

For example, the supervisor's job is to maintain discipline, and if disciplinary action is necessary, the supervisor should take action without discussing it with the union's representative. The supervisor should understand that usually there is no co-determination clause, and he or she should not set any precedent of determining together with the union what the supervisor's rights are in a particular disciplinary case. Of course, before any disciplinary measures are taken, a prudent supervisor will examine all the facts in the case, fulfill the preliminary steps, and think through the appropriateness of the action. This is more fully discussed in the next chapter.

In a few cases the union contract will call for consultation or advance notice before the supervisor can proceed. Advance notice or consultation, however, does not mean agreement on the final decision. Repercussions or protests from the union can still occur, although prior communication on anticipated action can avoid some of them. In any event the right to decide on day-to-day issues of contract administration still rests with the supervisor and not with the union.

The Supervisor and the Shop Steward

The supervisor will probably have the most union contact with the shop steward, who is the first-line official of the union and is sometimes referred to as shop *committeeperson,* or *departmental chairperson.* The shop steward is not the same as a union business agent or business representative; these are normally full-time union officials who are employed and paid by the local or national union. At times the supervisor will also have to deal with them.

The shop steward normally remains an employee of the healthcare facility and is subject to the same regulations as every other employee. He or she is expected to put in a full day's work for the employer, regardless of this person having been selected by fellow workers to be their official spokesperson with both the institution and the union. This obviously is a difficult position, since the shop steward has to serve two masters. As an employee, he or she has to follow the supervisor's orders and directives; as a union official, he or she has responsibilities to co-workers.

Just as individuals vary in their approach to their jobs, so shop stewards vary in their approach to their position. Some are unassuming; others are overbearing. Some are helpful and courteous, whereas others are difficult. Unless special provisions exist, the shop steward's rights are the same as those of any other union member. Moreover, the shop steward is subject to the same regulations regarding quality of work and conduct as the other employees of the department. Certain privileges may be specified in the union contract, however, such as how much "company" time the shop steward can devote to union business or other matters, whether or not solicitation of membership or collection of dues may be carried on during working hours, time off to attend union conventions, and similar questions.

As stated, the role of the shop steward will depend considerably on the makeup of the individual. Some will take advantage of their position to do as little work as possible, whereas others will perform a good day's work. The supervisor should always remember that the shop steward is an employee of the organization and should be treated as such. The supervisor should also remember, however, that the shop steward is the representative of the other employees; in this capacity the shop steward learns quickly what the other employees are thinking and what is going on in the grapevine. Thus, the supervisor will come to understand and take advantage of the fact that the dual role can make the shop steward a good link between management and employees.

Although shop stewards perform a number of union functions, such as collecting dues, soliciting membership, and promoting political causes, the supervisor should realize that the shop steward's most important responsibility probably concerns employees' complaints and grievances. The shop steward's job is to bring such complaints and grievances before the supervisor. The supervisor's job is to settle them to the best of his or her ability, using the grievance procedures described in great detail in every union contract. Throughout these procedures, which we will discuss more fully in the next chapter, the supervisor represents management, and the shop steward represents the employees for the union.

In most cases the shop steward is sincerely trying to redress the aggrieved employee by winning a favorable ruling. At times, however, the supervisor may be under the impression that he or she is out looking for grievances merely to stay busy. This may be partly true, since the shop steward does have a political assignment, and it is necessary to assure the employees that the union is working on their behalf. The shop steward must be able to convince the employees that they can rely on him or her, and therefore on the union, to protect them. On the other hand, an experienced shop steward knows that normally a sufficient number of real grievances must be settled. He or she sees no need to look for complaints that do not have a valid background and would rightfully be turned down by the supervisor.

Most unions will ensure that the shop steward is well trained to present the complaints and grievances so that they can be carried to a successful conclusion. The shop steward is usually well versed in understanding the content of the contract, management's obligations, and employees' rights. Before presenting a grievance, the shop steward should determine such matters as whether or not the contract has been violated, the employer acted unfairly, the employee's health or safety has been put in jeopardy, etc. In grievance matters the union is usually on the offensive and the supervisor is on the defensive. The shop steward will challenge the management decision or action, and the supervisor must justify what he or she has done.

Because the shop steward's main interest is in the union, at times this may antagonize the supervisor. In some instances it will be difficult for the supervisor to keep a sense of humor and remain calm. Often the supervisor also will have difficulty discussing a grievance with a shop steward on an equal footing, since the shop steward is a subordinate within the normal working situation. When assuming the role of shop steward, however, the position as representative of the union members gives him or her equal standing. The supervisor should always bear in mind that the shop steward's job is political and as such carries certain weight. At the same time the supervisor should understand that a good shop steward will keep any supervisor on the alert and force him or her to be a better manager.

■ SUMMARY

About 15 to 20 percent of the labor force in the United States are members of an employee association or a labor union. Since unions are attempting to represent more and more employees from services, it is essential that supervisors in healthcare undertakings are familiar with some basic aspects of labor union relations.

The supervisor's role in the union relations of a healthcare facility cannot be minimized. Although the supervisor is not normally a member of the management team that sits down with union negotiators to settle the terms of the labor contract, he or she does play an important indirect role in this meeting. Many of the difficulties and problems discussed at a negotiating meeting can be traced back to the daily activities of the supervisor. At best the union contract resulting from the negotiations can set forth only the broad outline of labor-management relationships. It is the day-to-day application and administration of the agreement that will make the difference between harmonious labor relations and a situation filled with unnecessary tensions and bad feelings.

The supervisor is the person who, through daily decisions and actions, gives the contract real meaning. The supervisor must therefore be thoroughly familiar with the contents of the contract and with the general philosophy of management toward the union. He or she must understand the difficult and important political role of the union shop steward, who serves in a dual capacity as one of the regular employees and as the representative of the union members. In grievance cases the supervisor must learn to regard the shop steward as an equal, as one who is trained to present the complaints of union members as effectively as possible. The shop steward will challenge management's decision, and the supervisor must justify it. Although at times it may be difficult to keep a balanced perspective, the supervisor should always remember that an alert shop steward can serve to force him or her to be a better manager.

28

HANDLING GRIEVANCES

A grievance can be defined as a complaint that usually results from a misunderstanding, misinterpretation, or violation of a provision of the labor agreement. This complaint has been formally presented to management by the union. Almost all union contracts contain provisions for a grievance procedure. The first step of the procedure begins at the departmental level, with the supervisor or the foreperson and the shop steward. If the grievance is not settled there, it can be appealed to the next higher level of management; at this point usually a chief steward or a business agent of the union will enter into the picture. At times the contract may provide for an appeal to an even higher level of management.

The grievance procedure usually sets a time limit for each of these steps to be finished. If the dispute cannot be settled by the first two or three steps to the mutual satisfaction of both parties, the agreement usually has an arbitration provision. This means that the issue may be submitted to an impartial outsider, an arbitrator. After hearing testimony and evidence, the arbitrator will render a final decision, which is binding on both parties.

This points to the necessity for the supervisor to be well qualified in handling complaints and settling grievances. Indeed, in a unionized setting one of the supervisor's most important duties is to make certain that most complaints and grievances are properly disposed of during the first step of the grievance procedure. Most organizations require that supervisors check and consult with a labor relations specialist in the personnel department when handling complaints. This is important because many complaints could have institution-wide or organization-wide implications. Grievances that refer to discrimination and equal employment opportunities could have legal implications for the entire organization.

Many additional reasons exist why the human resources department should be involved in the grievance procedure. The supervisor is not shirking responsibility or admitting ignorance by consulting and checking with these specialists. In some organizations management even has conferred on the staff of the labor relations division in the human resources department the final authority to adjust grievances by giving them functional authority, as discussed in Chapter 12.

The following discussion is based on an organizational setup in which the human resources and labor relations experts are in a strictly staff position, and the initial formal authority and responsibility to handle grievances rest with the line supervisor. In every unionized organization, line supervisors know that handling grievances is part of their job and that it takes judgment, tact, and often more patience than comes naturally. Supervisors should not feel threatened by grievances. Supervisors frequently may think that too much of their time is taken up in discussing complaints and grievances instead of getting the job done in the department. They may also believe that they have to be more of a labor lawyer than a supervisor. Supervisors should also realize, however, that higher management regards the skill in handling grievances to be an important index of supervisory ability. The number of grievances that arise within a department is considered a good indication of the state of employee-management relations.

A fine distinction can be made between the terms *complaint* and *grievance*. From the supervisor's point of view, however, a grievance simply means a complaint that has been formally presented either to the supervisor as a management representative or to the shop steward or any other union official. As mentioned, a grievance usually is a complaint resulting from a misunderstanding, misinterpretation, or violation of the provisions of the labor agreement. The supervisor must learn to distinguish between those grievances that are admissible and those that are gripes and merely indicate that the employee is unhappy or dissatisfied. In every case the supervisor should listen carefully to what the employee has to say in order to decide what action can be taken other than the grievance procedure to correct the situation. The grievance procedure, for the purposes of this chapter, means a process to resolve a misunderstanding, misinterpretation, or violation of the union contract.

■ THE SHOP STEWARD'S ROLE

The shop steward is usually the spokesperson for the employee in a grievance procedure. He or she is familiar with the labor agreement and has been well indoctrinated as to how to present the employee's side of the grievance. A good shop steward is eager to get the credit for settling a grievance. Therefore, the question arises as to what the supervisor should do if an employee approaches him or her without the shop steward or without having consulted the shop steward. In such a case it is appropriate for the supervisor to listen to the employee's story to see whether or not the case is of interest to or involves the union. If the indications are that the contract or the union are involved, then the supervisor should call in the shop steward to listen to the employee's presentation. Although it is unlikely that a union member would present a grievance without the shop steward, the supervisor will do well to notify the shop steward if this should happen.

Similarly, if the shop steward submits a grievance by himself or herself, the supervisor should also listen carefully and with understanding. It is always preferable, however, to listen to complaints when both the shop steward and the complaining employee are present. If the shop steward does not bring the employee along, it still is necessary to listen to what he or she has to say. Nothing can keep the supervisor from speaking directly to the employee later on, either with or without the shop steward. If the shop steward is not present, the supervisor should take great care not to give the impression that he or she is undermining the shop steward's authority or relationship with the union members. There should always be free and open communication between the supervisor and the shop steward, even though the shop steward's job is to represent employees and to fight hard to win their cases.

■ THE SUPERVISOR'S ROLE

One of the supervisor's prime functions is to dispose of all grievances at the first step of the grievance procedure. This means that part of the supervisor's job, usually with help from staff people in the labor relations department, is to explore fully the details of the grievance, deal with the problems brought out, and try to settle them. The supervisor will quickly learn that it pays to settle grievances early, before they grow from molehills into mountains. Occasionally some grievances will go beyond the first step and have to be referred to higher levels of management. Normally, however, if many grievances go beyond this step, this may indicate that the supervisor is not carrying out the supervisory duties properly. Unless circumstances are beyond his or her control, the supervisor should make every effort to handle grievances within reasonable time limits and bring them to a successful conclusion. To achieve prompt and satisfactory adjustments of grievances at this early stage, the supervisor should observe the following points in dealing with the grievance procedure.

Availability

The supervisor must be readily available to the shop steward and to the aggrieved employee. Availability does not only mean being physically present. It also means being approachable and ready to listen with an open mind. The supervisor must not make it difficult for a complaining employee to see him or her and sound off. This does not mean that the supervisor must stop immediately what he or she is doing, but every effort must be made to set a time as quickly as possible for the first hearing. An undue delay could be interpreted by the employee and the union as stalling, indifference, or resentment on the part of management.

Listening Skills

Everything stated about communication (Chapter 5) and interviewing (Chapter 17) is applicable to the grievance procedure as well. When a complaint is brought to the supervisor, the shop steward and the employee should be given the opportunity to present their case fully. Sympathetic listening by the supervisor is likely to minimize hostilities and tensions during the settlement of the case. The supervisor must know how to listen well. He or she must give the shop steward and the employee a chance to say whatever they have on their minds. If they believe that the supervisor is truly listening to them and that fair treatment will be given, the complaint will not loom as large to them as it did. Halfway through the story the complaining employee may even realize that he or she does not have a true complaint at all. Sympathetic listening can often produce this result. Also, sometimes the more a person talks, the more likely he or she is to make contradictory and inconsistent remarks, thus weakening the argument. Only an effective listener will be able to catch these inconsistencies and use them to help resolve the case. Frequently supervisors are so preoccupied with defending themselves or trying to justify their point of view that they simply do not listen.

Emotional Control

The supervisor must take great caution not to get angry at the shop steward or the employee. The shop steward's job is to represent the employee even when the shop steward knows that the grievance is not valid. In such a situation the supervisor's job is to point out objectively that there are no merits in the grievance. The supervisor cannot expect the shop steward to do this since he or she must serve as the employee's spokesperson at all times.

Sometimes a union deliberately creates grievances to keep things stirred up. Even this situation must not arouse the anger of the supervisor. If the supervisor does not know how to handle such occurrences successfully, he or she should discuss the matter with higher management and experts in the labor relations or human resources department. By no means, however, must the supervisor get upset, even if a grievance is phony.

If arguments, tempers, and emotional outbursts run high and make good communication difficult, the supervisor may want to terminate the meeting and reschedule it. The supervisor must use caution not to participate in a shouting match. It is hoped that at the next meeting tempers have cooled down and a calmer discussion will be possible.

Defining the Problem

Often the shop steward and the employee are not sufficiently clear in their presentations. It is then the supervisor's job to summarize clearly what has been presented and make certain that everyone understands the problem the complaint is trying to solve. Sometimes the complaint merely deals with the symptoms of the problem. The supervisor must know how deeply to delve in order to get at the root of the situation. It is necessary to define the employee's complaint and the extent of the problem precisely to determine whether a grievance is valid under the contract. Once the real problem is clarified and handled properly, it is unlikely that similar grievances will come up again.

Obtaining the Facts

It is necessary to obtain all the facts as quickly as possible to arrive at a solution of the problem and a successful adjustment of the grievance. The supervisor can probably get most of the facts by asking the complaining employee pertinent questions. In so doing, the supervisor should be objective and try not to confuse either the shop steward or the employee. The supervisor must ascertain who, what, where, when, and why. In other words, the supervisor must find out who or what caused the grievance, where and when it happened, and whether there was unfair treatment. He or she must also determine whether any connection exists between the current grievance and other grievances. Although it sometimes may be tempting to hide behind the excuse of searching for more facts, the supervisor must not do so. He or she must make a decision on the basis of those facts that are available and that can be obtained without undue delay.

Sometimes, however, it is impossible to gather all the information at once, and therefore the grievance cannot be settled immediately. In this case the supervisor must inform the aggrieved employee and the shop steward. If they see that the supervisor is working on the problem, they are likely to be reasonable and wait for an answer to be given at a specific future date.

Familiarity with the Contract and Consultation

After having determined the facts, the supervisor now must ascertain whether or not this is a legitimate grievance in the context of the contract. As mentioned earlier, a grievance is usually not a grievance in the legal sense unless provisions of the labor contract have been violated or administered inconsistently. Therefore, it is necessary to check the provisions in the contract when any reference to a violation is made. If the supervisor has any question about this, he or she should consult with someone in the personnel or labor relations department or higher management. Provisions in the labor agreement may not be clearly stated, and a question may exist about whether a certain provision in the contract is applicable at all. In such a situation the complaining employee should be told that additional clarification in reference to the agreement is needed and that the answer will be delayed for a few days.

Time Limits

Usually the grievance procedure sets a time limit within which the grievance must be answered. The supervisor must see that all grievances are settled as promptly and justly as possible. Postponing an adjustment in the hope that the complaint may disappear is courting trouble and more grievances. Moreover, an unnecessary postponement is unfair because the employee and the shop steward are entitled to know the supervisor's position as quickly as the facts can be obtained.

Speed is definitely important in the settlement of grievances, but not if it will result in unsound decisions. If a delay cannot be avoided, the aggrieved parties must be informed by the supervisor instead of leaving them under the impression that they are getting the runaround. Waiting for a decision is bothersome to everybody concerned. In such a situation it may be a good idea to put the grievance in writing and sign it so the parties involved do not forget the details.

Adjustment of Grievances

Part of the supervisor's job is to see that all grievances are properly adjusted, preferably at the first step of the grievance procedure. As already pointed out, this is included in the managerial aspects of the supervisory function. It is far better to settle a minor issue at this stage before it escalates into a major issue. The only cases that should be referred to higher levels of management are those that are unusual, require additional interpretation of the meaning of the union contract, contain problems that have not shown up before, or involve broad policy considerations.

Consistency of Action

In the adjustment of grievances, the supervisor must make certain that the rights of management are protected and that the policies and precedents of the institution are followed. If the supervisor must deviate from previous adjustments, he or she must explain the reasons to the employee and the shop steward. The supervisor must make certain that both of them fully understand that this exception does not set a precedent. In such cases the supervisor is always obliged to have this checked out and approved by higher-level administration and/or the human resources department before informing the parties involved.

Consequences of the Settlement

The supervisor should not reach a decision that is inconsistent with previous settlements. The supervisor must check previous settlements and make certain that the current intended decision is consistent with past decisions, the institution's policy, and the labor agreement. The supervisor should avoid making an exception because this decision is likely to become a precedent. In adjusting grievances, the supervisor must consider not only what effect the adjustment will have in this instance, but also its implications for the future. Whenever the supervisor settles a grievance, the possibility exists that this settlement will show up as part of the labor contract in following years. Also, if the case goes to arbitration, the arbitrator is likely to look for precedents, consider them almost as binding as the labor agreement, and use them as a valid basis for the final decision.

Providing a Clear Answer

The supervisor must answer the grievance in a straightforward, reasonable manner that is perfectly clear to the aggrieved parties. The answer must not be phrased in language that the aggrieved parties cannot understand, regardless of whether or not the adjustment is in favor of the employee. If the supervisor rules against the employee, the employee is that much more entitled to a clear, straightforward reply stating the reasons for the decision, not simply a "no." Although the employee may disagree with such a reply, at least it will be understood.

Clarity is even more necessary if the supervisor has to reply to the grievance in writing. In that case the answer must be restricted to the specific complaints involved, the words used must be appropriate, and any reference to a particular provision of the labor agreement or to the organization's rules must be clearly cited. Unless required, a written reply should not be rendered. If such a reply is required under the labor agreement, however, it is appropriate for the supervisor to discuss all the implications with higher management or with the human resources department so that a properly worded reply is given.

Record Keeping

It is essential for the supervisor to keep records and documents whenever a grievance decision is made. If the employee's request is satisfied, this decision may become a precedent. If the complaint cannot be settled in the first step, this grievance probably will go farther, possibly to arbitration or to a government agency, as in cases of discrimination. The case will certainly go to higher levels of management, and the supervisor should not defend the action by depending on memory. Diligent records of the facts, reasoning, and decisions should be available. With this documentation at hand, the supervisor will be able to substantiate the actions whenever asked. Good records are an absolute necessity because the burden of proof is usually on the supervisor and management. Management has the right to decide, but the union has the right to submit a grievance. Whenever the employee or the union maintains that the supervisor has violated the agreement or has administered its provisions in an unfair or inconsistent manner, the supervisor must defend the action. Without good records and documentation, this will often be difficult, if not impossible.

Supervisors should familiarize themselves with all the previous points as aids in handling grievances. The supervisors' decisions and actions will have some impact on employee-union relations at the healthcare facility. For this impact to be favorable, supervisors not only must be familiar with the points just covered, but also must apply them during honest, face-to-face discussions with employees and the shop steward whenever grievances do arise.

■ SUMMARY

The labor agreement sets forth a broad, general outline of labor-management relationships. This outline must be filled in with intelligent supervisory decisions. Occasions to make such decisions arise mainly in the settlement of grievances. Indeed, the proper adjustment of grievances is one of the important components of the supervisory position. Whenever the supervisor settles grievances, the labor contract is referred to and interpreted; the settlements may have far-reaching implications because they set precedents. Much of what the union will discuss at the next contract negotiations originates with day-to-day supervisory decisions. If a grievance should go to arbitration, the impartial arbitrator will also attach great importance to precedents set by the supervisor. Often it is not so much what the contract says that counts, but how it has been interpreted by management's front-line representative, the supervisor. This shows how important a role the supervisor actually plays in the adjustment of grievances and how necessary it is to gain considerable skill in the use of adjustment techniques. In most organizations specialists in labor relations will be involved in arriving at the appropriate settlement.

To apply adjustment techniques appropriately, the supervisor should always be available and listen without losing his or her temper, even if the grievance is a "phony" one. The supervisor must learn to define the problem, obtain the facts, and then draw on a thorough knowledge of the contract's clauses. It is also important to avoid unnecessary delays and settle grievances at an early stage. Moreover, the supervisor must be fair in all decisions, protecting the rights of the institution and respecting the content and spirit of the agreement. The supervisor also must keep good records, give clear replies, and above all, remain consistent.

Formal Organizational Charts and Manuals

Appendix

Many conflicts in organizations are often caused by the employees not understanding their assignments and those of their co-workers. Proper use of organizational charts, manuals, and job descriptions defining and spelling out authority and informational relationships will help to reduce misunderstandings substantially and to clarify doubts. Organizational charts, manuals, and job descriptions are tools to clarify the organization's structure to everyone concerned. The healthcare institution's structure is formalized *graphically* in the chart and *in words* in the manual. These tools help explain to everyone involved in the organization how it works. To be helpful, they must be available all the time and be up-to-date, which means changes must be incorporated promptly.

Once the chief executive officer (CEO) has established the formal structure of the organization by setting up departments and levels, determining the span of supervision and deciding which positions are to be line and which are to be staff, the entire structure can be depicted graphically in organizational charts and in words by using manuals. These are important organizational tools because they provide a clear-cut picture of the overall institution that can be used by all levels of management. For the supervisor organizational charts and manuals can be particularly helpful in understanding the formal organizing process and the goals and intent of the administration. By studying them, the supervisors can see the positions and relations of their own department within the overall structure and learn about the functioning and relationships of all other departments as well. However, it should be mentioned that they do not show the informal organizational relationships discussed in Chapter 15.

The responsibility for preparing an organizational chart rests with the CEO. A number of individuals, especially those in staff positions, will probably help in the collection of information and preparation of charts, but in the final analysis it is one of top-level administration's duties. Although the administrator is responsible for preparing charts and manuals for the institution as a whole, it will be necessary for the supervisor to devise some of these organizational tools on a departmental level if they are not available or not up-to-date. Thus, we must look more carefully at how such tools are prepared and at the information they supply.

■ ORGANIZATIONAL CHARTS

Organizational charts are a means of graphically portraying the organizational structure at a given time; it is a snapshot. The chart shows the skeleton of the structure, depicting the basic formal relationships and groupings of positions and functions. The chart maps the lines of decision-making authority. Most of the time the chart starts out with the individual position as the basic unit, which is shown as a rectangular box. Each box represents one function. The various boxes are then interconnected horizontally to show the groupings of activities that make up a department, division, or whatever other part of the organization is under consideration. They are connected vertically to show scalar relationships. Thus, one can readily determine who reports to whom merely by studying the position of the boxes in their scalar relationships. For example, we saw in the organizational charts in Figure 10-1 some of the scalar relationships that can be found in a typical hospital.

Advantages

One of the advantages is the analysis and work that is necessary for the preparation of a chart, whether it is for the overall organization or a department. As the chart is prepared, the organization must be carefully analyzed. Such analysis might uncover structural faults and possibly duplications of effort, complexities, or other inconsistencies. One might also uncover cases of dual-reporting relationships (one person reporting to two superiors), overlapping positions, and so on. Moreover, charts might indicate whether the span of supervision is too wide or too narrow. An unbalanced organization can also be readily revealed. Charts afford a simple way to acquaint new members of the organization with its makeup and how they fit into the entire structure. Most employees within the organization have a keen interest in knowing where they stand, in what relation their supervisor stands to the higher echelons, and so forth. Charts are also helpful in human resources administration. They can indicate possible routes of promotions for managers as well as for other employees.

Another advantage of charts is their assistance in developing better communications and relations. Charts can also be valuable for future planning purposes. A supervisor may want to have two charts for his or her department, one showing the existing arrangements and another depicting the ideal organization. The latter may be used so that all the gradual changes planned fall within the design of the ideal, representing the ultimate organizational goal of the department in the future. Charting shows what is changing and how the change affects the members of the organization.

Limitations

There are also some limitations to charts, especially if they are not continually kept up-to-date. It is imperative that organizational changes be recorded speedily because failure to do so makes charts outdated; managers often hesitate or neglect to redraft charts. Another shortcoming of charts is that the information they give is limited. A chart is a snapshot, not an x-ray film or a CT scan; it shows only what is on the surface, not the inner workings of the structure. A chart shows only formal authority relationships; it does not show the many informal relationships. (See Chapter 15.) The chart also does not show the amount of authority and responsibility.

Another problem with charts is that individuals confuse authority relationships with status. Sometimes people read into charts interpretations that charts are not intended to portray. For example, a person may interpret the degree of power and status by checking how distant a position is on the chart from the box of the CEO, or on which level it is shown. Despite these shortcomings, charts are still a very useful tool for every member of the organization.

Types of Charts

There are three main types of charts: vertical, horizontal, and circular. Of these, the vertical chart is the one used most often in organized activities.

Throughout this text and especially in Figures 10-1 and 13-1, the charts shown and referred to are the vertical type. *Vertical charts* show the different levels of the organization in a step arrangement in the form of a pyramid. The CEO is placed at the top of the chart, and the successive levels of administration are depicted vertically in the pyramid shape.

One of the main advantages of the vertical chart is that it can be easily read and understood. It also shows clearly the downward flow of delegation of authority, chain of command, functional relationships, and how those activities relate to one another. As previously stated, there are a number of shortcomings with charts. One of the disadvantages is that the information conveyed is incomplete; the vertical chart can also convey a wrong impression about the relative status of certain positions. This is because some positions have to be drawn higher or lower on the chart, when in reality they are on the same organizational plane. For example, an incorrect impression can result if one division of an organization has more levels than another. An organizational unit of three levels may show a supervisor on the lowest level, whereas in a five-level unit that person would be on the third level.

In addition to the vertical chart, some healthcare institutions may occasionally prefer a *horizontal chart,* which reads from left to right. (See Figure A-1.) The advantage of a horizontal chart is that it stresses functional relationships and minimizes hierarchical levels. The left-to-right chart of a matrix or project organization is a combination of these two arrangements. Horizontal relationships are superimposed on the vertical chart.

A *circular chart* can also be used. It depicts the various levels on concentric circles rotating around the top-level administrator, who is at the hub of the wheel. (See Figure A-2.) Positions of equal importance are on the same concentric circle. This graphic portrayal eliminates positions at the bottom of the chart.

A few organizations might prefer an *inverted pyramid chart,* showing the chief administrator at the bottom and the associate administrators farther up. This type tries to express the idea of the ''support'' given to each manager by the ''superior.''

■ ORGANIZATIONAL MANUALS

The organizational manual is another helpful tool for achieving effective organization. It provides in comprehensive *written* form the decisions that have been

■ FIGURE A-1 Horizontal chart.

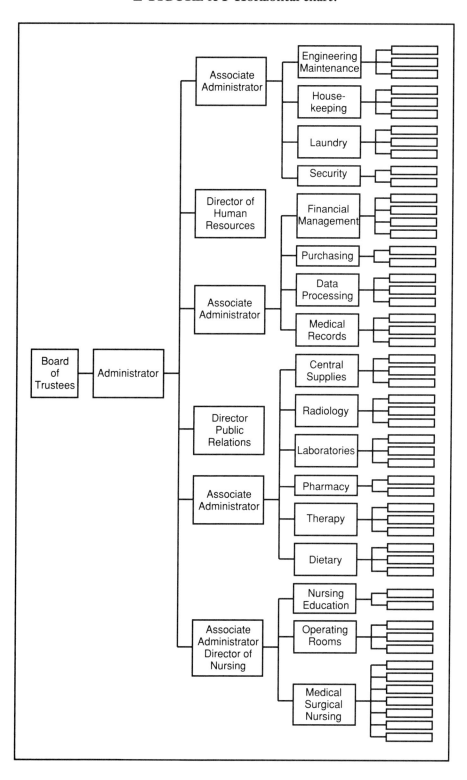

■ FIGURE A-2 Circular chart.

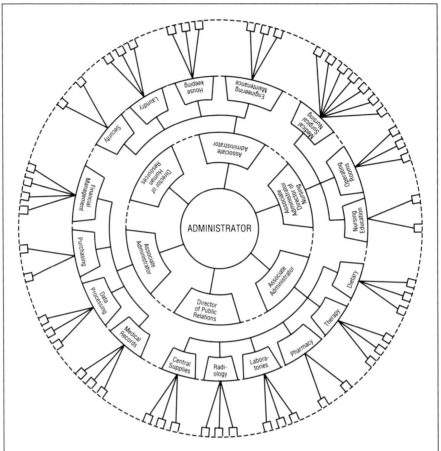

made with regard to the institution's structure. It defines the institution's major policies and objectives. It contains organizational charts of the institution and of specific departments; it also provides job descriptions. Moreover, the organizational manual, is a readily available reference defining the scope of authorities, responsibilities of managerial positions, and channels to be used in obtaining decisions or approval of proposals.

One of the chief advantages of a manual is the analysis and thinking necessary before one can be written. Another advantage is that the manual will also be of great assistance in the indoctrination and development of managerial personnel. The manual should clearly specify for each manager what the responsibilities of the job are and how they are related to other positions within the organization. In addition, the manual reiterates for the individual manager the objectives of the enterprise and of the department, and it provides a means of explaining the complex relationships within the organization. Supervisors should familiarize themselves with the contents of the institution's manual, especially those parts affecting their own department.

Organizational manuals are a valuable tool only if they are up-to-date. Since the manual is written, it is more difficult to change. Unless manuals are kept current and incorporate changes, they are more of a hindrance than a valuable aid. As stated before, another difficulty with a manual is the initial great effort it takes to compile one.

Content

Although the content of the manual varies from one healthcare institution to another, almost all include statements of objectives, overall policies, job descriptions, organizational charts of the institution and specific departments, and possibly an explanation of titles.

Objectives and Policies

In the manual, as we have said, top-level management states the major objectives and goals of the institution. For a hospital the manual would state the institution's creed, philosophies, and broad policies in regard to patient care, the quality of medicine practiced, social responsibility, and many other areas of activities. The manual would mention, for example, the hospital's objectives concerning the education of medical and many other professionals, investigative studies, and possibly research in the fields of medical sciences and services. It may state for healthcare providers the objective to be alert and responsive to the changing needs of the community and the environment. The manual would also include a statement of overall hospital policies.

■ POSITION DESCRIPTIONS

All manuals contain position descriptions, also known as job descriptions. There is some confusion, however, in the use of the term *job description* as compared to *job specification*. Generally, job descriptions objectively describe the elements of a position, that is, the principal duties and functions and scope and kind of authority. A job description is an accurate, up-to-date record of all pertinent information about a job as performed in a given department. Job specifications, on the other hand, specify the human qualities required, the personal qualifications necessary to perform the job adequately, such as education, training, experience, and disposition. In most enterprises position descriptions are extended to include such human qualities.

Position descriptions in the manual will vary depending on the size of the departments and type of work involved. For instance, in the section for nursing services, all jobs starting with the director of nursing services down to the jobs of aides should be described. If a job is particularly complicated or involves numerous activities, its description will probably be rather lengthy; otherwise, most descriptions are fairly short. (See Figure A-3).

■ FIGURE A-3 Staff nurse position description.

Date: _____ April 1989 _____	Job Title: _____ Nurse, Staff _____

Number of Employees
   Supervised: _____ NA _____
	Department: Nursing Service and
	    Operating Room

Supervised by: _____ Head Nurse _____	Section: Various Nursing Areas and 4430, 3620
Approved: _____	Job Grade: __15__ Job Code No: __126__

Purpose of Position

Provides direct patient care activities including assessment, planning, implementation, and evaluation.

Primary Responsibilities

Functions include admission and ongoing assessments of patients utilizing physical and psychosocial assessment skills, diagnostic data, and medical evaluations. Evaluate effectiveness of care provided as related to short and long term patient goals. Develops a plan for patient care including actions in anticipation of discharge needs. Implements nursing actions and medical orders to meet complex needs of patients and significant others. Documents care provided and patient responses to care in appropriate forms in the patient's record.

Assumes Charge Nurse responsibilities (once licensed) and accountability for care provided by LPNs and nonlicensed nursing personnel as assigned. Leadership abilities are demonstrated in functioning as a professional role model, consumer relations and communication skills, problem solving and decision making, and assistance in orienting and training personnel.

Participates in continued professional development and research activities for the improvement of patient care.

Performs other job related duties as assigned.

Training, Education, Experience, or Other Requirements

Graduate of a state approved school of nursing, possesses current RN licensure with the Missouri State Board of Nursing or current RN Missouri temporary work permit or has applied for licensure examination. Required to work rotating shifts.

Physical Demands

Stands and walks most of time on duty. Lifts and pushes patients on stretchers and in wheelchairs. Usually works in a clean, air-conditioned area. May be subject to infectious patients, contaminated specimens, toxic drugs, and radiation.

Replaces Job Description

Nurse, Staff; dated June 1985.

PERFORMANCE EXPECTATIONS

EXPECTATION I: Assessment/Evaluation of Patient Care

Demonstrates the ability to assess and evaluate appropriate patient care to promote optimal levels of wellness.

1. Patient Care:
   a. Assesses/evaluates patient understanding of disease process or present condition.
   b. Assesses patient utilizing a body systems approach.
   c. Identifies nursing care problems/diagnoses.

Reprinted with special permission from Barnes Hospital, St. Louis. For illustrative purposes only.

■ FIGURE A-3 Staff nurse position description. (cont.)

    d. Evaluates outcomes of nursing care/medical therapies related to body system assessment.

    e. Assesses discharge and/or transfer needs based on medical, nursing, and home care problems.

2. Diagnostic Data:

    a. Correlated diagnostic data with patient's assessment and recognizes changes in patients' condition relative to that data.

    b. Interprets and utilizes diagnostic data specific to patients on the patient care area.

3. Goals:

    a. Identifies short and long term goals for patients based on acute and chronic needs.

    b. Evaluates outcomes of nursing care with specific focus on the patients' progress toward achievement of short and long term goals.

EXPECTATION II: Planning/Implementation of Patient Care

Utilizes assessment data and problem identification to plan and provide appropriate nursing care toward patient's optimal level of wellness.

1. Patient Care:

    a. Plans nursing care based on medical treatment regimen nursing assessment data, identified nursing problems, and significant other/patient participation.

    b. Demonstrates competence in performance of nursing skills relative to area of practice.

    c. Collaborates with other health team members to plan and provide holistic nursing care.

    d. Provides nursing care which reflects consideration of discharge and/or transfer needs.

    e. Organizes patient care to be completed within designated shift.

2. Diagnostic Data:

    a. Reviews available diagnostic information to develop a holistic approach to patient care for assigned group of patients.

    b. Utilizes diagnostic data to report significant findings and initiate changes in therapies.

3. Goals:

    a. Organizes care in order to plan for meeting both acute and chronic needs of the patient.

    b. Focuses nursing care to assist the patient/significant other in identifying and achieving short and long term goals.

    c. Establishes care plan to meet short and long term goals.

EXPECTATION III: Patient/Significant Other Education

Initiates patient and significant other education of routine therapies and procedures, and begins discharge planning and teaching upon admission.

1. Performs consistent ongoing assessment/evaluation of patients' learning needs, e.g., upon admission—reason for hospitalization, basic understanding of illness/condition, understanding of relationship between illness and routine therapy.

    a. Assesses factors which enhance or interfere with teaching/learning.

    b. Evaluates success of teaching through patient's ability to verbalize implications of illness, treatment plan, and complications and return demonstration of basic healthcare concepts.

    c. Assess patients/significant others learning needs for discharge.

    d. Evaluates patients' and significant others' understanding of patients discharge health status.

■ FIGURE A-3 Staff nurse position description. (cont.)

2. Develops/implements plan of care based on patients/significant others' learning needs.
   a. Revises teaching plan as patients' needs become more complex, diverse, or resolved.
   b. Explains routine therapies, procedures, and surgeries.
   c. Explains and/or reinforces teaching regarding disease process.
   d. Performs healthcare teaching as outlined in care plans.
   e. Provides pertinent educational resources, e.g., educational classes, audio visual aids, booklets, and clinical specialists.
   f. Consults with other health team members regarding readiness for discharge.
   g. Develops/implements plan of care for discharge education.
   h. Refers to appropriate outside agencies, groups, and resources for outpatient follow-up prior to discharge.

EXPECTATION IV: Documentation
Documents pertinent data in a concise manner that is consistent with the approved Barnes Hospital system of documentation.
1. Documents assessment of patients' physical and nonphysical needs from admission to discharge utilizing nursing diagnoses.
2. Documents plan of care and patients/significant others response to plan.
3. Documents care given, medications, treatments, and other therapeutic diagnostic measures including any omissions and patients' response to same.
4. Documents and reports patient/visitor/employee incidents.
5. Maintains current and accurate nursing care plans.
6. Documents teaching and patient/significant other response to teaching.
7. Charts in a manner which reflects the patient's current status and condition using pertinent nursing diagnoses.
8. Documents nursing referrals/consultations for patients' care, discharge, or support services.

EXPECTATION V: Consumer Relations
Identifies the patient, significant others, staff, and physicians as consumers and demonstrates techniques for providing an open, professional, congenial atmosphere.
1. Communicates with and listens to the patient, significant others, and members of the health team in a concise, tactful, and considerate manner.
2. Demonstrates cooperative and effective relationships with all other personnel/departments.
3. Recognizes potential and actual consumer concerns in a timely manner.
4. Investigates all information pertinent to concerns to clearly define problem.
5. Assesses methods for meeting consumer needs.
6. Acts to resolve consumer problems and reports results of action taken to the appropriate manager.
7. Assists co-workers in dealing with consumer problems as needed.
8. Demonstrates effective/courteous telephone communication skills.
9. Maintains patient confidentiality in regard to the patient's Bill of Rights.
10. Encourages patient and significant others to evaluate nursing care by encouraging completion of patient questionnaire.

EXPECTATION VI: Leadership Skills Teamwork
Identifies potential and actual problems in patient care area. With other patient care providers, recommends solutions and intervenes appropriately. Is accountable for the care of assigned patients and the care assigned to other healthcare providers whom the RN covers. Communicates pertinent information to appropriate person.

■ FIGURE A-3 Staff nurse position description. (cont.)

1. Makes rounds on assigned patients.
2. Identifies problems occurring throughout shift.
   a. Assesses/evaluates problems identified.
   b. Seeks assistance from head nurse/assistant head nurse/designated others as needed to develop plan to intervention.
   c. Implements plan for intervention and reports to head nurse/assistant head nurse results of action taken.
3. Assigns patient care with patient needs and staff capability taken into account.
   a. Assesses/evaluates capabilities of nursing care providers assigned for coverage.
   b. Provides information/demonstrates skills to assigned nursing care providers as indicated.
4. Delegates tasks effectively when indicated.
5. Recognizes staff noncompliance with policies and procedures. Instructs staff regarding current policy/procedure when possible and informs appropriate manager (head nurse, assistant head nurse, supervisor).
6. Functions as charge nurse when assigned by head nurse/assistant head nurse (after successful completion of State Board examination).
   a. Review/revises patient care assignments with patient needs and staff capability taken into account.
   b. Adjusts patient care assignment during shift as need arises.
   c. Revises assignments as indicated to prevent overtime.
   d. Provides adequate orientation and appropriate assignment of float pulled staff, nursing students, and orientees.
   e. Assures oncoming shift of appropriate staff complement bases on patient census and acuity. Takes action to arrange coverage.
   f. Communicates all pertinent information occurring during shift to head nurse/ assistant head nurse/supervisor and/or other appropriate person.
   g. Supervises/evaluates nursing care provided during shift.

EXPECTATION VII: Policies and Procedures
Knowledgeable and supportive of Barnes' hospital and nursing philosophy, policies, and procedures as demonstrated in personal conduct and provision of nursing care.
1. Demonstrates professional conduct consistent with policies and procedures.
2. Organizes time to review policies and procedures on an ongoing basis and demonstrates compliance in nursing practice.
3. Provides input to head nurse and/or policy and procedure committee for development and revision of policies and procedures.

EXPECTATION VIII: Budgetary Awareness
Provides cost-effective, quality patient care through appropriate use of supplies and personnel.
1. Completes and signs time sheet properly.
2. Recognizes the budgetary impact of numbers and mix of personnel.
3. Makes appropriate charges.
4. Uses supplies and equipment judiciously.
5. Communicates problems in acquisition or use of supplies and services to head nurse/assistant head nurse/nursing supervisor.

EXPECTATION IX: Professional Development
Participates in continuing education programs for the improvement of patient care and demonstrates interest in professional growth.
1. Assumes responsibility and accountability for own practice.
2. Identifies strengths and limitations of professional practice.

■ FIGURE A-3 Staff nurse position description. (cont.)

3. Utilizes identified strengths and limitations as a basis for selecting developmental opportunities.
4. Verbalizes rationale for decisions/actions based on current principles of nursing practice.
5. Acknowledges errors or omissions in care and takes action to correct these.
6. Remains updated and current in unit activities by attending unit staff meetings/reading minutes.
7. Accompanies physician and/or head nurse in patient rounds when possible.
8. Attends and participates in patient care conferences and presents at least one conference or inservice per year.
9. Completes at least two continuing education programs per year relative to area of practice.
10. Incorporates new knowledge into daily nursing practice.
11. Participates in programs for career development and/or attainment of BSN.
12. Acts as preceptor for orienting personnel as requested by head nurse/assistant head nurse.
13. Assists head nurse/assistant head nurse in orientation and development of students and staff unfamiliar with the patient care area.
14. Maintains and submits to head nurse current licensure and educational record/qualification permits as relevant to practice.

EXPECTATION X: Problem Solving Research
Utilizes problem-solving methodologies for benefit of patients/significant others, the patient care area, and the nursing profession.
1. Recognizes and proposes solutions to patient and/or divisional problems.
2. Utilizes appropriate resources in investigation of problems, e.g., patient record documentation, patients/families, colleagues, journals.
3. Participates in data collection and implementation of investigational protocols as directed by head nurse.
4. Identifies problems on assigned patients and/or patient care area amenable to research and recommends these to head nurse/clinical nurse specialists for investigation.
5. Implements applicable research findings relative to care of assigned patients, consistent with policy/protocols in collaboration with head nurse/clinical specialist.

Initially position descriptions should be written by the CEO and his or her staff as they proceed with the organizing process. If an institution does not have job descriptions, the departmental supervisors should see that they are drawn up. To help in this endeavor, the supervisors should be able to call on the human resources department, which has the necessary expertise to facilitate the job. Even when job descriptions are available, it is the supervisor's duty to become familiar with them to make sure they are realistic, accurate, and up-to-date. Job descriptions have a tendency to become obsolete, and this can have serious consequences. Thus, it is necessary for the supervisor to check with employees who hold the various positions in the department and compare their jobs with those descriptions in the manual. If the manual is outdated or incorrect, the supervisor must have it revised. Times are changing, and in all likelihood the content of some jobs has changed without the administrator being aware of it. Furthermore, requirements for background, education, and training have undergone significant changes in many cases. All this should be recorded on the job description.

If they are kept current, position descriptions will prove invaluable to many people throughout the organization. They inform the incumbent and whoever needs or wants to know what he or she is supposed to do. The position description usually includes some statement of authority and informational relationships. The position description has many additional benefits. For example, the human resources director will refer to the job description when requests are made by the supervisor to recruit applicants for an open position. Further, someone in the human resources department will use them in the preliminary interview. The supervisor will also keep the job description in mind when applicants for positions in the department are interviewed.

Position descriptions help in drawing up candidate requirements. The new employee should have a chance to see the description of the job for which he or she has been hired. In some healthcare facilities it is standard practice to hand new employees a copy of it for them to keep and study. In this respect position descriptions serve as a basis of common understanding between employees and management. The job description is also used when the supervisor evaluates and appraises the employee's performance at regular intervals. For all of these reasons both the supervisor and the administrator should be vitally concerned that the content of the position description is proper and current.

■ TITLES

No standard agreement exists on the use and meaning of titles, especially in the upper echelons of healthcare centers. This is because of the recent trend toward the use of corporate titles for the top-level person. The role of the executive head has evolved from superintendent to hospital administrator to executive director to president. The job of the CEO in larger hospitals is no longer concerned only with the internal operations of the hospital, but also with the external relations in the larger field of community responsibilities. The title of president is gaining more and more acceptance, and the CEO of the healthcare center will be known as the hospital president just as his or her counterpart in industry. This will assist those who are not familiar with healthcare operations to identify the president's organizational role properly. Before too long, the term president for the healthcare center's CEO will be the most appropriate designation. (Throughout this text the terms *president, chief executive officer,* and *administrator* have been used interchangeably.) This title will communicate to patients, relatives, visitors, physicians, and the general public that the president is the CEO in the organization.

Following corporate usage of titles, this would lead to an executive vice president on the second level, several senior vice presidents (e.g., for patient care, for fiscal affairs), then vice presidents on the next level (e.g., vice president of nursing, of professional services, of human resources, of environmental affairs).

Although the titles of the upper echelons vary from one healthcare institution to another, there must be internal consistency. Within a healthcare institution titles must be clear and consistent. The best way to do this is to use a basic title, such as director, and then add adjectives to indicate the rank and area of activity (executive, associate or assistant director, nursing, medical and surgical; or chief technologist, radiology, outpatient section).

The supervisor's job will be greatly facilitated by having all these organizational tools available. Charts, manuals, and position descriptions properly maintained and updated explain to everyone involved in the organization how it works and how the individual department and its members fit into the overall organization.

• Index •

About the Author

Theo Haimann, PhD, is the Mary Louise Murray Professor of Management at St. Louis University, St. Louis, MO, where he has been professor in the department of management for many years. In 1988 he was awarded the Outstanding Teacher Award by the St. Louis University chapter of Beta Gamma Sigma. Haimann has lectured extensively in the healthcare field at seminars and workshops sponsored by individual hospitals, their associations, and other societies and universities. For many years, the Catholic Health Association regularly presented Dr. Haimann's seminars for middle level and supervisory personnel engaged in all aspects of the healthcare field. In addition, he has spoken at seminars for business executives and government employees. Haimann is a member of the board of St. Mary's Health Center, St. Louis, MO.

Dr. Haimann is the author of *Management*, now in its Fifth Edition, published by Houghton Mifflin Co., and *Supervision: Concepts and Practices of Management*, in its Fourth Edition, published by South-Western Publishing Co. Both of these texts are used as college textbooks throughout the U.S. and have been translated into Spanish.